THE LAST CENTURY
IN THE HISTORY OF JUDAH

ANCIENT ISRAEL AND ITS LITERATURE

Thomas C. Römer, General Editor

Number 37

THE LAST CENTURY
IN THE HISTORY OF JUDAH

The Seventh Century BCE in Archaeological, Historical, and Biblical Perspectives

Edited by

Filip Čapek and Oded Lipschits

SBL PRESS

SBL PRESS

Atlanta

Copyright © 2019 by Society of Biblical Literature

Library of Congress Cataloging-in-Publication Data

Names: Čapek, Filip, 1971– editor. | Lipschits, Oded, editor.
Title: The last century in the history of Judah / edited by Filip Čapek and Oded Lipschits.
Description: Atlanta : SBL Press, [2019] | Includes bibliographical references and index.
Identifiers: LCCN 2019031771 (print) | LCCN 2019031772 (ebook) | ISBN 9780884143994 (hardcover) | ISBN 9781628372526 (paperback) | ISBN 9780884144007 (ebook)
Subjects: Bible. Old Testament—History of Biblical events. | Bible. Old Testament—Criticism, interpretation, etc.—History. | Judaea (Region)—History. | Judaea (Region)—Antiquities.
Classification: LCC DS110.J78 L37 2019 (print) | LCC DS110.J78 (ebook) | DDC 933/.4903—dc23
LC record available at https://lccn.loc.gov/2019031771
LC ebook record available at https://lccn.loc.gov/2019031772

Printed on acid-free paper.

Contents

Abbreviations

AASOR	Annual of the American Schools of Oriental Research
AB	Anchor Bible
ABRL	Anchor Bible Reference Library
AcBib	Academia Biblica
ADPV	Abhandlungen des Deutschen Palästina-Vereins
AIL	Ancient Israel and Its Literature
A.J.	Josephus, *Antiquitates judaicae*
ANEM	Ancient Near East Monographs
ANET	Pritchard, James B., ed. *Ancient Near Eastern Texts Relating to the Old Testament.* 3rd ed. Princeton: Princeton University Press, 1969.
AOAT	Alter Orient und Altes Testament
AOS	American Oriental Series
Apoc. Ab.	Apocalypse of Abraham
Apos. Con.	Apostolic Constitutions
ArBib	The Aramaic Bible
ASORAR	American Schools of Oriental Research Archaeological Reports
ATANT	Abhandlungen zur Theologie des Alten und Neuen Testaments
ATD	Alte Testament Deutsch
Atiquot	*'Atiqot*
BA	*Biblical Archaeologist*
BAR	*Biblical Archaeology Review*
BARIS	British Archaeological Reports International Series
BASOR	*Bulletin of the American Schools of Oriental Research*
BBB	Bonner Biblische Beiträge
BCAW	Blackwell Companions to the Ancient World

BETL	Bibliotheca Ephemeridum Theologicarum Lovaniensium
BJS	Brown Judaic Studies
BN	*Biblische Notizen*
BVB	Brem- und Verdische Bibliothek
BZAW	Beiheft zur Zeitschrift für die alttestmentliche Wissenschaft
CCSA	Corpus christianorum, series apocryphorum
CEJL	Commentaries on Early Jewish Literature
CHANE	Culture and History of the Ancient Near East
ConBOT	Coniectanea Biblical: Old Testament Series
CRINT	Compendia Rerum Iudaicarum and Novum Testamentum
DCLS	Deuterocanonical and Cognate Literature Studies
DJD	Discoveries in the Judaean Desert
Dtr	Deuteronomist
EJL	Early Judaism and Its Literature
EncJud	Skolnik, Fred, and Michael Berenbaum, eds. *Encylopedia Judaica*. 2nd ed. 22 vols. Detroit: Macmillan Reference USA, 2007.
ErIsr	*Eretz Israel*
ESI	*Excavations and Surveys in Israel*
FAT	Forschungen zum Alten Testament
FOTL	Forms of Old Testament Literature
frag.	fragment
FRLANT	Forschungen zur Religion und Literatur des Alten und Neuen Testaments
ha	hectare
HA	*Hadashot Arkheologiyot: Excavations and Surveys in Israel*
HSM	Harvard Semitic Monographs
HSS	Harvard Semitic Studies
HThKAT	Herders Theologischer Kommentar zm Alten Testament
HTS	*HTS Teologiese Studies/Theological Studies*
IAAR	Israel Antiquities Authority Reports
IEJ	*Israel Exploration Journal*
JAJ	*Journal of Ancient Judaism*
JAOS	*Journal of American Oriental Society*
JBL	*Journal of Biblical Literature*

JCSSS	*Journal of the Canadian Society for Syriac Studies*
JSJ	*Journal for the Study of Judaism*
JSJSup	Journal for the Study of Judaism Supplement
JSOT	*Journal for the Study of the Old Testament*
JSOTSup	Journal for the Study of the Old Testament Supplement Series
JSP	*Journal for the Study of the Pseudepigrapha*
JSPSup	Journal for the Study of the Pseudepigrapha Supplement Series
KAT	Kommentar zum Alten Testament
LHBOTS	Library of Hebrew Bible/Old Testament Studies
Liv. Pro.	Lives of the Prophets
LXX	Septuagint
Mart. Ascen. Isa.	Martyrdom and Ascension of Isaiah
MT	Masoretic Text
NCB	New Century Bible Commentary
NEA	*Near Eastern Archaeology*
NEAEHL	Stern, Ephraim, ed. *New Encyclopedia of Archaeological Excavations in the Holy Land*. 4 vols. Jerusalem: Carta & Israel Exploration Society; New York: Simon & Schuster, 1993.
NovTSup	Supplements to Novum Testamentum
OBO	Orbis Biblicus et Orientalis
OBO.SA	Orbis Biblicus et Orientalis, Series Archaeologica
OLA	Orientalia Lovaniensia Analecta
OTP	Charlesworth, James H., ed. *Old Testament Pseudepigrapha*. 2 vols. New York: Doubleday, 1983, 1984.
OTS	Old Testament Studies
PEQ	*Palestine Exploration Quarterly*
Pesiq. Rab.	Pesiqta Rabbati
QD	Questiones Disputatae
Rab.	Rabbah (+ biblical book)
RB	*Revue biblique*
RlA	Ebeling, Erich, et al., eds. *Reallexikon der Assyriologie*. Berlin: de Gruyter, 1928–2018.
RSF	*Rivista di studi fenici*
Sanh.	Sanhedrin
SC	Sources chrétiennes
SCJ	*Stone-Campbell Journal*

SECA	Studies on Early Christian Apocrypha
Sem	*Semitica*
SJOT	*Scandinavian Journal of the Old Testament*
StBibLit	Studies in Biblical Literature (Lang)
STDJ	Studies on the Texts of the Desert of Judah
SVTP	Studia in Veteris Testamenti Pseudepigraphica
SymS	Symposium Series
TA	*Tel Aviv*
ThW	Theologische Wissenschaft
TSAJ	Texts and Studies in Ancient Judaism
Transeu	*Transeuphratène*
UF	*Ugarit-Forschungen*
VeEc	*Verbum et Ecclesia*
VT	*Vetus Testamentum*
VTSup	Supplements to Vetus Testamentum
WBC	Word Biblical Commentary
Yebam.	Yebamot
ZAW	*Zeitschrift für die alttestamentliche Wissenschaft*
ZDPV	*Zeitschrift des deutschen Palästina-Vereins*

The Last Century in the History of the Kingdom of Judah: New Data, New Queries, New Interpretations

Oded Lipschits and Filip Čapek

The seventh century BCE, the last century in the history of the kingdom of Judah, is well defined historically and archaeologically. On the one hand, the region was devastated by the Assyrian campaign of Sennacherib (701 BCE), which subsequently caused several destruction levels. An additional series of destruction levels caused by the Babylonian campaign of Nebuchadnezzar (588–586 BCE) were discovered all over Judah and mark not only the end of this century, but also the end of the monarchic period in Judah—the end of the First Temple period.

From an archaeological perspective, the material culture of the late eighth century BCE (as discovered in the 701 destruction levels) and the late seventh–early sixth century BCE (as discovered in the 586 destruction levels) are considered to be familiar to research and easy to identify. The material culture of this period can be added to the historical sources from and related to the seventh century BCE, which include mainly Assyrian and Babylonian sources that mention kingdoms, places, events, and people that are well known from archaeological research and from biblical descriptions of the history of the kingdom of Judah during this period.

From the historical perspective, the kingdom of Judah became an Assyrian vassal kingdom already during the days of King Ahaz and continued to exist as such for the next century. Only after one hundred years and after the Assyrian withdrawal from the Levant and the cancellation of all the Assyrian geopolitical measures did Judah become, for a short period, an Egyptian vassal kingdom and later, after the Babylonian conquest of the region, a Babylonian vassal kingdom. The outcome of this history is that Judah was under the direct rule of great empires for approximately 150 years (732–586 BCE) before the Babylonian destruction of Jerusalem and the demotion of its status to a province. The economy and administration of the kingdom of Judah was established already at the beginning of this period, when Judah, like other vassal kingdoms, was obliged to send regular intelligence reports on the movements of Assyria's enemies, pay annual taxes to the Assyrian throne, and participate in Assyrian military campaigns. The settlement pattern, economy and administration were changed and adapted to this new political and geopolitical situation, especially during the seventh century BCE, after Sennacherib's campaign (701 BCE) and the loss of the Shephelah. It can be assumed that Ramat Raḥel was the center of this rural administration, and the main development occurred in the area of Benjamin to the north of Jerusalem and to its south. This is likely also the reason why from this same period there are numerous Judahite ostraca, seals, weights, stamp impressions, bullae, and other administrative finds. Such material remains render the seventh century BCE the most documented and well-known era in the history of Judah.

Further to this, the seventh century BCE was the period when, according to many scholars, biblical historiographers ("the Deuteronomistic school") wrote and edited parts of the biblical historiography, describing the history of Judah from the time of Joshua to the time of Josiah, and when prophets such as Isaiah, Jeremiah, and Ezekiel lived in Jerusalem, side by side with other prophets and prophetesses, leaving a rich library of scrolls with a abundant historical, theological, political, and social information.

From all these perspectives, the information and knowledge of the seventh century BCE is incomparable with any other century in the history of the kingdoms of Israel and Judah.

This collective volume is the result of international cooperation between researchers who, coming from different academic disciplines and having different viewpoints, have concentrated on a single common theme, the kingdom of Judah in the last full century of its existence. Altogether, eleven chapters in four main sections develop the current ongoing discussion about Judah in the seventh century BCE and extend it to include further important insights. These are based on the specific results of the most recent research in the fields of archaeology, history, cult, and the interpretation of Old Testament texts. Although the academic disciplines involved differ in character, their perspective is influenced by the other scholarly fields, so that thanks to this interdisciplinary approach the reader has a vivid picture of the period under examination, in which mainstream historical developments merge with the events of everyday life.

The first section, "Judah in Extended Perspective," deals first of all with the definition of "the long century," as the seventh century BCE is known. To begin, Oded Lipschits demonstrates how little we actually know about the history, archaeology, and geopolitical situation of the land of Israel and in particular the history of Judah during the seventh century BCE. Based on a geopolitical analysis of the history of the land, its administrative and economic development, Lipschits suggests an alternate solution to the current understanding of the seventh century BCE and a different perspective on the development of its material culture. He further suggests to expand the limits of this seventh century, both backward for thirty-four years (734 BCE) and forward about fourteen years (586 BCE), effectively creating the long seventh century. A new chronological frame for the Iron Age IIB–IIC is suggested in which the long seventh century is divided to two subphases, each one of them approximately one hundred years: the late Iron IIB (734–630 BCE) and the Iron IIC (630–539 BCE), with each one of these periods further categorized into two subphases, employing the destruction levels as a spotlight on the middle of a chronological phase in the development of the material culture, rather than as a marker for the end of the archaeological period: the late Iron IIB1 (734–701 BCE) and the late Iron IIB2 (701–630 BCE), when the Sennacherib campaign places the spotlight on the material culture of this period and facilitates a historical separation between these two phases, and the Iron IIC1 (630–586 BCE) and the Iron IIC2 (586–539 BCE), when the Babylonian destruction shifts the spotlight onto the material culture of this period and historically separates these two phases.

In the next chapter Filip Čapek focuses on the strange tension that is associated with the figure of Josiah, king of Judah (639–609 BCE), if we attempt to understand his period and Josiah himself through the material culture, on one hand, and the biblical texts, on the other. This tension is due not only to the silent epigraphic evidence about the long reign of this king, but also to the conflict between the material culture, in particular cult artifacts, and what the biblical texts try to communicate. These texts, written from a later perspective, have a marked religious and literary stylization and portray Josiah as a prominent reformer of the Yahwistic cult, which according to them should be strongly monolatrous or even directly monotheistic. Čapek outlines an interpretational scenario that resolves this conflict positively by using the different disciplines to complement each other. In this scenario the later perspective found in the biblical texts is also significant, because if it is analyzed critically it, too, helps extend our understanding of the late seventh century BCE in which, from the viewpoint of material culture, it is as if Josiah has been forgotten.

The second section, "Material Culture under Scrutiny," primarily examines the settlement of Judah in the towns and the countryside. On the basis of his own current research in Hebron, David Ben-Shlomo describes the appearance of the architecture from the eighth and seventh centuries BCE, in particular town walls, in its archaeological and historical context, including the seals and ostraca that have been found there. A notable discovery is the evidence of the continued use of Middle Bronze IIB–C fortifications during the Iron Age and specifically their reinforcement in the southern part of the tell dated to the Iron Age IIB–C, which has its parallel in the City of David, where Middle Bronze II fortifications were used during Iron Age II.

Yuval Gadot, together with Sivan Mizrahi, Liora Freud, and David Gellman, analyze the changes in the agricultural landscape around Jerusalem, the appearance and usage of which were derived from the organization of the political, religious, and economic system. These authors' research reveals the important role played by Assyria, whose hegemony is evident both outside the capital, where the cultivation of previously unused areas occurs, and from the material culture, in particular the architecture, in Jerusalem itself. The last chapter in this section, written by Liora Freud, focuses on a specific type of ceramic that was used, the holemouth jar, which is associated with the end of the Iron Age. The detailed description of the typology of the holemouth jar provided by the author makes it possible both to date more exactly the settlement of selected sites in the vicinity of Jerusalem and to determine the extent to which some other types of ceramic were used after the fall of the kingdom of Judah in the year 586 BCE.

The third section, "Iconography, Cult, and Cultural Interaction," deals with the broad field of religion, cult, and the associated political contexts. Ido Koch examines in detail how the iconographic material in Judah adopts the models of the Assyrian hegemony. An important aspect observed by the author is the adaptation of the imperial symbols and their transformation in many different ways. After the fall of their principal bearers these symbols became the sign of the proclaimed sovereignty of Judah, as can be seen, for example, from the use of the rosette in the late seventh century BCE and the start of the following century. The religious symbols of the deities underwent a similar transformation, being adapted to the setting of the southern Levant, where innovation of the already existing iconography of the local lunar deities also occurred.

David Rafael Moulis considers the subject of the cult under the reign of Hezekiah. By using existing archaeological evidence, including the latest discoveries from Tel Moza, he shows that the reform of the cult took place over a lengthy time period. According to Moulis, this is also connected with the various forms it took, which developed out of the different ways that the local authorities understood the assumed instructions for centralization issued in Jerusalem.

The chapter by Josef Mario Briffa concentrates on a different aspect of the cult. It puts forward the thesis that the Judean pillar figurines need to be seen as part of a miniature figural world that includes female figurines but also other anthropomorphic types, figurines of riders and horses, and the like. This assertion stands against a restrictive paradigm that isolates the female figurines, notably the Judean pillar figurines, from the rest of the repertoire, linking them with rituals of fertility and protection. Informed by semiotic and poststructural debate, the figurines are seen as a medium for the production and manipulation of social identities and meanings, offering a window, a pale reflection, on the persons and communities who made and used them, as though "looking through a glass darkly."

The fourth section, "Judah in the Seventh Century BCE, Reflected Not Only in Biblical Texts," contains three chapters and deals with the theme of how the events in this century were treated in the Old Testament traditions and in texts from later historical periods. Adam Mackerle questions the historical reliability of the preexilic prophetic texts. Analyzing studies on this theme by Rainer Kessler, Devadasan Premnath, and Gunther Fleischer, he argues that the assumption of a preexilic date is based more on a preconceived view of the time at which they were supposed to have been written than on any genuine proof. This means that the interpretation, including the social, economic, and religious contexts, ends up in a vicious circle. The reliability of a monarchic dating for texts in the books of Kings, and particularly the lists of Israelite and Judahite kings, is explored by Jan Rückl. Contrary to the notion that the first edition of Kings climaxed with the depiction of Josiah's reign and that it was composed under this king's rule in the last quarter of the seventh century BCE, Rückl demonstrates that accounts of the reigns of Manasseh, Amon, and Josiah do not support the Josianic date of origin of the book but point rather to a first edition of the book during the exilic/postexilic period. On the basis of textual criticism, Rückl argues that the way the seventh century is described in Kings does not point to a seventh-century BCE edition of the book culminating with Josiah's reign.

The final chapter, by David Cielontko, examines seven early Jewish texts dealing with King Manasseh (Animal Apocalypse, Apocalypse of Abraham, 2 Baruch, Martyrdom of Isaiah, Greek Prayer of Manasseh, Prayer of Manasseh in 4Q381, and a prayer in Apos. Con. 7.37). Cielontko comes to the conclusion that these literary sources provide unique insights into the ongoing development of the tradition and recollections about this Judahite king from the seventh century BCE. Manasseh has been remembered in two very distinct ways, on the one hand, as the most wicked sinner guilty of the worst possible deeds and, on the other hand, as a blessed righteous example for following generations.

This collective volume extends the horizons of our knowledge about the kingdom of Judah in the seventh century BCE. New archaeological data and their analysis, together with a detailed study of the iconography, cult, and texts relating to this period, shed new light on this long century, the last full one, which is essential for an understanding of the history of the kingdom of Judah, a small state in the region of the southern Levant.

Part 1
Judah in Extended Perspective

The Long Seventh Century BCE: Archaeological and Historical Perspectives

Oded Lipschits

The final century of the kingdom of Judah, the seventh century BCE, is considered a well-understood period in the history of this small and hilly kingdom and is possibly even the most notable century in its history.[1] In contrast to every other century in the four hundred years of the kingdoms of Israel and Judah, from an archaeological perspective, the seventh century BCE is considered a well-defined period. The region was devastated by military events, which subsequently caused several destruction levels at the turn of the century (the Assyrian campaign of Sennacherib, 701 BCE) and generated an additional series of destruction levels at its end (the Babylonian campaign of Nebuchadnezzar, 588–586 BCE). Since several of these destruction levels were identified at the same sites, especially in the lowland (Shephelah) sites (with Lachish Levels III and II considered the most indicative of the late Iron Age II material culture in Judah), such layers became the chronological framework for the seventh century

---

This chapter is based on two lectures that were presented at the Annual Meeting of Tel Aviv University and Charles University: "Archaeology of the Days of Josiah" and "Chronology of the Iron IIC." Although each lecture will also be published separately, here I wish to present a synthesis of my views on the history and archaeology of this period from historical and archaeological perspectives.

1. See, e.g., the detailed reconstruction of the second half of the seventh century BCE by Nadav Na'aman, "The Kingdom of Judah under Josiah," *TA* 18 (1991): 3–71; and the collected essays edited by Lester L. Grabbe, *Good Kings and Bad Kings: The Kingdom of Judah in the Seventh Century BCE*, LHBOTS 393 (London: T&T Clark, 2005), dealing especially with the first half of this century. Even according to Mario Liverani, *Israel's History and the History of Israel* (London: Equinox, 2005), translated from the 2003 Italian original publication, 143–99, this part of the history can be reconstructed, as against the "invented history" of the periods before and after.

in Judah. From an archaeological perspective, the material culture of the late eighth century BCE (Lachish Level III) and the late seventh–early sixth century BCE (Lachish Level II) are now considered to be familiar to research and easy to identify.[2]

Furthermore, there are historical sources from, and related to, the seventh century BCE. These sources are primarily Assyrian and Babylonian and mention kingdoms, places, events, and people that are well known from archaeological research and biblical descriptions of the history of the kingdoms of Israel and Judah in the second half of the eighth and seventh century BCE.[3]

The kingdom of Israel's confrontation with the Assyrian Empire during this period triggered a series of events during which (1) the kingdom was conquered and its territory annexed, (2) three different provinces were established on the former territory of the kingdom, and (3) a large portion of the population was deported elsewhere and replaced with large groups of resettled deportees.[4] During this same time (already during the days of King Ahaz), the kingdom of Judah became an Assyrian vassal kingdom and continued to exist as such for the next century.[5] Only after one

---

2. On the material culture of Lachish Levels III and II, see Orna Zimhoni, "Two Ceramic Assemblages from Lachish Levels III and II," *TA* 17 (1990): 3–52; Zimhoni, "The Pottery of Levels III and II," in *The Renewed Archaeological Excavations at Lachish (1973–1994)*, ed. David Ussishkin, Sonia and Marco Nadler Institute of Archaeology Monograph Series 22 (Tel Aviv: Emery and Claire Yass Publications in Archaeology, 2004), 4:1789–1900; Ussishkin, *Renewed Archaeological Excavations at Lachish*, 1:92. For a modern and detailed evaluation of the pottery assemblages from the late Iron Age II, see Liora Freud, "Judahite Pottery of the Transition Phase between the Iron Age and Persian Period" [Hebrew] (PhD diss., Tel Aviv University, 2018).

3. See Angelika Berlejung, "The Assyrians in the West: Assyrianization, Colonialism, Indifference, or Development Policy?," in *Congress Volume Helsinki 2010*, ed. Martti Nissinen, VTSup 148 (Leiden: Brill, 2012), 21–60.

4. See, e.g., Nadav Na'aman, "Province System and Settlement Pattern in Southern Syria and Palestine in the Neo-Assyrian Period," in *Neo-Assyrian Geography*, ed. Mario Liverani, Quaderni di geografia storica 5 (Rome: Università di Roma, Istituto di studi del Vicino Oriente, 1995), 103–15; Israel Finkelstein, *The Forgotten Kingdom: The Archaeology and History of Northern Israel*, ANEM 5 (Atlanta: Society of Biblical Literature, 2013), 119–40.

5. For this during the time of King Ahaz, see Oded Lipschits, "The Changing Faces of Kingship in Judah under Assyrian Rule," in *Changing Faces of Kingship in Syria-Palestine 1500–500 BCE*, ed. Agustinus Gianto and Peter Dubovský, AOAT 459 (Münster: Ugarit-Verlag, 2018), 116–38. For a discussion of the policies that the Assyr-

hundred years and following the quick collapse and withdrawal of Assyria from all of its holdings in the Levant did Judah become (for a short period) an Egyptian vassal kingdom and later, after the Babylonian conquest of the region, a Babylonian vassal kingdom.[6] The outcome of this history is that Judah was under the direct rule of great empires for approximately 150 years (732–586 BCE) before the Babylonians destruction of Jerusalem and the demotion of its status to a province.[7] During this period the small kingdom of Judah was integrated into the economy and administration of the Assyrian, and later Babylonian, Empire. This is likely also the reason why, starting with this period, there are numerous Judahite ostraca, seals, weights, stamp impressions, bullae, and other administrative finds. Such material remains render the seventh century BCE the most documented and well-known era in the history of Judah.[8]

Further to this, the seventh century BCE is the period when, according to a multitude of scholars, the biblical historiographers ("the Deuteronomistic school") wrote and edited large parts of the biblical historiographic books. Such work described the history of Israel and Judah from the time of Joshua to the time of Josiah, when prophets such as Isaiah, Jeremiah, and Ezekiel lived in Jerusalem, side by side, along with other minor prophets and prophetesses. In their stead, they are understood to have left behind a rich library of scrolls that contained a wealth of historical, theological, political, and social information.[9]

---

ians employed to rule and administer their external regions, both the annexed provinces and the semiautonomous vassal kingdoms, see Bradley J. Parker, *The Mechanics of Empire: The Northern Frontier of Assyria as a Case Study in Imperial Dynamics* (Helsinki: Neo-Assyrian Text Corpus Project, 2001). See also Berlejung, "Assyrians in the West," 28; Ariel M. Bagg, "Palestine under Assyrian Rule: A New Look at the Assyrian Imperial Policy in the West," *JAOS* 133 (2013): 119–44; Lipschits, "Changing Faces of Kingship," 119–21.

6. Na'aman, "Kingdom of Judah under Josiah," 34–41. Oded Lipschits, *The Fall and Rise of Jerusalem: The History of Judah under Babylonian Rule* (Winona Lake, IN: Eisenbrauns, 2005), 3–67.

7. Oded Lipschits, *The Age of Empires: History and Administration in Judah in Light of the Stamped Jar Handles* [Hebrew] (Jerusalem: Yad Ben Zvi, 2018), 237–72.

8. Lipschits, "Changing Faces of Kingship," 116–28.

9. See the summary in Lipschits, *Fall and Rise of Jerusalem*, 272–89. For a balanced discussion on the time and the process of development of the Deuteronomistic literature, see Thomas Römer, *The So-Called Deuteronomistic History: A Sociological, Historical and Literary Introduction* (London: T&T Clark, 2005), and see also his recent discussion: Römer, "The Rise and Fall of Josiah," in *Rethinking Israel: Stud-*

From all these perspectives, the information and knowledge of the seventh century BCE is incomparable with any other century in the history of the kingdoms of Israel and Judah. In spite of that, the aims of this paper are to demonstrate how every definition of the seventh century BCE is problematic and flexible and how this century can be defined in several different ways, based on archaeological material, historical sources, and the biblical historiography. I will further demonstrate how every definition of the seventh century BCE must consider the geographical region, be it the coastal area, the territory of the (former) kingdom of Israel, or different regions from within the territory of the kingdom of Judah. Furthermore, I will demonstrate more generally how little we actually know about the history, archaeology, and geopolitical situation of the region and in particular the history of Judah during the seventh century BCE. I will expand upon this and note how critical it is that scholars remain careful when adopting this period for the study of cultic and theological developments, the history of Judah, and biblical historiography and prophecy. Rather, I will suggest an alternate solution to the current understanding of the seventh century BCE, based on a geopolitical analysis of the history of the land, its administrative and economic development, and a different perspective on the development of its material culture. Such an approach will expand the limits of this seventh century, both backward for thirty-four years (734 BCE) and forward about fourteen years (586 BCE), effectively creating "the long seventh century."

Since, according to my view, every definition of a period in history is a reflection of historiographical perspectives and only after such a definition can one examine the characteristics of the material culture in different regions and see how the geopolitical and historiographical observations are reflected in it, I will suggest a new chronological frame for the Iron Age IIB–IIC and within it also to the long seventh century. Following previous suggestions that were based on a careful examination of the material culture of Judah and in the former kingdom of Israel, I will suggest that we define the long seventh century as a *part* of the Iron

---

ies in the History and Archaeology of Ancient Israel in Honor of Israel Finkelstein, ed. Oded Lipschits, Yuval Gadot, and Matthew J. Adams (Winona Lake, IN: Eisenbrauns, 2017), 329–40. Israel Finkelstein and Neil A. Silberman, *The Bible Unearthed, Archaeology's New Vision of Ancient Israel and the Origin of Its Sacred Texts* (London: Simon & Schuster, 2001), 275, described the late seventh century, especially the days of King Josiah as "the climax of Israel's monarchic history."

IIB–IIC and split this archaeological/historical period into two subphases, each one approximately one hundred years: *the Iron IIB* (734–630 BCE) and *the Iron IIC* (630–539 BCE).[10]

Based on archaeological and historical considerations, I will further suggest that each one of these periods be further categorized into two subphases, employing the destruction levels as a spotlight on the middle of a chronological phase in the development of the material culture, rather than as a marker for the end of the archaeological period. In the *late Iron IIB* (734–630 BCE) one can differentiate between the Iron IIB1 (734–701 BCE) and the Iron IIB2 (701–630 BCE), when the Sennacherib campaign places the spotlight on the material culture of this period and facilitates a historical separation between these two phases. During the *Iron IIC* one can differentiate between the Iron IIC1 (630–586 BCE) and the Iron IIC2 (586–539 BCE), when the Babylonian destruction shifts the spotlight onto the material culture of this period and historically separates these two phases.

1.1. Traditional Definitions of the Seventh Century BCE

From the simplest numerical perspective, the seventh century BCE is the one hundred years between the first day of the year 700 and the last day of the year 601 BCE. Yet besides this numerical perspective, defining the seventh century in such a way is meaningless from any other standpoint. Therefore, to define this century from a more historical perspective, the seventh century BCE should be defined according to alternate criteria.

The standard relative chronological-archaeological framework applied to the seventh century BCE (and up until the Babylonian destruction of 586 BCE) is defined as the "Iron IIC" and, for example, is presented as such in the *New Encyclopedia of Archaeological Excavations in the Holy Land* (*NEAEHL*) and in numerous other archaeological publications.[11] This

---

10. For the material culture of Judah, see Avi Ofer, "The Highland of Judah during the Biblical Period" (PhD diss., Tel Aviv University, 1993), 2:44–50. For the material culture of the former kingdom of Israel, see Lily Singer-Avitz, "The Pottery of Megiddo Strata III–II and a Proposed Subdivision of the Iron IIC Period in Northern Israel," *BASOR* 372 (2014): 123–45, esp. 138–40.

11. It is not clear why Dafna Langgut et al., "Vegetation and Climate Changes during the Bronze and Iron Ages (~3600–600 BCE) in the Southern Levant Based on Palynological Records," *Radiocarbon* 57 (2015): 217–35, employs the date of 680

definition is centrally based on the history and archaeology of Judah and concerns the period between the Assyrian military campaign of Sennacherib (701 BCE) and the Babylonian military campaign of Nebuchadnezzar (586 BCE). On the one hand, the intense trauma inflicted on Judah by the Assyrians had disastrous consequences for all matters (especially in relation to the Shephelah) and led to a grave weakening of its military might and human resources.[12] The destruction of this event was clearly detected in several sites, especially in the Shephelah and at Lachish (Level III). These remains were thus applied as a clear marker for the separation between the material culture of the late eighth and the material culture of the seventh century BCE. The destruction of Jerusalem and other urban centers (among them Lachish [Level II]) during the Babylonian campaign of 588–586 BCE was the main indication for the end of the material culture of the seventh and the early sixth century BCE.[13]

1.2. Problems with the Definition of the Seventh Century BCE as Iron IIC

The core problem with this definition of the seventh century BCE as Iron IIC is that these two very distinct assemblages of pottery and associated finds are representative of the material culture that characterized Judah during the long period prior to and immediately after 701 BCE and later prior to and immediately after 586 BCE.[14] These destructions provide an important spotlight on the material culture that existed during the destruction of the sites at the moment that they were destroyed. It is clear that these assemblages existed prior to the destruction, but it is not clear how much time before such destructions that this material culture

---

BCE as the beginning of the Iron IIC. It may be because of the date presented by Oded Lipschits, Omer Sergi, and Ido Koch for the transition between the late *lmlk* and the concentric circle incision, but in any case, there is no explanation for this date. See Lipschits, Sergi, and Koch, "Royal Judahite Jar Handles: Reconsidering the Chronology of the *lmlk* Stamp Impressions," *TA* 37 (2010): 3–32; Lipschits, Sergi, and Koch, "Judahite Stamped and Incised Jar Handles: A Tool for the Study of the History of Late Monarchic Judah," *TA* 38 (2011): 5–41.

12. Lipschits, *Age of Empires*, 243–53.

13. Ussishkin, *Renewed Archaeological Excavations at Lachish*, 1:92.

14. Lynn Tatum, "Jerusalem in Conflict: The Evidence for the Seventh-Century B.C.E. Religious Struggle over Jerusalem," in *Jerusalem in Bible and Archaeology: The First Temple Period*, ed. Andrew G. Vaughn and Ann E. Killebrew, SymS 18 (Atlanta: Society of Biblical Literature, 2003), 291–306.

existed, when the characteristics of this material culture were developed, and until when they continued to develop afterward in areas and sites that were not destroyed. Even if there are clear destructions and a settlement gap in Lachish and other sites that were destroyed during one or even in both of these military campaigns, the characteristics of the material culture discovered from within these destruction levels are only spotlights on a certain point in a long process of ongoing change in the material culture. Neither in Lachish nor in any other site in Judah can one find further evidence for the gradual development of the material culture during the late eighth century (before 701 BCE), the gradual change and transition of distinctive assemblages from the late eighth to the late seventh century BCE, and the further development of the material culture after the 586 BCE destruction. There is no reason to assume that the Lachish III repertoire, which characterizes the material culture in Judah just prior to 701 BCE, ceased to exist as a result of the events of 701 BCE, particularly in the many sites that were not destroyed during this event, such as Jerusalem and the hill country around it. Furthermore, it is reasonable to assume that this same material culture continued to exist in this region during the early seventh century BCE and changed gradually through a slow process during the first half of the seventh century BCE.[15] There are no destruction levels in Judah from this period, when the mid-seventh century material culture could have been recovered and clearly defined. Yet a careful study

---

15. On the understanding that the material culture that characterizes Lachish Level III continued in places that did not suffer a destruction of 701 BCE and (even if not identified) continued during the early seventh century BCE until the crystallization of the typical pottery types of Lachish Level II, see already Nadav Na'aman, "When and How Did Jerusalem Become a Great City? The Rise of Jerusalem as Judah's Premier City in the Eighth–Seventh Centuries B.C.E.," *BASOR* 347 (2007): 25–26; Israel Finkelstein, "Comments on the Date of Late-Monarchic Judahite Seal Impressions," *TA* 39 (2012): 204–5; Alon De Groot, "Discussion and Conclusions," in *Area E; Stratigraphy and Architecture*, vol. 7a of *Excavation at the City of David 1978–1985 Directed by Yigal Shiloh*, ed. Alon De Groot and Hannah Bernick-Greenberg, Qedem 53 (Jerusalem: Institute of Archaeology, Hebrew University of Jerusalem, 2012), 162; Yuval Gadot, "In the Valley of the King: Jerusalem's Rural Hinterland in the Eighth–Fourth Centuries BCE," *TA* 42 (2015): 8; Liora Freud, "Production and Widespread Use of Holemouth Vessels in Jerusalem and Its Environs in the Iron Age II: Typology, Chronology, and Distribution" [Hebrew], in *New Studies in the Archaeology of Jerusalem and Its Region: Collected Papers, Volume 11*, ed. Yuval Gadot et al. (Jerusalem, 2017), 93–97.

of the development of building phases in sites such as Ramat Raḥel and other hill country sites, reveals a separation between different building phases in Jerusalem (Strata 12–10), and a clear definition of the differences between fills below the floor of structures from the late seventh and early sixth century BCE and the finds above it (especially finds that were sealed by the 586 destruction of these phases) can aid the identification of the main characteristics of the material culture of these phases from within the seventh century BCE.[16] Developing upon this further, the use of the stamped jar handles for dating different phases in the late eighth, early to mid-seventh, and late seventh century, alongside further development in the sixth century BCE, can assist in refining the dates assigned to the different phases of the material culture from this period and the changes in material culture during these chronological phases.[17]

The conclusion here is that there is no reason to argue that the entire corpus of material culture that characterizes Lachish Level III is limited to the end of the eighth century BCE or that the known material culture from Lachish Level II is limited to the late seventh and early sixth century BCE. Nor is there cause to argue that there is a gap between these two corpora of pottery, architecture, stamp impressions, and other finds. On the contrary, transitions in pottery traditions were always gradual and may take a significant amount of time. Hence the fact that Lachish Level III pottery vessels were found in sites that were not destroyed in 701 BCE does not mean that the date of these sites should be limited to the late eighth

---

16. In area E of the City of David, the transitional Stratum 11 was identified as dated to the first half of the seventh century BCE, with a gradual change and few new vessel types, as compared with Stratum 12 (similar to Lachish Level III) and Stratum 10 (similar to Lachish Level II). See Yigal Shiloh, *Excavations at the City of David I 1978–1982: Interim Report of the First Five Seasons*, Qedem 19 (Jerusalem: Hebrew University, 1984), 3; Alon De Groot and Hannah Bernick-Greenberg, "The Pottery of Strata 12–10 (Iron Age IIB)," in *Area E; The Finds*, vol. 7b of *Excavations at the City of David 1978–1985 Directed by Yigal Shiloh*, ed. Alon De Groot and Hannah Bernick-Greenberg, Qedem 54 (Jerusalem: Institute of Archaeology, Hebrew University of Jerusalem, 2012), 100–101; Freud, "Production and Widespread Use of Holemouth Vessels," 93–97. Liora Freud, "The Longue Durée of the Seventh Century BCE: A Study of the Iron Age Pottery Vessels from Ramat Raḥel" [Hebrew] (MA thesis, Tel Aviv University, 2011); Freud, "Judahite Pottery of the Transition Phase."

17. Lipschits, *Age of Empires*, 123–65. See already Lipschits, Sergi, and Koch, "Royal Judahite Jar Handles," 3–32; Lipschits, Sergi, and Koch, "Judahite Stamped and Incised Jar Handles," 5–41.

century BCE. Even in sites that have been established in the early seventh century BCE and continued to exist with no disturbance until the end of the seventh century BCE, the pottery would likely include both Lachish III and Lachish II forms.

Throughout this period, in the first two-thirds of the seventh century BCE, Judah enjoyed the economic prosperity of the entire region under Assyrian rule.[18] The eastern and southern border areas (in particular the Negev) integrated into the Assyrian and international commercial system and flourished both demographically and economically.[19] In the Judean highland and the Benjamin region, a gradual process of rehabilitation took place, and the status of Jerusalem was established as the central city.[20] All of these data add a great deal to existing perceptions of the "dark era" between the luminous historical and archaeological points of 701 and 586 BCE.

The same conclusions as expressed in relation to the material culture discovered in the destruction levels from 701 BCE can also be aligned with the material culture that characterizes the end of the First Temple period, as discovered in the 586 BCE destruction levels. There is no reason to assume that this pottery repertoire, which characterizes the material culture in Judah just before 586 BCE, ceased to exist as a result of the events of 586 BCE.[21] Several

---

18. For a summary of the archaeological finds and historical reconstruction of this period, see Lipschits, *Age of Empires*, 243–53; see also Israel Finkelstein, "The Archaeology of the Days of Manasseh," in *Scripture and Other Artifacts: Essays on the Bible and Archaeology in Honor of Philip J. King*, ed. Michael D. Coogan, J. Cheryl Exum, and Lawrence Stager (Louisville: Westminster John Knox, 1994), 169–87.

19. For the Negev, see Dafna Langgut and Oded Lipschits, "Dry Climate during the Early Persian Period and Its Impact on the Establishment of Idumea," *Transeu* 49 (2017): 135–62, with further literature. See also Nadav Na'aman, "The Negev in the Last Century of the Kingdom of Judah" [Hebrew], *Cathedra* 42 (1987): 4–15; Na'aman, "Province System and Settlement Pattern," 113–14; Israel Finkelstein, "Edom in the Iron I," *Levant* 24 (1992): 161; Itzhak Beit-Arieh, *Tel 'Ira—A Stronghold in the Biblical Negev*, Monograph Series of the Institute of Archaeology 15 (Tel Aviv: Institute of Archaeology of Tel Aviv University, 1999), 1–3. For the Jordan Valley, see Ephraim Stern, "The Jericho Region and the Eastern Border of the Judean Kingdom in Its Last Days" [Hebrew], *ErIsr* 24 (1993): 192–97; Oded Lipschits, "Was There a Royal Estate in Ein-Gedi by the End of the Iron Age and During the Persian Period?" [Hebrew], in *Jerusalem and Eretz Israel (Arie Kindler Volume)*, ed. Joshua Schwartz, Zohar Amar, and Irit Ziffer (Tel Aviv: Eretz Israel Museum and The Ingeborg Center for Jerusalem Studies, 2000), 31–42.

20. Gadot, "In the Valley of the King."

21. Lipschits, *Fall and Rise of Jerusalem*, 192–206.

rural sites continued to exist in Judah after 586 BCE (mainly to the north and to the south of Jerusalem), the remains of which indicate that there was a continuation of the well-known and familiar material culture.[22] This means that the transition from this Iron Age II ceramic repertoire to the assemblage of pottery types that characterize the Persian period took place sometime in the middle or even toward the end of the sixth century BCE.[23] There is no reason to argue that the entire corpus of material culture that characterize Lachish (Level II) and Jerusalem (Stratum 10) at the beginning of the sixth century BCE was immediately and uniformly replaced by the known material culture of the Persian period. The fact that these typical and well-known pottery vessels were recovered from sites that were not destroyed in 586 BCE does not mean that these sites should be dated to events that predate the 586 BCE destruction.[24] Even in sites that were established in the sixth or even in the early fifth century BCE (and continued to exist with no disturbance during the Persian and even the early Hellenistic period), the pottery would include both Late Iron Age II and Persian period forms.[25]

---

22. Oded Lipschits, "Shedding New Light on the Dark Years of the 'Exilic Period': New Studies, Further Elucidation, and Some Questions Regarding the Archaeology of Judah as an 'Empty Land,'" in *Interpreting Exile: Interdisciplinary Studies of Displacement and Deportation in Biblical and Modern Contexts*, ed. Brad E. Kelle, Frank R. Ames, and Jacob L. Wright, AIL 10 (Atlanta: Society of Biblical Literature, 2011), 57–90.

23. Freud, "Judahite Pottery of the Transition Phase."

24. This hypothesis is opposed to that expressed by Israel Finkelstein in Yitzhak Magen and Israel Finkelstein, eds., *Archaeological Survey of the Hill Country of Benjamin* [Hebrew] (Jerusalem: Israel Antiquities Authority, 1993), 27. Finkelstein hypothesized that in the early sixth century BCE, parallel to the destruction of Jerusalem, a severe crisis beset the settlement in the Benjamin region, and the picture was even grimmer than that reflected in the archaeological survey. In the fifth and fourth centuries BCE, by comparison, a certain recovery took place, which is the historical situation that the survey reflects. In my opinion, this is a general historical assessment with no archaeological evidence. The only possible point of comparison is to the sites that were excavated in the region of Benjamin, which indicate the opposite picture. In the sixth century BCE, the settlement in Benjamin continued to flourish and prosper, and the dwindling of the settlement began in the late sixth and early fifth centuries BCE. The historical centrality of Mizpah (Tel en-Naṣbeh) and the indications for the centrality of Gibeon at this time (as a wine-producing center) also warrant an exploration of the notion that there was a strong agricultural hinterland in the region.

25. Freud, "Judahite Pottery of the Transition Phase." See also Oded Lipschits et al., "Judah in 'the Long Third Century': An Archaeological Perspective" [Hebrew], in

1.3. Defining the Higher Border of the Long Seventh Century

From a broader historical and archaeological perspective, the beginning of the seventh century BCE should be defined by the appearance of the Assyrian Empire and its effect on the local kingdoms. On the one hand, there are a series of destructions caused by the Assyrian army, all of which are well dated and clearly defined, mainly in the territory of the former kingdom of Israel. These destructions terminated the prosperous settlements of the Iron IIB in northern Israel, including its prosperous olive oil production centers and economy.[26] In the northern and western regions of this kingdom there are major destructions from the 732 BCE campaign, and in the Samaria hills such destructions are dated to 722–720 BCE.[27]

From this perspective, the seventh century BCE begins in the northern vicinity of the region in 732 BCE, when the material culture of this phase, for example, as it was defined in Megiddo Stratum III, is characterized by a continuation from the Iron IIB, alongside the emergence of new forms and pottery types that appear only in the post-732 BCE destruction horizon.[28] The arrangements made by Tiglath-pileser III in the former areas of the kingdom of Israel existed without any marked change until the Babylonian, Persian, and even the early Hellenistic periods. These arrangements included establishing two provinces in the lands wrested from the kingdom as early as 732 BCE: the province of Dū'ru (Dôr) extended through the narrow expanse of the Carmel coast and reached to the Yarkon River in the south, while the province of Magidû encompassed the upper and lower Galilee, Beth Shean Valley, and the Jezre'el Plain.[29] Following the

---

vol. 8 of *New Studies in the Archaeology of Jerusalem and Its Region: Collected Papers*, ed. Guy D. Stiebel et al. (Jerusalem, 2014), 134–52.

26. For the termination of settlements, see Singer-Avitz, "Pottery of Megiddo Strata III–II," 137. For the olive oil centers and economy, see Avraham Faust, "Settlement, Economy, and Demography under Assyrian Rule in the West: The Territories of the Former Kingdom of Israel as a Test Case," *JAOS* 135 (2015): 765–89.

27. See Singer-Avitz, "Pottery of Megiddo Strata III–II."

28. See Singer-Avitz, "Pottery of Megiddo Strata III–II."

29. For the province of Dôr, see Ephraim Stern, "The Dor Province in the Persian Period in the Light of the Recent Excavations at Dor," *Transeu* 2 (1990): 147–55; Stern, "Hazor, Dor and Megiddo in the Time of Ahab and under Assyrian Rule," *IEJ* 40 (1990): 12–30; Stern, *The Assyrian, Babylonian, and Persian Periods (732–332 B.C.E.)*, vol. 2 of *Archaeology of the Land of the Bible*, ABRL (New York: Doubleday, 2001),

destruction of the kingdom of Israel, Sargon II annexed the remainder of the territory to Assyria in 720 BCE and established a third province, the province of Sāmerīna.[30] The lands of this province consisted of the entire Samarian hills, as well as the eastern part of the Sharon and the northern coastal plain, including Apqu (Tel Aphēk) and Gazru (Gezer/Gazra).[31]

The success of the Assyrian arrangement in the northern and central parts of the land of the kingdom of Israel, as well as in Syria, is well reflected archaeologically. It is noteworthy that following the Assyrian retreat, there are no documented changes in the geopolitical situation, no known major destructions have been uncovered by archaeological excavations, and no clearly defined change can be discerned in the material culture.

These regions continued to develop in a slow and gradual process (with no clear archaeological anchor) until the Hellenistic period. With this in mind, from an archaeological perspective, the seventh century BCE in the northern regions of the former kingdom of Israel has no clearly defined lower border. The clear upper border of the seventh century BCE in the kingdom of Israel applies to the northern and western areas in 732 and in the hill country in 722–720 BCE. The lack of a lower border that can separate the seventh from the sixth century BCE in these regions is a phenomenon unique to the area of the former kingdom of Israel and is very distinct from what is known about areas that did not undergo such destruction during the first wave of the Assyrian takeover of this region, that is, the coastal area, Transjordan, and Judah.

In Philistia, no such border can be detected at the beginning, or at the end, of the seventh century BCE. Instead, it appears that from all aspects of the material culture there is a continuation from the eighth to the sev-

---

12, 385–407; Na'aman, "Province System and Settlement Pattern," 106; Ayelet Gilboa, "Assyrian Pottery in Dor and Notes on the Status of the City During the Period of Assyrian Rule" [Hebrew], *ErIsr* 25 (1996): 122–35; Yifat Thareani-Sussely and Nadav Na'aman, "Dating the Appearance of Imitations of Assyrian Ware in Southern Palestine," *TA* 33 (2006): 61–82. For Magidû, see Na'aman, "Province System and Settlement Pattern," 107; Stern, *Assyrian, Babylonian, and Persian Periods*, 46–49.

30. On this subject, see Hayim Tadmor, "On the History of Samaria in the Biblical Period," in *Eretz Shomron: The Thirtieth Archaeological Convention, September 1972* [Hebrew], ed. Joseph Aviram (Jerusalem: Israel Exploration Society, 1973), 67–74. For additional literature see Nadav Na'aman, "Population Changes in Palestine Following the Assyrian Deportations," *TA* 20 (1993): 107 n. 3.

31. See Na'aman, "Province System and Settlement Pattern," 106–7, and fig. 1, p. 105; Stern, *Assyrian, Babylonian, and Persian Periods*, 49–51.

enth and early sixth centuries BCE. The Assyrian arrangement in this region had already been established in the late eighth century BCE during the reign of Sargon II and Sennacherib. These arrangements remained in effect until the death of Assurbanipal and the outbreak of the revolt in Babylonia in 627 BCE.[32]

Asdūdu (Ashdod) was an isolated Assyrian province among the vassal city-states in the region. The head of the province was a local vassal king alongside an official Assyrian governor.[33] North and south of Ashdod, the vassal city-states of Isqalūna (Ashkelon), Anqarrūna (Ekron), and Ḥazzat (Gaza) continued to maintain their existence.[34] These city-states were

----

32. Lipschits, *Fall and Rise of Jerusalem*, 7–9.

33. An inscription of Sargon II notes that an Assyrian governor was stationed in Asdūdu (apparently in 712 BCE), and a governor of the city is mentioned as the eponym of the year 669 BCE. The province of Asdūdu continued to exist in the Persian period and apparently even before under Babylonian rule. Thus, it would seem that Assyrian arrangements remained throughout the Assyrian rule and were the territorial and administrative basis for the arrangements of the Babylonian and Persian rule. In contrast, we know that in the days of Sennacherib a king governed in the city. For an explanation of this special and extraordinary duality, see Hayim Tadmor, "The Assyrian Campaigns to Philistia" [Hebrew], in *The Military History of the Land of Israel in Biblical Times*, ed. Joseph Liver (Tel Aviv: Bialik, 1964), 272–76. For a critique of Tadmor's proposal, see Nadav Na'aman, "The Brook of Egypt and Assyrian Policy on the Border of Egypt," *TA* 6 (1979): 72; Na'aman, "Esarhaddon's Treaty with Baal and Assyrian Provinces along the Phoenician Coast," *RSF* 22 (1994): 3–8, with further literature.

34. Isqalūna (Ašqelôn/Ashkelon) was an important port and central commercial hub, wherein a vast wine production industry thrived. At the end of the eighth century BCE, prior to the campaign of Sennacherib, the territory of this kingdom included the enclave near Iappû (Yafo/Jaffa). See Lawrence E. Stager, "Ashkelon and the Archaeology of Destruction: Kislev 604 BCE," *ErIsr* 25 (1996): 61*–74*; Seymour Gitin, "The Neo-Assyrian Empire and Its Western Periphery: The Levant, with a Focus on Philistine Ekron," in *Assyria 1995: Proceedings of the Tenth Anniversary Symposium of the Neo-Assyrian Text Corpus Project, Helsinki, September 7–11, 1995*, ed. Simo Parpola and Robert M. Whiting (Helsinki: Neo-Assyrian Text Corpus Project, 1997), 84; Nadav Na'aman, "Two Notes on the History of Ashkelon and Ekron in the Late Eighth–Seventh Century B.C.E.," *TA* 25 (1998): 222–23. There is no evidence that the territorial situation in this region changed at any stage under Assyrian rule, although one may accept the premise that at some stage, the enclave was transferred to the administration of neighboring Ekron. See Na'aman, "Two Notes on the History of Ashkelon," 223–25. Ekron was an important center for the production of oil, and apparently of textiles as well. See Gitin, "Neo-Assyrian Empire and Its Western Periphery," 87–93. Ekron was the main party to profit from the harsh blow dealt to Judah during the 701 BCE Assyrian campaign. Its growth during the seventh century

strengthened territorially and economically under the reign of Assyrian kings, seemingly because they recognized Philistia's strategic importance as the gateway to Egypt, as well as its economic importance.[35]

To the south of the former kingdom of Israel and to the east of Philistia, Judah operated as a small, peripheral, and mountainous kingdom within the region's seventh century BCE political, economic, and military systems. There is no evidence to indicate that the traumatic events that the kingdom of Israel underwent in any way affected the kingdom of Judah.

BCE, under Assyrian rule, is directly connected to the weakening of the kingdom of Judah and the harsh damage to the territories of the kingdom in the coastal plain. On this subject, see Trude Dothan and Seymour Gitin, "Tel Miqne/Ekron: The Rise and Fall of a Philistine City," *Qadmoniot* 105–106 (1996): 18–25; Seymour Gitin, "The Philistines in the Prophetic Texts: An Archaeological Perspective," in *Hesed ve-Emet: Studies in Honor of Ernest S. Frerichs*, ed. Jodi Magness and Seymour Gitin, BJS 320 (Atlanta: Scholars Press, 1998), 274–78; Amihai Mazar, "The Northern Shephelah in the Iron Age: Some Issue in Biblical History and Archaeology," in *Scriptures and Other Artifacts, Essays on the Bible and Archaeology in Honor of Philip J. King*, ed. Michael D. Coogan, J. Cheryl Exum, and Lawrence E. Stager (Louisville: Westminster John Knox, 1994), 260–63. It is hard to accept, though one cannot totally rule out, the suggestion by Stager ("Ashkelon and the Archaeology of Destruction," *70–*71) and David S. Vanderhooft (*The Neo-Babylonian Empire and Babylon in the Later Prophets*, HSM 59 [Atlanta: Scholars Press, 1999], 75), who prefer to link the growth of Ekron with the Egyptian period of rule, after the withdrawal of Assyria from the region. Ḥazzat (Gaza) was the southernmost of the Philistine kingdoms and served as the major outlet port for merchandise that arrived from Arabian trade. During the reign of Tiglath-pileser III and the early days of Sargon II, major Assyrian effort was focused toward Gaza and its surroundings, as a direct result of their importance. Accordingly, it is not surprising that Gaza remained a loyal Assyrian vassal kingdom from the days of Sargon II until the collapse of the Assyrian rule in this region. See Tadmor, "Assyrian Campaigns to Philistia," 271; H. Jacob Katzenstein, "Gaza in the Neo-Babylonian Period (626–539 B.C.E.)," *Transeu* 7 (1994): 37–38.

35. In the days of Sennacherib, territory was wrested from Judah and awarded to three Philistine kingdoms, so as to establish them more firmly. The Assyrian gain was twofold as it was able to both strengthen its rule in the southwestern border of its empire near the Egyptian border and increase economic gain as a result of the prosperity of these kingdoms and the integration of their ports into the Arabian trade. For further literature on this subject, see Gitin, "Neo-Assyrian Empire and Its Western Periphery," 99–100. For Philistia's economic importance, see Moshe Elat, "The Economic Relations of the Neo-Assyrian Empire with Egypt," *JAOS* 98 (1978): 30–34; Elat, "International Commerce in Palestine under the Assyrian Rule," in *Commerce in Palestine throughout the Ages*, ed. Benjamin Zeev Kedar, Trude Dothan, and Shmuel Safrai (Jerusalem: Yad Ben Zvi, 1990), 67–88.

The events of 732 BCE, and later of 722–720 BCE, are not visible in the material culture of Judah (in the sense of clear destruction levels).

1.4. The Implications of the Beginning of the Long Seventh Century on Judah and Its Existence in the Shadow of the Empire

From the historical perspective, the greatest difference between the seventh century and the former, the eighth century BCE, is the destruction and disappearance of the kingdom of Israel after the destructions of 732 and 720 BCE. As such, from this historical perspective, the beginning of the seventh century BCE is the "postkingdom of Israel" period, when Judah was left alone in the hill country. Developing from this perspective is the notion that, for Judah also, the seventh century had begun already in 732 BCE.

From a Judean perspective this date is also justified as the historical beginning of the seventh century, since in 734 BCE Judah became an Assyrian vassal kingdom.[36] The story that symbolizes the subjugation to Assyria is Ahaz's call to Tiglath-pileser for assistance (2 Kgs 16:8).[37] Without dealing with the tone of the description or the negative evaluation of Ahaz and the deliberate use of negative expressions, from a historical perspective the narrative relays an important issue, that Ahaz's appeal to Tiglath-pileser marks the beginning of the subjugation of Judah to Assyria.

By accepting Assyrian rule and changing its status from independent state to vassal kingdom, Judah was one of only a handful of small kingdoms to survive the Assyrian conquest of Syria and the Levant in the second half of the eighth century BCE.[38] Similarly to other kingdoms in the peripheral regions of the empire that submitted to Assyrian demands, the ruling

---

36. Nadav Na'aman, "Hezekiah and the Kings of Assyria," *TA* 21 (1994): 235; Lipschits, "Changing Faces of Kingship," 116–28.

37. On the story of Ahaz's visit to Damascus, its sources, and goal, see Nadav Na'aman, "Royal Inscriptions and the Histories of Joash and Ahaz, Kings of Judah," *VT* 48 (1998): 344–49.

38. For a comprehensive review of the dynamic expansion of the Neo-Assyrian Empire and the economic and ideological strategies behind such expansion, see Simo Parpola, "Assyria's Expansion in the Eighth and Seventh Centuries and Its Long-Term Repercussions in the West," in *Symbiosis, Symbolism, and the Power of the Past: Canaan, Ancient Israel, and Their Neighbors from the Late Bronze Age through Roman Palaestina*, ed. William Dever and Seymour Gitin (Winona Lake, IN: Eisenbrauns, 2003), 100.

Judean elite were allowed to remain in power and granted autonomy. In exchange, the Assyrians imposed vassal obligations on Judah, including the payment of an annual tribute (not only in material goods but in labor as well), submission of intelligence reports and information related to political and military matters in the area, participation in Assyrian military campaigns, and provision of supplies for the Assyrian army during battles. These obligations were monitored by an Assyrian official and had immediate consequences on Judah's material culture and on its local administration and economy.

The subjection of Judah to Assyria in the early days of King Ahaz and the change in its status from independent state to vassal kingdom was the most significant and influential economic and administrative event in its entire history.[39] It marked the beginning of a roughly six-hundred-year period during which Judah remained under the rule of great empires, first as an Assyrian, Egyptian, and Babylonian vassal kingdom (734 to 586 BCE) and then as a Babylonian, Persian, Ptolemaic, and Seleucid province (586 to the middle of the second century BCE, when the Hasmonaean state was established). The administrative and economic arrangements established by the Assyrians and developed by local Judean leadership remained in effect and continued to develop during the following centuries. Such practices evolved into some of the most typical and well-known characteristics of the Judean economy, administration, and material culture.[40]

1.5. Characteristics of Judah as a Vassal Kingdom during the Long Seventh Century BCE

The administrative and economic arrangements that were established by the Assyrians and developed by the local Judean leadership continued to be in effect and develop during the coming centuries as they became some of the most typical and well-known characteristics of the Judean economy, administration, and material culture. The existence of these characteristics in the Judean economy, administration, and material culture over so long a timespan is a clear indication of how well suited such systems were to the Judean elite and ruling classes. Furthermore, such characteristics reflect just how critical they were to an internal development of the

---

39. Lipschits, "Changing Faces of Kingship."
40. Lipschits, *Age of Empires*, 48–124.

region, one that reflects what its elite could and would accept, agree to, and pay the ruling empires in order to protect the national and cultic independence inside Jerusalem. Such independence was essential in enabling Judean political, spiritual, and religious life to blossom in the shadow of the empires.[41]

From an agricultural and industrial aspect, Judah was still in its "non-centralized, kinship based" mode during the eighth century BCE, and there is no archaeological evidence of mass manufacture of olive oil in Judah before the mid- and late eighth century BCE.[42] As part of the dramatic change that occurred in the Judean administration and economy (already in the last decades of the eighth century BCE, probably immediately after the subjugation of Judah to Assyria), one should mention the appearance of a new system of marked shekel weights.[43] Such finds are a clear indication of the maturing of the economy and evolving process of standardization. The adaptation of an Egyptian system as well as the use of hieratic numbers, when Judah was under Assyrian rule, indicate that the system likely emerged under Assyrian pressure but was not an Assyrian decision or forced by an Assyrian system, as a Judahite development, derived from known sources as well as close and familiar systems.[44] To this

---

41. Lipschits, "Changing Faces of Kingship."

42. Aren M. Maeir and Itzik Shai, "Reassessing the Character of the Judahite Kingdom: Archaeological Evidence for Non-Centralized, Kinship-Based Components," in *From Sha'ar Hagolan to Shaaraim: Essays in Honor of Prof. Yosef Garfinkel*, ed. Sa'ar Ganor et al. (Jerusalem: Israel Exploration Society, 2016), 323–40. For the manufacture of olive oil, see Faust, "Settlement, Economy, and Demography under Assyrian Rule in the West," 27–29; Israel Finkelstein and Neil A. Silberman, *David and Solomon: In Search of the Bible's Sacred Kings and the Roots of Western Tradition* (New York: Free Press, 2006), 263.

43. Raz Kletter, *Economic Keystones: The Weight System of the Kingdom of Judah*, JSOTSup 276 (Sheffield: Sheffield Academic, 1998), 145–47; Haya Katz, *"A Land of Grain and Wine ... A Land of Olive Oil and Honey": The Economy of the Kingdom of Judah* [Hebrew] (Jerusalem: Yad Ben Zvi, 2008), 77–79, with further literature; Berlejung, "Assyrians in the West," 44–45. Kletter, *Economic Keystones*, 43, demonstrated that only 4 percent of the shekel weights were discovered in pre-seventh century BCE. The meaning of it is that the system of weights was introduced during the late eighth century BCE, and the system was integrated and became fully operational in the period of the *pax Assyriaca* in the seventh century BCE.

44. For hieratic numbers, see Kletter, *Economic Keystones*, 148–49. Assyrian weights are rarely attested in the Levant; see Kletter, *Economic Keystones*, 125–27; Berlejung, "Assyrians in the West," 44 and n. 105.

period one should also assign the technological changes in the agricultural production installations and the development of the state-organized olive oil industry that flourished in Judah during the last quarter of the eighth century BCE, a time when Judah had already become an Assyrian vassal kingdom.[45]

At the same time, a significant change occurred in all aspects of the ceramic repertoire of Judah, which evolved from unstandardized, small-scale production in local workshops to a standardized mass-production industry, with a broad range of distribution and a limited variety of shapes.[46] The development of ceramic industry included the construction of storage jars that were larger than had previously been fashioned.[47] Such vessels are a clear sign of a centralized royal economy, which improved agricultural production and its mobility under the guidance of a central authority.

The best example of this change can be found in the study of the local production of storage jars and their change in production in the late eighth century BCE.[48] From the oval storage jars dated to the late ninth and the early eighth centuries BCE (which appeared mainly in the Shephelah and were characterized by the manufacturing of nonstandardized subtypes), the standardized jars became more common in the early mid-eighth century BCE and in the late eighth century BCE. One jar type in particular was adopted for use by the royal administrative system of Judah, as can be demonstrated by the appearance of stamp impressions on the handles of jars from this type. This royal administrative system

---

45. For technological changes, see Avraham Faust and Ehud Weiss, "Judah, Philistia and the Mediterranean World: Reconstructing the Economic System of the Seventh Century BCE," *BASOR* 338 (2005): 71–92; Katz, *Land of Grain and Wine*, 55–59. For the olive oil industry, see Israel Finkelstein and Nadav Na'aman, "The Shephelah of Judah in the Late Eighth and Early Seventh Century BCE: An Alternative View," *TA* 31 (2004): 74.

46. Amihai Mazar, *Archaeology of the Land of the Bible*, ABRL (New York: Doubleday, 1990), 509; Orna Zimhoni, *Studies in the Iron Age Pottery of Israel: Typological, Archaeological, and Chronological Aspects*, Institute of Archaeology of Tel Aviv University Occasional Publications 2 (Tel Aviv: Tel Aviv University, Institute of Archaeology, 1997), 171–172; Zimhoni, "Pottery of Levels III and II," 1705–7; Katz, *Land of Grain and Wine*, 52–53.

47. Zimhoni, "Pottery of Levels III and II," 1706.

48. Omer Sergi et al., "The Royal Judahite Storage Jar: A Computer Generated Typology and Its Archaeological and Historical Implications," *TA* 39 (2012): 64–92, with further literature.

expanded the distribution of these standardized jars and transported them to the various geographic regions in the kingdom of Judah. However, it is clear that all jars continued to be manufactured in the same place and that this one main production center was ultimately integrated into the royal administrative system connected with the stamped jar handles, which effectively dictated their main function.

The same progression was observed in the development in the system of the stamped jar handles. This system began in the last third of the eighth century BCE, when Judah became an Assyrian vassal kingdom, and developed throughout the six hundred years that Judah was under the rule of the great empires. About three thousand stamped jar handles were discovered in Judah during archaeological excavations and surveys covering these six hundred years.[49] This is precisely the period when Ramat Raḥel existed as the region's administrative center and main depot for agricultural products, primarily wine and oil stored in jars. No other Judahite site, not even Jerusalem, can challenge Ramat Raḥel's record: over three hundred stamped handles from the late Iron Age II were recovered there, including *lmlk-* and private-stamp impressions dated to the late eighth and early seventh centuries BCE, concentric circle incisions dated to the mid-seventh century BCE, and rosette-stamp impressions dated to the late seventh–early sixth centuries BCE.[50] In the Babylonian, Persian, and Hellenistic periods Ramat Raḥel was the main center of stamped jar handles, with about seventy-seven lion-stamped handles dated to the sixth century BCE, more than three hundred *yhwd*-stamp impressions dated to the late sixth–mid-second centuries BCE, and thirty-three *yršlm*-stamp impressions dated to the second century BCE.[51] All in all, the phenomenon of

---

49. Lipschits, *Age of Empires*, 237–65.

50. For Iron II, see Lipschits, Sergi, and Koch, "Judahite Stamped and Incised Jar Handles," 16–17; Oded Lipschits et al., *What Are the Stones Whispering? Ramat Raḥel 3000 Years of Forgotten History* (Winona Lake, IN: Eisenbrauns 2017), 34–39, 64. For late eighth and early seventh centuries, see Lipschits, Sergi, and Koch, "Royal Judahite Jar Handles," 3–32. For mid-seventh century, see Lipschits, Sergi, and Koch, "Royal Judahite Jar Handles," 7–8. For late seventh–early sixth centuries, see Ido Koch and Oded Lipschits, "The Rosette Stamped Jar Handle System and the Kingdom of Judah at the End of the First Temple Period," *ZDPV* 129 (2013): 60–61.

51. For lion-stamped handles, see Lipschits, *Age of Empires*, 91–98. For *yhwd*-stamp impressions, see Oded Lipschits and David S. Vanderhooft, *Yehud Stamp Impressions: A Corpus of Inscribed Stamp Impressions from the Persian and Hellenistic Periods in Judah* (Winona Lake, IN: Eisenbrauns, 2011), 107–10. For *yršlm*-stamp

stamped jar handles collected and stored at Ramat Raḥel continued for more than half a millennium as part of a continuous, systemized administrative system.[52]

Just as the administrative and economic system represented by the stamped jars endured throughout the six hundred years of Judah's existence under the rule of the empires, so too did Ramat Raḥel's function as the center of this system. The earliest building phase at Ramat Raḥel should be dated to the late eighth or early seventh century BCE.[53] The pottery and stamp impressions from the earliest building phase represent the entire chronological span from the end of the eighth at least until the middle or even until the last third of the seventh century BCE. Several architectural features are unique to Ramat Raḥel, indicating that already in this early phase (parallel to the Assyrian period of control in Judah) the site served as an administrative and governmental center. The numerous volute capitals (the so-called Proto-Aeolic capitals), as well as a series of small, carved stone columns with tiny palmette capitals (that had been part of a window balustrade, similar to those that appear in the reliefs known as "the woman in the window"), should all be assigned to the same architectural assemblage.[54] Even at this initial stage, the edifice at Ramat Raḥel was unparalleled in its might, beauty, and architectural technique by any other in the kingdom of Judah. The abundance of stamp impressions on jar handles found at the site testifies to its role as the Judahite administrative center for the collection of agricultural produce, probably

---

impressions, see Efrat Bocher and Oded Lipschits, "The Corpus of *yršlm* Stamp Impressions—The Final Link," *TA* 40 (2013): 103–4.

52. The renewed excavations at Ramat Raḥel and the final publication of the architecture and finds from Aharoni's excavations have made it possible to reevaluate the archaeology of the site and its significance vis-á-vis the political history of Judah as a province in the Achaemenid Empire. See Lipschits et al., *What Are the Stones Whispering?*, 22–26; Oded Lipschits, Yuval Gadot and Liora Freud, *Ramat Raḥel III: Final Publication of Yohanan Aharoni's Excavations (1954, 1959–1962)*, Sonia and Marco Nadler Institute of Archaeology Monograph Series 35 (Winona Lake, IN: Eisenbrauns, 2016).

53. The Western Tower is the main architectural structure assigned to this early phase. This structure probably functioned as a tower fortress, situated at the top of the hill for all to see, effectively controlling the main roads leading to Jerusalem. Additional structures were built to the east of the tower, though they were later integrated into the complex of buildings that composed the edifice of the second building phase or were dismantled to their foundations.

54. Lipschits et al., *What Are the Stones Whispering?*, 30–43.

exchanged for silver and gold and paid as tax to the Assyrian Empire. This administrative role would continue to grow in importance during the subsequent stages of its existence.

1.6. From Late Iron IIB to Iron IIC: Judah in the Transition from Assyrian to Egyptian and Babylonian Rule

The geopolitical and administrative character of the Levant only slightly changed under the Egyptian rule during the last third of the seventh century BCE.[55] In the short period of the Egyptian rule (for which there is scant historical documentation), it seems that the Egyptian economic and strategic interests were primarily concentrated in the coastal region, from Philistia to Phoenicia.[56] It is not clear to what extent Egypt was interested in the hill country or what effort it invested in establishing its rule there. However, it appears as though Egypt established its rule throughout the entire area and that Judah was enslaved by Egypt and was subsequently unable to conduct an independent foreign policy of its own, certainly not

---

55. Lipschits, *Fall and Rise of Jerusalem*, 20–35.

56. At a fairly early stage in the Egyptian rule of the region, Egypt established itself up to the borders of Phoenicia, subjugating Tyre, and apparently also Arwad. It seems that Tyre was restored at this point to its status as a vassal kingdom. It is also possible that upon the Assyrian's retreat, the Egyptians immediately established their foothold in Philistia. The establishment of Egyptian rule in this overland gate to Egypt was rapid, and apparently the Egyptians fought only against Ashdod. One may conjecture that already, during the long years of the *pax Assyriaca*, the Philistine coastal cities maintained close ties with Egypt, as they were the first to recognize its status as a successor state. In any case, the Philistine city-states continued to pledge fealty to Egypt, even in the early years of Babylonian rule in the region. See Donald B. Redford, *Egypt, Canaan, and Israel in Ancient Times* (Princeton: Princeton University Press, 1992), 435–42; Vanderhooft, *Neo-Babylonian Empire and Babylon in the Latter Prophets*, 70–71, 92–99. For a summary and further bibliography see Bernd Schipper, "Egyptian Imperialism after the New Kingdom: The Twenty-Sixth Dynasty and the Southern Levant," in *Egypt, Canaan and Israel: History, Imperialism, Ideology and Literature; Proceedings of a Conference at the University of Haifa, 3–7 May 2009*, ed. Shay Bar, Dan'el Kahan, and Judith J. Shirley, CHANE 52 (Leiden: Brill, 2011), 268–90; Alexander Fantalkin, "Coarse Kitchen and Household Pottery as an Indicator for Egyptian Presence in the Southern Levant: A Diachronic Perspective," in *Ceramics, Cuisine and Culture: The Archaeology and Science of Kitchen Pottery in the Ancient Mediterranean World*, ed. Michela Spataro and Alexandra Villing (Oxford: Oxbow, 2015), 233–41.

in the Shephelah, the coastal region, or the Jezreel Valley.[57] The Egyptians were unhindered in establishing their rule on the former Assyrian provinces in Syria and up to the western bank of the Euphrates. Yet as the Euphrates became the most important border with Babylon, Egypt had to turn it into its first line of defense in a bid to prevent the establishment of Babylonian outposts on the western side of the Euphrates and its use as a springboard for future attacks beyond the Euphrates.[58] The ease with which Syria fell into the hands of the Babylonians (summer 605 BCE) and the ease with which the Babylonians conquered the remainder of the Egyptian-controlled Asian territories (up to the border of Egypt) is evidence that the Egyptians were not successful in truly establishing their rule there. Rather, Egyptian control had largely relied on filling the power vacuum that remained once the Assyrians withdrew.

In the military campaign conducted between June 604 and January/February 603 BCE, Nebuchadnezzar conquered all of the Levant up to Gaza. None of the local kings dared stand up to Nebuchadnezzar, except for the king of Ashkelon. The Babylonian response was decisive, and the fate of the city served as an example to the other kingdoms in the region.[59] Judah became a Babylonian vassal kingdom at this stage, after about a generation of Egyptian rule, which probably lasted during most of Josiah's rule (640–609 BCE) and during the first years of Jehoiakim's rule (609–598 BCE).

---

57. Neco's presence in Megiddo and the killing of Josiah (2 Kgs 23:29), then later deposing Jehoahaz from the throne (v. 33) and appointing Eliakim-Jehoiakim (v. 34), attest to Egypt's intention of establishing its rule over Judah. For a summary of this subject, see Lipschits, *Fall and Rise of Jerusalem*, 36–67.

58. The military ventures that the Egyptians initiated along the Euphrates, especially in 608–605 BCE, are evidence of the great importance that they attributed to this region. It seems that besides the chief Egyptian stronghold in Carchemish (on the banks of the Euphrates), the main Egyptian center in Syria was at Riblah (cf. 2 Kgs 23:33). For a summary of this subject, see Lipschits, *Fall and Rise of Jerusalem*, 32–35.

59. It may have been at this time that the territory of Ashkelon was annexed to Ashdod. If this is the case, it could be considered as evidence of the single change that the Babylonians made in the geopolitical and administrative character of the Levant during the first phase of their rule. During this time, there is no reason to ascribe any other destruction to the Babylonian army. Most of the country was still arranged in a line of provinces as dictated during the Assyrian period, and it appears as though the Egyptian retreat left the country unopposed to the rule of Nebuchadnezzar. On the background to the Babylonian military campaign, its main events and consequences, see Lipschits, *Fall and Rise of Jerusalem*, 36–67.

Some scholars claimed that the recovery of Judah from the Assyrian 701 BCE destruction (mainly in the Shephelah, the southern Judean hills, and the Negev area) had already begun during the first half of the seventh century BCE. They have described this process as a part of the glorious days of King Manassaeh, when Judah, as a loyal Assyrian vassal kingdom, used the quiet days of the Assyrian dominancy in the Levant (the so-called *pax Assyriaca* era) to integrate the empire's economy and administration.[60] Writing in opposition to such descriptions, Ido Koch and Oded Lipschits demonstrated that during the first half of the seventh century BCE Judah did not recover from the harsh blow of the 701 BCE Assyrian campaign. This delayed recovery related to the Assyrian geopolitical and administrative arrangements that were still valid until the complete Assyrian withdrawal from the Levant, as during the days of King Manasseh, Judah was left as a small and damaged kingdom. Rather, it was only during the days of Josiah (after the withdrawal of the Assyrians from the Levant) that the post-701 BCE arrangements were canceled and Judah was able to begin repopulating the Shephelah and the Negev areas and rebuild border fortresses. This period most clearly represents distinctive historical change and is when, from an archaeological perspective, one can describe the point of change from the late Iron IIB to the Iron IIC.[61]

The stamped jar handles are the key to a greater understanding of this pivotal point of change in the history of Judah. While hundreds of early *lmlk*-stamped handles (dated to the late eighth century BCE) were found in lowland sites, only six late *lmlk*-stamped handles (dated to the early seventh century BCE) and eight handles bearing concentric circle incisions

---

60. See Itzhak Beit-Arieh, "Tel-'Ira and Horvat 'Uza: Negev Sites in the Late Israelite Period" [Hebrew], *Cathedra* 42 (1987): 34–38; Avraham Biran, "Tel-'Ira and 'Aro'er towards the End of the Judean Monarchy" [Hebrew], *Cathedra* 42 (1987): 26–33; Na'aman, "Negev in the Last Century of the Kingdom of Judah," 4–15; Finkelstein, "Archaeology of the Days of Manasseh," 169–87; Stern, *Assyrian, Babylonian, and Persian Periods*, 161; Yifat Thareani-Sussely, "The 'Archaeology of the Days of Manasseh' Reconsidered in the Light of Evidence from the Beersheba Valley," *PEQ* 139 (2007): 69–77; Ernst Axel Knauf, "The Glorious Days of Manasseh," in Grabbe, *Good Kings and Bad Kings*, 170–71; Avraham Faust, "Settlement and Demography in Seventh-Century Judah and the Extent and Intensity of Sennacherib's Campaign," *PEQ* 140 (2008): 168–94.

61. Koch and Lipschits, "Rosette Stamped Jar Handle System and the Kingdom of Judah."

(dated to the middle of the seventh century BCE) were found there.[62] This stands in clear contrast to the hill country, where 370 late *lmlk*-stamped handles, and 240 incised handles were found. Furthermore, about half of the total corpus of each system was recovered in the environs of Jerusalem and 25 percent at Ramat Raḥel, which was already an administrative center for the storing and distribution of commodities, which likely originated from royal estates.[63]

The administrative picture drawn from the late seventh century BCE is similar. The majority of the rosette-stamped handles (well dated to the late seventh and the early sixth century BCE)[64] were found in the hill country, whereas 37 percent were discovered in Jerusalem and 20 percent at Ramat Raḥel. The Benjamin Plateau (situated to the north and west of Jerusalem) prospered during the seventh century BCE.[65] Almost a quarter of the late *lmlk*-stamped handles and the concentric incised handles (dated to the first two-thirds of the seventh century BCE) were found in this region, mainly at el-Jib (biblical Gibeon) and Khirbet el-Burj (biblical Beeroth).[66] This vast amount of stamped handles renders the Benjamin Plateau the third most important region of the Judahite administration in the early and middle seventh century BCE. The centrality of the region probably came as a result of the loss of the Shephelah, wherein Judah had to refocus its economic goals toward substitute areas that still remained within its boundaries, such as Benjamin and the Rephaim Valley, which evolved during the early seventh century BCE.[67] During the final phase of the seventh century BCE, there is a clear change in the his-

---

62. Lipschits, Sergi, and Koch, "Royal Judahite Jar Handles," 3–32; Lipschits, Sergi, and Koch, "Judahite Stamped and Incised Jar Handles," 5–41.

63. Lipschits, Sergi, and Koch, "Judahite Stamped and Incised Jar Handles," 10–20.

64. Analyses of the new archaeological data and the distribution of the rosette stamped handles all indicate that this administrative system be dated to the last third of the seventh century BCE. See Koch and Lipschits, "Rosette Stamped Jar Handle System and the Kingdom of Judah," 342–55; Lipschits, *Age of Empires*, 253–65.

65. Alongside important sites such as Tell en-Naṣbeh and el-Jib, there was Tell el-Fûl; and Nebi-Samwil, in which the main activity took place in that period.

66. See Lipschits, Sergi, and Koch, "Royal Judahite Jar Handles," 21; Lipschits, *Age of Empires*, 141–65, 243–53.

67. Oded Lipschits and Yuval Gadot, "Ramat Rahel and the Emeq Rephaim Sites: Links and Interpretations" [Hebrew], in vol. 2 of *New Studies in the Archaeology of Jerusalem and its Region: Collected Papers*, ed. David Amit and Guy D. Stiebel (Jerusalem, 2008), 88–96; Gadot, "In the Valley of the King," 3–26.

tory of the region of Benjamin, with only fifteen rosette-stamped handles (approximately 7 percent of the corpus) unearthed at Benjamin sites. As the demographic landscape indicates that this was a prosperous period, it seems that the reason for such change may lie elsewhere, namely, in the Shephelah. Due to the renewed Judahite activity in the Shephelah, there was a lesser need for the royal estates located in Benjamin. Thus, the region lost its importance to the administrative system. The main shift in Judahite administration during the seventh century BCE is the renewed appearance of lowland sites as part of the Judahite administration. The twenty-four rosette-stamped handles recovered from Lachish (11 percent of the corpus) render this site the third most important center of the system (after Jerusalem and Ramat Raḥel). In the new excavations in Azekah, eight additional rosette-stamped handles have been found, bringing the number of handles recovered from this site to seventeen. The number of impressions recovered at Azekah classifies this site as the fourth most important center of this system.[68] It seems that Lachish Level II and the settlement at Azekah were each founded during the same period that the rosette system was introduced or even used.[69]

These archaeological data from the Shephelah strengthen the conventional historical reconstruction regarding the date of the region's recovery.[70] While during the first half of the seventh century BCE the Shephelah (excluding its easternmost part, and Tel Socoh) remained largely outside of the Judahite administration, it was reintegrated during the second half of the same century. During this period this region was without doubt one of critical importance for the kingdom, but its character was weaker and diminished in scale when compared to what it had been during the late

---

68. Lipschits, *Age of Empires*, 124, and personal information from the 2018 excavation season at the site.

69. Despite some indications for a resettlement immediately after the 701 BCE destruction, most scholars concur that Level II was founded in the second half of the seventh century BCE. See Ussishkin, *Renewed Archaeological Excavations at Lachish*, 1:90–93; Naʾaman, "Kingdom of Judah under Josiah," 33–41.

70. Naʾaman, "Hezekiah and the Kings of Assyria," 235; Naʾaman, "When and How Did Jerusalem Become a Great City," 25–27; Finkelstein, "Archaeology of the Days of Manasseh," 169–87; Finkelstein and Naʾaman, "Shephelah of Judah in the Late Eighth and Early Seventh Century BCE," 84; Ussishkin, *Renewed Archaeological Excavations at Lachish*, 1:90–91; Faust, "Settlement and Demography in Seventh-Century," 173.

eighth century BCE.[71] In the late seventh century the area was sparsely settled, less urban and fortified, without the economic importance that it had previously maintained.

As with the Shephelah, during the early seventh century BCE there was a decrease in the administrative involvement of the central regime in the Beersheba-Arad Valley, as only four late *lmlk*-stamped handles and two concentric incised handles were unearthed in the region, all at the site of Arad.[72] Yet some scholars argue for complete Judahite control of the region, already established during the first half of the seventh century.[73] At the very least, when the administrative system based on stamped jar handles is evaluated, it is clear that it did not reach the region until the late seventh century BCE, and only then did Judah return to the Beersheba-Arad Valley.[74] Thus, it may be that the Judahite population did return to the Beersheba-Arad Valley following the Sennacherib campaign, though there is no evidence for royal administrative involvement until the late seventh century BCE.

Just as with the Beersheba-Arad Valley sites, the establishment of the eastern fringe sites has also been dated by some scholars to the first half of the seventh century BCE.[75] Indeed, it might be that several farmsteads already existed during the early seventh century but were probably already

---

71. Oded Lipschits and David Amit, "Eighteen Stamped Jar Handles Not Published So Far" [Hebrew], in *New Studies in Jerusalem 17*, ed. Eyal Baruch and Avraham Faust (Ramat Gan: Rennert Center for Jerusalem Studies, 2011), 179–98, with English Summary on pp. 54*–55*.

72. Lipschits, Sergi, and Koch, "Judahite Stamped and Incised Jar Handles," table 1; Lipschits, *Age of Empires*, 124.

73. According to this view, King Manasseh opted for a degree of compensation for Judah (post-701 BCE) in the eastern fringe and the Beersheba-Arad Valley, under Assyrian auspices. See Beit-Arieh, "Tel-'Ira and Horvat 'Uza," 25; Biran, "Tel-'Ira and 'Aro'er towards the End of the Judean Monarchy," 32; Na'aman, "Negev in the Last Century of the Kingdom of Judah," 11; Finkelstein, "Archaeology of the Days of Manasseh," 165; Stern, *Assyrian, Babylonian, and Persian Periods*, 161; Thareani-Sussely, "'Archaeology of the Days of Manasseh' Reconsidered"; Knauf, "Glorious Days of Manasseh," 171–180; Faust, "Settlement and Demography in Seventh-Century Judah," 168–94.

74. Four stratified rosette stamped handles were excavated in the Judahite administrative center at Tel 'Ira Stratum VI. Three more stamped handles were unearthed at Arad Strata VII–VI, and four rosette-stamped handles unearthed at Tel Malḥata Stratum III. See Lipschits, *Age of Empires*, 124.

75. Finkelstein, "Archaeology of the Days of Manasseh," 177–78; Faust, "Settlement and Demography in Seventh-Century Judah," 181.

founded during the eighth century BCE.[76] However, not a single rosette-stamped handle was found below the floors of Stratum V at ʿEin-Gedi, and the three concentric incised handles recovered were unearthed in mixed contexts.[77] It seems, therefore, that the eastern fringe centers and the array of fortresses and their adjunct sites were mainly founded during the administrative phase of the rosette-stamped handles, toward the end of the seventh century BCE, and not before the Assyrian withdrawal from the Levant. In any case, it appears that Judah was not capable of expansion into the vicinity of Jericho prior to this period.[78]

When evaluated, the above data suggest that around the beginning of the last third of the seventh century BCE, a new era began in the history and archaeology of Judah. During this period a new administrative system was established, with the rosette-stamp impressions in its center. The distribution of the rosette-stamped handle system reflects the expansion of the Judahite administration into regions that, as long as Assyria dominated the Levant, were out of its reach. The recovery of the Shephelah began with the rebuilding of the administrative centers at Lachish and possibly also Azekah. In the Beersheba-Arad Valley the Judahite administration was renewed by the founding of the administrative center at Tel ʿIra and the array of fortresses situated along the valley. In the eastern fringe, the natural resources of the Dead Sea were exploited by the industrial site at En-Gedi, which was protected by an array of fortresses and parking sites. Thus, a new settlement pattern was established, likely as the outcome of the Assyrian withdrawal from the Levant and the cancellation of territorial and geopolitical arrangements that had remained in place since the last third of the eighth century BCE. This is also the period when Ramat Raḥel underwent a second building phase, and it became the center of the new administrative system of the rosette-stamped handles. The renewed archaeological excavations at Ramat Raḥel demonstrated that during the late seventh century BCE—just before or during the period when the rosette system was introduced—the second and monumental phase at the site was erected. The natural hill was reshaped and a fortified

---

76. Faust, "Settlement and Demography in Seventh-Century Judah," 174–75.

77. Ephraim Stern, *En-Gedi Excavations I—Conducted by B. Mazar and I Dunayevsky: Final Report (1961–1965)* (Jerusalem: Israel Exploration Society, 2007), 145, and pls. 4.7.2.1:1–6.

78. Naʾaman, "Kingdom of Judah under Josiah," 23, with further literature; Stern, "Jericho Region and the Eastern Border of the Judean Kingdom," 192–97.

edifice was built with a vast garden and central courtyard.[79] As a result of these changes, archaeological research is able to date the introduction of the pottery assemblages and practices that characterize Judah in the late seventh and early sixth century BCE.

As such, the term "the archaeology of the days of Manasseh," coined by Finkelstein to describe the expansion of Judah during the first half of the seventh century BCE, should be abandoned.[80] Instead, the term "the archaeology of the days of Josiah" of the last third of the seventh century BCE should take its place, when the changing geopolitical conditions of the late seventh century BCE resulted in a significant shift in Judah's positioning and status. The reconfiguration of Judah was enabled by the withdrawal of Assyria from the Levant, the change in the policies of Twenty-Sixth Dynasty, and Judah's successful attempt to reconsolidate its control over territories beyond the highlands.[81]

1.7. The Former Territories of the Kingdom of Israel in Transition from Late Iron IIB to Iron IIC

The same transition process from late Iron IIB to Iron IIC, following the Assyrian withdrawal from the Levant, can be detected in the northern parts of the land. As observed by Lily Singer-Avitz, Megiddo Strata III and II represent these two periods, as both follow the 732 BCE Assyrian conquest.[82]

---

79. See Lipschits et al., *What Are the Stones Whispering?*, 57–75; Lipschits, Sergi, and Koch, "Judahite Stamped and Incised Jar Handles," 20–34.

80. Finkelstein, "Archaeology of the Days of Manasseh," 169–87.

81. Na'aman, "Kingdom of Judah under Josiah," 34–41; Lipschits, *Fall and Rise of Jerusalem*, 20–29. Following the Egyptian expansion and under their auspices, it is plausible to assume that under Egyptian hegemony, the role of Judah in international trade included the production of grain in the fertile lands of the Shephelah, the production of olive oil and wine, as well as monitoring the trade routes from the Mediterranean to the Arabian Peninsula. Ashkelon grew and became the most important trade center in the region. See Stager, "Ashkelon and the Archaeology of Destruction," 61*–74*; Daniel M. Master, "From the Buqeʿah to Ashkelon," in *Exploring the Longue Durée: Essays in Honor of Lawrence E. Stager*, ed. David Schloen (Winona Lake, IN: Eisenbrauns, 2009), 305–17; see also Alexander Fantalkin, "Why Did Nebuchadnezzar II Destroy Ashkelon in Kislev 604 B.C.E.?," in *The Fire Signals of Lachish: Studies in the Archaeology and History of Israel in the Late Bronze Age, Iron Age, and Persian Period in Honor of David Ussishkin*, ed. Israel Finkelstein and Nadav Na'aman (Winona Lake, IN: Eisenbrauns, 2011), 87–111.

82. Singer-Avitz, "Pottery of Megiddo Strata III–II."

The late Iron IIB is represented by Megiddo Stratum III, when the city was established as the capital of the Assyrian province; aside from Megiddo, the remains were located only in Kinnereth (Stratum I) and probably also in Ta'anach (period V). At both Megiddo and Kinnereth, the fortifications of the earlier stratum were reused.

It may be that during the days of Assurbanipal, the Assyrians deported new groups into the region of the Megiddo province and resettled them.[83] This process triggered an increase in the number of settlements in the region, likely a process that continued long after the Assyrian withdrawal from the Levant, and may explain the resettlement of sites that parallel the building of Megiddo Stratum II, that is, Dan (Stratum I), Yoqne'am (Stratum XI), and possibly Beth Shean (Stratum P-6).[84] The organization of the Assyrian province of Tyre, which took place either in the late years of Esarhaddon or in the early years of Assurbanipal, could be the starting point for the establishment of sites in the territory of this province, for example, Kabri (Stratum E2) and Tell Keisan (Stratum 5).[85] It might be that following the Assyrian withdrawal from the region, during the early last third of the seventh century BCE, this settlement wave continued on throughout the period of Egyptian domination in the region, when the connections between Greece and the East were renewed under Egyptian domination.[86] This phase in the material culture in the north continued until the Babylonian campaigns of the late seventh century BCE, and thus, this marks the end of the early Iron IIC horizon in this region.[87]

---

83. Na'aman, "Population Changes in Palestine," 116; Singer-Avitz, "Pottery of Megiddo Strata III–II," 139.

84. Singer-Avitz, "Pottery of Megiddo Strata III–II," 138.

85. For the organization of Tyre, see Na'aman, "Esarhaddon's Treaty with Baal," 7–8. For Kabri and Tell Keisan, see Na'aman, "Esarhaddon's Treaty with Baal," 3–8; Gunnar Lehmann, "Area E," in *Tel Kabri: The 1986–1993 Excavation Seasons*, ed. Aharon Kempinski, Sonia and Marco Nadler Institute of Archaeology Monograph Series 20 (Tel Aviv: Emery and Claire Yass Publications in Archaeology, Institute of Archaeology, Tel Aviv University, 2002), 85; Singer-Avitz, "Pottery of Megiddo Strata III–II," 139–140.

86. For the Assyrian withdrawal, see Na'aman, "Kingdom of Judah under Josiah," 34–41. For the renewal of connections between the East and Greece, see Alexander Fantalkin, "Contacts between the Greek World and the Southern Levant during the Seventh–Sixth Centuries BCE" (PhD diss., Tel Aviv University, 2008).

87. Singer-Avitz, "Pottery of Megiddo Strata III–II," 138.

1.8. The Effect of the 586 Events on the Judean Economy, Administration, and the Chronological Frame of the Iron IIC

Already Gabriel Barkay has noted:

> The date of the destruction 587/586 BCE is not at all relevant to the history of most parts of the Land of Israel—the Galilee, the Samarian Hills, the coastal plain, the Negev, and eastern Transjordan.... It seems that the destruction of the Temple and the fall of Jerusalem influenced modern scholarship which fixed the date of the end of the Iron Age according to a historical fact and not on the basis of the archaeological picture.[88]

After the Babylonian destruction of Jerusalem and other main urban and military Judahite centers at the beginning of the sixth century BCE, "the people who were left in the land of Judah" (2 Kgs 25:22) continued to live in close proximity to the north and south of Jerusalem, maintain a rural economy, pay the annual tribute in the same way as before, produce pottery in the same Iron Age tradition (including stamped jars used for the taxation system), and serve under the same administration.[89] The administrative center at Ramat Raḥel continued to function as the collection center of taxes, mainly in the form of jars filled with wine and oil. This continuation included no marked change aside from the introduction of new lion-stamp impressions on the handles of jars, which replaced the rosette-stamp impressions on the same type of jars.[90] The capital of the newly established province of Yehud moved to Tell en-Naṣbeh (Mizpah), which served as the *Bîrāh* for 141 years (from 586 BCE, through the Neo-Babylonian period, until the time of Nehemiah).[91] These observations confirm the conclusion that in many aspects, the Babylonian Empire continued the Assyrian ideology and administration,

---

88. Gabriel Barkay, "The Iron Age III: The Babylonian Period" [Hebrew], in *Is It Possible to Define the Pottery of the Sixth Century B.C.E. in Judeah?*, ed. Oded Lipschits (booklet of lecture summaries from the conference held in Tel Aviv University, 21.10.1998, Tel Aviv), 25.

89. See Lipschits, "Shedding New Light on the Dark Years of the 'Exilic Period.'"

90. Lipschits, *Age of Empires*, 91–98.

91. Oded Lipschits, "Persian Period Judah: A New Perspective," in *Texts, Contexts and Readings in Postexilic Literature: Explorations into Historiography and Identity Negotiation in Hebrew Bible and Related Texts*, ed. Louis Jonker, FAT 2/53 (Tübingen: Mohr Siebeck, 2011), 187–212, with further literature.

took over the Assyrian provincial system, and only made minimal and necessary adjustments.[92]

The most conspicuous and significant archaeological phenomenon of sixth-century BCE Judah (after the destruction of Jerusalem) was the sharp decline in urban life. Such a decline rests in contrast to the continuity of the rural settlements in the region of Benjamin and in the area between Bethlehem and Beth-Zur.[93] This settlement pattern also continued throughout the Persian period when, despite the rebuilding of Jerusalem and the restoration of its status as the temple city of Yehud and later on also as the capital of the province, there was no strengthening of urban life in this area, and the settlement in Judah remained largely based on the rural population.[94]

The sharp decline in urban life had wider implications on the material culture, for example, the disappearance of the typical family burial caves, usually associated with urban and other elite social classes.[95] This shift is a reflection of deep religious and social change. Since there is a continued use of some of the burial caves in the area of Benjamin, in Jerusalem, and other sites, there is no need to connect the phenomenon to the isolated crisis of 586 BCE.[96] Instead, such processes may be better understood as a broader and gradual change in religion and society, which occurred during the sixth century BCE and possibly mainly at the beginning of the Persian

---

92. See, e.g., Ronald H. Sack, "Nebuchadnezzar II and the Old Testament: History versus Ideology," in *Judah and the Judeans in the Neo-Babylonian Period*, ed. Oded Lipschits and Joseph Blenkinsopp (Winona Lake, IN: Eisenbrauns, 2003), 229. A similar opinion was expressed by Ephraim Stern, "Assyrian and Babylonian Elements in the Material Culture of Palestine in the Persian Period," *Transeu* 7 (1994): 51–62, as against later statements (see, e.g., Stern, *Assyrian, Babylonian, and Persian Periods*, 307–8). An alternate view was expressed by Vanderhooft, *Neo-Babylonian Empire and Babylon in the Later Prophets*, 90–114. Against his views, see Sack, "Nebuchadnezzar II and the Old Testament," 226–27.

93. Lipschits, "Shedding New Light on the Dark Years of the 'Exilic Period.'"

94. Oded Lipschits, "Demographic Changes in Judah between the Seventh and the Fifth Centuries BCE," in Lipschits and Blenkinsopp, *Judah and the Judeans in the Neo-Babylonian Period*, 326–55; Lipschits, *Fall and Rise of Jerusalem*, 206–71; Lipschits, "Persian Period Judah," 187–212.

95. Gabriel Barkay, "Burial Caves and Burial Practices in Judah in the Iron Age," in *Graves and Burial Practices in Israel in the Ancient Period*, ed. Itamar Singer (Jerusalem: Yad Ben Zvi, 2004), 96–104.

96. Avraham Faust, "Judah in the Sixth Century BCE: Continuity or Break?," *ErIsr* 29 (2009): 341, with further literature.

period, when other changes, such as the disappearance of iconography in the stamp impressions on jar handles (e.g., the change from the lion to the *yhwd*-stamp impressions), occurred. Other elements that emphasize the change in material culture from the Iron Age II to the Persian period, for example, the disappearance of the typical Judahite house, are probably a part of a gradual change that had already begun during the seventh century BCE and continued for hundreds of years afterward, with some typical four-room houses still built during the sixth century BCE.[97] In this regard one should remember that, aside from the monumental building at Ramat Raḥel and the industrial site at En-Gedi, there are scanty architectural remains in Judah dated to the Persian period.[98]

The implication of the above is that as with the analysis of the 701 BCE destruction and its impact on the characteristics of local material culture, so too must scholarship resist employing the 586 BCE destruction as a marker for the end of the Iron IIC. The harsh blow delivered to urban settlements, especially the destruction of Jerusalem and the temple and the deportation of the Judahite elite and the House of David, were of major importance to the existence of Judahite national and cultic life. Further to this, such historical realities impacted social unity and the national memory and historiography. That said, from many different aspects of the material culture, life continued as before: local pottery production, agricultural economy and the stamped jar handles administration, the pattern of the rural settlement in the Judean hill country to the north and to the south of Jerusalem, imperial rule, and the existence of Ramat Raḥel as a central administrative center.

The central difference in the material culture between the periods of pre-586 BCE destruction and post-586 destruction is primarily the outcome of the Babylonian deportation of "all the men of valor, seven thousand, and the craftsmen and the smiths, one thousand, all strong and fit for war" (2 Kgs 24:16). The lack of skilled artisans during the Babylonian and the Persian periods in every field of the economy, administration, and

---

97. Jeffery R. Zorn, "Mizpah: Newly Discovered Stratum Reveals Judah's Other Capital," *BAR* 23.5 (1997): 34–35.

98. For more on the reason for the absence of architectural remains in Judah from the Persian period, see Oded Lipschits, "Achaemenid Imperial Policy, Settlement Processes in Palestine, and the Status of Jerusalem in the Middle of the Fifth Century BCE," in *Judah and the Judeans in the Persian Period*, ed. Oded Lipschits and Manfred Oeming (Winona Lake, IN: Eisenbrauns, 2006), 24–30.

daily life is one of the prominent characteristics of these periods. The situation also did not improve in the Persian period, and the poor province (with its nominated governors) did not acquire the means, ability, and perhaps not even the permission to undertake building projects in Jerusalem or in any other urban center in the land. The inferior building techniques and shabby quality of the pottery and the seals (probably also a result of the scarcity of raw materials and need to reuse existing resources, i.e., building stones and metals, or inexpensive substitutes) are all an expression of this situation during the Babylonian and Persian periods. It seems to me that this is one more explanation for the lack of architectural remains and other finds from the Babylonian and Persian periods and for the relatively easy way in which Persian-period building remains and additional finds could have been removed and lost during the Hellenistic period and later on.

1.9. Summary

The first point in the summary of this paper is the understanding that destructions provide an important and crucial spotlight on existing material culture and do not represent the end of it. The Assyrian destruction of 701 BCE effectively froze the material culture that had been developed by the first generation of Judeans under Assyrian rule and was included in the administration and economy of Judah after it became an Assyrian vassal kingdom in 734 BCE. This material culture continued to develop in the early seventh century, although it is difficult to locate. This difficulty is due to the absence of destruction levels during the *pax Assyriaca* period. It seems, however, that modern archaeological research, which has included a careful study of the development of the pottery assemblages of this period and exploration of the importance of the stamped jar handles to the study of the development processes during this period, enable a separation between early and late seventh century material culture.

The material culture of the early seventh century BCE is the further development of the local material culture of the late eighth century BCE and is different from the well-defined pottery assemblages of the end of the seventh and the early sixth century BCE, which can be clearly located within the 586 BCE destruction levels. Characteristics of this later material culture represent the continued developments under Egyptian and Babylonian rule in the latter part of the seventh century BCE.

The two destructions are not two ends of development processes, and the seventh century BCE is not a period that should be defined in between them. Every destruction symbolizes the creation of a frozen state in history and archaeology, but in reality, this material culture developed before such events and continued to develop immediately afterward in other areas that were not impacted by the outcome of the military campaigns. One should view the 701 and 586 BCE destructions as a milestone and not as the endline.

1.10. Chronological Implications

Based on the preceding discussion and suggestions, I suggest an alternate definition to the long seventh century, the expansion of the chronological frame of this archaeological/historical Iron IIB–IIC period to the time between the Assyrian occupation of the Levant (734 BCE) and the Persian period (539 BCE), and a split of the periodical divisions into two subphases, each one approximately one hundred years: the late Iron IIB (734–630 BCE) and the Iron IIC (630–539 BCE).[99]

The beginning of this period is marked by destructions of the northern parts of the kingdom of Israel (a process well attested in the archaeological research) and the subjugation of Judah to Assyria, which caused many changes in its economy, administration, and material culture. The transition between these two periods is centrally based on historical grounds, as the disappearance of the Assyrian Empire caused quick changes in settlement patterns in the northern parts of the land, in the Shephelah, and in the southern and eastern parts of Judah. This period is marked by slow changes in material culture, the building of the second building phase in Ramat Raḥel, the rebuilding of Level II in Lachish, possibly the late Iron Age II settlement in Azekah, and the beginning of the rosette-stamp impression phase.[100]

Based on archaeological and historical considerations, I also suggest defining two subphases for each of these periods. In the late Iron IIB (734–

---

99. For a first suggestion to differentiate between these two periods, see Singer-Avitz, "Pottery of Megiddo Strata III–II."

100. In this suggestion, I in part follow Ofer, who distinguishes between the Iron IIC, which corresponds mainly to the seventh century BCE, and the period that he calls Iron IID, which corresponds to the late seventh and early sixth century BCE. See Ofer, "Highland of Judah during the Biblical Period," 2:44–50. For a critique of Ofer's conclusions regarding the ceramic finds, see Finkelstein, "Archaeology of the Days of Manasseh," 174–75.

630 BCE) one can distinguish between the late Iron IIB1 (734–701 BCE) and the late Iron IIB2 (701–630 BCE), when the Sennacherib campaign spotlights the material culture of this period and can historically separate between these two phases. The loss of the Shephelah and changes in the settlement pattern of the hill country (especially the growth of the importance of the region of Benjamin) are the main markers for this change, as well as the transition from the early to the late *lmlk*-stamp impressions. In the Iron IIC one can distinguish between the Iron IIC1 (630–586 BCE) and the Iron IIC2 (586–539 BCE), when the Babylonian destruction spotlights the material culture of this period and enables the historical separation between these two phases, as well as the change from the rosette to the lion-stamp impressions and other more gradual changes, such as the disappearance of the traditional four-room house and the family burial caves. The end of this stage in the material culture is marked by the transition from Babylonian to Persian rule with the change from lion to *yhwd*-stamp impressions, the third building phase in Ramat Raḥel, and the early appearance of the Persian period local pottery forms, a process that probably further crystalized into a more developed stage in the middle of the fifth century BCE.

King Josiah between Eclipse and Rebirth: Judah of the Seventh Century BCE in History and Literature

Filip Čapek

The scene provided by biblical texts focused on Judah of the seventh century BCE and especially on King Josiah is peculiar in many respects. It is *the* time of the prosperous and flourishing Judah that possibly gave birth to the concept of Judean historiography as best represented by the literary work of the Deuteronomistic History. Nevertheless, this is the very same period that is absent in nonbiblical textual evidence. As stated by Lester Grabbe, "we are left with archaeology and biblical text."[1] This leads some scholars to consider this king to be of a very marginal role and to proclaim his reform as only a literary fabrication of authors, generally called Deuteronomists. There is a wide range of theories of exilic, postexilic, Persian, or even later provenance of accounts of the time of Josiah. The growth of biblical texts has been correctly identified as spread over centuries, but to anchor its beginning means to know about the first historical topos of the constitutive events, persons, and decisions that subsequently became an inspirational reservoir for further reflections. There are generally two lines of questioning to follow. The first is to search along lines provided by the biblical account of Josiah, and the second is to search for what is behind the biblical narration about Josiah with help of material culture of the period in question.

This chapter is a result of the research funded by the Czech Science Foundation as project GA ČR P401/12/G168 "History and Interpretation of the Bible."
1. Lester L. Grabbe, *Ancient Israel: What Do We Know and How Do We Know It?* (London: T&T Clark, 2007), 204.

A third line, which might be called synthesis, aims to prove that historical reading has the potential to increase not only understanding of the historical realities related to the text but also helps to shed new light on the function of the same text in the context of material culture related to it. This third line requires tight interdisciplinary teamwork of historians, archaeologists, and biblical scholars all searching for function in its many-sided aspects that is our common task. Joint work deepens knowledge, makes it more extensive, more balanced, and, therefore, applicable to more critical enterprises in each respective field of science.

2.1. Foiling and Following Josiah (Kings, Chronicles, Jeremiah)

There are three fundamental sources in the biblical texts on Josiah. The first is in 2 Kings, the second in 2 Chronicles, and the third in Jeremiah. Each provides a particular and unmistakable perspective on Judah in last decades of the seventh century BCE and, in the case of Jeremiah, also on the first two decades of the following century.

2.1.1. Kings

When reading the last chapters of 2 Kings as literature, it turns out that the Judean kings serve as a foil for Josiah, who is depicted in a substantially more extensive narrative. Josiah is *not* acting badly in God's eyes, as were his predecessors and successors.[2] On the contrary, he acts as one who is right in the sight of the Lord and who walks in all the ways of David, his father.[3]

Accordingly, Josiah is responsible for restoration of the temple, multiple religious purifications, and reforms that bespeak clearly of monotheistic traits and that go even beyond the historically probable and that positions the king on the same level as David. The impact that Josiah has extends beyond the territory of Judah to the north. Reform hits Bethel and high places in Samarian towns (עָרֵי שֹׁמְרוֹן). This happens in accord with 1 Kgs 13:2, where Josiah is foreseen in a proleptic way in the time of Jeroboam as one who will burn the priests of the high places, that is in Bethel. At the end of 2 Kgs 22, Passover is celebrated. Not surprisingly,

---

2. Cf. 2 Kgs 23:32 where Jehoahaz, despite being the son of Josiah, is described as
וַיַּעַשׂ הָרַע בְּעֵינֵי יְהוָה כְּכֹל אֲשֶׁר־עָשׂוּ אֲבֹתָיו.

3. For the literary means of foil see Filip Čapek, "David's Ambiguous Testament: The Role of Joab in 1 Kings 2:1–12," *Communio Viatorum* 1 (2010): 4–26.

the king is praised as unique since there was no one like him either before (כמהו לא־היה לפניו) or after (ואחריו לא־קם כמהו). Moreover, Huldah's oracle in 2 Kgs 22:20 seems to confirm harmonious living and the passing away of the king.

> Therefore, I will gather you to your ancestors, and you shall be gathered to your grave in peace; your eyes shall not see all the disaster that I will bring on this place. (NRSV)

Nevertheless, there is a drastic change in the course of events. The impressive royal account is radically interrupted by a statement about God's continuous (cf. Ps 30:6) wrath that had not ceased (see vv. 26–27) and that also fatally affects Josiah's destiny. The king goes to Meggido to meet Neco II (610–595 BCE) on his campaign to the Euphrates and is killed. The circumstances of this occurrence are not very clear from the text. Although there are many explanations as to why and how Josiah was killed, the account *as such* is here short-spoken and, in a way, also sarcastic.[4] In brief, one king goes to meet (לקראתו, LXX: καὶ ἐπορεύθη Ἰωσιας εἰς ἀπαντὴν αὐτοῦ) the other king, and the latter, the pharaoh, kills the first (וימיתהו במגדו כראתו אתו) and thus ends the most hopeful king of Judah!

There are substantial questions relating to the text: Do we face in the narration of 2 Kings a collision of expectations and facts? There was a good king, *but* he was killed. Or, to put it differently, do we face a retrojection of expectations backward in history in which real facts are deliberately reused to frame a narration in which an ideal-typical prototype of a king meets a drastically human dimension? There was a good king, *and* he was killed (see the phrase: "no one was like ... except David"). If the second is the case, which I would favor, the death confirms on the synchronic level of the text what was to be expected. On the human side of history, there are no infinite victories and victors but only persons advisable to follow, since their conduct was right, proper, righteous. Nevertheless, even these paradigmatic figures *do die* either violently or in a peaceful way, no matter what or how Huldah had prophesied. The last episode from Josiah's life is, on the level of diachrony, more complex, but the final text supports the

---

4. For an overview of the explanations offered, see Joseph Blenkinsopp, "Remembering Josiah," in *Remembering Biblical Figures in the Late Persian and Early Hellenistic Period: Social Memory and Imagination*, ed. Diana V. Edelman and Ehud Ben Zvi (Oxford: Oxford University Press, 2013), 236–56.

interpretation mentioned above. This interpretation rests on the propo-
sition of the terrifying absurdity of human existence in its fragility and
nakedness, however, both being only consequences of previous guilt,
which has a transpersonal scope. As for history in general, this is proven
not only by the fall of Israel, but also of Jerusalem and Judah that comes
closer and closer no matter what Josiah achieved or not.

2.1.2. Chronicles

The book of Chronicles, as is well known and documented in scholarship,
follows different, and in part intentionally opposing, interpretative interests. To start with Manasseh, he sins, then repents under pressure of the
Assyrians, and does not serve therefore as a foil to Josiah (2 Chr 33:12–16).
Compared to 2 Kings, the account about Josiah is longer, in many respects
more detailed (Passover), but also more general (the purification of Bethel
is not mentioned directly) and in the sphere of cult betraying postexilic
traits. The last episode about the encounter with Neco bespeaks, if read
cursorily, of the characteristics of heroic tragedy. Moreover, as noted by
Sara Japhet, it is text quoting from other biblical texts that makes potential
reconstruction impracticable.[5] The explicit geopolitical context is weaker
since the Assyrians are not mentioned and the main emphasis is laid on
the Egyptian and Judean kings being two equal partners. The contours
of battle, including its prologue (the sending of a messenger), resemble
the clash between Jehu, Joram, and Ahaziah from 2 Kgs 9, including the
result—which is death. At some point, there is also some similarity with
1 Kgs 22:29–37 and the death of Jehoshaphat.[6] Close reading reveals that
that story incorporates some ironic features. The Egyptian king deals as
one informed about God's plan when he warns Josiah as follows: "What
have I to do with you, king of Judah? I am not coming against you today,
but against the house with which I am at war; and God has commanded
me to hurry. Cease opposing God, who is with me, so that he will not

---

5. Sara Japhet, *2 Chronik*, HThKAT (Freiburg im Breisgau: Herder, 2003), 481.

6. See Steve Delamarter, "The Death of Josiah in Scripture and Tradition: Wrestling with the Problem of the Evil?," *VT* 54 (2004): 34–36, who draws attention to the
Hebrew verb (*hithpael* התחפש) in meaning "disguise," which connect these two texts.
Yet, in 2 Chronicles there is no suggestion of the masking of the king's identity except
for an intertextual link to 1 Kgs 22:29–37 in any sense (cf. LXX translating ἐκραταιώθη,
i.e., "[he] strengthens himself").

destroy you" (2 Chr 35:21 NRSV). However, Neco himself goes on to lose his own subsequent battle. In the following scene, Josiah in a disguise fights with the pharaoh and is hit by archers. The Judean king dies on the way to Jerusalem or shortly afterward.

There are substantial questions relating to the text, too: What is the point of the alternative account of Josiah? Why is there a missing link to Manasseh as a contrasting figure? Especially, why are the circumstances of the death radically transformed? From the above-mentioned, the text from Chronicles suggests a different understanding of human existence. The destiny of man is more individualized, and sin is not necessarily transferable. That is the reason why Manasseh is not serving as a foil, since he repents. Josiah, though righteous up to his Megiddo-gate, stumbles due to being fascinated by the possibility of becoming a part of the great history of the Levant. As it turns out, the opposite is the case. His fight with Neco is a total fiasco with fatal personal consequences. Writers of the Chronistic account of Josiah follow a different agenda compared to the Deuteronomists. Josiah "does not die because of the sins of another. He dies for his own sin," since he caused the battle that should not have taken place at all.[7] To add to these two narrative traditions, the Septuagint reading should also be mentioned, since it deals with 2 Kings and 2 Chronicles creatively but also critically in its own theological and historiographical terms. Thus, for instance, 4 Kingdoms combines the accounts of 2 Chronicles with 2 Kings to form its own story about the battle in which Josiah does not hide but acts in a "much nobler stance."[8]

2.1.3. Jeremiah

The third biblical literary source about Josiah is the prophetic account in the book of Jeremiah. It covers the time of the last rulers of Judah: Josiah, Jehoiakim, and Zedekiah. Josiah is mentioned in prophecy as a starting point for time reference that "God said ... in the days of King Josiah" (3:6) or as a point from which onward the destruction of Judah comes closer and closer. Oracles are addressed to the following kings, especially to Jehoiakim. Reform is not mentioned and a reference to Neco in Jer 46:2 does not hint at any direct military conflict with Judah:

---

7. Quotation from Delamarter, "Death of Josiah in Scripture and Tradition," 34.

8. Delamarter, "Death of Josiah in Scripture and Tradition," 39.

Concerning Egypt, about the army of Pharaoh Neco, king of Egypt, which was by the river Euphrates at Carchemish and which King Nebuchadrezzar of Babylon defeated in the fourth year of King Jehoiakim son of Josiah of Judah. (NRSV)

Though many wonder why reform is missing, the composition and genre explain this issue itself. The biblical text just quoted introduces the last part of the book representing so-called oracles against the nations.[9] Here, Egypt and Babylonia serve as the first and the last of nations, both as the very existing threats to Judah at the turn of seventh and sixth century BCE. Other nations, the Philistines, Moab, Amon, Edom, Damascus, Kedar, Hazor, and Elam illustrate geopolitically that the impact of God's judgment is universal. The key political entity, Persia, which brings new conditions for Judah, consistently termed here as Israel or Jacob (except for 51:5), remains intentionally unmentioned since all this is what would be fulfilled only later. An important reference to the *new* Josiah is present in Jer 23:5–7.

The days are surely coming, says the LORD, when I will raise up for David a righteous Branch, and he shall reign as king and deal wisely, and shall execute justice and righteousness in the land. In his days Judah will be saved and Israel will live in safety. And this is the name by which he will be called: "The LORD is our righteousness" [יהוה צדקנו]. Therefore, the days are surely coming, says the LORD, when it shall no longer be said, "As the Lord lives who brought the people of Israel up out of the land of Egypt." (NRSV)

In this text, though only implicitly, Josiah or a king like him is prophesied as an idealized prototype of a postexilic king. The reference in the previous chapter (22), in which Josiah, again not explicitly mentioned in verses 1–9, is significant and serves as a last possible carrier of obedience to God expressed in terms of social justice, avoiding bloodshed, and heeding the covenant. This reference has its place in the past days of Josiah and is projected as a promise of the Davidide king to come in the future.[10]

Again, there are substantial questions relating to the text of Jeremiah: first, what historical reference it conveys and, second, what Jeremiah says about Josiah. As for history, the account is quite scanty about the end of the

---

9. See Grabbe, *Ancient Israel*, 206.

10. See Georg Fischer, *Jeremia 1–25*, HThKAT (Vienna: Herder, 2015), who also considers Josiah to be the best candidate to whom Jer 22–23 refers.

seventh century BCE and its events should be discussed. Memories are relatively vague. Concerning Josiah, he serves as a two-directional referential figure for past and future. Compared to successive Judean rulers, he is *the one* who encapsulates hopes of recent memories and also events to come. He is David that is to be revived (*David redivivus*).[11] However, to interpret Jeremiah adequately means to emphasize that the central message goes to the very factual and present situation of the exilic or postexilic community that draws strength from the paradigmatized past and idealized future to fight off the challenges of the present time, either in Babylonia, or Egypt, or back in the land. Any access to the past is inferred from texts that unquestionably reflect upon past events, but this reflection has its peculiarities in genre, intention, and scope.

2.2. Josiah in History: Embroidered

Any search for events, facts, and persons firmly anchored in history is similar to a police investigation. When a homicide has been committed, for instance, criminologists speak of hot footprints that should be traced within twenty-four hours, otherwise they change to cold traces that make investigation more difficult. After one day of chasing hot traces, the team is changed, and those involved afterward "embroider" or "sew" with the various data available. Criminologists leave the scene and not pathologists, but historians, archaeologists, and biblical scholars take the initiative to revive past events in terms of their respective disciplines. What appears within their work is a fabric woven from more or less solid threads. This also applies to history and archaeology and the issues related to the second half of the seventh century BCE. Factors dictating examination are extant. As for material culture, the kingdom of Judah under Josiah comes back to life and sight in particular by analysis of rosetta stamps and by items of an iconographic nature.

2.2.1. Borders, Administration, and Interactions

The extent of Judah under Josiah has been discussed for decades. According to A. Alt, who dated the list from Josh 15 to the time of Josiah, the kingdom

---

11. See Antti Laato, *Josiah and David Redivivus: The Historical Josiah and the Messianic Expectations of Exilic and Postexilic Times*, ConBOT 33 (Stockholm: Almqvist & Wiksell, 1992).

expanded westward up to the Mediterranean.[12] Yohanan Aharoni assumed that the territory expanded to the north and that part of it was Bethel and the surrounding hilly region. As for the coastal area, according to him, ostraca from Mesad Hashavayahu "reflects Judaean rule in the area during the late seventh century B.C."[13] However, in recent research, this find is nearly univocally interpreted as proof of a Judean presence in terms of commerce and not as political supremacy over the fortress and adjacent territory. This explanation is much more plausible with respect to the geopolitical situation in the coastal region of Levant and to material culture excavated, namely, Judahite fiscal seals and ostraca from the Moussaieff collection, documenting economic subjugation of Judah under Egyptian control, according to Bernd Schipper at the latest in 610 BCE.[14] There is a problem with how to interpret the time interval between the Assyrian withdrawal and new control over the territory by the Twenty-Sixth Egyptian Dynasty under Psammetichus (664–610 BCE). It was probably not the time of *Machtvakuum*, as advocated by some. There was hardly time for an expansion of Judah up to the Mediterranean, and, moreover, strong Philistine cities dominated the region. Possibly, there was no such interval at all, and Egypt became in fact a continuously successive hegemon in the region and took advantage of the previous Assyrian administration and only adapted the system to its demands.[15] As pointed out by Othmar Keel and Oded Lipschits, one should not look only at the backs of the retreating Assyrians, but also at the increasing expansion of the Twenty-Sixth Dynasty, which "immediately filled in the 'Machtvacuum'" in southern Levant.[16] There was no time or place for Judah to expand beyond what was politically practicable.[17] Judah was unquestion-

---

12. Cf. Albrecht Alt, *Kleine Schriften zur Geschichte des Volkes Israel* (Munich: Beck 1953), 176–92.

13. Yohanan Aharoni, *The Land of the Bible* (Philadelphia: Westminster, 1979), 348.

14. See Bernd U. Schipper, "Egypt and the Kingdom of Judah under Josiah and Jehoiakim," *TA* 37 (2010): 200–226, esp. 215–20; and Schipper, "Egyptian Imperialism after the New Kingdom: The Twenty-Sixth Dynasty and the Southern Levant," in *Egypt, Canaan and Israel: History, Imperialism, Ideology and Literature*, ed. Shay Bar, Dan'el Kahn, and Judith J. Shirley, CHANE 52 (Leiden: Brill, 2011), 268–90, esp. 281.

15. For discussion, see Oded Lipschits, *The Fall and Rise of Jerusalem* (Winona Lake, IN: Eisenbrauns, 2005), 24–29.

16. Cf. Othmar Keel, *Die Geschichte Jerusalems und die Entstehung des Monotheismus* (Göttingen: Vandenhoeck & Ruprecht, 2007), 512.

17. For the presence of the Twenty-Sixth Dynasty in Palestine documented by numerous scarabs see Keel, *Geschichte Jerusalems*, 513.

ably an integral part of trade and cultural exchange in the region, powered either by the Assyrians or the Egyptians, but was not a tax collector, but a contributor, not dominating but dominated. It was constantly a vassal state on the outskirts.[18]

The above-mentioned more restrained judgment is confirmed by a distribution analysis of more than 250 rosetta stamps in the very territory of Judah. This represents one of the most effective tools for historical reconstruction. It has been proved that the two main centers were in Jerusalem and the adjacent Ramat Raḥel, and then also in the lowlands, especially in Azekah, Lachish, and Tel Batash, but not further west on the coastal plain except for a few finds from Tel Miqne and Tel Erani. As for the dating of these stamps and affiliation to a particular Judean king, there are three positions advocated. The first, which connects the administration system of rosetta stamps to Manasseh and the first half of the seventh century BCE, has been challenged recently by a second option, according to which the administration system comes from the last third of the same century and relates to renewed expansion under Josiah to the Shephelah that had been previously abandoned or nearly desolated after Sennacherib's campaign.[19] A third option, proposed by Jane Cahill in the mid-1990s and expanded on in the following decade, relates, on the basis of the stratigraphy of Tel Batash II and six rosetta impressions from there, to a period after Josiah.[20] According to Cahill, vessels impressed with a rosetta date after

---

18. Cf. Nadav Naʾaman, "The Kingdom of Judah under Josiah," *TA* 18 (1991): 40.

19. For the Manasseh option, see Israel Finkelstein, "The Archaeology of the Days of Manasseh," in *Scripture and Other Artifacts: Essays on the Bible and Archaeology in Honor of Philip J. King*, ed. Michael D. Coogan, J. Cheryl Exum, and Lawrence E. Stager (Louisville: Westminster John Knox, 1994), 169–87. For the second option, see Ido Koch and Oded Lipschits, "The Rosette Stamped Jar Handle System and the Kingdom of Judah at the End of the First Temple Period," *ZDPV* 129 (2013): 55–78. For a response see Israel Finkelstein, "Comments on the Date of the Late-Monarchic Judahite Seal Impressions," *TA* 39 (2012): 203–11; see also Yuval Gadot, "In the Valley of the King: Jerusalem's Rural Hinterland in the Eighth–Fourth Centuries BCE," *TA* 42 (2015): 3–26.

20. Jane M. Cahill, "Rosette Stamp Seal Impression from Ancient Judah," *IEJ* 45 (1995): 230–52; Cahill, "Royal Rosettes Fit for a King," *BAR* 23.5 (1997): 48–57, 68–69; Cahill, "Rosette-Stamped Handles," in *Inscriptions*, vol. 6 of *Excavations at the City of David 1978–1985 Directed by Yigal Shiloh*, ed. Donald T. Ariel, Qedem 41 (Jerusalem: Institute of Archaeology, Hebrew University of Jerusalem, 2000), 85–108; Cahill, "Rosette Stamp Seal Impressions," in *The Finds from Areas A, W and X-2*, vol. 2 of *Jewish Quarter Excavations in the Old City of Jerusalem*, ed. Hillel Geva (Jerusalem: Israel Exploration Society, 2003), 85–98.

605 BCE and the Egyptian defeat at Carchemish, and as such represent the Jehoiakim effort to support the Philistines (Ekron) against the rising Neo-Babylonian Empire. A destruction layer from 603 BCE attests that the city was Philistine but with commercial ties to neighboring Judah.[21]

There are two remarks to be mentioned about embroidering the delicate fabric of the history of seventh-century BCE Judah. Cahill's dating that aspires to an accuracy of a two-year range rests on stratigraphy and the ethnic affiliation of Tel Batash, which are both very complex and ambiguous.[22] Whereas she regards the site as Philistine with rosette-impression stamps documenting Judean commercial support against the Babylonians, Ido Koch and Lipschits consider Tel Batash to be a Judean city loyal to the Babylonians.[23] The difference lies in the analysis of pottery and in the view whether there is a connection between the destruction of Ekron and Tel Batash. Second, there is a different perspective on playing a card of the northern border of Judah in Benjamin sites, specifically in respect to the presence of *lmlk* impressions and the concentric incised handles, on the one side, and the drop in the number of rosettes, on the other. Whereas Cahill interprets this disproportion as proof for the diminished map of post-Josianic Judah of the very end of the seventh century BCE, others take the same evidence as a sign of deliberate relocation of administrative activities in the days of Josiah back to territories in the lowlands lost after the Assyrian campaign.[24] The issue seems to confirm Grabbe's realistic comment that "mixed archaeological artifacts cannot fix borders, maximally temporary dominance in places where they were found."[25]

---

21. See Cahill, "Rosette Stamp Seal Impression from Ancient Judah," 247, stating that Timnah "does not appear in the city list of Joshua 15 currently recognized as a detailed record of Judah's holdings during the reign of Josiah." However, the list contains this geographical place in v. 10 (וירד בית־שמש ועבר תמנה).

22. Amihai Mazar and Nava Panitz-Cohen, *Timnah (Tel Batash) II: The Finds from the First Millennium BCE (Text, Plates)*, Qedem 42 (Jerusalem: Institute of Archaeology, Hebrew University of Jerusalem, 2001); and Panitz-Cohen and Mazar, *Timnah (Tel Batash) III: The Finds from the First Millennium BCE*, Qedem 45 (Jerusalem: Institute of Archaeology, Hebrew University of Jerusalem, 2006); see also Filip Čapek, "The Shephelah in the Iron Age I and IIA: A New Survey of the Emergence of the Early Kingdom of Judah," *Oriental Archive* 80 (2012): 475–504.

23. Koch and Lipschits, "The Rosette Stamped Jar Handle System," 66.

24. Cahill, "Rosette Stamp Seal Impression from Ancient Judah," 248.

25. See Grabbe, *Ancient Israel*, 206; for further study see Nadav Na'aman, "The *lmlk* Seal Impressions Recosidered," *TA* 43 (2016): 111–25.

2.2.2. Iconography and Cult

Other material culture, especially cultic and iconographical items, will be discussed with respect to the reforms of Josiah. Herein, biblical texts are related to, some directly, or come as if through a back door and substantially affect the interpretation of material culture. Sometimes this uneasy relation is a reminder of gorgonizing by a snake. There are scholars who deny the existence of the reform and others who favor it as a part of real history.[26] Outcomes rely on the evaluation of artifacts and biblical texts, not only in terms of dating but of the factual range of impact. In the case that texts, or at least their original core, are taken against the preexilic monarchic backdrop, the collision of religious praxis is more sweeping compared to the idea of exilic or postexilic provenance of texts. Existence of figurines of horse and horse with rider, both with a sun-like disk, pillar figurines, and other artifacts do not as such exclude the reform and speak for a continuity of religious traditions that developed in parallel, but also probably highly independently. It is more than conceivable that the religion of Judah was, in the late monarchic period, a tricky complex of mixed religious practices. It was stratified socially, geographically, and intellectually and should be so interpreted. It should not be perceived as a monolith of commonly practiced religion, since evidence does not support such a clear concept. There was a process of monotheizing moving ahead and the biblical texts document it in many ways. The question is: to what extent was this process fully set in motion only by the fall of Jerusalem and to what extent was this national catastrophe theologically transformed into the account about the golden age of Josiah? Similarly, it is a matter of discussion whether cult centralization was inspired by cult reforms in ancient empires over ages (cf. Nadav Na'aman), here especially by Assyrians.[27] Another contributory factor was the sociopolitical context of *translatio imperii* in interim, when the interests of small states in the Levant had thrived before a new power

---

26. Thus, e.g., Ernst Axel Knauf, "The Glorious Days of Manasseh," in *Good Kings and Bad Kings: The Kingdom of Judah in the Seventh Century BCE*, ed. Lester L. Grabbe, LHBOTS 393 (London: T&T Clark, 2005), 164–88, esp. 166–68; or Juha Pakkala, "Why the Cult Reforms in Judah Probably Did Not Happen," in *One God–One Cult–One Nation: Archaeological and Biblical Perspectives, ed. Reinhard G. Kratz and Hermann Spieckermann, BZAW 405 (Berlin: de Gruyter, 2010), 201–35.

27. Thus especially Keel, *Geschichte Jerusalems*, 555–64.

took control.[28] To sum up and to admit it openly, this is very unsafe ground with many questions and uneasy answers.

To give just one example of how complex historical embroidering is, horse figurines excavated in Iron Age B–C Judah in their hundreds are frequently related to 2 Kgs 23:11.[29] In this text is written:

> He removed the horses that the kings of Judah had dedicated to the sun, at the entrance to the house of the LORD, by the chamber of the eunuch Nathan-melech, which was in the precincts; then he burned the chariots of the sun with fire. (NRSV)

There is a connection discussed between the horses in front of the temple and terracotta horse figurines. Some relate the *hapax legomenon* פרורים (LXX only transliterates as φαρουριμ) further in the text to the Hittite deity of Parwa (1400–1200 BCE) whose attribute was a horse. The text clearly refers to destruction of sun chariots (מרכבות השמש). However, in the ancient Near East, these chariots are nowhere iconographically pictured as being ridden by the deity of the sun until the Greek image of quadriga with the deity of Helios from the late sixth century BCE.[30] It has been suggested by Othmar Keel and Christoph Uehlinger that horse figurines should not be interpreted as a deity but as an artifact mediating between YHWH (in his sun-line context) and a worshiper as a part of family piety (*Familiefrömigkeit*). Figurines served as a mediator of divine protection or blessing.[31] Moreover, the sun disk between the ears is probably not a sun disk but a floral embellishment.[32] Tension between domestic or private cult and official religious prescription in Judah has been commented on by many without providing a broader consensus on this issue.[33]

---

28. Cf. Keel, *Geschichte Jerusalems*, 546: "Der Zusammenbruch übergreifender Imperien wie der des assyr. Reiches geht in der Regel mit einer Neubesinnung auf lokale Structuren und Werte einher und fördert übertriebene lokale Ansprüche."

29. For presumably the earliest occurrence of these artifacts see Shua Kisilevitz, "The Iron IIA Judahite Temple at Tel Moza," *TA* 42 (2015): 147–64.

30. Keel, *Geschichte Jerusalems*, 537.

31. Othmar Keel and Christoph Uehlinger, *Göttinen, Götter und Gottessymbole: Neue Erkenntnisse zur Religionsgeschichte Kanaans und Israels aufgrund bislang unerschlossener ikonographischer Quellen*, 4th ed., QD 134 (Freiburg: Herder, 1999), 394.

32. Keel and Uehlinger, *Göttinen, Götter und Gottessymbole*, 394; Keel, *Geschichte Jerusalems*, 527.

33. See Knauf, "Glorious Days of Manasseh," 166–68.

2.3. Synthesis

As for the third line, that is, for possible synthesis, it is necessary to concede that both lines have been outlined as separate, but methodological perfection has gradually lost its focus. There were moments where these lines touched or crossed each other, overlapped or contradicted each other. The question that results from this unsettled relation sounds like this: *Is a synthesis of biblical and archaeological records practicable?* The answer that might sound like "yes" has to be limited by many reservations and also propositions that keep this synthesis under scientific control from the side of various respective disciplines. In other words, both the eclipse and rebirth of Josiah fundamentally rests on the correlation of biblical texts and material culture. I offer eight interpretative propositions.

(1) Material culture and texts can be taken as synchronous only to a limited extent. Most texts are later and there is an intensive debate on preexilic Isaiah, Jeremiah, and also the account of Josiah and his reform in the Deuteronomistic History, which is a result of a many-fold redactional effort.

(2) From the perspective of biblical scholarship of the European tradition, adopted by many in Israel and by some in the United States, it is clear that an uncritical reading of texts incurs circular reasoning and noninventive or truistic interpretations. The key issue is to detect to what extent the Deuteronomistic account is a literary invention and work providing retrospective thoughts and ideas. We are dealing with complex *theological* transformations of the texts on Josiah. Questions implied sound as if Josiah was a renascent David of late preexilic time, or, possibly, also Hezekiah (i.e., a tenth to seventh century BCE transformation), or if Josiah in a similar way was construed by later exilic and postexilic reflection as *the* king embodying all substantial features of the paradigmatic monarchic trio David–Hezekiah–Josiah.

(3) As for the realm of religion, the biblical account about reform is not a single testimony about religious practice in the late seventh century BCE. This applies to various biblical texts since they indicate that monotheism and purity of the cult was more wishful thinking than fact on the ground. There might have been reform amid a variety of other religious phenomena taking place simultaneously. This author would not dare to postulate monotheism as a reality only of sixth century BCE, as Christopher Rollston, Brian Mastin, Ephraim Stern, and many others have, on the one side, but would be careful and reserved to build up a construal of a

fully reformed and purified Judah of the late seventh century under Josiah, on the other.[34]

(4) There are tasks beyond resolution of the available data. Researchers often have to deal with concepts that relate to texts and artifacts only to a limited extent or in a specific constellation.

(5) Though pushing scholars to give new insights to a respective issue, scholarly honesty requires us also to admit that it is not possible simply to know if we are asked to say whether this was a real fact of history or not. Negative evidence is evidence, too.

(6) The probabilities being dealt with are on a scale going from 0 to 100 percent. As for the death of Josiah in Megiddo, to give an example, this author's impression from all the available data, and from all the interpretations suggested, is that while it is known that death in battle is *improbable*, being killed for disloyalty is *thinkable but not necessarily true*, to take all this as fiction is *too much*.[35] The last option is skeptical but touches on the ground of the available factual knowledge, namely, that "Necho II met Josiah at the traditional Egyptian base at Megiddo, killed him for unknown reasons, and then continued onwards to the Orontes."[36]

(7) In the context of biblical texts, the inquiry is about *the meaning of the death of Josiah*. Was he a victim of a Deuteronomistic puristic view that leaves even the most righteous king to disappear in a peculiar way (*eclipse*) so that he returns to biblical historiography in narrative emplotment as a semimythical paradigmatic king (*rebirth*)?

(8) Generally speaking, the two lines discussed represent two different and partly opposing processes. On the side of the biblical texts, we are unweaving the narrative emplotment to get at its basic constituents.

---

34. Christopher A. Rollston, "The Rise of Monotheism in Ancient Israel: Biblical and Epigraphic Evidence," *SCJ* 6 (2003): 95–115; Brian A. Mastin, "Yahweh's Asherah, Inclusive Monotheism and the Question of Dating," in *In Search of Pre-exilic Israel: Proceedings of the Oxford Old Testament Seminar*, ed. John Day, JSOTSup 406 (London: T&T Clark, 2004), 326–51; Ephraim Stern, "From Many Gods to the One God: The Archaeological Evidence," in Kratz and Spieckermann, *One God–One Cult–One Nation*, 395–403.

35. For being killed for disloyalty, see Zipora Talshir, "The Three Deaths of Josiah and the Strata of Biblical Historiography (2 Kings XXIII 29–30; 2 Chronicles XXXV 20–5; 1 Esdras I 23–31," *VT* 46 (1996): 213–36. See also Klaus Koenen, *Bethel: Geschichte, Kult und Theologie*, OBO 192 (Fribourg: Presses Universitaires; Göttingen: Vandenhoeck & Ruprecht, 2003).

36. Schipper, "Egyptian Imperialism," 282.

On the side of material culture, we are embroidering and weaving from the artifacts an available fabric that might resist critical testing. These two processes cannot be fully separated. However, their controlled interfusion is necessary.

2.4. Summary

To conclude, any historical investigation, though in many respects tentative, relying on hypothesis and taking various pieces of evidence to reach an interpretive clue, increases the understanding of the biblical texts. It uncovers multilayered dimensions of textual testimony and reveals its theological function in a particular historical context. Similarly, it indicates what the functions are of past events in a new context.[37] As for Josiah, it seems that later developments written down in biblical literature preserved an awareness of this king through plotted theological reflections for his time, about which we know less than is assumed. In other words, the eclipse of Josiah and his time has its counterweight in his rebirth by means of literature.

---

37. Thus, especially in his pioneering studies on this issue, see James Barr. Among many see Barr, "Historical Reading and the Theological Interpretation of Scripture," in *The Scope and Authority of the Bible* (London: SCM, 1980), 30–51; see also Blenkinsopp, "Remembering Josiah."

Part 2

Material Culture under Scrutiny

New Evidence of Iron Age II Fortifications at Tel Hebron

David Ben-Shlomo

New evidence on the fortifications of Tel Hebron (Rumeida) was uncovered during the 2014 excavation at the site conducted by the author and Emanuel Eisenberg. In the new excavations a further 70 m of the cyclopean city wall was exposed from the outside on the southeastern part of the site, continuing the area excavated by Philip Hammond during the 1960s. In addition, late Iron Age fortification elements, combined within the city wall as a tower, support walls, and glacis were also uncovered. Within this context a Hebrew seal and a fragmentary ostracon were also found. These finds will be discussed in their archaeological and historical framework of the late eighth and seventh century BCE. In addition, recent suggestions as well as data regarding the dating of the Hebron and Jerusalem Middle Bronze and Iron Age fortifications will also be discussed.

3.1. Introduction

The site of Tel Hebron (Tell Rumeida), about 30 km south of Jerusalem, had been accepted as the location of biblical Hebron already in the 1950s. Hebron was a major town in Judah throughout ages and the seat of the kingdom of David during its first seven years. The site was excavated in the past by Hammond (1964–1966), Avi Ofer (1984–1986) and Emauel Eisenberg (1999), yet the results from these excavations have only been published very briefly so far.[1] Recently (2014) the excavations at the site were renewed by Eisenberg and David Ben-Shlomo.[2] The excavation areas

---

1. Hammond and Ofer excavations: Avi Ofer, "Hebron," *NEAEHL* 2:606–9; Eisenberg 1999 excavations: Emanuel Eisenberg, "The Fortifications of Hebron in the Bronze Age" [Hebrew], *ErIsr* 30 (2011): 14–32.

2. Emanuel Eisenberg and David Ben-Shlomo, eds., *Tel Hevron 2014 Excavations: Final Report* (Ariel: Ariel University Press, 2017).

(Plots 52 and 53) were located on the western and southwestern fringes of Tel Hebron (fig. 3.1). The eastern part of the larger area (fig. 3.1, Area 53B) is adjacent to Hammond's Area I.3 (fig. 3.2) where the city's ancient fortification were exposed and dated to the Middle Bronze Age IIB–C (the city wall was eventually dated by pottery and scarabs according to the 1999 excavation results on the other side of the tell).[3] The current excavation took place just south and outside of the fortification line and further exposed the Bronze Age city wall to a continuous length of nearly 70 m (figs. 3.1, 3.2). This paper will review the cyclopean Bronze Age fortifications at Tel Hebron exposed so far and the Iron Age fortification elements that were linked to them.

Table 3.1. Phases in Areas 53A and 53B of Tel Hebron 2014 Excavations

Phase	Period	Area 53A	Area 53B
Phase 9	MB IIB–C	Not represented	City wall
Phase 8	IA I	Only Area 52	Not represented
Phase 7	IA IIB–C	Pottery in fills	Fortification and support walls, glacis
Phase 6	Hasmonean	Scanty plastered installations	Not represented
Phase 5	Early Roman	Paved street, mikveh, water channels	Not represented
Phase 4	Early Roman	Two houses, mikveh(s), industrial area	Not represented
Phase 3	Early Roman	House, paving, mikveh, industrial area(?)	Not represented
Phase 2	Late Roman–early Byzantine	Mikveh pools reused, winepress reused	Mill, installations (2B, 2A)
Phase 1	Late Byzantine–Ottoman	Thick accumulation of terrace soil in south	Up to 1 m accumulation of terrace soil

3. See Eisenberg, "Fortifications," 26–28, 30.

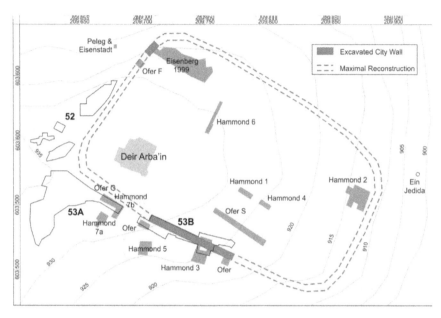

Fig. 3.1. Plan of Tel Hebron showing exposed fortification lines and a suggested contour of the city wall. Figure by author.

Fig. 3.2. The fortifications in Area 53B, general view. Photograph by author.

3.2. The Cyclopean Fortifications at Tel Hebron

The Bronze and Iron Age fortification at Tel Hebron was visible in certain areas of the tell on the ground before excavations were begun. This massive, cyclopean fortification wall was first identified by Garstang in 1931, then by Hammond, Ofer, and most recently described by Eisenberg, who summarized the results prior to the current excavations.[4] A cyclopean wall would be defined as a wall primarily built of rubble, unworked, polygonal stones, substantially larger than 0.5 m each; the stones are not laid in horizontal courses, rather courses are adapted to the polygonal lines of the individual stones. Hammond dated the fortification to the Middle Bronze IIB–C and suggested this wall surrounded an area of only 2 ha, while Ofer suggested the Middle Bronze IIB–C wall surrounded a city of 2.4–3 ha.[5] Jeff Chadwick suggested a similar size, whereas Eisenberg suggested a larger area of 3.5 ha (fig. 3.1).[6] Several segments of the wall are either connected or have a very similar construction technique and are thus assumed to be contemporary. Nevertheless, fortification walls of a different character also appear, built with smaller hued rectilinear stones (see below). As will be shown, the two types of construction may be used to tentatively classify their construction date.

Altogether, the continuous exposure of the fortification wall is of approximately 69.20 m (figs. 3.2–3.4), yet it seems that a maximum 60.80 m of this length belongs to the earlier Middle Bronze IIB–C wall, while the rest are later additions. The wall is identified by its large polygonal rubble stones. The original building technique of the wall can be clearly observed in most locations where it was exposed. The large stones and boulders were set on the bedrock, which was leveled by a layer of small stones (ca. 10–25 × 10–25 × 10–20 cm; figs. 3.4–3.6). The stones were laid with their straight side facing outward, creating a flat smooth surface that would have prevented climbing on the wall. The lower part overlying the bedrock was seemingly enforced by a layer of stones and yellowish marl soil, although this marl may have eroded from the top of the wall or from between the stones, as it may have been used as bonding material. The

---

4. Eisenberg, "Fortifications," 20, fig. 11. See also Jeff R. Chadwick, "Discovering Hebron: The City of the Patriarchs Slowly Yields its Secrets," *BAR* 31.5 (2005): 28.

5. Ofer, "Hebron"; see Eisenberg, "Fortifications," 28.

6. For Chadwick's suggested size, see "Discovering Hebron," 27; Eisenberg, "Fortifications," fig. 16. For Eisenberg's suggestion, see "Fortifications," 28, fig. 17.

wall itself was built of large roughly cut rubble stones of polygonal shapes, with their size ranging from 140 × 85 × 45–65 cm and 115 × 100 cm to larger stones reaching 200 × 90 × 70 cm. The cavities created between the large stones were filled by small stones, sized 10–25 × 10–20 cm. Whereas the external faces of the wall were built in this manner, the wall's core was filled with medium-sized rubble stones, sized 15–30 × 15–30 × 10–25 cm. The core of the wall as well as gaps between the large stones were filled with chunks of stones and relatively small amounts of soil or marl, thus creating a solid strong wall that was able to stand for centuries. The wall was clearly higher in antiquity, with the uppermost portion of the super-structure not having survived. It seems reasonable to assume that while larger stones were used in the lower courses, the top of the wall was built of smaller stones (as those found in the fallout layers to the south, see below). The outer face of the wall was built relatively straight, and was probably reinforced in several locations by buttresses (figs. 3.3, 3.4), creating a series of insets and outsets.[7]

The long, now continuous, line of exposure (denoted Wall 2151 or Wall B, figs. 3.2–4) includes a part the wall's western external face exposed completely for a length of approximately 12.7 m (to the east its continuation is masked by tower 2403, see below), which rises from the bedrock to a preservation of up to 4.30 m (fig. 3.4), up to five courses high. The wall was excavated from the outside, yet, in one location, the full 3.4–3.6 m width of the wall was revealed (fig. 3.5 left). This section was exclusively excavated in the 2014 excavations. The wall was clearly higher in antiquity, and many fallen stones from the top of the wall were found adjacent to it.

Although Hammond already suggested dating the fortification in this area to the Middle Bronze IIB–C, the entire area outside the city wall down to bedrock (elevations 925.50–924.00 m) was covered by eroded, later, accumulations and no Middle Bronze Age floors were preserved (or existed?).[8] The dating is therefore determined only according to floor levels from the 1999 excavation in the northwestern part of the tell (see below).[9] Here, floors that abut the city wall were excavated on the inner face of the wall and according to well-dated pottery and scarabs found on

---

7. See also Eisenberg, "Fortifications," 26.

8. For the dating, see Phillip C. Hammond, "Hebron," *RB* 73 (1966): 566–69; Chadwick, "Discovering Hebron."

9. Emanuel Eisenberg and Alla Nagorski, "Tel Hebron," *HA* 114 (2002): 92; Emanuel Eisenberg, *The 1999 Excavations at Tel Hebron*, forthcoming.

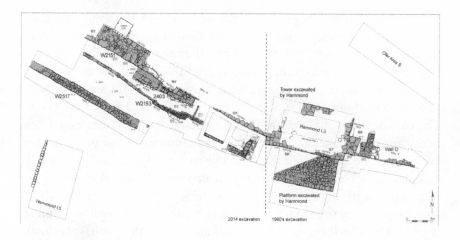

Fig. 3.3. The Bronze and Iron Age fortifications in Area 53B, general plan (Iron Age additions are darker colored). Figure by author.

Fig. 3.4. The cyclopean wall fortifications in Area 53B. Photograph by author.

Fig. 3.5. The cyclopean wall from the top (Wall 2517 on the right). Photograph by author.

them are dated to the Middle Bronze IIB–C, that is, the final stages of the Middle Bronze Age.[10] In that area this wall also overlies the better-preserved Early Bronze Age city wall. The finds from the 2014 excavations do not contribute to the dating of the construction of this wall to the Middle Bronze IIB–C period. Yet the current fortification wall from Area 53B is of a similar construction technique and thus assumed to be part of the same wall. Moreover, fortification walls built in a similar fashion were dated elsewhere in the southern Levant, especially in the central hill country of Israel, to the same period (see below).

The style of this fortification wall, as well as its dating, is in particular very similar to the various fortifications found in the City of David.[11] In addition, similar city walls were built in other important Middle Bronze

---

10. Eisenberg, "Fortifications," 19–20, 30; Strata IX–VIII, "Wall B" and structure 141 abutting it; Eisenberg, *Excavations*, figs. 3.80–3.93.

11. Margreet L. Steiner, *The Settlement in the Bronze and Iron Ages*, vol. 3 of *Excavations by Kathleen M. Kenyon in Jerusalem 1961–1967*, Copenhagen International Series 9 (London: Sheffield Academic, 2001), 10–11; Yigal Shiloh, *Excavations at the City of David I 1978–1982: Interim Report of the First Five Seasons*, Qedem 19 (Jerusalem: Hebrew University, 1984), 12; and particularly the fortifications leading to and surrounding the spring: Ronny Reich and Eli Shukron, "Jerusalem, City of David," *HA* 114 (2003): 92–94; Reich and Shukron, "A New Segment of the Middle Bronze Fortification in the City of David," *TA* 37 (2010): 141–53; Reich, *Excavating the City of David: Where Jerusalem's History Began* [Hebrew] (Jerusalem: Israel Exploration Society, 2011); Joe Uziel and Nachshon Szanton, "Recent Excavations near the Gihon Spring and Their Reflection on the Character of Iron II Jerusalem," *TA* 42 (2015): 233–50.

IIB–C centers of the central hills country, such as Shechem and Shiloh.[12] The earliest wall at Gezer also seems similar as well as the Middle Bronze IIC wall at Jericho.[13] This similarity both strengthens the suggested date for the construction of this wall, as well as indicates a possibly common cultural and architectural tradition for these hill sites during this period.

3.3. The Iron Age II Fortifications at Tel Hebron

The results of the 2014 excavations in Area 53B clearly indicate that during the Iron Age II the earlier (MB IIB–C) cyclopean fortification wall was still in use and, furthermore, was amended, with various fortification elements added to it (fig. 3.3).[14] The Iron Age construction was in a different style using smaller, hued, rectilinear stones. This is visible also in inspection of areas previously excavated by Hammond and Ofer in several spots.

In the area excavated by Ofer during the early 1980s (denoted Area G1 by him, in a 5 × 5 m square) the upper courses of the wall were exposed on the surface before excavation.[15] Ofer already recognized that this wall was an Iron Age fortification element (denoted Wall 351). This area was expanded in 2014 and excavated down to bedrock, exposing the base of the wall. Along this section, exposed for a length of 7.3 m long, the wall stands to a height of up to approximately 4 m and four to five courses high (fig. 3.4), with the modern terrace wall built on top of it. Here, within the earlier city wall, a later buttress or tower was built (figs. 3.3, 3.6 W2403). A section of this buttress was already exposed by Ofer (Area G1, fig. 1.5,

---

12. Edward F. Campbell, *Text*, vol. 1 of *Shechem III: The Stratigraphy and Architecture of Shechem/Tell Balatah*, ASORAR 6 (Boston: American Schools of Oriental Research, 2002), 105–9; Israel Finkelstein, Shlomo Bunimovtz, and Zvi Lederman, *Shiloh: The Archaeology of a Biblical Site*, Sonia and Marco Nadler Institute of Archaeology Monograph Series 10 (Tel Aviv: Institute of Archaeology Tel Aviv University, 1993), 37, 47; see also Joe D. Seger, "The MB II Fortifications at Shechem and Gezer: A Hyksos Retrospective," *ErIsr* 12 (1975): 34*–45*; Eisenberg, "Fortifications," 28–30 for a general overview of such fortifications.

13. For Gezer, see William G. H. Dever, Darrell Lance, and Ernest G. Wright. *Gezer I: Preliminary Report of the 1964–66 Seasons* (Jerusalem: Glueck School of Biblical Archaeology, 1970), 41–43. For Jericho, see Chiara Fiaccavento and Daria Montanari, "The MB III Rampart and Cyclopean Wall of Tell es-Sultan/Jericho," *Scienze dell'Antichità* 19.2–3 (2013): 58–61.

14. Eisenberg and Ben-Shlomo, *Hevron*, 78–92.

15. Avi Ofer, "Tel Hebron" [Hebrew], *HA* 90 (1988): 48.

denoted outset 351). This structure is 12.7 m long and approximately 1.7 m thick. It is notable that the inner stones are combined within the earlier construction and were part of an earlier, smaller, buttress, while the outer stones, which thicken and widen this protrusion, are not similarly combined (fig. 3.6). Furthermore, the outer stones are of different sizes and shapes than the earlier city wall stones, being more rectilinear and forming an outer line of a slightly different orientation than the original wall. These observations indeed indicate a later date for the construction of this addition, and the latest sherds from the fill abutting this structure are dated to the Iron Age IIB (see below, fig. 3.13). This dates its final use, yet, its construction can be earlier. It seems that the tower enfolds the earlier wall outset, and uses various stones from the wall, including larger stones possibly reused after the original wall collapsed in this area.

Fig. 3.6. Iron Age II tower showing its addition to the city wall. Photograph by author.

At the base of the original city wall a layer of sediment of stones and yellowish marl was found as well as in the western corner of this buttress, indicating that an earlier glacis or fill served as a reinforcement for the lower courses of the city wall, protecting it from erosion. This element, related to the cyclopean wall of the Middle Bronze IIB–C, was also noticed by the previous excavators of the tell.[16]

Parallel to the fortification, a reinforcement wall (figs. 3.3, 3.9, W2153) was exposed for a total length of approximately 26.50 m (fig. 3.7); it is located 1.5–3 m south of the city wall and clearly surrounds the tower. This wall was built to support a stone glacis between it and the city wall. It is cut

---

16. Ofer, "Tel Hebron," 48.

in the east by a Late Roman-Byzantine (Phase 2) wall. The top of this stone glacis was already excavated by Ofer.[17] The wall is built against a sloping fill of earth and small-sized stones with a solid coating made of rubble stone. Larger blocks were used as foundations built directly on bedrock (fig. 3.8). Only the outer, southern face of the wall is built by stones, creating a line parallel more or less to the city wall. The inner, northern face was not straight (as in the terrace walls), and the area between the supporting wall and the city wall was filled with stones and dirt. The latest sherds from this fill are dated to the Iron Age IIB. The wall, which thins toward the top, is slightly inclined to the north toward the city wall (fig. 3.9). This wall at its full exposure was over 2 m and nine courses high and was built directly on the bedrock. Due to the inward inclination of the wall, it appears that in antiquity the top of it probably abutted the city wall. From the outer, southern face, layers of fill, stones and fine dirt can be seen in the section (fig. 3.9, L.2158). Particularly notable are the yellowish and brown layers, each about 1–15 cm thick, sloping down gently to the south (fig. 3.8). The latest sherds from the excavation of these layers were also dated to the Iron Age IIB (see fig. 3.13), thus dating the final use; again the date of construction can be earlier.

The supporting wall and the glacis served as a reinforcement of the city wall, protecting the fortification against military attacks as well as weather and earthquake damage. In particular, the glacis provided support to the base of the wall, preventing stones from being washed away due to erosion. A similar supporting wall was found at Tell en-Naṣbeh, dating to the Iron Age II.[18] Other possibly similar Iron Age II glacis or ramparts can be noted at Tell el-Fûl and Tel Beit Mirsim.[19] Note that all these sites were in the territory of Judah during the end of the eighth and seventh centuries BCE, and thus possibly there is a historical connection between all these fortification efforts.

---

17. Ofer, "Hebron," 608.

18. Chester C. McCown, *Tell en-Nasbeh I: Excavated under the Direction of the Late William Frederic Bade* (New Haven: American Schools of Oriental Research, 1947), 192–193, pl. 69.

19. Willian F. Albright, *Excavations and Results at Tell el-Fûl (Gibeah of Saul)*, AASOR 4 (New Haven, Yale University Press, 1924), fig. 17, pl. XXIV; William F. Albright, James L. Kelso, and J. Palin Thorley, *The Iron Age*, vol. 3 of *The Excavation of Tel Beit Mirsim*, AASOR 21–22 (New Haven: American Schools of Oriental Research, 1943), pl. 40.

Fig. 3.7. Iron Age II supporting wall (center). Photograph by author.

Fig. 3.8. The Iron Age II glacis close-up. Photograph by author.

Fig. 3.9. Section of fortification walls in Area 53B. Figure by author.

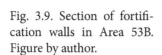
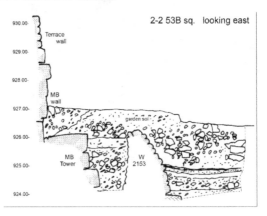

About 8.5 m from the cyclopean city wall and parallel to it, an additional stonewall was built (fig. 3.5 right; fig. 3.3, Wall 2517). This wall, exposed for a length of 22.5 m, was 1.6–1.7 m thick and preserved to a height of 2 m on the western side. It was built of medium to large stones laid in horizontal courses, with the lowest courses built on bedrock. The direction of the glacis is lined up with the outer tower unearthed in 1964 by Hammond (see fig. 3.10, Hammond Area I.3a). This wall may have continued further to the west, although this area remains unexcavated; it slopes gradually up to the west, following the natural slope of the bedrock. The westernmost exposed portion is built of larger stones, possibly indicating the presence of a corner. The width of this wall and its orientation, and lack of any connection to a structure to the south, indicates this wall also functioned as part of the fortification system at the site, serving as a reinforcement of the city wall and/or an additional barrier. A possibly similar example comes from Tell en-Naṣbeh and dated to the Iron II.[20] It is also possible that the wall was originally constructed in an earlier period, serving a different function—possibly a support wall for a pathway leading to a gate in the wall.

Fig. 3.10. Tower and wall excavated by Hammond (in the rear) looking west; Wall D in front. Photograph by author.

---

20. McCowen, *Tell en-Nasbeh*, pl. 69.2 on the left, denoted as "retaining wall."

The area between the later supporting walls and the city wall was found covered with building stones of various sizes (fig. 3.5, center). These stones most likely represent the collapse of the fortification walls after they were destroyed and/or went out of use. The finds from this accumulation represent the final stage of the fortification's use in the Iron Age, as indicated by the pottery found and a Hebrew seal of an official (fig. 3.14:8, see below). Above this layer, a layer of loose stones mixed with fallen stones from the fortification wall was excavated, sealed by a 1–2 m layer of topsoil containing large quantities of Roman and early Byzantine pottery.

In the eastern part of the area two wall segments (fig. 3.3, W2372, W2387) likely also belong to later fortifications, with sherds below the upper level of the wall dating to the Iron Age II or earlier. Since it was only partly excavated beneath the later remains, its relationship and connection to the stone glacis and to Hammond's exterior tower in his Area I.3a–b remains unclear. A drainage channel was exposed (fig. 3.3, L. 2413), apparently beneath Wall 2372. This feature comprises two walls built of upright stones, covered by flat capstones, creating a channel 0.6 m wide with an internal width of approximately 0.35 m. This may have been a channel that drained water from beneath the city wall.

To the east of Area 53B, remains from Hammond's excavation were cleaned and further clarified during the 2014 excavations. The rectangular tower excavated by Hammond in this area measures 15.5 × 9.2 m (figs. 3.3, 3.10).[21] It is integrated into the city wall, as also seen in the similar construction notable in the polygonal stones of the lower courses. The upper horizontal courses, however, indicate a later (Iron Age?) addition. Another outset or tower (Wall 2) abutting the face of this inner tower was unearthed by Hammond in 1964.[22] Hammond dated the wall to the Middle Bronze period.[23] This structure (covered and no longer visible today), extended 6.5 m outward from the line of the main wall, and its length was exposed for 12 m (fig. 3.3, in blue). It was founded on bedrock with large square-cut boulders laid in horizontal courses. It seems that it was first built as a smaller tower and later extended with outer walls to create a full block of stones. Due to the discovery of the fortifications in the 1999 excavations, Chadwick related this tower to the Early Bronze III, however, as shown

---

21. Chadwick, "Discovering Hebron"; Eisenberg, "Fortifications," 28.

22. See Eisenberg, "Fortifications," fig. 15; Eisenberg and Ben-Shlomo, *Hevron*, fig. 4.45.

23. Phillip C. Hammond, "Hebron," *RB* 72 (1965): 268.

above, the results of the current excavation indicate it most likely belongs to the Iron Age II activity along the original city wall.[24]

Chadwick, who studied the results from Hammond's Area I.3, presumed the inner tower is the western tower of a gateway, which would have a matching eastern tower. He based it on a clear seam that looked like a blocked entrance, constructed with smaller stones.[25]

About 10 m east of Hammond's site I.3, Ofer excavated a 5 × 5 m square in 1984 and reached the top of the of the city wall. Based on this discovery, Ofer claimed that the walled city continued further down to lower terraces and in a straight line.[26] In 2014, this area was cleaned and the soil between these two sections cleared, uncovering an additional 13.5 m portion of Wall D (fig. 3.3, Wall D; figs. 3.10, 3.11). It stands to a height of 3.6 m, with nine to ten courses built above the bedrock, up to the modern terrace wall built above it. It became apparent however that this wall is attached to the original cyclopean city wall, built with larger stones that, for an unknown reason, stop at this point (possibly making an angle or a turn to the north). Wall D is built of smaller, partly hued and more rectilinear stones measuring 0.65 × 0.65–0.70 × 0.50–0.60 m as opposed to the polygonal stones, measuring over 1 m in size, of the earlier (MB II) wall. Thus, this wall is a later attachment, tentatively dated to the Iron Age II. This is supported by the results of the current excavations further west (see above).

Fig. 3.11. Wall D exposed east of Area 53B. Photograph by author.

24. Chadwick, "Discovering Hebron," 27–28.
25. Chadwick, "Discovering Hebron," 28.
26. Ofer, "Tel Hebron," 48.

3.4. Other Iron Age IIB–C Remains at Tel Hebron:
Previous Excavations and Finds

During 1999, a large-scale salvage excavation was directed by Eisenberg on the northwestern part of the tell (Plot 67) and exposed approximately 500 m² with eleven strata defined (table 3.2).[27] The main results were an Early Bronze III city wall: a 5.7–6.2 m thick wall made of medium-sized rubble stones, preserved for a length of 14 m and a height of 3.1 m (table 2, Phase XI).[28] Adjacent to the wall on its inner face, a structure containing several rooms was excavated and yielded an assemblage of restorable Early Bronze III pottery and small finds.

Strata IX–VIII date to the Middle Bronze IIB–C and include a poorly preserved small section of a city wall (of a somewhat different orientation than the EB III wall) made of large polygonal rubble stones and remains of several rooms attached to it from the inside.[29] The finds from the floors abutting the fortification wall from the inside can date this fortification securely for the first time to the Middle Bronze IIB–C, based on pottery vessels and scarabs.[30] Other finds included metal artifacts, silver jewelry, and bone tools.

Stratum VII is dated to the Iron Age I and included a silo and two refuse pits. In Stratum VI, dated to the Iron IIB (eighth–seventh century BCE), a large part of a well-preserved four-room house was exposed (fig. 3.12; reconstructed on the site). The building, a typical pillared four-room house, was violently destroyed and contained some thirty restorable pottery vessels, stone weights, loom weights, and a stone roof roller. Nearby an oval silo within an open area was discovered, and to the northeast were remains of another building and two smaller silos. Remains of an Iron IIB–C building (Stratum V) cut this structure. The Stratum V building contained eight *lmlk*-jar handles, of which five legible ones read "*hbrn*."

Iron Age II remains were reported from Hammond's excavation as well; roughly in the center of the tell, the main structure exposed was a well-built pillared house from the Iron Age II.[31] Two phases dating to the

---

27. Eisenberg and Nagorski, "Hebron"; Eisenberg, "Fortifications"; Eisenberg, *Excavations*.
28. Eisenberg, "Fortifications," figs. 3, 7.
29. Eisenberg, "Fortifications," 19–20, figs. 10–14.
30. Eisenberg, "Fortifications," 26–28.
31. Hammond, "Hebron" (1966).

Fig. 3.12. The four-room house (reconstructed) excavated in 1999 by Eisenberg. Photograph by author.

Iron II with remains of a room and installations are reported from Ofer's main section (Area S) as well.[32]

In the 2014 excavations in Area 52 in which architectural remains were poorly preserved a segment of a wall dated to the Iron Age IIB was also unearthed; under it an Iron Age I lime kiln was exposed.[33]

Table 3.2. The Different Strata in Eisenberg 1999 Excavations at Tel Hebron

Stratum	Period	Main finds
XI	EB III	City wall; domestic structures
X	EB III	Raising of floor level; staircase along the outer wall
IX	MB IIB–C	Fragment of city wall; inner floor levels
VIII	MB IIB–C	Fragment of city wall; inner floor levels
VII	IA I	Silos
VI	IA IIB	Four room house
V	IA IIC	Fragmentary building

32. Ofer, "Hebron."

33. For the wall segment, see Eisenberg and Ben-Shlomo, *Hevron*, 19–20. For the lime kiln, see Adi Eliyahu-Behar, Naama Yahalom-Mack, and David Ben-Shlomo, "Excavation and Analysis of an Early Iron Age Lime Kiln," *IEJ* 67 (2017): 14–31.

IV	Hellenistic	Domestic houses, cancelling the city wall
III	Early Roman	Floor levels
II	Late Roman–Byzantine	Complex winepress
I	Middle Ages–Ottoman period	Terraces, burials

3.4.1 Finds from the Iron Age II in Area 53B

Within the debris and fallen stones near the city wall and adjacent loci, the finds included pottery of which the latest can be dated to the Iron Age IIB–C (fig. 3.13). The pottery from the fills between these walls can be dated to the Iron Age IIB–C, similar to Lachish Levels III–II, City of David Strata 12–10, or Batash Strata III–II. Typical forms include red slipped and wheel burnished "Judean folded rim" bowls and kraters (fig. 3.13:1–4), grooved cooking pots (fig. 3.13:5), holemouth jars (fig. 3.13:6, 7), holemouth pithoi with thickened rims (fig. 3.13:8, 9) and lamps with thick bases (fig. 3.13:10). These types appear in the Iron IIB while some continue to the Iron IIC; in particular, the cooking pot (fig. 3.13:5) and thick-based lamp (fig. 3.13:10) appear in the seventh century BCE. Yet other types more typical of the late seventh century BCE are missing, as the closed type cooking pots, mortaria bowls, jars with rosette stamp, and decanter jugs. It should be noted, however, that the assemblage is rather small in size, and absence of types can be incidental. Thus, it seems that this fill-related pottery assemblage should be dated to the late eighth or early seventh centuries BCE. Therefore, the date of the construction stage of the Iron Age fortification walls and their final use was not earlier than this period, and thus was probably during the Iron Age IIC.

Additional stratified Iron IIB–C finds come from Area 52 where a fragment of supporting wall was excavated.[34] Most common types are again the "Judean folded rim" bowls and kraters, holemouth jars, and holemouth pithoi.

Other noteworthy Iron Age IIB–C finds from the 2014 excavations include *lmlk*-jars handles (fig. 3.14:1–3; two winged, without script), zoomorphic figurine fragments (fig. 3.14:4–7), a stone seal (fig. 3.14:8), and a

---

34. Eisenberg and Ben-Shlomo, *Hevron*, figs. 2.14, 2.15.

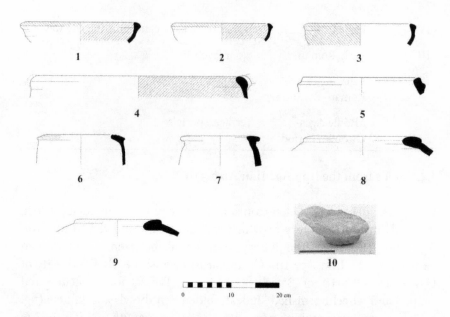

Fig. 3.13. Iron Age IIB–C pottery from the Tel Hebron 2014 excavations. Figure by author.

worn ostracon (fig. 3.14:9). Both the seal and the ostracon were found in the same context of the accumulation representing the fallout of the fortification walls.[35] The stone seal with three engraved lines is worn but the lower two lines can be read (fig. 3.14:8), reading:

לשפטיהו (בן) סמך   Belonging to Shepaṭyahu (son of) Samak

Similar or identical names are known both from the biblical text and provenanced and unprovenanced epigraphic material (mainly bullae) and their date, as well as the style of the letters, also points to a date of the late eighth and seventh centuries BCE.[36]

On the upper line of the base, a quadruped was engraved, likely a grazing deer/gazelle crouching toward the ground (very similar to other examples especially an impression at Tel 'Eton).[37] Very similar decorations

---

35. Daniel Vainstub and David Ben-Shlomo, "A Hebrew Seal and an Ostracon from Tel Hebron," *IEJ* 66 (2016): 151–60.

36. Vainstub and Ben-Shlomo, "Hebrew Seal," 157.

37. Avraham Faust and Esther Eshel, "An Inscribed Bulla with Grazing Doe from

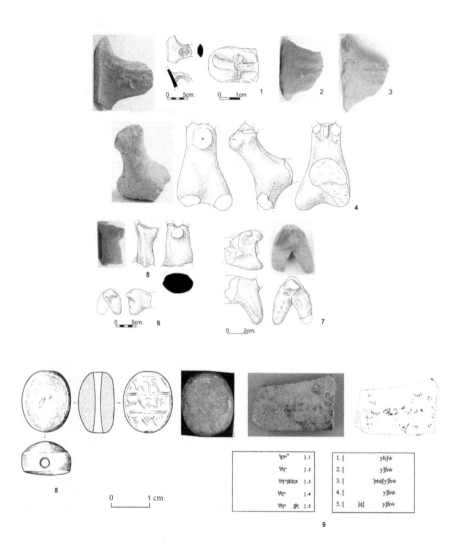

Fig. 3.14. Iron Age IIB–C finds from the Tel Hebron 2014 excavations. Figure by author.

are known from Hebrew seals and stamps from unknown provenances.[38] This iconographic motif may be popular on private seals of officials in Judah during the late Iron Age II also as it may symbolize dedication and devotion as well as the "one beloved by god," picturing the verse: "As a deer longs for flowing streams, so my soul longs for you, O God" (Ps 42:2 NRSV).[39] The motif of course has a long history in Near Eastern iconography, probably representing well-being, fertility, or something similar.[40] Note that the seal from Tel Hebron is the only known seal retrieved so far in a controlled excavation in Judah that bears the motif.

The ostracon is very worn and fragmentary yet it is possible to read the typical Judahite theophoric ending יהו at the end of each of the five rows (fig. 3.14:9). This leads to the conclusion that the document is a list of personal Judahite names, a well-known document type. The proximity of the endings of the names to the border of the ostracon indicates that our list holds only names and no numerals or quantity signs after each name as many such ostraca contain. However, name lists without numerals or signs are known, for example, Lachish 1 and Arad 39.

3.5. The Date of the Cyclopean Fortifications in the Central Hills

The dating of the construction of fortification systems is not easy, since these elements, which require much labor in their construction, were often in use for long periods of time with amendments and modifications along the years. Most of the finds associated with these walls represent their final period of use rather than their construction period, which could be many centuries earlier. In the hill country this becomes even more difficult since

---

Tel 'Eton," in *Puzzling the Past: Studies in Northwest Semitic Languages and Literature in Honor of Bruce Zuckerman*, ed. Marilyn J. Lunberg, Steven Fine, and Wayne T. Pitard, CHANE 55 (Leiden: Brill, 2012), 63–70.

38. See, e.g., Nachman Avigad, *Corpus of West Semitic Stamp Seals*, rev. and completed by Benjamin Sass (Jerusalem: Israel Exploration Society, 1997), nos. 144, 181, 204, 301; Tallay Ornan, "The Beloved, Neʿehevet, and Other Does: Reflections on the Motif of the Grazing or Browsing Wild Horned Animal," in *Alphabets, Texts and Artefacts in the Ancient Near East: Studies Presented to Benjamin Sass*, ed. Israel Finkelstein, Christian Robin, and Thomas Römer (Paris: Van Dieren, 2016), 279–302.

39. See Ornan, "Beloved"; Othmar Keel and Christoph Uehlinger, *Gods, Goddesses and Images of God in Ancient Israel* (Minneapolis: Fortress, 1998), 147–50.

40. Ornan, "Beloved," 291–99.

every new layer built on the rock surfaces erases the previous layers rather than overlays them (as in classical tell sites).

Recently, David Ussishkin suggested that the cyclopean fortification walls of the City of David near the Gihon Spring as well as those of Tel Hebron should not be dated to Middle Bronze IIB–C as previously suggested but much later to the Iron Age IIB–C.[41]

In regard to Tel Hebron, as noted, the Middle Bronze IIB–C dating of the original cyclopean city wall in Area 53B is based on the both the results of the 1999 excavations from the northwest (where floors with MB IIB–C finds were found reaching a segment of the cyclopean wall) and indeed on typological reasoning linking this very exceptional construction technique to other sites mainly in the central hills, such as the City of David, Shechem, and Shiloh. This dating could be also inspired from the biblical text from the story of Caleb and the spies: "They went up into the Negeb, and came to Hebron; and Ahiman, Sheshai, and Talmai, the Anakites, were there. (Hebron was built seven years before Zoan in Egypt.)" (Num 13:22 NRSV). This passage suggests that the city wall of Hebron was exposed, well known, and was built much before the text was written; it also alludes to its cyclopean nature by the referral to the giants (Anaq).

For Tel Hebron our direct archaeological data for dating the cyclopean walls is, however, so far relatively limited. The results of the 1999 excavations, not yet fully published, include a small and not very well-preserved portion of the cyclopean city wall, overlying the EB III city wall (see above). Furthermore, the walls of the rooms dated according to finds on the floor and abutting the city wall are not in a right angle to the city wall.[42] However, this is so far the only direct evidence for dating this wall, and therefore, the cyclopean wall in Area 53B and in Hammond's excavations on the southeast of the tell were thus tentatively dated to the Middle Bronze IIB–C. The supporting wall and glacis described above, of which their final use is dated to the Iron Age IIB–C, are clearly linked with later additions and modifications to the city wall, which was apparently still in use during this period but were built in a completely different style. Nevertheless, in order to achieve a final and definite dating of the original construction date for the cyclopean wall of Tel Hebron it will be necessary

---

41. David Ussishkin, "Was Jerusalem a Fortified Stronghold in the Middle Bronze Age? An Alternative View," *Levant* 48 (2016): 135–51.

42. As noted by Ussishkin, "Jerusalem," 150.

to excavate more and larger floors and houses abutting the city wall, as well as to excavate a section of the wall itself.

Therefore, we are still highly dependent on the typological reasoning of the parallels to other cyclopean construction techniques in the central hills. One of the important cases is the cyclopean fortifications of the City of David dated by Kathleen Kenyon and Yigal Shiloh and more recently by Ronny Reich and Eli Sukrun to the Middle Bronze II (in particular the Spring Tower and Pool Tower).

Ussishkin discusses the evidence for fortification in the City of David unearthed in Kenyon's (Wall NB/Wall), Shiloh's (Area E, Wall 285/219), and Reich and Sukron's excavations (the Spring Tower and the Pool Tower).[43] According to his reanalysis of the finds, there is no proof that these fortification walls date to the Middle Bronze II since no Middle Bronze II floor clearly reaches these walls.[44] Alternatively, he suggests an Iron Age IIB–C date, linking this construction with the substantial expansion of the city in the Western Hill. Similarly Ussishkin suggests an Iron Age IIB date for the construction of the cyclopean fortification at Tel Hebron.[45]

The main arguments raised by Ussiskin for rejecting the excavators datings of these walls, in particular those from Area E and the area of the Gihon Spring (especially Walls 108 and 109 of the Pool Tower), is that floor material from houses reaching the wall from the inside (as in Area E Strata 17–18; as well various spots in the interior of the Pool Tower) cannot be used to date the wall and should be treated as early constructional fills. The main stratigraphical argument is that fortification walls built in a sloped terrain do not cut older strata on their inner face, but rather lean on them.[46] Therefore, material from floors seemingly abutting the wall from the inside cannot give a *terminus ante quem* for the construction of the fortification wall. This argument relates mostly to terrace-type walls, which have the

---

43. For Kenyon's excavations, see Steiner, *Settlement in the Bronze and Iron Ages*. For Shiloh's, see Alon De Groot and Hannah Bernick-Greenberg, eds., *Area E: Stratigraphy and Architecture*, vol.7A of *Excavations at the City of David 1978–1985 Directed by Yigal Shiloh*, Qedem 53 (Jerusalem: Institute of Archaeology, Hebrew University of Jerusalem, 2012). For Reich and Shukrun's, see "New Segment"; Uziel and Szanton, "Recent Excavations."

44. Ussishkin, "Jerusalem," 141–43.

45. Ussishkin, "Jerusalem," 148–50.

46. Ussishkin, "Jerusalem," 141–42, quoting Yigal Yadin, "The Nature of the Settlements during the Middle Bronze IIA Period in Israel and the Problem of the Aphek Fortifications," *ZDPV* 94 (1978): 14–15.

characteristic of a nonaligned inner face built of smaller stones, as they merely support fill and soil and are not free-standing walls. This is clearly not the case here, at least for Wall 108 in the Pool Tower.[47] Furthermore this argument usually does not hold in areas of the central hills such as the City of David, since the massive freestanding walls were not built on sloped surface but rather of a relatively flat step in the rock. In that case they must cut earlier remains and therefore walls and finds from floors that do abut them from the inside can indeed reflect the time they were existing and thus provide a *terminus ante quem* for their construction date. Therefore, I believe there is no reason so far not to date the original construction of the cyclopean walls of the Pool Tower to the Middle Bronze II.

Clearly, these massive walls stood and were used, whether as intact fortification walls of the city or otherwise for very long periods, especially during the Iron Age when the city expanded. Recent excavations in the area of the Spring Tower and the Pool Tower unearthed domestic houses abutting or leaning on the cyclopean walls.[48] Two phases were identified, an earlier dated to the late Iron Age IIA (Stratum 9, ninth–early eighth century BCE) and a later phase to the late Iron Age IIB (Stratum 8, late seventh century BCE, or Lachish III).[49] Recent radiocarbon datings in the base of the Spring Tower seem to indicate that much of the construction in this area is dated to the Iron Age IIA or the ninth century BCE.[50] While these results do not indicate a Middle Bronze II construction date of the cyclopean elements in this area, they clearly show the massive walls were standing and used during the ninth century BCE and thus constructed at that time, or more likely before it. Therefore, the dating of the cyclopean elements in the City of David to the late eighth century BCE (or later) suggested by Ussishkin cannot be accepted.[51] Furthermore, if we examine, for example, the construction technique of the Broad Wall in the Western Hill dated to the Iron Age IIB–C, we can see it is not built with large polygonal

---

47. Reich and Shukrun, "New Segment"; Reich, *Excavating*, 12; Ussishkin, "Jerusalem," 142–43, fig. 10.

48. Uziel and Szanton, "Recent Excavations."

49. For the earlier phase, see Uziel and Szanton, "Recent Excavations," 237–39, fig. 3.

50. Johanna Regev, Joe Uziel, Nachshon Szanton, and Elizabetta Boaretto, "Absolute Dating of the Gihon Spring Fortifications, Jerusalem," *Radiocarbon* 59 (2017): 1171–93.

51. See also Yuval Gadot and Joe Uziel, "The Monumentality of Iron Age Jerusalem Prior to the Eighth Century BCE," *TA* 44 (2017): 123–40.

stones and represents a completely different style than the cyclopean walls at the City of David.[52] Since in the Pool Tower area at the base of the wall only Middle Bronze II remains were found, while this area hardly yielded Late Bronze Age, Iron I, and early Iron IIA remains, the Middle Bronze II construction dating for the cyclopean walls is so far the most likely.

Another question arising from Ussishkin's reanalysis is whether we should change the date of the construction of the cyclopean city walls in other sites in the central hills, such as Shechem/Tell Balatah and Shiloh, as well as other sites as at Gezer and Jericho, from the traditional Middle Bronze II to the Iron Age IIB–C.[53] Apparently, Ussishkin does not redate these other cyclopean city walls, probably due to historical reasons. Therefore, it seems strange that this very exceptional and unique construction technique, not known in the southern Levant from any other period during the Bronze and Iron Ages, should be dated otherwise only at the City of David and Tell Hebron, which were the two main towns in the area geographic of Judah in this period.[54] This difference between the area of the Judean hills and other areas such as Samaria and the Bethel hills is not explained. Therefore, maybe we also have to reexamine the dating of these other cyclopean wall systems as at Shechem and Shiloh?

3.6. Conclusions

The Iron Age II fortification elements at Tel Hebron indicate the usage and maintenance of the cyclopean city wall, currently dated to the Middle Bronze IIB–C, at Tel Hebron during end of the Iron Age, thus about one thousand years later. It is likely the walls were visible and standing throughout this period, as the passage from the book of Numbers implies, and testifies to the antiquity and impressiveness of this fortification.

---

52. Hillel Geva, "Western Jerusalem at the End of the First Temple Period in Light of the Excavations in the Jewish Quarter," in *Jerusalem in Bible and Archaeology: The First Temple Period*, ed. Andy G. Vaughn and Ann E. Killebrew, SymS 18 (Atlanta: Society of Biblical Literature, 2003), 192–95, fig. 7.5:1.

53. For Shechem, see Campbell, *Text*; for Shiloh, see Finkelstein, Bunimovitz, and Lederman, *Shiloh*, 37, 71, fig. 5.6. For Gezer, see Dever, Lance, and Wright, *Gezer*, 41–43; for Jericho, see Fiaccavento and Montanari, "Jericho."

54. An exception would be the cyclopean walls of Khirbet Qeiyafa constructed during the early Iron Age IIA (e.g., Yosef Garfinkel and Sa'ar Ganor, *Excavation Report 2007–2008*, vol. 1 of *Khirbet Qeiyafa* (Jerusalem: Israel Exploration Society, 2009).

The excavations in Area 53B unearthed an impressive fortification wall, constructed in the Middle Bronze IIB–C period and used for over one thousand years as the wall of the city. The Middle Bronze IIB–C fortification of Hebron was known before the 2014 excavations, but the current project cleaned a very large, well-preserved section of this wall, showing its construction technique. This has great value for the presentation of the ancient site to the public. The primary scientific contribution of the current excavations in this area is the evidence for the continued use of the Middle Bronze IIB–C fortifications during the Iron Age and, specifically, its reinforcement in the southern part of the tell dated to the Iron Age IIB–C. A similar phenomenon, of the continuous use of Middle Bronze II fortifications during the Iron Age II, was found at the City of David.[55]

During the late eighth century BCE period the *lmlk* jars bearing the impression reading "[belonging] to the king - *hbrn*" were made and used, of which several were found at the site as well.[56] These stamped jars further testify to the importance of Hebron in the administration of the Judean kingdom during these days as a major administrative center. The private Hebrew seal found in an Iron Age IIB–C level at Tel Hebron is another evidence for such administration at the site.

The Iron Age II remains also testify to special fortification efforts to strengthen the defense of the city (as the construction of the support wall and an additional thick wall outside of it), probably in the days of Hezekiah, as preparation against the Assyrian campaigns, and also afterward. The final usage of the walls may probably be related to defense efforts during the seventh century BCE against Egyptian (?) campaigns, which would have been expected especially from the south. Similar fortifications were found in other sites controlled by Judah in the same period, such as Tell en-Naṣbeh, Tell el Fûl, and Tel Beit Mirsim. The effort to fortify the site from the south by the Judahite kings (Josiah?) may be related to threats from the Edomites or the Egyptians during this period.

55. Uziel and Szanton, "Recent Excavations."
56. E.g., Ofer, "Hebron," 608.

What Kind of Village Is This?
Buildings and Agroeconomic Activities Northwest of Jerusalem during the Iron IIB–C Period

Yuval Gadot, Sivan Mizrahi, Liora Freud, and David Gellman

4.1. Introduction

The economy of Jerusalem has always been dependent on a network of agricultural villages that were located along the Soreq and Rephaim Valleys, north, west, and southwest of the city. Archaeological surveys and excavations in these areas over the years have documented hundreds of sites, of all sizes and types, that attest to the importance and complexity of this network.[1] In terms of number of sites as well as its complexity, the system reached its peak during the Iron IIC, the seventh century BCE, a time when the city of Jerusalem was at its largest.[2] The relatively large number of sites dating to this period has not been ignored by scholars, who have attempted to understand the nature of the agricultural activity and the events that led to the wide spread of these sites.[3] Avraham Faust

---

1. E.g., Amos Kloner, *Survey of Jerusalem: The Northwestern Sector, Introduction and Indices*, Archaeological Survey of Israel (Jerusalem: Israel Antiquities Authority, 2003); Gershon Edelstein, Ianir Milevski, and Sara Aurnat, *Villages, Terraces and Stone Mounds: Excavations at Manahat, Jerusalem, 1987–1989*, IAAR 3 (Jerusalem: Israel Antiquities Authority, 1998).

2. Hillel Geva, "Jerusalem's Population in Antiquity: A Minimalist View," *TA* 41 (2014): 131–60.

3. Gershon Edelstein and Mordechai Kislev, "Mevasseret Yerushalayim: The Ancient Settlement and Its Agricultural Terraces," *BA* 44 (1981): 53–56; Nurit Feig, "The Environs of Jerusalem in the Iron Age II," in *The History of Jerusalem: The Biblical Period*, ed. Shmuel Ahituv and Amihai Mazar [Hebrew] (Jerusalem: Yad Ben-Zvi, 2000), 387–409; Yigal Moyal and Avraham Faust, "Jerusalem and Its Daughters: Moza, Ramat Rahel, and Jerusalem's Hinterland in the Seventh Century BCE" [Hebrew], in

followed by Yuval Gadot noted that most of these sites are not enclosed villages but rather isolated buildings or farmsteads.[4] In this paper we aim at examining a specific group of such sites, consisting of two large buildings, two small buildings, and several stone clearance heaps, along the western slopes of the Soreq Valley, in the modern neighborhood of Ramot, northwest of Jerusalem. This group of sites is unique in its spatial distribution and the nature of the buildings, thus challenging the accepted distinctions between a village and an isolated farmstead (fig. 4.1). This group joins a similar group of buildings that served as field towers, preserved to a height of two stories, stone clearance heaps, and winepresses hewn into bedrock, that were excavated along the opposite bank of the wadi, as well as several buildings documented on the hill east of the Soreq channel (inside the modern neighborhood of Ramat Shlomo) and along the western slopes of the hill toward Shemuel Valley.[5]

In their larger context, these sites are near large administrative and settlement sites, such as Tel Moza to the west, Khirbet el-Burj and Nebi Samuel to the north, and Tel el-Fûl to the northeast. A closer look at these sites may help to better understand the nature of this cluster of sites, the

---

New Studies on Jerusalem 21, ed. Eyal Baruch and Avraham Faust (Ramat Gan: Bar-Ilan University, 2015), 25–46.

4. Avraham Faust, "Jerusalem's Hinterland and the City's Status in the Bronze and Iron Ages" [Hebrew], *ErIsr* 28 (2007): 165–72, with English summary p. 15*; Yuval Gadot, "In the Valley of the King: Jerusalem's Rural Hinterland in the Eighth–Fourth Centuries BCE," *TA* 42 (2015): 3–26.

5. Uri Davidovich et al., "Salvage Excavation at Ramot Forest and Ramat Bet-Hakerem: New Data Regarding Jerusalem's Periphery during the First and Second Temple Periods" [Hebrew], in *New Studies on Jerusalem 11*, ed. Eyal Baruch and Avraham Faust (Ramat Gan: Bar-Ilan University, 2006), 35–111. Yehudah Rapuano and Alexander Onn, "An Iron Age Structure from Shu'afat Ridge, Northern Jerusalem," *Atiqot* 47 (2004): 119–29; Ron Be'eri, "Jerusalem, Shu'fat Ridge," *HA* 124 (2012): https://tinyurl.com/SBL2643b; Benyamin Storchan, "Jerusalem, Ramat Shelomo," *HA* 129 (2017): https://tinyurl.com/SBL2643h; Y. Elgart-Sharon, "Settlement Patterns and Land Use in the Upper Soreq Area: Longue Durée Approach" [Hebrew] (MA thesis, Tel Aviv University, 2017); Yuval Gadot et al., "OSL Dating of Pre Terraced and Terraced Landscape: Land Transformation in Jerusalem's Rural Hinterland," *Journal of Archaeological Science, Report* 21 (2018): 575–83. A survey and community excavations (A-6496) took place at Ramot forest under the management of D. Levi, H. Neuboern, and D. Tanami. The excavation included cleaning a winepress they dated to the Iron Age. We would like to thank the managers of the survey and the excavation for sharing the information.

Fig. 4.1. Aerial photograph of the channel of the Soreq Valley and the location of the buildings described throughout this essay, as well as additional buildings published by Uri Davidovich et al. Map prepared by H. Bithan; all rights reserved to Survey of Israel, 2018. Used by permission.

circumstances that brought about the development of the agricultural network, and the forces behind its foundation.

4.2. Results of the Excavations

Six areas (A–F) in the Ramot Forest were excavated between 2014 and 2017, including stone clearance heaps, terrace walls, a winepress, a lime-kiln, remains of an ancient road, and buildings dating to the Iron IIC period.[6] In this paper we describe the buildings dated to the Iron Age that may add important information to the aforementioned subjects (fig. 4.1).[7]

4.2.1. The Rectangular Building (Area A)

In Area A, a rectangular building, built on three topographical steps along a steep slope was uncovered (figs. 4.2 and 4.3). The infrastructure of the building required much effort, including building thick foundation walls, especially in the middle and lower steps, and laying a fill of stones in an area of 24 m² to a depth of 1.5 m. The fill was used to create a horizontal floor level along the three steps. The bedrock was incorporated into some of the walls, probably in order to prevent them from being swept away. The upper step consists of a square room (Room I) with a flagstone floor laid above the bedrock. In the southern part of the room a staircase was uncovered, leading to a parallel room to the east (the middle step) and a second floor that was not preserved, which may have served as a lookout point. The middle step consists of a rectangular room whose floor was not preserved (Room II). A mixture of brown soil with medium-sized field-stones was used as a constructive fill in order to level the bedrock's natural slope. The lower step has a narrow rectangular space (Room III). The eastern closing wall is integrated with the bedrock. Below the red-brown

---

6. For earlier publications, see Sivan Mizrahi and Renee Forestani, "Jerusalem, Ramot Alon, Preliminary Report," *HA* 128 (2016): https://tinyurl.com/SBL2643f; Sivan Mizrahi, Natalya Katanelson, and Donald T. Ariel, "Jerusalem, Ramot Alon," *HA* 128 (2016): https://tinyurl.com/SBL2643g.

7. Salvage excavations were held in the Ramot Forest (permit no. A-7917) during the year 2017. The excavations were initiated by the ministry of housing prior to erecting a swimming pool in the neighborhood. The excavations were managed by D. Gellman and S. Mizrahi, assisted by N. Nechama (administrator), A. Weigman (photography and aerial photography), V. Esman, M. Kahn, and A. Hagian (measurements and plans), A German-Levanon (digital documentation), and C. Amit (photography).

silt, mixed with medium-sized stones and pottery, a support wall, built of medium-sized fieldstones was found. The aforementioned constructive fill adjoins this wall on its north and south sides.

The partial preservation does not allow an understanding of whether the space on the lower step was a third room with a floor leveled with that of the higher rooms or whether it was a constructive fill meant to support the other parts of the building. Either way, the many support walls integrated with the fill show the high level of effort put into keeping the building stable on the slope.

Wall 11, 3 m wide and oriented north-south, was found to the north of the building. The northern part of the wall is built of two rows of large stones while in the southern part only a few stones were preserved, making it difficult to reconstruct the continuation of the wall. Beyond the northern end of the wall there are no architectural remains to the north, east, and west. The wall may have originally ended there, but it is also possible that the northern end of the wall was part of an opening, and Wall 11 continued further to the north. The nature of the remains is such that the use of the wall remains unclear.

Several changes, made in a later phase, were identified. Wall 24 was built adjacent to Wall 30 on the western end of the higher step, connecting the building to Wall 11. Adjacent to Walls 24 and 11 a small, rectangular room was built, with small fieldstones making up the walls that meet in a rounded corner. East of the room and adjacent to it, a half-circle installation was found. Both the room and the installation were filled with silt, stones, and pottery.

Few pottery sherds were found in connection with the building, between its walls and the terrace, above the floor, and in the fills beneath the wall (fig. 4.4:1–6). These sherds represent the time that the structure was built and its first phase of use. The majority of the sherds are of bowls and kraters with out-folded rims (fig. 4.4:1, 3), and the minority are of carinated bowls (fig. 4.4:2).[8] These bowls are typical of the end of the eighth century and beginning of the seventh century BCE. The cook-

---

8. For the bowls and kraters, see Alon De Groot and Hannah Bernick-Greenberg, "The Pottery of Strata 12–10 (Iron Age IIB)," in *Area E; The Finds*, vol. 7B of *Excavations at the City of David 1978–1985 Directed by Yigal Shiloh*, ed. Alon De Groot and Hannah Bernick-Greenberg, Qedem 54 (Jerusalem: Hebrew University, 2012), 64, type B8. For the carinated bowls, see De Groot and Bernick-Greenberg, "Pottery of Strata 12–10," 58, type B4.

Fig. 4.2. The rectangular building in Area A, looking east. Photograph by Assaf Peretz.

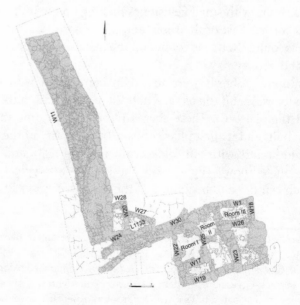

Fig. 4.3. Plan of the rectangular building. Prepared by Noa Evron.

ing pot (fig 4.4:4) is a transitional form of the beginning of the seventh century BCE.[9] An additional sherd of a cooking pot has a neck with a single ridge in its middle (fig. 4.4:5) from the seventh century BCE.[10] The holemouth jar (fig. 4.4:6) appears from the middle of the seventh century BCE and onward.[11] Based on this assemblage, the rectangular structure should be dated to the end of the eighth century and/or the beginning of the seventh century BCE.

4.2.2. Three-Room Building (Area B)

Beneath an ovular stone clearance heap, a rectangular structure was found, divided into three clear areas: two long rooms divided by a wall and pillars and a third wide room, perpendicular to the two long rooms (fig. 4.5). The building had two floors laid one above the other. The long rooms are divided between north and south by Wall 235 with three square pillar bases integrated in it.

The northern room has a floor made of hewn fieldstones that was only partially preserved. In the eastern part of the room the floor was not preserved and a collapse layer was uncovered. Underneath the collapse an earlier floor was found, made of densely packed, dark brown soil, mixed with crushed limestone. The southern room is rectangular, filled with dark brown soil and collapsed stones that originated from the walls of the structure. Under a partially preserved stone floor an earlier phase of brown soil mixed with crushed limestone was found, identical to that of the northern room. A test trench excavated in the western part of the room showed that this layer is laid on the bedrock. Wall 236 separates the two rooms from the wide room perpendicular to them. This wide space is divided into two rooms, south and north, by Wall 232. The northern room is square with the entrance on its west. The floor is made of flagstones. The small finds in this room include pottery dating to the Iron Age (see below) and a limestone weight. In the corner of the room a tabun of orange clay, with pottery sherds

---

9. De Groot and Bernick-Greenberg, "Pottery of Strata 12–10," 68 and fig. 4.3:8.

10. De Groot and Bernick-Greenberg, "Pottery of Strata 12–10," 70–71; type CP3.

11. Liora Freud, "Production and Widespread Use of Holemouth Vessels in Jerusalem and Its Environs in the Iron Age II: Typology, Chronology, and Distribution" [Hebrew], in vol. 11 of *New Studies in the Archaeology of Jerusalem and Its Region: Collected Papers*, ed. Yuval Gadot et al. (Jerusalem, 2017), 95, type HMJ1; an English version of this essay is published on pages 119–50 in this volume.

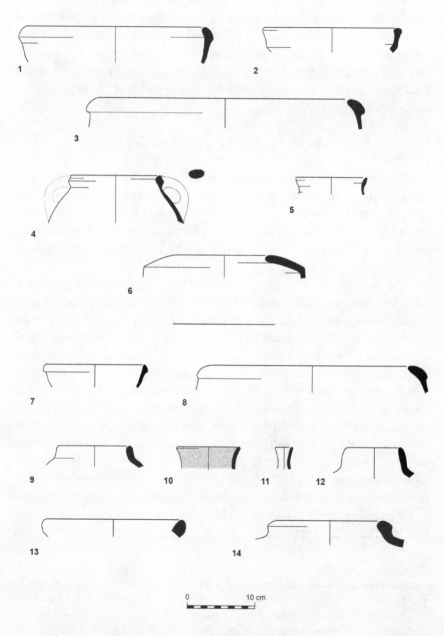

Fig. 4.4. Select pottery found in the rectangular building, Area A (1–6) and in the three-room building, Area B (7–14). Scanning by the IAA digital laboratories; preparation by Yulia Gotleib.

Fig. 4.5. Plan of the three-room building in Area B. Drawing by Noa Evron.

along its walls, was found. The pottery and the tabun suggest that this room was used for preparation of food. In the southern room a collapse of floor stones with brown soil mixed with ash and crushed limestone was found.

Wall 236 creates two parallel corridors, on the east and west, that connect the various rooms of the building. In the eastern corridor, between Wall 236 and Room L2326, floor stones were uncovered. The flooring continues to the western corridor, between Wall 236 and the eastern edge of Wall 235, beneath Wall 236 until the eastern pillar base of Wall 235. These finds show that this building had an earlier phase.

Over the course of the excavation no clear entrance to the building was found, though based on comparisons to similar, contemporary buildings (see discussion below), it seems likely that the entrance was on the narrow side, in the western wall.

Most of the pottery found in this building dates to the Iron Age IIB–C (fig. 4.4:7–12). The small bowl with a folded rim is typical of the late seventh century BCE (fig. 4.4:7).[12] The rest of the pottery is more typical of the eighth century BCE, including kraters (fig. 4.4:8–9), a red jug (fig. 4.4:10), a

---

12. Liora Freud, "Pottery of the Iron Age: Typology and Summary," in *Ramat Raḥel III: Final Publication of Yohanan Aharoni's Excavations (1954, 1959–1962)*, ed. Oded Lipschits, Yuval Gadot, and Liora Freud, Sonia and Marco Nadler Institute of

black juglet (fig. 4.4:11), and a *lmlk*-type storage jar (fig. 4.4:12).[13] Because of the relatively small amount of diagnostic sherds found, the precise use of the building is difficult to suggest. Approximately one-third of the sherds found in the building date to the Persian period (fig. 4.4:13, 14) and the Hellenistic period, most found on the surface and in the stone clearance heap that covered the building. These facts lead to the conclusion that the building was in use mostly during the Iron Age IIB–C.

4.2.3. The Storerooms Building (Area D)

On the upper slopes a building that was used for storage was found (figs. 4.6 and 4.7). The building had been previously identified in the Jerusalem survey and in a predevelopment survey conducted in 2013.[14] The building was divided into eight rooms: an entrance room, a stairwell, a large main room, four storage rooms in different sizes, most likely used to store agricultural produce (fig. 4.7).

The entrance is a narrow, rectangular enclosure that led, through a narrow opening, to a square stairwell. Adjacent to the opening a second, wider opening was found, which led to the eastern corridor. In the southern closing wall the remains of a drainage channel were noticed. The eastern corridor (Room II) is long and narrow and in its center stands a pier. Remnants of a plastered floor were noted adjacent to the pier. In the northern part of the corridor a blocked entrance, inside Wall 138, was found. Originally this entrance allowed access into the eastern storage room (Room VI).

The main room (Room III) is a wide space, in which a layer of collapsed stones and pillar fragments was found. In the eastern part of the room a small segment of a floor, made of medium-sized fieldstones, was preserved. In the collapse layer in the center of the room a handle with incised concentric circles was found, most likely washed here from one of the rooms to the west. In the northwestern part of the room a large

---

Archaeology Monograph Series 35 (Winona Lake, IN: Eisenbrauns, 2016), table 16:1, type B5.

13. For the kraters, see De Groot and Bernick-Greenberg, "The Pottery of Strata 12–10," 62–64, type B8a. For the red jug, see De Groot and Bernick-Greenberg, "The Pottery of Strata 12–10," fig. 4.4:17. For the black juglet, see De Groot and Bernick-Greenberg, "The Pottery of Strata 12–10," fig. 4.44:20.

14. Site number 29 in Kloner, *Survey of Jerusalem.*

Fig. 4.6. The large storage building in Area D, looking south. Photograph by Assaf Peretz.

Fig. 4.7. Plan of the storage building. Drawing by Noa Evron.

amount of holemouth jars was found, probably originating from the western storage room (Room V), and swept here down the slope (see below).

Three rooms have been identified as storage facilities: two (the eastern and western rooms) are rectangular, and the third (the northern room) is square. In the western room (Room V) two floors of yellowish crushed limestone were found. On the upper floor many sherds of holemouth jars were found. In the northern part of the storage room broken pieces of plaster were found above the upper floor and within the collapse layer. These may attest to the existence of a second story. Alternately, they may have originated from Wall 104, of which the eastern face was plastered (see below). In the eastern storage room (Room VI) a collapse layer was found, above the remains of a crushed limestone floor. These collapse stones may have been part of a second story that collapsed into the storage room. In a narrow test trench excavated in the northern part of the storage room, a thick collapse layer and the remains of an earlier floor were found underneath the crushed limestone floor. In the northern corner of the storage room a round cupmark installation, which was cut into the bedrock, was found. The pottery assemblage in the fill included mostly holemouth jars, identical to those found on the floors in the other storage rooms. The northern storage room (Room VII) had a crushed limestone floor that canceled the use of a wall from an earlier stage, attesting to changes made in the complex of storage rooms during the last phase of use.

Room IV is rectangular with an entrance from the east. In the northeastern corner a narrow test trench was excavated, finding a rectangular, stone-cut pillar, standing in situ. This pillar most likely supported the room's roof; probably a second pillar was standing to the south of the one found. No floor was found in this room. Room VIII is cut into the bedrock. On its floor the upturned base of a cooking vessel was found.

Wall 104 closed the northern and western storage rooms from the west. This is a massive built wall, with two faces of large and medium-sized hewn fieldstones and between them a core of medium and small fieldstones. The inner face of the wall was plastered. In the southern part of the wall the remains of a surface made of crushed limestone were found, possibly a ramp or an observation post that collapsed from above.

In several of the points described above changes in the layout of the buildings, or the elevation of the floors, were identified. The original layout of the building may have been only the western and eastern storage rooms, which were originally longer. The change included shortening the rooms on their northern end and building the northern and the small storage rooms.

The pottery assemblage found in this building is mostly vessels typical of the end of the seventh and beginning of the sixth centuries BCE, such as a fine, well-fired bowl (fig. 4.8:1), a bowl with an elongated, folded-out rim (fig. 4.8:2, 3), and a krater (fig. 4.8:4).[15] The basin (fig. 4.8:5) is of a type common in the eighth century BCE but also found in assemblages of the seventh century BCE.[16] The cooking pots found throughout the building (fig. 4.8:6, 7) are of the variety without a neck, which continued to be in use during the sixth century BCE.[17]

The storage building is characterized by a large number of holemouth jars (approximately one hundred) of a variety of types, found mixed together in the same loci. Most of the holemouth jars have a smooth, elongated rim, with a rounded and thickened end. They belong to two types, differentiated from one another by the form of the connection of the rim to the wall: in one type (fig. 4.8:8, 9) the rim is perpendicular to the wall, while in the other type (fig. 4.8:10, 11) there is a protrusion, perpendicular to the rim, that sticks out at the point of connection between the rim and the wall. Both types are equally as common and constitute most of the assemblage. The holemouth jars are dated to the second-half of the seventh and the beginning of the sixth century BCE.[18] Some of the holemouth jars have a thick, dome-like rim (fig. 4.8:12), others have a short rim with a triangular profile (fig. 4.8:13). These vessels are typical of the end of the eighth and beginning of the seventh centuries BCE.[19] It is important to note that no preference for any specific type of holemouth jar was identified in any specific location or phase.

---

15. For the well-fired bowl, see De Groot and Bernick-Greenberg, "The Pottery of Strata 12–10," 65–66, fig. 4.2:7, 8. For the bowl with an elongated rim, see De Groot and Bernick-Greenberg, "The Pottery of Strata 12–10," type Bb. For the krater, see De Groot and Bernick-Greenberg, "The Pottery of Strata 12–10," fig. 4.3:4.

16. See Orna Zimhoni, "The Pottery of Levels III and II," in *The Renewed Archaeological Excavations at Lachish (1973–1994)*, ed. David Ussishkin, Sonia and Marco Nadler Institute of Archaeology Monograph Series 22 (Tel Aviv: Emery and Claire Yass Publications in Archaeology, 2004), 4: fig. 26.2:4.

17. De Groot and Bernick-Greenberg, "The Pottery of Strata 12–10," 68, type cp8.

18. Freud, "Production and Widespread Use of Holemouth Vessels," types HMJ1, HMJ5.

19. Freud, "Production and Widespread Use of Holemouth Vessels," 97, types HMJ4a–b.

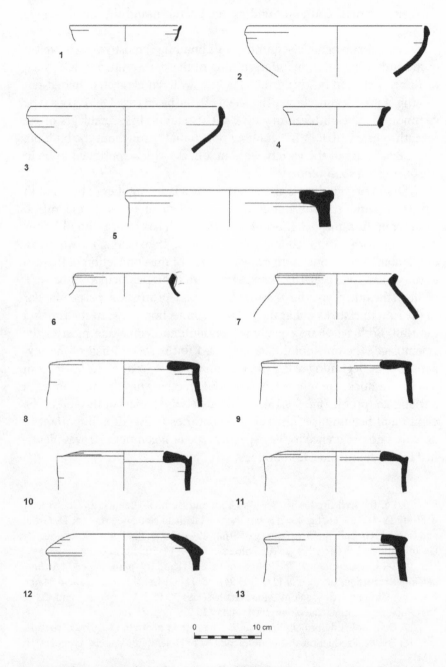

Fig. 4.8. Select pottery from the storage building. Scanning by the IAA digital laboratories; preparation of the table by Yulia Gotleib.

4.2.4. Open-Courtyard Building (Area F)

West of the three-room building in Area B is an additional building with a long eastern room, a large courtyard in the northwest, a plastered installation in the west, and an outdoor activity zone in the north, along with other installations (fig. 4.9).

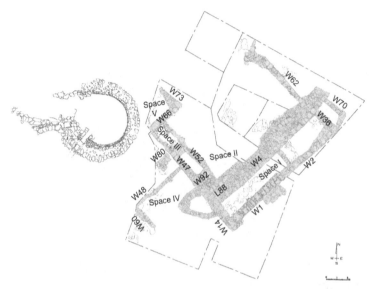

Fig. 4.9. Plan of open-courtyard building in Area F. Drawing by Noa Evron.

The building was found partially built over by a limekiln dating to the Ottoman period, making the complete excavation of the structure impossible. The floor plan indicates this building was of the open-courtyard building type, similar to buildings found in Mamilla, Khirbet er-Ras, and Area E in the City of David.[20]

The eastern room (Enclosure I) is rectangular. Two architectural phases were identified: In the earlier phase the entrance was from the southeastern corner, between Walls 14 and 92, and may have also led to

---

20. Yuval Gadot and Efrat Bocher, "The Introduction of the Open-Courtyard Building to the Jerusalem Landscape and Judean-Assyrian Interaction," in *Archaeology and History of Eight-Century Judah: Papers in Honor of Oded Borowsky*, ed. Zev I. Farber and Jacob L. Wright, ANEM 23 (Atlanta: SBL Press, 2018), 205–27; and see earlier references.

a stairwell. In the second phase this entrance was blocked and the stairs were dismantled. To the north of the elongated room a small, rectangular room was built, probably to serve as an entrance room. In the main room two floors of crushed limestone were found, atop one another, showing that the room was in use for a significant amount of time.

The courtyard was approximately 62 m², spanning along the west side of the elongated eastern room. The entrance to the courtyard was through the northern wall. In a later phase, the entrance was also blocked, and no alternate entrance was identified. The southern wall of the courtyard was preserved in its entirety, and in a later phase was thickened by adding a row of hewn fieldstones on its north face. Of the western wall (W80) only a few hewn stones were preserved. The northwestern corner of the courtyard was not preserved. The courtyard may have been enlarged to the west when Wall 47 was thickened, thus making it necessary to dismantle Wall 80.

Southwest of the courtyard the remains of a room or installation (Enclosure III), built on the bedrock, were found. The floor was covered in greenish plaster (7 cm thick) that climbed slightly on the western wall. In a later phase the plaster floor was covered by flagstones. In a third phase a wall oriented east-west was built over the floor, adjoining the southern wall of the courtyard. The excavation did not continue to the west due to the presence of the later limekiln, but it is possible that this wall was built when the courtyard was enlarged to the west (see above).

In the southern activity area (Enclosure IV) two round cupmarks were hewn into the straightened bedrock. It seems that these cupmarks predate the erection of the rest of the parts of this complex. A square room with a layer of collapsed building stones and rectangular pillar stones, probably originating from the area west of the room, was also dug. Beneath the collapse a layer of compressed soil was found, that may have been the foundation of a floor that was not preserved. A small, triangular installation, similar to that of Area A, was found to the east of the square room.

West of the building, in the western corner of the excavation area, part of an additional room (Enclosure V), later than the main building, was found. Floors 84 and 85, which belong to the main building, continue west underneath the walls of this room, which are on a higher elevation than the southern wall of the courtyard. All these show that the main building was not in use when this room was active.

The majority of the pottery in the open-courtyard building dates to the eighth to seventh centuries BCE. A few Persian sherds were found as well, in secondary use of the building. The Iron Age pottery includes cooking pots with a ridged neck with an everted, simple rim, typical of the seventh century BCE (fig. 4.10:1), and storage jars with a short, straight or slightly inward inclining neck, and a rounded, thickened rim (fig. 4.10:2). Sherds of these vessels were found, among other locations, in the sealed fill beneath the floor of the first phase of the building, providing a *terminus post quem* for the entire structure to the seventh century BCE.

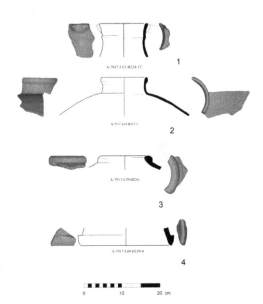

Fig. 4.10. Select pottery from the open-courtyard building. Scanning by the IAA digital laboratories; preparation of the table by Yulia Gotleib.

Further sherds dating to the eighth and seventh centuries BCE were found, some that have also been found in sixth century BCE contexts. These include: bowls and kraters with a folded rim (for similar bowls and kraters see figs. 4.4:3 and 4.4:7); *lmlk*-type storage jars (for a similar type jar, see fig. 4.4:12); storage jars with no neck or a very short neck, and a rounded rim folded outward (fig. 4.10:3), a type that originated from the coastal plain and is found in contexts of the eighth through sixth centuries BCE; holemouth jars of various types (figs. 4.4:6; 4.8:8–9, 12); one fragment of a stand (fig. 4.10:4); a few thick bases of oil lamps (not drawn); two handles with incised potter's marks, a phenomenon common throughout the eighth through the beginning of the sixth century BCE; and two handles with incised, concentric circles, a phenomenon common from the end of the eighth century and the beginning of the seventh century BCE.[21]

4.2.5. Stone Clearance Heaps

Due to the hard dolemitic rock formation of the area, intensive clearing of stones was necessary for making the land suitable for agricultural activities. In the predevelopment survey conducted in Area 20, stone clearance heaps were documented, five of them in Areas A–C.[22] In a previous study, Uri Davidovich et al. suggested that some of these heaps are related to the buildings found nearby, and therefore should be dated to the Iron Age.[23] Dating of stone heaps is extremely difficult as some have no pottery at all, while other do but they are related to different phases of activity. The three-roomed building found in Area B was found under one such stone heap, showing that the act of stone clearing was done after the building ceased to be in use. The remaining stone heaps have not been dated. Most have support walls that show that the heaps were planned in a way that prevents the scattering of stones in the area.

4.3. Neighboring Sites

The structures described above are not alone in the region. Similar buildings, unearthed in nearby salvage excavations, show that the significant agricultural activity had spread all over. The excavations of the Ramot Forest, along the northern banks of the Soreq Valley, documented eight structures, some used for storage and others for residence.[24] The buildings were dated to the Iron Age IIC, the seventh century BCE—the same period as the structures described above—based on the small pottery assemblages found. Twenty-nine stone clearance heaps were identified and excavated in between the structures. Some were dated to the Iron Age based on the assumption that the agricultural activity required aggressive

---

21. For the holemouth jars, see Freud, "Production and Widespread Use of Holemouth Vessels," HMJ1, HMJ3, HMJ4, and HMJ5.

22. Mizrahi and Forestani, "Jerusalem, Ramot Alon, Preliminary Report."

23. Davidovich et al., "Salvage Excavation at Ramot Forest and Ramat Bet-Hakerem," 46–51.

24. Davidovich et al., "Salvage Excavation at Ramot Forest and Ramat Bet-Hakerem."

Fig. 4.11. A stone heap from N. Shemuel after excavation and the results of the OSL sampling. Photograph by Yuval Gadot.

stone clearing. The map of the area (fig. 4.1) shows that the group of buildings was an integral part of the group described here (and see below).

Further away surveys and excavations along the slopes leading from the channel of the Soreq eastward, toward the watershed line (today's Ramat Shlomo and Shuafat neighborhoods) identified 350 rock-cut installations, stone clearance heaps, guard towers, and other buildings, most dated to the Iron Age.[25] From excavations in three towers, in which a second story was preserved, pottery dating to the Iron Age IIC was found. Tower 304 is similar in its floor plan to the rectangular building found in Area A.[26]

Towers, stone heaps, and rock-cut winepresses have also been found on the western slopes of the Ramot ridge, in the direction of Shemuel Valley, a tributary of the Soreq Valley.[27] At least three towers have been found in this area, between them dozens of stone heaps and at least three rock-cut winepresses. One of the stone heaps was sampled using OSL

25. Alexander Onn and Yehuda Rapuano, "Jerusalem—Kh. er-Ras," *ESI* 13 (1993): 71.

26. Be'eri, "Jerusalem, Shu'fat Ridge."

27. Gadot et al., "OSL Dating of Pre Terraced and Terraced Landscape"; Elgart-Sharon, "Settlement Patterns."

dating techniques. The test showed that the soil at the base of the heap had last been exposed to sunlight approximately 2,400 years ago (±160 years), a date that allows a possible connection of the act of clearing the stones to the end of the Iron Age or the Persian period.[28] That said, it is clear that the act of stone clearing was not limited to the Iron Age, and in some cases stone heaps were laid upon ruins of abandoned buildings. An ongoing study has excavated several more such stone heaps and taken samples for OSL dating. When the results are received, it will be possible to differentiate dates acquired from soil samples below the heaps from those acquired from soil samples inside the heaps, and thus to narrow the margin of error regarding the dates the samples give.

The three rock-cut winepresses documented in this area include, beside the pressing area and collection vat, niches cut into the back bedrock wall, used to house beams. It has been suggested that this type of winepress dates to the Iron Age.[29] A sample of the soil that covered the pressing area of one of the winepresses was taken for dating, and it showed that the winepress ceased to be in use in the transition between the Byzantine and the Early Islamic periods.[30] It is possible, of course, that the winepress was hewn much earlier, but at this point there is no way to date the initial use of the winepress.

4.4. Discussion

Based on the ceramic assemblage, the buildings described above, as well as the stone heaps between them, existed perhaps in the late eighth century BCE and definitely throughout the seventh and beginning of the sixth centuries BCE. The storage building in Area D may have continued to be in use throughout the sixth century BCE, and some additional buildings show evidence of use in the Persian period. The pottery from the buildings on the opposite side of the valley show a similar chronological picture.

A comparison of the four buildings described here with the eight buildings from the other side of the valley and the complete building documented uphill to the east show that almost every structure had its own unique floor plan. In some buildings, for example, the rectangular

---

28. Gadot et al., "OSL Dating of Pre Terraced and Terraced Landscape," 581.

29. David Amit and Irit Yezerski, "An Iron Age II Cemetery and Wine Presses at an-Nabi Danyal," *IEJ* 51 (2001): 171–93.

30. Gadot et al., "OSL Dating of Pre Terraced and Terraced Landscape," 581.

building, the construction technique was fitted to the rocky topography of the slope. This building resembles the width-axis building found in Kh. Abu-Shwan, Manahat, and Ras Abu Ma'aruf.[31] The area of the building (approximately 40 m²) is similar to that of most buildings found on the opposite side of the valley (38 m²) and of the building on the Shuafat ridge (approximately 27 m²).[32] It is safe to assume that if these buildings had an enclosed courtyard, it was external and not part of the built space.

The plan of the three-room building in Area B is similar to that of other buildings of this type (pillared buildings), which are divided into three or four enclosures by one or several row(s) of pillars.[33] Pillared homes or, as they are more commonly known, three- or four-roomed buildings are common throughout Judea and Israel, including Jerusalem and its surroundings, throughout the entire Iron Age.[34] The building in Area B is similar in its floor plan and area to building 36 excavated on the opposite side of the valley.[35] Like the other buildings previously described, if this building had a courtyard for various activities, it was external to the structure, and not a part of it. This characteristic separates the pillared building from Area B and building 36 from the rest of the pillared buildings, in which usually one of the inner enclosures is identified as a general use courtyard. On top of that, the two buildings at hand are smaller than the majority of such buildings throughout Israel and Judea. Davidovich has already noted this difference, which shows that there was a difference of function between the buildings and the people using them.[36]

The open-courtyard building excavated in Area F is fundamentally different from the rest of the buildings described, since the courtyard is in the center and is a fundamental component of the structure (with an area of 62 m²). Buildings of this type have been found in the City of David as

---

31. Gadot and Bocher, "Introduction of the Open-Courtyard Building," 205, and further references there.

32. Davidovich et al., "Salvage Excavation at Ramot Forest and Ramat Bet-Hakerem," 92; Be'eri, "Jerusalem, Shu'fat Ridge."

33. Gadot and Bocher, "Introduction of the Open-Courtyard Building," 205, and further references there.

34. Avraham Faust and Shlomo Bunimovitz, "The Four Room House: Embodying Iron Age Israelite Society," *NEA* 66 (2003): 22–31.

35. Davidovich et al., "Salvage Excavation at Ramot Forest and Ramat Bet-Hakerem," 71–72.

36. Davidovich et al., "Salvage Excavation at Ramot Forest and Ramat Bet-Hakerem," 92.

well as in the surrounding rural area, such as in Mammilla and Khirbet er-Ras.[37] Farmsteads like this have been found in the Judean Shephelah and the hills of Rosh Ha'ayin, dating mainly to the Persian and Hellenistic periods.[38] Some argue that the first appearance of this form of building in the southern Levant is connected to the Assyrian presence, and that the presence of such buildings in and around Jerusalem is another expression of the cultural relations between Jerusalem and Assyria.[39]

The storage building in Area D is unique in its size and complexity compared to the rest of the buildings on both sides of the valley. Though it was not completely excavated, it is clearly divided into more rooms (eight, as opposed to the more common three). The building occupies an area of approximately 300 m², and its outer walls give it the look of a fortified structure. No similar buildings have been found in Jerusalem and its surroundings.

4.5. A Village or Isolated Buildings?

In archaeological research, several attempts have been made to define types of sites and organize them in order to create unity in discussions, and recognize settlement patterns in rural areas. In the vicinity of Jerusalem, it is customary to differentiate enclosed villages from farmstead buildings.[40] Examples of contemporary enclosed villages are Khirbet el-Burj, a site about 2 km away from the sites described here, along the northeastern ridge, and Khirbet er-Ras in the Rephaim Valley.[41] Lone farmsteads have been found in numerous additional locations.[42] A third

---

37. Gadot and Bocher, "Introduction of the Open-Courtyard Building," 202–4.

38. Elena Kogan-Zehavi, "The Rural Settlement in the Judaean Foothills in the Persian and Early Hellenistic Periods, in Light of the Excavations in Ramat Beit Shemesh" [Hebrew], in vol. 8 of *New Studies in the Archaeology of Jerusalem and its Region: Collected Papers*, ed. Guy D. Stiebel et al. (Jerusalem, 2014), 120–33.

39. Ruth Amiran and I. Dunayevsky, "The Assyrian Open-Court Building and Its Palestinian Derivatives," *BASOR* 149 (1958): 25–32; Gadot and Bocher, "Introduction of the Open-Courtyard Building," 206.

40. Faust, "Jerusalem's Hinterland"; Gadot, "In the Valley of the King."

41. Alon De Groot and Michal Weinberger-Stern, "Wine, Oil and Gibeonites: Iron II–III at Kh. el-Burj, Northern Jerusalem" [Hebrew], in *New Studies on Jerusalem 19*, ed. Eyal Baruch and Avraham Faust (Ramat Gan: Bar-Ilan University, 2013), 95–102, with English summary; Gadot, "In the Valley of the King."

42. See Gadot, "In the Valley of the King," table 1.

pattern of sites has been defined by Nurit Feig as a "rural settlement," consisting of buildings separated from one another by a significant distance.[43] An example of such a site is in 'Alona, with at least two buildings and a guard tower separated from each other by several dozen meters.[44] It seems that the 'Alona site is a remnant of a tradition that started in the Middle Bronze Age, of erecting structures with each being an autonomous unit, and very few public buildings or areas exist in the area.[45] That said, the difference between the size of the buildings in 'Alona and those in Ramot, and the fact that each building in 'Alona is surrounded by a series of agricultural installations, show that the buildings discussed in this paper were different in usage from those in sites defined as rural settlements. Therefore, we chose to use the term "buildings cluster" for the Ramot sites, a worthy title for these finds, one that set them apart from rural settlements as defined by Fieg.

The size and nature of the storage building in Area D place it in the center of the cluster. Its storage rooms, in which a large concentration of one hundred holemouth jars was found, may have been used for storing the agricultural product brought from the adjacent buildings. Large concentrations of holemouth jars have been found in most contemporary sites in and around Jerusalem.[46] Due to the finds of the excavations in Moza, which included granaries, Zvi Greenhut and Alon De Groot suggested a connection between the holemouth jars found there and moving and storing of grain.[47] At Khirbet er-Ras in the Rephaim Valley a large concentration of holemouth jars was found adjacent to a winepress.[48] Based on these examples, and on the large amount of vessels in all the sites around Jerusalem, it seems logical to conclude that their use was

---

43. Feig, "Environs of Jerusalem," 388. According to Feig ("Khirbat er-Ras, Jerusalem: Iron Age and Ottoman-Period Remains," *HA* 128 [2016]: https://tinyurl.com/SBL2643d), the site of Kh. er-Ras should also be designated a rural settlement, but further excavations there found a row of at least five buildings adjacent to one another, see Gadot, "In the Valley of the King," fig. 2.

44. Shlomit Weksler-Bdolah, "'Alona," *HA* 19 (1997): 68*–70*.

45. E.g., Naḥal Rephaim; see Emanuel Eisenberg, "Naḥal Rephaim: A Bronze Age Village in Southwestern Jerusalem" [Hebrew], *Qadmoniot* 103–104 (1993): 82–95.

46. Freud, "Production and Widespread Use of Holemouth Vessels."

47. Zvi Greenhut and Alon De Groot, *Salvage Excavations at Tel Moza: The Bronze and Iron Age Settlements and Later Occupations*, IAAR 39 (Jerusalem: Israel Antiquities Authority, 2009).

48. Freud, "Production and Widespread Use of Holemouth Vessels," 101.

not uniform and in each site they had their own use. The finds from the storage building do not allow for a precise determination of what the jars were used to store. A large concentration of rock-cut winepresses attributed to the Iron Age found west of the site may attest to specialization in growing grapes on the rocky hillsides.[49] The produce of the grapes may have been transferred to Khirbet el-Burj, where a concentration of twenty-four pits were used for a winery.[50] The strips of land between the rock outcrops could have been used for orchards as well. The fact that only one olive press dating to the Iron Age was found nearby suggests that olive groves were not a central part of the economy of the area. This fact sits well with the botanical reconstruction of the surroundings of Jerusalem from environmental research based on pollen from the Dead Sea.[51] The large concentration of granaries found in the Moza excavations shows that much of the alluvial soil in the valley bed was used to grow grain, and this may have also been what was stored in the storage building in Ramot. The building may have also been used to store produce later distributed to the smaller buildings.

Reconstructing the relations between the buildings is based, among others, on understanding the activities that took place in each of the smaller buildings. The nature and preservation of the finds from most of the buildings do not allow for a reconstruction of the function of each room.[52] That said, the small area occupied by each building cannot be

49. Gadot et al., "OSL Dating of Pre Terraced and Terraced Landscape." For a similar designation of the slopes of the Rephaim Valley and its tributaries for the growing of grapes and preparation of wine, see Raphael Greenberg and Gilad Cinamon, "Stamped and Incised Jar Handles from Rogem Ganim, and Their Implications for the Political Economy of Jerusalem, Late Eighth–Early Fourth Centuries BCE," *TA* 33 (2006): 229–43.

50. De Groot and Weinberger-Stern, "Wine, Oil and Gibeonites," 96.

51. In Khirbet el-Burj, see De Groot and Weinberger-Stern, "Wine, Oil and Gibeonites," 97–98; Israel Finkelstein and Dafna Langgut, "Climate, Settlement History, and Olive Cultivation in the Iron Age Southern Levant," *BASOR* 379 (2018): 153–69.

52. Past researchers reconstructed the activity areas of buildings based on the size of the rooms and the built installations in them. See Lawrence E. Stager, "The Archaeology of the Family in Ancient Israel," *BASOR* 260 (1985): 1–35. Thanks to application of research methods from the area of microarchaeology in recent years, it seems that such reconstruction not based on evidence from the excavation is no longer relevant, see, e.g., Avraham Faust et al., "The Birth, Life and Death of an Iron Age House at Tel 'Eton, Israel: A Preliminary Analysis," *Levant* 49 (2017): 136–73.

ignored in any attempt of reconstruction of activity. Davidovich rejected the possibility that they were used as residential buildings for extended families or farmsteads for rich people, such as those identified by Faust in other sites around the country.[53] They instead suggested two further options: the buildings were used as dwellings for nuclear families, or they were seasonal buildings inhabited only in the main agricultural season.[54]

The building found in Area B is the only one with clear evidence of cooking and consumption of food. The lack of similar finds in the other buildings may be related to the way in which they were abandoned or to the fact that they initially were not used for residence and therefore had no household activities. The buildings may have had specific purposes year-round, or on a seasonal basis. Some may have in fact been only used for storage alongside agricultural plots and not for residential needs.

4.6. The Building Cluster in Its Regional Context

As described above, the hills that the upper channel of the Soreq River go through north of Jerusalem are characterized by small strips of soil between rocky outcrops. This is not a natural place for large-scale agricultural activities to develop, as is seen in maps and aerial photographs from the beginning of the twentieth century, in which only small parts of the area were developed with terraces for dryland farming, as opposed to the nearby villages of Lifta and Bet Iksa.[55] These data further emphasize the uniqueness of the Iron Age buildings, whose spatial placement shows that they were connected to significant agricultural activity. Meticulous collection of the data from archaeological excavations held in the area shows how exceptional the number of sites from the late Iron Age is. Apparently only in the Early Roman period the Soreq basin was used similarly, while in all other periods until today the number of settlements and agricultural sites in the area was significantly lower.[56]

---

53. Avraham Faust, "Differences in Family Structure between Cities and Villages in Iron Age II," *TA* 26 (1999): 233–52; Davidovich *et al.*, "Salvage Excavation at Ramot Forest and Ramat Bet-Hakerem," 92.

54. For stone huts, see Zvi Ron, "Agricultural Terraces in the Judean Mountains," *IEJ* 16 (1966): 111–22.

55. Elgart-Sharon, "Settlement Patterns," fig. IV.3.

56. Elgart-Sharon, "Settlement Patterns," 121–49.

While the hills on which the buildings were erected had very low agricultural value, the surrounding areas, that is, the Soreq channel and its six tributaries, the hilltops and the slopes of the neighboring hills, are the most fertile agricultural region near Jerusalem.[57] It is not surprising, therefore, that near the building cluster important agricultural administration buildings were found, such as Tel Moza, with its concentration of granaries, Khirbet el-Burj and Nebi Samuel, with their rock-cut winepresses, winery pits, and one olive press, and Tel el-Fûl, which was probably a central site.[58] The activities in the building cluster could have taken place in connection to any one of these sites, or directly with Jerusalem.

In this context it is important to note that at the time this cluster of buildings was active, at least part of the administration of the kingdom of Judea was processed using a system of stamp impressions on storage jar handles.[59] Hundreds of handles with these marking have been found in central sites such as Jerusalem, Ramat Raḥel, and Lachish, and in secondary sites around Jerusalem. Contrary to that, in this building cluster only three such handles with incised, concentric circles were found, one in the storage building and two in the open-courtyard building. These incisions date to the middle of the seventh century BCE and were mainly incised on the type of storage jars that previously bore *lmlk*-stamps impressions.[60] No *lmlk*-stamped handles, or handles with a rosette stamp, of the kind found commonly in nearby contemporary sites, were found here. In Khirbet el-Burj, for instance, which was inhabited throughout the Iron Age, twenty-one *lmlk* handles, thirteen concentric circle incisions on handles, and four rosette handles were found.[61] Similar Iron Age handles were found in smaller sites, such as Rogem Ganim, and recently in a site named Arnona, adjacent to Ramat Raḥel, in which thirty-two incised and

---

57. Edelstein and Kislev, "Mevasseret Yerushalayim."

58. For Moza, see Greenhut and De Groot, *Salvage Excavations at Tel Moza*; for El Burj, see De Groot and Weinberger-Stern, "Wine, Oil and Gibeonites"; and for Tel el-Fûl, see Yuval Baruch and Joe Uziel, "Tell el-Ful and Its Environs during the Second Temple and Late Roman Period," in New Studies on Jerusalem 21, ed. Eyal Baruch and Avraham Faust (Ramat Gan, Bar-Ilan University, 2015), 163–83.

59. Oded Lipschits, Omer Sergi, and Ido Koch, "Royal Judahite Jar Handles: Reconsidering the Chronology of the *lmlk* Stamp Impressions," *TA* 37 (2010): 3–32; Lipschits *The Age of Empires: History and Administration in Judah in Light of the Stamped Jar Handles* [Hebrew] (Jerusalem: Yad Ben Zvi, 2018).

60. Lipschits, *Age of Empires*, 76–81.

61. De Groot and Weinberger-Stern, "Wine, Oil and Gibeonites," 98.

imprinted handles of various types dating to the eighth and beginning of the seventh century BCE were found.[62]

It seems that the lack of incised and imprinted storage jars shows that the system to which the building cluster belonged to was not part of the estates that brought their produce in *lmlk* jars or other incised and impressed jars. At Tel Moza excavations, in which a royal granary that held much produce was found, only two *lmlk* handles, six concentric circle handles, and three rosette handles were found.[63] The connection between Moza and the building cluster, via the Soreq Valley, is more natural and much easier than the connection to hilltop sites such as Khirbet el-Burj, Nebi Samuel, or Tel el-Fûl. According to this explanation, the building cluster, the stone clearance heaps, and the rock-cut installations are an expression of the presence of laborers who worked in the plots of land belonging to an estate. The produce of these plots was collected in the storage building, and from there moved to the administrative center in Moza, and from there to Jerusalem. This system was distinct from the one used to collect wine, and perhaps also olive oil, of which evidence has been found in Giv'on and Khirbet el-Burj, as well as north of and along the Rephaim Valley.[64]

4.7. Conclusions

The building cluster is one factor of many that together comprise the agricultural landscape around Jerusalem in the late Iron Age and continuing to exist in the Persian period.[65] This is an example of a different form of utilizing the ground, combining relatively small buildings separated by large distances making it difficult to reconstruct the cluster as a part of an enclosed or scattered village on the one hand, or autonomous farmsteads on the other hand. The decision to utilize the rocky terrain around the

---

62. Greenberg and Cinamon, "Stamped and Incised Jar Handles." Our thanks to N. Sapir and Oded Lipschits for sharing this information with us.

63. Zvi Greenhut, "Impressed and Incised Sherds," in Greenhut and De Groot, *Salvage Excavations at Tel Moza*, 129–37.

64. De Groot and Weinberger-Stern, "Wine, Oil and Gibeonites"; Greenberg and Cinamon, "Stamped and Incised Jar Handles"; Haya Katz, *"A Land of Grain and Wine ... A Land of Olive Oil and Honey": The Economy of the Kingdom of Judah* (Jerusalem: Yad Ben Zvi, 2008), 33.

65. Gadot, "In the Valley of the King."

Soreq Valley is unique and raises several questions. The act of intensive stone clearing needed to prepare the land for agriculture shows that the settling in the area required cooperation, based on ties beyond those of nuclear families. Therefore, it seems that the cause of this unique development must be searched for in the historical circumstances of the time.

The political and demographic rise of Jerusalem began in the ninth century BCE and reached its peak in the seventh century BCE, when Jerusalem was already under the rule of the Assyrian Empire.[66] This presence had various forms of influence over the happenings in Judea. The Assyrian campaigns and political instability of the late eighth century BCE no doubt brought many refugees to Jerusalem, from the kingdom of Israel and/or from the Sennacherib campaign.[67] On top of that, the loss of control over significant Judean agricultural territories due to Sennacherib's campaign, combined with the need to pay tribute and taxes to the Assyrian Empire, forced the leadership of Jerusalem to reorganize the rural and agricultural hinterland near the city.[68] This brought forth a sharp increase in the number of sites around the city, of which the Ramot building cluster is but one.

A precise reconstruction of the organization of activities in the buildings is difficult to make. The first possibility is to assume that the buildings were seasonal, occupied by the population of the enclosed villages, which were organized as extended families. If this explanation is accurate, the

---

66. Nadav Na'aman, "When and How Did Jerusalem Become a Great City? The Rise of Jerusalem as Judah's Premier City in the Eighth–Seventh Centuries B.C.E.," *BASOR* 347 (2007): 21–56; Joe Uziel and Nahshon Szanton, "New Evidence of Jerusalem's Urban Development in the Ninth Century BCE," in *Rethinking Israel: Studies in the History and Archaeology of Ancient Israel in Honor of Israel Finkelstein*, ed. Oded Lipschits, Yuval Gadot, and Matthew J. Adams (Winona Lake, IN: Eisenbrauns, 2017), 429–39; Israel Finkelstein, "Jerusalem and Judah 600–200 BCE: Implications for Understanding Pentateuchal Texts," in *The Fall of Jerusalem and the Rise of the Torah*, ed. Peter Dubovský, Dominik Markl, and Jean-Pierre Sonnet, FAT 107 (Tübingen: Mohr Siebeck, 2016), 3–18. For Assyrian influence on the kingdom see Lipschits, *Age of Empire*, 237.

67. Geva, "Jerusalem's Population in Antiquity"; Alon De Groot, "Discussion and Conclusions," in *Area E; Stratigraphy and Architecture*, vol. 7A of *Excavation at the City of David 1978–1985 Directed by Yigal Shiloh*, ed. Alon De Groot and Hannah Bernick-Greenberg, Qedem 53 (Jerusalem: The Institute of Archaeology, Hebrew University of Jerusalem, 2012), 155–56.

68. Gadot, "In the Valley of the King."

small buildings were part of an agricultural system, without central organization or administration, and the produce was sent directly to the villages and from there to Jerusalem. Though this explanation is theoretically possible, the placement of the buildings in an ecological niche in which agricultural activity is difficult and was not in use after the Persian period show that this was not a natural growth of a system of villages, rather this was the fruit of external initiative.

A second explanation is that settlement in a decentralized form is evidence of refugees from Sennacherib's campaign settling into the rough terrains of the area. According to Haya Katz, the arrangement of land in Iron Age Judea was based on family estates: the richer and more important the family, the more lands it controlled. The royal family also held significant estates, and it is safe to assume that the temple in Jerusalem did as well.[69] The lands of the Ramot hills were probably on the edges of those estates, thus allowing for refugees to settle in them.

A third possible explanation that we would like to propose to elucidate this unique form of building cluster is that it, especially the storage building of Area D, was part of an estate established in the area during the Iron Age that may have continued to be in use during the Persian period. According to Israel Finkelstein and Yuval Gadot, the lands of the upper Soreq were traditionally part of a royal or holy estate.[70] Turning to rocky lands required comprehensive stone clearing, which was no doubt beyond the capabilities of a nuclear family, therefore must have been done cooperatively by many workers. The management of manpower is a characterization of estates based on surpluses and cooperative work.

Similar research on the central parts of the Assyrian Empire has found similar patterns of activity in areas previously unfit for agriculture, and a different dispersal of agricultural population.[71] Naturally, research tends to focus on the destruction that Sennacherib spread throughout Judea, but it is important to remember as well that the campaign also brought with it new opportunities that some of the Jerusalem elite knew how to exploit. Relationships were built between these elites and the Assyrian Empire, allowing those loyal to the new order to flourish. Evi-

---

69. Katz, *Land of Grain and Wine*.

70. Israel Finkelstein and Yuval Gadot, "Mozah, Nephtoah and Royal Estates in the Jerusalem Highlands," *Semitica et Classica* 8 (2015): 227–34.

71. T. J. Wilkinson et al., "Landscape and Settlement on the Neo-Assyrian Empire," *BASOR* 340 (2005): 23–56.

dence of these relationships throughout the seventh century BCE can be found in many aspects of the material culture in Jerusalem, such as in the appropriation of the open-courtyard building.[72] The establishing of agricultural estates, as suggested in the third option, may be another aspect of these relationships, perhaps via importation of knowledge and resources from the Assyrians, while the local elites began strengthening their hold over fields near their homes.

Additional evidence that the Soreq region was part of an estate can be found in the pottery assemblage, which included typical sixth-century BCE forms, as well as some typical Persian period pottery and perhaps some Hellenistic sherds. The activity in the region continued, though to a lesser extent, after the destruction of Jerusalem by the Babylonians. A similar picture is shown in the dates from OSL samples taken from the agricultural installations in the Shemuel and Halilim Valleys.[73] These data sit well with the historical information, that after the Babylonian destruction, Mizpah (Tell en-Nasbeh) became an administrative center, and the surrounding areas were designated as an estate related to Moza.[74] It seems that the practice of utilizing lands in the area as part of the estate (be it royal, temple, or belonging to another body) was renewed with the reorganization of the political, religious, and economic systems of the area.

72. See Ido Koch, "New Light on the Glyptic Finds from Late Iron Age Jerusalem and Judah," in vol. 12 of *New Studies in the Archaeology of Jerusalem and its Region: Collected Papers* [Hebrew], ed. Joe Uziel et al. (Jerusalem, 2018), 29–44.

73. Gadot et al., "OSL Dating of Pre Terraced and Terraced Landscape."

74. Liphshits, *Age of the Empires*, 101.

The Widespread Production and Use of Holemouth Vessels in Jerusalem and Its Environs in the Iron Age II: Typology, Chronology, and Distribution

Liora Freud

At the end of the Iron Age, a small cylindrical storage jar appears in Jerusalem and its environs: the holemouth jar. Already common in the Iron Age IIB, it became the most common jar type toward the end of the Iron IIC, with dozens of jars recovered from many rural sites around Jerusalem. Given the findings from new excavations conducted in recent years at several sites, including Ramat Raḥel, Khirbet er-Ras, and Ramot Alon, a new typology of these jars and an analysis of their chronological horizon within the Iron Age IIB–C may contribute to our understanding of the material culture in the late seventh–early sixth centuries BCE.

In this article I define several subtypes of holemouth jars and attribute them to various chronological horizons. I then discuss changes in their production and distribution and address the question why they became the most common storage vessel in Judah at the very end of the Iron Age IIC.

5.1. The Chronology of the Iron Age IIB–C in Jerusalem

In Jerusalem and especially in the small rural settlements in its environs, the absence of destruction layers makes it difficult to date pottery assemblages from phases between the end of the Iron IIB (City of David Stratum 12) and

This essay was originally published in Liora Freud, "Production and Widespread Use of Holemouth Vessels in Jerusalem and Its Environs in the Iron Age II: Typology, Chronology, and Distribution" [Hebrew], in vol. 11 of *New Studies in the Archaeology of Jerusalem and Its Region: Collected Papers*, ed. Yuval Gadot et al. (Jerusalem, 2017), 93–110.

the end of the Iron IIC (City of David Stratum 10). The distinction between Strata 12–10 is based on a comparison with assemblages from Lachish, where two destruction layers are associated with historical events and thus function as chronological anchors: the Level III destruction, attributed to the city's conquest by Sennacherib in 701 BCE; and the Level II destruction, identified with Nebuchadnezzar's conquest in 586 BCE.[1] It is widely accepted that, after the Level III destruction, Tel Lachish remained abandoned throughout the first half of the seventh century BCE.[2] Despite the existence of a few architectural elements pointing to resettlement immediately after the destruction, most scholars concur that Layer II was founded in the second half of the seventh century BCE and that the pottery assemblages found in the destruction layer represent the city's final decades.[3]

Jerusalem's history was different from that of Lachish. The city was not destroyed in 701 BCE, and there was no settlement gap in the first part of the seventh century. Many researchers therefore argue that the Lachish dating should not automatically be compared to that of the City of David, the Western Hill, and the rural sites around the city. According to these scholars, pottery types parallel to the ones uncovered in Lachish Level III continued in use after Lachish was destroyed in places that did not suffer a destruction, and it took some time until the typical pottery types of Level II began to appear.[4] This explains the difficulty in dating stratigraphic levels and in differentiating between late eighth-century pottery types and

1. David Ussishkin, *The Renewed Archaeological Excavations at Lachish (1973–1994)*, 5 vols., Sonia and Marco Nadler Institute of Archaeology Monograph Series 22 (Tel Aviv: Emery and Claire Yass Publications in Archaeology, 2004), 1:92.

2. See Ussishkin, *Renewed Archaeological Excavations at Lachish*, 1:90–91; Seymour Gitin, "Iron Age IIC: Judah," in *The Ancient Pottery of Israel and Its Neighbors from the Iron Age through the Hellenistic Periods*, ed. Seymour Gitin, 2 vols. (Jerusalem: Israel Exploration Society, 2015), 1:345–63, table 3.3.1.

3. Ussishkin, *Renewed Archaeological Excavations at Lachish*, 1:93; Nadav Na'aman, "The Kingdom of Judah under Josiah," *TA* 18 (1991): 33–41.

4. Nadav Na'aman, "When and How Did Jerusalem Become a Great City? The Rise of Jerusalem as Judah's Premier City in the Eighth–Seventh Centuries B.C.E.," *BASOR* 347 (2007): 25–27; Israel Finkelstein, "Comments on the Date of Late-Monarchic Judahite Seal Impressions," *TA* 39 (2012), 204–5; Alon De Groot, "Discussion and Conclusions," in *Area E; Stratigraphy and Architecture*, vol. 7A of *Excavation at the City of David 1978–1985 Directed by Yigal Shiloh*, ed. Alon De Groot and Hannah Bernick-Greenberg, Qedem 53 (Jerusalem: Institute of Archaeology, Hebrew University of Jerusalem, 2012), 162; Yuval Gadot, "In the Valley of the King: Jerusalem's Rural Hinterland in the Eighth–Fourth Centuries BCE," *TA* 42 (2015): 8.

those of the early or mid-seventh century, when production continued for a longer period, almost without change. The difficulty arises when dealing with the rural settlements, where the variety of vessel types was usually smaller and the vessels were often less well preserved.

These reservations notwithstanding, Strata 12–10 assemblages in Area E in the City of David serve as a reference anchor for dating Iron IIB–C pottery in the area of Jerusalem. In their publication of Area E, Alon De Groot and Hannah Bernick-Greenberg presented a transitional stratum, Stratum 11, dated to the first half of the seventh century BCE, with a small number of new vessel types, uncovered only in this stratum.[5] In contrast to Lachish, it appears that it is possible to trace a gradual transition between two clear ceramic horizons in Jerusalem.

The assemblage of the latter part of the Iron IIB is designated by Stratum 12 in the City of David, which is dated to the later part of the eighth century BCE, and by Stratum 11, which is dated to the early part of the seventh century; the assemblage of the Iron IIC is designated by Stratum 10, which is dated to the later part of the seventh and the early part of the sixth century.[6] The transition between these horizons was gradual, and we have no destruction layer that can function as a *fossile directeur*. However, we can still identify the process whereby certain types disappeared and new types came into existence. To date, most ceramic studies have focused on the typology of cooking pots and storage jars. I suggest that the holemouth jar too should be considered a chronologically significant typological tool.

5.2. The Holemouth Jars and Their Contribution to the Chronological Debate

The first to discuss holemouth jars was Ruth Amiran, who identified them as typical Judean, rather than northern, vessels.[7] According to Miriam and

---

5. De Groot, "Discussion and Conclusions," 161–62; De Groot and Hannah Bernick-Greenberg, "The Pottery of Strata 12–10 (Iron Age IIB)," in *Area E; The Finds*, vol. 7B of *Excavations at the City of David 1978–1985 Directed by Yigal Shiloh*, ed. Alon De Groot, and Hannah Bernick-Greenberg, Qedem 54 (Jerusalem: Institute of Archaeology, Hebrew University of Jerusalem, 2012), 100–101.

6. Yigal Shiloh, *Excavations at the City of David I 1978–1982: Interim Report of the First Five Seasons*, Qedem 19 (Jerusalem: Hebrew University, 1984), 3.

7. Ruth Amiran, *Ancient Pottery of the Holy Land: From Its Beginning in the Neolithic Period to the End of the Iron Age* (Ramat Gan: Massada, 1969), 242.

Yohanan Aharoni, the ribbed rim on the holemouth jar was replaced by the flat rim in the Iron Age IIC.[8] Amihai Mazar and Nava Panitz-Cohen demonstrated that the ribbed rim continued, in fact, to appear in the Shephelah in the seventh century BCE, in Timna-Tel Batash.[9] Gabriel Barkay, Alexander Fantalkin, and Oren Tal discussed the holemouth jars from the fortress uncovered in Ora Negbi's 1969 excavation of Givʿat Shapira (French Hill).[10] The thick-walled fortress, strategically located, was used, according to Barkay, Fantalkin, and Tal, as part of a series of citadels defending Jerusalem. The holemouth jars, the main finds at the site, are classified into two main types, which must be contemporaneous as they were uncovered together in one locus. Barkay, Fantalkin, and Tal, however, claimed that the type with the bulbous rim, triangular in section preceded the type with the flat rim with an oblong section.[11] The excavators date the two types to the eighth–seventh centuries BCE, without narrowing the chronological range any further. Their typological and chronological classification is accepted and is cited by many researchers.[12] In recent years much information has accumulated on holemouth jars from various sites, mainly from Ramat Raḥel (from the final publication of Aharoni's excavations and the renewed excavations at the site), as well as other rural sites from the Jerusalem vicinity, such as Khirbet er-Ras, Ramot Alon, Diplomat Hotel, and Ras el-ʿAmud.[13] In light of their popularity in the Jerusalem

8. Miriam Aharoni and Yohanan Aharoni, "The Stratification of Judahite Sites in the Eighth and Seventh Centuries BCE," *BASOR* 224 (1976): 83.

9. Amihai Mazar and Nava Panitz-Cohen, *Timnah (Tel Batash) II: The Finds from the First Millennium BCE (Text, Plates)*, Qedem 42 (Jerusalem: Institute of Archaeology, Hebrew University of Jerusalem, 2001), 105–7.

10. Gabriel Barkay, Alexander Fantalkin, and Oren Tal, "A Late Iron Age Fortress North of Jerusalem," *BASOR* 328 (2002): 49–71.

11. Barkay, Fantalkin, and Tal, "Late Iron Age Fortress," 64–65.

12. Alla Nagorski and Zvi Greenhut, "Iron Age and Second Temple-Period Remains at Ras el-ʿAmud, Jerusalem" [Hebrew], *Atiqot* 80 (2015): 1*–21*; Zvi Greenhut and Alon De Groot, *Salvage Excavations at Tel Moza: The Bronze and Iron Age Settlements and Later Occupations*, IAAR 39 (Jerusalem: Israel Antiquities Authority, 2009); Nurit Feig, "Khirbat er-Ras, Jerusalem: Iron Age and Ottoman-Period Remains," *HA* 128 (2016): https://tinyurl.com/SBL2643d.

13. For Ramat Raḥel, see Oded Lipschits, Yuval Gadot and Liora Freud, *Ramat Raḥel III: Final Publication of Yohanan Aharoni's Excavations (1954, 1959–1962)*, Sonia and Marco Nadler Institute of Archaeology Monograph Series 35 (Winona Lake, IN: Eisenbrauns, 2016); Oded Lipschits et al., *What Are the Stones Whispering? Ramat Raḥel: 3000 Years of Forgotten History* (Winona Lake, IN: Eisenbrauns, 2017), 83. For

area and the abundant knowledge that has accumulated about them in recent years, there is a need to discuss various aspects beyond their function as a storage vessel associated with wine and olive presses and silos for the collection of agricultural products.[14] A typological analysis and comparative study of good assemblages that include these holemouth jars may make it possible to derive more precise typological conclusions and narrow the timespan of the end of the Iron Age IIB and during the Iron IIC, when the type was most common.

5.2.1. Typology and Distribution

The holemouth jar is a small cylindrical jar, without a neck and generally lacking handles. The rim varies between a triangular or elongated section (ca. 4–5 cm long), perpendicular to the wall or elevated above it. The base is wide and rounded, making it impossible for the jar to stand alone unless it is placed within a stand, sunken into the floor or leaned against a wall or another vessel. The great variety in rim shape and size stems from the long timespan of the type and from the variety in regions and workshops. The jars are on average approximately 30–35 cm high, 20–30 cm in diameter, and 6–15 L in capacity.[15]

Khirbet er-Ras, see Gadot, "In the Valley of the King." For Ramot Alon, see Sivan Mizrahi and Renee Forestani, "Jerusalem, Ramot Alon, Preliminary Report," *HA* 128 (2016): https://tinyurl.com/SBL2643f. For Diplomat Hotel, see Fanny Vitto, "A First Century CE Mint South of Jerusalem? Archaeological Context," in *New Studies in the Archaeology of Jerusalem and Its Region: Collected Papers*, ed. D. Amit, G. D. Stiebel, and O. Peleg-Barkat, vol. 5 (Jerusalem, 2011), 14*. For Ras el-ʿAmud, see Nagorski and Greenhut, "Ras el-ʿAmud."

14. Barkay, Fantalkin, and Tal, "Late Iron Age Fortress," 59–64; Nagorski and Greenhut, "Ras el-ʿAmud," 12–13.

15. The volume of the holemouth jars from Khirbet er-Ras, scanned by Ortal Haroch (personal communication), is 14–19 L (external volume) and 11–17 L (internal). Four holemouth jars from Moza, measured by Elena Zapassky ("Volume Estimation of Four Iron Age Holemouth Jars," in Greenhut and De Groot, *Salvage Excavations at Tel Moza*, 111–14), yielded 5.7, 6.2, 6.9, and 8.2 L respectively. Feig ("Khirbat er-Ras," 20) noted a volume of 6.8–7.3 L for holemouth jars from her excavation at Khirbet er-Ras. The calculation of the volume from holemouth jars (type HMJ1 below) from Ramat Raḥel (according the formula $v = \pi r^2 h$) yielded a volume of 15–16 L (Liora Freud, "The Longue Durée of the Seventh Century BCE: A Study of the Iron Age Pottery Vessels from Ramat Raḥel" [Hebrew] [MA thesis, Tel Aviv University, 2011], 70). The inaccuracy stemming from the rounded base and the differences is

The classification into types proposed here is based mainly on the reprocessing of the Ramat Raḥel material from Aharoni's excavations and the renewed excavations at the site, in addition to the material from rural sites around Jerusalem, such as Khirbet er-Ras, Bet Ha-Kerem, Ramot Alon, and Givʿat Ḥoma.[16]

In order to differentiate the various types, the following categories were taken into account: rim length, rim thickness, thickness of the tip of the rim, finish of the tip of the rim, and the way it was attached to the wall. The holemouth jars were divided into five main types. Subtypes occur, but since their differences are minimal, parallels are given to the main type only.

5.2.1.1. HMJ1 (Fig. 5.1:1–9)

This type has a smooth rim, elevating slightly like a dome. There is great diversity in the rim shape, which sometimes is of uniform thickness and sometimes thickens on the inside toward the edge. The edge of the rim is either rounded or straight, as if sliced with a knife (average rim dimensions: circa 5 cm in length and 1.0–1.5 cm in thickness). Occasionally, there is a small depression on the inside, where the rim is attached to the body. Each site exhibited its own typical version of the holemouth

---

negligible, since the HMJ are not all identical in dimensions. The significant discrepancies stem both from the different sizes, but also because in some cases (such as at Moza) the inner volume is calculated and in others (such as at Khirbet er-Ras), the external volume is given.

16. For Ramat Raḥel, see Yohanan Aharoni, *Excavations at Ramat Raḥel I: Seasons 1959 and 1960*, Centro di Studi Semitici, Serie Archaeologica 2 (Rome: Università degli studi, Centro di studi semitici, 1962); Aharoni, *Excavations at Ramat Raḥel II: Seasons 1961 and 1962*, Centro di Studi Semitici, Serie Archaeologica 6 (Rome: Università degli studi, Centro di studi semitici, 1964); Lipschits, Gadot, and Freud, *Ramat Raḥel III*; Oded Lipschits et al., "Palace and Village, Paradise and Oblivion: Unraveling the Riddles of Ramat Raḥel," *NEA* 74 (2011): 1–49. For Khirbet er-Ras, see Gadot, "In the Valley of the King"; Feig, "Khirbat er-Ras." For Bet Ha-Kerem, see Yaʿakov Billig, "Jerusalem, Bet Ha-Kerem, Preliminary Report," *HA* 123 (2011): https://tinyurl.com/SBL2643c. For Ramot Alon, see Mizrahi and Forestani, "Jerusalem, Ramot Alon." For Givʿat Ḥoma, see Natalya May, "Givʿat Ḥoma" [Hebrew], *ESI* 19 (1997): 93–94. The pottery from these excavations was processed within the framework of my PhD dissertation, part of which will be published as a monograph discussing rural settlement around Jerusalem. I wish to thank Eilat Mazar, Yuval Gadot, Yaʿakov Billig, Sivan Mizrahi, Zubair ʿAdawi, Natalya May, and Gideon Solimany for permitting me to process the ceramic findings from their excavations.

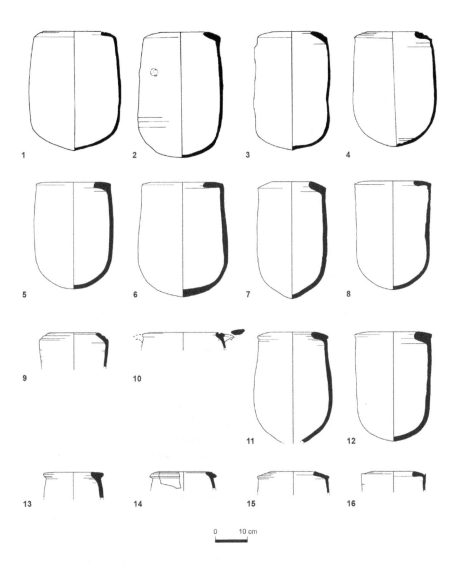

Fig. 5.1. Holemouth types: 1–9: HMJ1; 10: HMJ2; 11–13: HMJ4; 14: HMJ3; 15–16: HMJ5. Drawings nos. 1–4, 10, 14 from Ramat Raḥel by Ada Peri and Yulia Gotlib; nos. 5–8, 11–13 from Khirbet er-Ras by Avshalom Kerasik and Ortal Haroch; no. 15 from Bet Ha-Kerem and nos. 9 and 16 from Ramot Alon by Avshalom Kerasik; figure arranged by Yulia Gottlieb.

jar. This is probably due to different workshops and does not bear any chronological significance.

HMJ1 is the most common type of holemouth jar. Such vessels were found in sites all around Jerusalem, as well as in the city itself. In the City of David they first appear in Stratum 11 and are most common in Stratum 10, near the Gihon Spring from Stratum 7.[17] At Ramat Raḥel, many holemouth jars of this type were found in a room adjacent to Courtyard 380, the central courtyard of the palace.[18] The holemouth jars were uncovered in secondary use as a foundation of the floor of the second building phases.[19] In Structure 2 at Khirbet er-Ras, twenty-four complete and twenty partially restored holemouth jars were found, most of them belonging to this type.[20] Most of the many holemouth jars found in the storage buildings excavated in Ramot Alon, Givʿat Shaʾul, Ras el-ʿAmud, and the Diplomat Hotel belong to this type.[21]

One subtype has a wavy rim, slightly ribbed on its upper external part (fig. 5.1:4, 9; 5.2: HMJ6). The elongated and slightly lifted rim and the shape of its edge define it as HMJ1 and not as the ribbed HMJ3 (see below). Such holemouth jars were found in Ramot Alon (fig. 5.1:9), in Ramat Raḥel, and in ʿEin-Gedi Stratum V.[22] Two sherds of this subtype were found in the Babylonian Stratum 9/10 at the summit of the City of David, one of them with incised lines and small circles.[23]

---

17. De Groot and Bernick-Greenberg, "Pottery of Strata 12–10," 84–85; Joe Uziel and Nahshon Szanton, "Recent Excavations near the Gihon Spring and Their Reflection on the Character of Iron II Jerusalem," *TA* 42 (2015): fig. 12:9.

18. Lipschits et al., *What Are the Stones Whispering*, 83.

19. Freud, "Longue Durée," 30–31.

20. Gadot, "In the Valley of the King," fig. 2.

21. Mizrahi and Forestani, "Jerusalem, Ramot Alon, Preliminary Report"; Irina Zilberbod, "Jerusalem, Givʿat Shaʾul, Final Report," *HA* 127 (2015): fig. 13:1–13, fig. 14; Nagorski and Greenhut, "Ras el-ʿAmud," fig. 7:7–11; Vitto, "First Century CE Mint," 7.

22. For Ramat Raḥel, see Freud, "Longue Durée," fig. 27:10, 12. For ʿEin-Gedi, see Irit Yezerski, "Pottery of Stratum V," in *En-Gedi Excavations I: Final Report (1961–1965)*, ed. Ephraim Stern (Jerusalem: Israel Exploration Society, 2007), pl. 8:11–12.

23. Eilat Mazar, *Area G*, vol. 1 of *The Summit of the City of David Excavations 2005–2008: Final Reports* (Jerusalem: Shoham Academic Research and Publication, 2015), 25; Liora Freud, "Judahite Pottery in Transition Phase between the Iron Age and the Persian Period: Jerusalem and Its Environs" [Hebrew] (PhD diss., Tel Aviv University, 2018), fig. 59:68.

5.2.1.2. HMJ2 (Fig. 5.1:10)

Holemouth jar or deep krater with gutter or plain rim, with or without handles. The upper part of the wall inclines slightly inward; some specimens have a small ring base. This type is uncommon in the rural sites. It appears in the City of David in Area G; in Area E, Stratum 12; at the summit of the City of David Stratum 10; in Stratum 9/10; in the Ophel; in the Jewish Quarter in Stratum 7; in 'Ein-Gedi Stratum V; in Aharoni's excavations at Ramat Raḥel; and in Lachish Level II.[24] It is quite similar to the small holemouth jar of the Iron IIC with swollen body.[25]

5.2.1.3. HMJ3 (Fig. 5.1:14)

This type has a ribbed rim and is shorter than most smooth-rimmed jars (HMJ1); the wall is generally perpendicular to the rim and protruding outward. The type is widespread mainly in the Shephelah during the Iron IIC.[26] Several specimens were found in the City of David, in Lachish Level III, in 'Ein Gedi Stratum V, and at Ramat Raḥel, under the floor of Courtyard 380.[27]

---

24. For Area G, see Shiloh, *Excavations at the City of David*, fig. 30:2, with three handles. For Area E, Stratum 12, see De Groot and Bernick-Greenberg, "Pottery of Strata 12–10," fig. 4.8:2. For the summit of the City of David, Stratum 10, see Irit Yezerski and Eilat Mazar, "Iron Age III Pottery," in Mazar, *Area G*, fig. 5.12:170–174. For Stratum 9/10, see Freud, "Judahite Pottery of the Transition Phase," figs. 59:67; 63:129. For the Ophel, see Eilat Mazar and Benjamin Mazar, *Excavations in the South of the Temple Mount: The Ophel of Biblical Jerusalem*, Qedem 29 (Jerusalem: Institute of Archaeology, Hebrew University of Jerusalem, 1989), pl. 18:24, fills of upper floor 86/80. For the Jewish Quarter Stratum 7, see Alon De Groot, Hillel Geva, and Irit Yezerski, "Iron Age Pottery," in *The Finds from Areas A, W and X-2*, vol. 2 of *Jewish Quarter Excavations in the Old City of Jerusalem*, ed. Hillel Geva (Jerusalem: Israel Exploration Society, 2003), pl. 1.10:11, 13; Irit Yezerski, "Iron Age II Pottery," in *Area E and Other Studies*, vol. 3 of *Jewish Quarter Excavations in the Old City of Jerusalem*, ed. Hillel Geva (Jerusalem: Israel Exploration Society, 2006), pl. 3.2:20. For 'Ein-Gedi Stratum V, see Yezerski, "Pottery of Stratum V," pl. 8:18. For Ramat Raḥel, see Liora Freud, "Pottery of the Iron Age: Typology and Summary," in Lipschits, Gadot, and Freud, *Ramat Raḥel III*, table 1: HMJ2. For Lachish Level II, see Orna Zimhoni, "The Pottery of Levels III and II," in Ussishkin, *Excavations at Lachish*, fig. 26.50:5, with ribbed rim and four handles.

25. Gitin, "Iron Age IIC," pl. 3.3.4:3.

26. Mazar and Panitz-Cohen, *Timnah (Tel Batash) II*, 107, type 10b.

27. For the City of David, see De Groot and Bernick-Greenberg, "Pottery of Strata 12–10," fig. 4.6:3, Stratum 10 fills. For Lachish Level III, see Zimhoni, "Pottery

5.2.1.4. HMJ4 (Fig. 5.1:11–13)

This type has a short, plain bulbous rim, triangular in section, generally protruding beyond the wall, which turns slightly inward close to the rim. This type can be further divided into two subtypes: the first, HMJ4a (fig. 5.1:11–12), has a rim oblong in section, which grows thinner at the edge (3–4 cm in length). The second subtype, HMJ4b (fig. 5.1:13), has a shorter rim (ca. 3 cm in length) and a triangular section. The rim generally protrudes beyond the vessel's wall.

The subtypes parallel the ones defined by Barkay, Fantalkin, and Tal.[28] Their first type, with bulbous rim and triangular section, parallels our subtype HMJ4b, while their second type, with thinner flattened rim, square in section, parallels our HMJ4a. A few of the holemouth jars classified by Barkay, Fantalkin, and Tal as their second type have a rim 5 cm long; in this they resemble our HMJ1 but differ from it in the sharpened rim, which protrudes outward at the juncture of the rim and the wall.[29] There is a wide variety in both subtypes, and it is often difficult to determine to which subtype a certain sherd belongs. Types such as these were already found in Stratum 13 in the City of David; they are common in Stratum 12, for example, in Pit 317 in Area D, which contained some 130 holemouth jars, and in Stratum 11, Area E.[30] In Stratum 10 they are less common. Holemouth jars of this type uncovered near the Gihon Spring, City of David, have recently been published.[31] In Lachish they have been found in Level III, although they are not common there.[32] In Ramat Raḥel several items were found above and below the floor of Courtyard 380.[33] HMJ4 assemblages were

of Levels III and II," fig. 26.19:4. For ʿEin Gedi Stratum V, see Yezerski, "Pottery of Stratum V," pl. 8:11,12. For Ramat Raḥel, see Yuval Gadot et al., "Sub-Sectors ACS1, ACS2," in Lipschits, Gadot, and Freud, *Ramat Raḥel III*, fig. 8.17:23.

28. Barkay, Fantalkin, and Tal, "Late Iron Age Fortress," 61.

29. Barkay, Fantalkin, and Tal, "Late Iron Age Fortress," fig. 3:26.

30. For Stratum 13 in the City of David, see De Groot and Bernick-Greenberg, "Pottery of Strata 15–13," fig. 5.21:30. For Area D, see Alon De Groot and Donald T. Ariel, "Ceramic Report," in *Excavations at the City of David 1978–1985 Directed by Yigal Shiloh V: Extramural Areas*, ed. Donald T. Ariel, Qedem 40 (Jerusalem: Institute of Archaeology, Hebrew University of Jerusalem, 2000), 91–154, fig. 26:2–9. For Area E, see De Groot and Bernick-Greenberg, "Pottery of Strata 12–10," fig. 4.6:1.

31. Uziel and Szanton, "Recent Excavations," fig. 10:12, with elongated rim.

32. Zimhoni, "Pottery of Levels III and II," fig. 26.5:13.

33. Freud, "Pottery of the Iron Age," fig. 16.1, HMJ4.

found at Khirbet er-Ras, alongside characteristically Iron IIC pottery, such as the open neckless cooking pots, as well as in Ras el-ʿAmud.[34]

5.2.1.5. HMJ5 (Fig. 1:15, 16)

This type closely resembles HMJ1, differing only in the juncture, which protrudes upward or continues the same line of the rim (maybe because the rim was attached to the side wall by pinching both on the outside) and in the tip, which is thickened and finished with a diagonal cut.

This type is less common than HMJ1 and HMJ4. It was found in the City of David in Area G, in the Bulla House, and in Area E, Stratum 10A, as well as at the summit of the City of David Stratum 10 and the Babylonian Stratum 9/10.[35] A large assemblage of this type, most with the bulge at the juncture parallel to the wall, were found in a storage house in Ramot Alon (fig. 5.1: 16) and in Givʿat Shaʾul.[36] Smaller assemblages of this type were found in Bet Ha-Kerem (fig. 5.1: 15), alongside Iron IIC types and new vessel types from the sixth century BCE.[37]

5.2.2. Technology, Petrography and Chronology

Petrographic analyses conducted on eight HMJ1 vessels from Ramat Raḥel indicated that they were all made of clay originating from the Moza formation and of dolomite sand from the Aminadav formation (table 5.1). Many tiny white grits (dolomite sand) and big dark red and white grits (iron minerals and burnt chalk), which were added as temper, are visible to the naked eye. Some of these tempers, as well as the air bubbles in the clay,

---

34. For Khirbet er-Ras, see Gadot, "In the Valley of the King," fig. 3:12–22; Feig, "Khirbat er-Ras," fig. 10. For the open neckless cooking pot, see Gadot, "In the Valley of the King," fig. 3:7, 8; Feig, "Khirbat er-Ras," fig.11:9, 10; for Ras el-ʿAmud, see Nagorski and Greenhut, "Ras el-ʿAmud," figs. 6:8, 7:2.

35. For the Bulla House, see Yigal Shiloh, "A Group of Hebrew Bullae from the City of David," *IEJ* 36 (1986): fig. 6:17. For Stratum 10A, see De Groot and Bernick-Greenberg, "Pottery of Strata 12–10," fig. 4.13:12. For the summit of the City of David, Stratum 10, see Yezerski and Mazar, "Iron Age III Pottery," fig. 5.11:164, 166. For Stratum 9/10, see Mazar, *Area G*, 25; Freud, "Judahite Pottery of the Transition Phase," figs. 59:71–72, 63:124.

36. Mizrahi and Forestani, "Jerusalem, Ramot Alon, Preliminary Report"; Zilberbod, "Jerusalem, Givʿat Shaʾul," fig. 12:4, 5.

37. Billig, "Jerusalem, Bet Ha-Kerem."

caused cracks on the surface of the vessels. Some of the holemouth jars have an asymmetrical rim, and in some of these pieces of clay can be seen stuck to the rim from the inside.[38] The type of clay from which the HMJ1 vessels are made and the sloppy workmanship evident in some examples suggests that a change has begun in the pottery industry toward the Persian period. This is the most common type of clay in the Persian period, used in the vast majority of vessels, including jars, jugs, bowls, and lamps. This is further cause for dating the HMJ1 type to the very end of the Iron Age IIC, immediately before the Babylonian period and the beginning of the Persian period in the sixth century BCE.

The results of the petrographic analyses conducted by Cohen-Veinberger on sixteen holemouth jars from Ramot Alon are more diverse.[39] Of the eight HMJ1 vessels, six were made of Moza clay and dolomite sand, and two—one with an extremely thin rim and the other with a slightly ribbed rim (a subtype of HMJ1?)—were made of terra rossa clay. Three HMJ5 vessels were made of Moza clay and dolomite sand. Of the six HMJ4 vessels analyzed, four were made of Moza clay and dolomite sand, one of terra rossa combined with dolomite sand and another of terra rossa alone. Three holemouth jars from the French Hill were made of Moza clay with dolomite sand.[40] The results indicate a clear preference for production of holemouth jars from Moza clay mixed with dolomite sand. Hendricus Franken and Margreet Steiner reached similar conclusions while researching the clay types and the manufacturing techniques of rims uncovered in Kathleen Kenyon's excavations in the City of David.[41] They noted that holemouth jars, like other vessels from the Iron Age that continued in use after the 586 BCE destruction, were made after the destruction, of dolomite clay, a type that was widely common during the Iron Age I. The use of

---

38. Those clay pieces detached themselves during the manufacturing process, while the base was being closed. After the rim was shaped, the vessel was placed upside-down on the wheel, and the potter did not bother covering them up. For the manufacture technique, see Hendricus J. Franken and Margreet L. Steiner, eds., *Excavation in Jerusalem 1961–1967 II: The Iron Age Extramural Quarter on the South-East Hill* (Oxford: Oxford University Press, 1990), 97.

39. Cohen-Veinberger, personal communication.

40. Sampled by Amir Gorzalczany at the laboratory of the Institute of Archaeology, Tel Aviv University (Barkay, Fantalkin, and Tal, "Late Iron Age Fortress," n. 5). Although the types sampled were not specified in the report, all the holemouth jars published from the site belong to the HMJ4 type.

41. Franken and Steiner, *Excavation in Jerusalem*, 112–13.

this type of clay later declined, but became common again in the sixth century BCE, during the Persian period.[42] These petrography results indicate that the choice of Moza clay mixed with dolomite sand for the production of certain vessel types, such as the holemouth jars, already existed by the end of the Iron Age IIC, in contrast to other vessel types, such as bowls, kraters, lamps, and bag-shaped jars, which in the Iron Age IIC were made mostly from terra rossa and rendzina clay.[43]

The small size of the sample notwithstanding, the clear correspondence between the typological types analyzed and the clay source corroborates the typological distribution. The findings suggest that previous types, typical of the end of the Iron IIB or the beginning of Iron IIC (HMJ4a, HMJ4b), are made of terra rossa and Moza clay, whereas the vessels typical of the late Iron IIC (HMJ1, HMJ5) are mostly made of Moza clay. It is possible the transition to holemouth jars made of Moza clay signifies the beginning of a change in the Judean pottery industry, for by the Persian period most of the pottery from the Jerusalem area was manufactured with this type of clay.[44]

Table 5.1: Results of the Ramat Raḥel[45]
and Ramot Alon[46] petrography analysis

Type	Number Sampled	Moza Clay	Terra Rossa
HMJ1	13	12	1
HMJ2	1	1	–
HMJ3	1		1

42. Franken and Steiner, *Excavation in Jerusalem*, 83; Hendricus J. Franken, *A History of Pottery and Potters in Ancient Jerusalem: Excavations by K. M. Kenyon in Jerusalem 1961–1967* (London: Equinox, 2005), 65–66, 98; see also David Ben-Shlomo, "Jerusalem's Trade Networks in the Iron Age II as Seen through the Archaeometric Analysis of Pottery" [Hebrew], in vol. 11 of *New Studies in the Archaeology of Jerusalem and Its Region: Collected Papers*, ed. Yuval Gadot et al. (Jerusalem, 2017), 183, table 3.

43. Doron Boness and Yuval Goren, "Petrographic Study of the Iron Age and Persian Period Pottery at Ramat Raḥel," in *Ramat Raḥel V*, ed. Oded Lipschits, Yuval Gadot, and Liora Freud (forthcoming).

44. Amir Gorzalczany, "Appendix: Petrographic Analysis of Persian-Period Vessels," in De Groot and Bernick-Greenberg, *Excavations at the City of David*, 51.

45. Boness and Goren, "Petrographic Study."

46. Cohen-Weinberger, personal communication.

Type	Number Sampled	Moza Clay	Terra Rossa
HMJ4	6	4	1+1 with Amina-dav sand
HMJ5	3	3	–
Total	24	20	4

5.3. Discussion

5.3.1. Chronology

In light of the typology presented above and on the basis of the renewed Ramat Raḥel excavation results and other sites near Jerusalem, a reexamination of the relative dating of the various holemouth jar types is warranted. Gadot has shown that the growth in rural settlements in the seventh century BCE differs from the periods that precede and follow it.[47] Through the typography of holemouth jars suggested here, along with other vessels, such as typical seventh-century BCE cooking pots, I attempt to provide a more precise dating for Iron IIB sites, pinpointing it to the seventh century BCE.

The Ramat Raḥel palace is a key site in order to pinpoint the chronology. The excavators defined two Iron Age building phases, the transition between them including the construction of Courtyard 380 at the center of the site.[48] The courtyard is built over fill more than a meter thick, including many pottery sherds from vessels used in the first building phase. The pottery vessels uncovered under the floor, and thus related to the first stage, are dated to the end of the Iron Age IIB and the beginning of the Iron IIC. These include bowls and kraters with outfolded rim and cooking pots typical mainly of the Iron IIC.[49] In addition, many two-winged *lmlk*-stamp impressions, with incised circles, were uncovered, mostly of types IIb, IIc, and IIX, which have been attributed to the first half of the seventh century BCE.[50] It is noteworthy that all the rosette stamp impressions

---

47. Gadot, "In the Valley of the King," 13–18.

48. Gadot et al., "Sub-Sectors ACS1 ACS2," 97–100.

49. For bowls and kraters, see Freud, "Pottery of the Iron Age," figs. 16.1:B2.1, B7; 16.2:K1. For cooking pots, see Freud, "Pottery of the Iron Age," fig. 16.2:CP1, CP2, CP3.

50. Omer Sergi, "*lmlk* Stamp Impressions," in Lipschits, Gadot, and Freud, *Ramat Raḥel III*, 287–341; Oded Lipschits, Omer Sergi, and Ido Koch, "Royal Juda-

found at Ramat Raḥel were uncovered in mixed assemblages above the floor of Courtyard 380 and not in the fill, since the courtyard continued in use at least until the end of the Persian period.[51] The first appearance of the rosette stamps is dated to the end of the Iron IIC.[52] These data support Aharoni's assessment that the transition between the Ramat Raḥel building phases took place toward the end of the seventh century BCE.[53] A comparison between the finds uncovered in the fill under the floor and those recovered above it makes it possible to isolate the late part of the Iron IIC from the end of the Iron IIB and the early Iron IIC.

5.3.1.1. Ramat Raḥel

The many holemouth jars uncovered at Ramat Raḥel have been found in two main assemblages: (1) The holemouth jars from the first building phase were found under the floor of Courtyard 380, along with other pottery vessels. The jars are of the HMJ1, HMJ2, HMJ3, and HMJ4 types, with HMJ1 vessels appearing only rarely.[54] (2) The holemouth-jar assemblages, found in a room southwest of Courtyard 380, consist only of HMJ1.[55] The holemouth jars were in secondary use as a fill of the second building phase. A few vessels uncovered with them are identical to those found in Pit 14109 in the renewed excavations and in locus 477 of Aharoni's excavation, pits that are dated to the second building phase.[56] They include vessel

---

hite Jar Handles: Reconsidering the Chronology of the *lmlk* Stamp Impressions," *TA* 37 (2010): 3–32; Oded Lipschits, Omer Sergi, and Ido Koch, "Judahite Stamped and Incised Jar Handles: A Tool for the Study of the History of Late Monarchic Judah," *TA* 38 (2011): 5–41.

51. Ido Koch, "Rosette Stamp Impressions," in Lipschits, Gadot, and Freud, *Ramat Raḥel III*, 371–88.

52. Jane M. Cahill, "Rosette Stamp Seal Impressions from Ancient Judah," *IEJ* 45 (1995): 230–52; Ido Koch and Oded Lipschits, "The Rosette Stamped Jar Handle System and the Kingdom of Judah at the End of the First Temple Period," *ZDPV* 129 (2013): 60–61.

53. Aharoni, *Excavations at Ramat Raḥel II*, 119–22.

54. Freud, "Longue Durée," 25–29, 141; Freud, "Pottery of the Iron Age," 263.

55. Lipschits et al., *What Are the Stones Whispering*, 83; Freud, "Longue Durée," 27, 30–31.

56. Lipschits et al., *What Are the Stones Whispering*, 82–83; Deirdre N. Fulton et al., "Feasting in Paradise: Feast Remains from the Iron Age Palace of Ramat Raḥel and Their Implications," *BASOR* 374 (2015): 29–48; Gadot et al., "Sub-Sectors ACS1 ACS2," 156–58.

types such as the flat bowls with rims sharpened outward, the small bowls with outfolded rim, and the rounded hemispherical bowls, which are dated to the latter half of the Iron Age IIC.[57] The HMJ1 type should thus be dated to the second building phase. Other assemblages of holemouth jars were found around the central courtyard in Aharoni's excavations as well, mostly consisting of HMJ1.[58]

5.3.1.2. The City of David

At this site the HMJ1 type appears only in Strata 11–10 and not in previous strata.[59] Stratum 11 did not yield many assemblages, and only a few holemouth jars have been found. In general, the vessels of this stratum resemble those of Stratum 10.[60] Since Stratum 10 represents the 586 BCE destruction, the assemblages that contained HMJ1 holemouth jars, especially in large quantities, must be dated from the middle to the end of the Iron Age IIC. The other types of holemouth jars—HMJ2, HMJ3, and HMJ4—were already found in Strata 11 and 12.[61]

5.3.1.3. The Summit of the City of David

Holemouth jars resembling the HMJ1, HMJ5, HMJ2, and HMJ4 types have been found here in the stratified fills of Stratum 10.[62] In Stratum 9/10, termed the Babylonian stratum, most of the holemouth jars are of the HMJ1 type, a few are HMJ5, and several are HMJ2 or HMJ4.[63] It should be noted that alongside the familiar vessel types of the Iron Age IIC found in Stratum 9/10, some new vessel types have been uncovered, which did not appear in the 586 BCE destruction assemblages and are dated to the beginning of the Persian period, or as Babylonian type vessels.

---

57. Freud, "Pottery of the Iron Age," fig. 16.1:B2.2, B3, B8–9, B10; Fulton et al., "Feasting in Paradise," fig. 4.

58. Freud, "Pottery of the Iron Age," 263.

59. De Groot and Bernick-Greenberg, "Pottery of Strata 12–10," 84.

60. De Groot and Bernick-Greenberg, "Pottery of Strata 12–10," 98–100.

61. De Groot and Bernick-Greenberg, "Pottery of Strata 12–10," 82.

62. Yezerski and Mazar, "Iron Age III Pottery," figs. 5.11, 5.12, and tables 5.1–5.5. Here, the division into HJ1–HJ3 is slightly different, with HJ1 including mainly HMJ1 and HMJ5 jars, with a few HMJ4 jars; but note the increase in quantity from phase 10-4 to phase 10-1.

63. For naming the stratum Babylonian, see Mazar, *Area G*, 25.

5.3.1.4. The Giv'ati Parking Lot

Here, HMJ2 and HMJ4 rims were found in Stratum XIC; some HMJ1 and HMJ5 types were found in Stratum XIB and HMJ5 vessels were found in Stratum XIA.[64] Stratum XI was dated by the excavators to the eighth–seventh century BCE.[65] HMJ1 vessels were found in the Giv'ati Parking Lot in Stratum X, dated to the seventh century BCE, and in Stratum IX, from the end of the seventh–beginning of the sixth century BCE.[66] The excavators' dating is unlikely, as Stratum IX revealed some vessel types from the beginning of the Persian period and Stratum X contained vessel types from the end of the Iron IIC, alongside some early typical Persian-period vessels.[67] Thus, in my opinion, Stratum X is a transitional sixth-century layer. Stratum XIA should be dated, on the basis of the vessels found in it, to the second half of the Iron Age IIC.[68] No Iron IIB types were found in it, the jars resemble the rosette-stamped jars, and some bowls are also typical of the beginning of the Persian period.[69] Stratum XIB did not reveal distinctly Iron IIB vessel types. The only cooking pot from this stratum was erroneously identified as a jug, although it is of the neckless cooking-pot type common in the Iron Age IIC and throughout the sixth century BCE.[70] If one accepts the new dating proposed here, on the basis of the analysis

---

64. For Stratum XIC, see Doron Ben-Ami, *Jerusalem Excavations in the Tyropoeon Valley (Giv'ati Parking Lot)*, IAAR 52 (Jerusalem: Israel Antiquities Authority, 2013), fig. 3.4:2, 3. For Stratum XIB, see Ben-Ami, *Jerusalem Excavations in the Tyropoeon Valley*, fig. 3.5:7, 8. For Stratum XIA, see Ben-Ami, *Jerusalem Excavations in the Tyropoeon Valley*, fig. 3.7:3.

65. Ben-Ami, *Jerusalem Excavations in the Tyropoeon Valley*, 4.

66. For Stratum X, see Ben-Ami, *Jerusalem Excavations in the Tyropoeon Valley*, fig. 3.10:12, 13. For Stratum IX, see Ben-Ami, *Jerusalem Excavations in the Tyropoeon Valley*, fig. 3.11:10.

67. For Stratum IX, see Ben-Ami, *Jerusalem Excavations in the Tyropoeon Valley*, fig. 3.11:1, 9, 14, 15. For Stratum X Iron IIC vessels, see Ben-Ami, *Jerusalem Excavations in the Tyropoeon Valley*, fig. 3.10:2–8, 17. For Persian period vessels, see Ben-Ami, *Jerusalem Excavations in the Tyropoeon Valley*, fig. 3.10:1, 14, 15, 18.

68. Ben-Ami, *Jerusalem Excavations in the Tyropoeon Valley*, figs. 3.6–3.8.

69. For rosette-stamped jars, see Ben-Ami, *Jerusalem Excavations in the Tyropoeon Valley*, figs. 3.6:8, 19; 3.7:7, 8. For the bowls, see Ben-Ami, *Jerusalem Excavations in the Tyropoeon Valley*, figs. 3.6:8, 19; 3.7:7–8.

70. Ben-Ami, *Jerusalem Excavations in the Tyropoeon Valley*, fig. 3.5:12; see Gitin, "Iron Age IIC," plate 3.3.3:8.

of the pottery published from Strata IX–XI, it is clear that the HMJ1 and
HMJ5 jars should be dated to the Iron Age IIC.

5.3.1.5. Khirbet er-Ras

Several structural ruins, along with agriculture installations and terraces, have been recovered at this site, located on the lower northern
slope of Naḥal Refa'im. Three excavations were conducted here in five
Iron Age buildings.[71] In Building 3, approximately three hundred holemouth jars were found layered one on top of the other (only a few
have been restored and published).[72] The holemouth jars are smaller
than the Ramat Raḥel ones and have elongated rims (fig. 5.1:1–4); they
differ somewhat in their clay as well. Most of them belong to the HMJ4
type, with both subtypes represented. The discovery of a large quantity
of intact vessels of a single type suggests that this stratum represents
their actual period of use, whereas a few rims or sherds found in isolation might be accidental. The HMJ4 type is most common in City of
David Strata 11 and 12 (see above), dated to the end of the eighth and
the beginning of seventh century BCE. Since these holemouth jars were
found along with typical Iron IIC pottery types such as cooking pots,
one may conclude that the holemouth-jar storage room in Building 3
represents the end of the Iron IIB and the beginning of the Iron IIC.[73]
In Building 5 an assemblage was found close to the surface; in contains
mainly HMJ4 rims, along with a few HMJ1 and HMJ2 rim types.[74] This
assemblage resembles the one excavated by Feig in Building 3, and based
on the holemouth jars and cooking pots found in it, it should be dated to
the same period.[75] In Building 2, more than twenty holemouth jars were
found, as well as many other rims, mainly HMJ1 (fig. 5.1:5–8), with a
few HMJ4 (fig. 5.1:11–13).[76] The assemblage, containing typical Iron IIC

---

71. Gershon Edelstein, "A Terraced Farm at er-Ras," *Atiqot* 40 (2000): 39–63; Feig,
"Khirbat er-Ras"; Gadot, "In the Valley of the King."

72. For Building 3, see Feig, "Khirbat er-Ras," 3. For the holemouth jars, see Nurit
Feig, "The Agricultural Settlement in the Jerusalem Area in Iron Age II" [Hebrew],
in *Recent Innovations in the Study of Jerusalem I*, ed. Zeev Safrai, and Avraham Faust
(Ramat Gan: Bar-Ilan University, 1995), 5; Feig, "Khirbat er-Ras," fig. 10.

73. For the cooking pots, see Feig, "Khirbat er-Ras," fig. 11:8–10.

74. Gadot, "In the Valley of the King," figs. 2, 3.

75. E.g., Gitin, "Iron Age IIC," pl. 3.3.3.

76. For Building 2, see Gadot, "In the Valley of the King," fig. 2.

cooking pots, as well as other vessel types, is dated to the middle or latter half of the Iron Age IIC.[77]

From Building 1, most of the published jars are HMJ4, with a few HMJ1 vessels.[78] Although the excavator notes that a large quantity of holemouth jars was found, it is unclear whether they came from the building or from one of the caves or installations nearby. In the IAA storeroom we found early Persian pottery that originated mainly in the courtyard. The building apparently continued in use from the Iron Age IIC to the Persian period.[79]

5.3.1.6. Ras Abu Maʿaruf, Pisgat Zeʾev A

Many holemouth jars were found at this site in a building dated to the eighth–seventh until the beginning of the sixth century BCE.[80] The most common type uncovered there was HMJ1, while the HMJ2 and HMJ4 types were found in small numbers.[81] In a nearby cave, a large concentration of holemouth was found, only three of which were drawn (all HMJ1).[82] The large quantity of HMJ1 vessels, compared to the paucity of the others, is notable. Although Jon Seligman dated the cooking pots to the eighth–mid-seventh century BCE, they are more common in the beginning of the Iron Age IIC.[83] The finding of ten rims of this cooking pot type compared to nineteen rims of the neckless type that continued to the sixth century BCE makes it possible to date the structure to the middle of the Iron Age IIC, rather than the Iron Age IIB.[84]

---

77. See, e.g., Gitin, "Iron Age IIC," pl. 3.3.3.

78. Edelstein, "Terraced Farm," 47, fig. 13:1–8.

79. Efrat Bocher and Liora Freud, "Persian Period Settlement in the Rural Jerusalem Hinterland" [Hebrew], in *New Studies on Jerusalem 22*, ed. Eyal Baruch and Avraham Faust (Ramat Gan: Rennert Center for Jerusalem Studies, 2017), 150.

80. Jon Seligman, "A Late Iron Age Farmhouse at Ras Abu Maʿaruf, Pisgat Zeʾev A," *Atiqot* 25 (1994): 63–75.

81. Seligman, "Late Iron Age Farmhouse," 67, 71, fig. 6:1–3.

82. Seligman, "Late Iron Age Farmhouse," fig. 9:5–7.

83. For the cooking pots, see Seligman, "Late Iron Age Farmhouse," fig. 5:16–18. See Gitin, "Iron Age IIC," 347–48, cooking pots with outflaring rim and an emphasized ridge in the middle of the neck.

84. Seligman, "Late Iron Age Farmhouse," 67, fig. 5:13–18.

5.3.1.7. A Farmhouse in the French Hill

From this farmhouse, dated to the eighth century BCE, only a few hol-emouth jars were published, all of the HMJ4 type.[85] These cooking pots have a neck, an outflaring rim and an emphasized ridge typical of the early Iron IIC.[86] In my opinion, this dating—to the first half of the seventh century BCE—is correct.

5.3.1.8. Givʿat Shaʾul

Under a layer of dirt within a columbarium cave that had collapsed (the result of erosion or later deposition), some Iron II sherds dated no later than the seventh–sixth century BCE were found.[87] Most of the vessels uncovered were HMJ1 and HMJ5 holemouth jars, with no distinctly Iron IIB vessels.[88] It is therefore suggested that the assemblage should be dated to the latter half of the Iron Age IIC.

5.3.1.9. Ras el-ʿAmud

In the fill of a collapsed pit, many holemouth-jar rims were uncovered. One is attributed to the bulbous type (HMJ4b) defined by Barkay, Fan-talkin, and Tal, and ten belong to their elongated-rim type (HMJ4a).[89] An examination of the illustrations suggests that the latter are associated with the HMJ1 and HMJ5 jar types (and not to HMJ4, as suggested by Barkay, Fantalkin, and Tal). These types are dated here to the second half of the Iron Age IIC. This is also the date to which the excavators attributed the Iron Age fill on the basis of the rest of the pottery types and on the basis of Barkay, Fantalkin, and Tal's assumption that the type with the rectangular-section rim (HMJ4a) is the later type.[90]

---

85. Gaby Mazor, "A Farmhouse from the Late Iron Age and Second Temple Period in 'French Hill,' North Jerusalem" [Hebrew], *Atiqot* 54 (2007): fig. 6:10, 11.

86. For the cooking pots, see Mazor, "Farmhouse from the Late Iron Age," fig. 6:8, 9. Gitin, "Iron Age IIC," plate 3.3.3:1, 2.

87. Zilberbod, "Jerusalem, Givʿat Shaʾul," 1.

88. Zilberbod, "Jerusalem, Givʿat Shaʾul," figs. 12–14.

89. Barkay, Fantalkin, and Tal, "Late Iron Age Fortress." Nagorski and Greenhut, "Ras el-ʿAmud," 11, fig. 7.

90. Barkay, Fantalkin, and Tal, "Late Iron Age Fortress," 64.

5.3.1.10. Moza

Some HMJ4 holemouth jars were uncovered in the Stratum V Silo 760 in Area D.[91] In Area A, HMJ4 jars were found in storage Building 104, Strata V–IV, as well as some HMJ1 vessels.[92] Some 130 holemouth jars were recovered from this building; they had been stacked either on shelves or one on top of the other and had collapsed. The excavators attribute them all to the type with the bulbous rim (HMJ4b) as defined by Barkay, Fantalkin, and Tal.[93] An examination of the illustrations suggest that not all belong to that type, but since only a few were illustrated, it is difficult to determine which type was most common.[94] HMJ1, HMJ2, and HMJ5 jars were found in the collapse of Structure 500 of Stratum IV, alongside vessels similar to the ones found in City of David Stratum 10, such as the neckless cooking pot and a red-painted jug with funnel neck.[95] The contents of Silo 760 and the Area A storage house can therefore be dated to the final phase of the Iron Age IIB and the beginning of the Iron Age IIC, while Structure 500 can be dated to the second half of the Iron Age IIC.

5.3.1.11. Ramot Alon

A storehouse containing HMJ1 and HMJ5 jars alongside both HMJ4 sub-types was excavated.[96] Most of the cooking pots found in the building (eleven sherds) belong to the neckless type, which continued in use until the sixth century, while a few are of the type with outflaring rim and an emphasized ridge on the neck.[97] The building is, therefore, dated to the end of the Iron IIC period.

---

91. Greenhut and De Groot, *Salvage Excavations at Tel Moza*, fig. 3.15:8, 10.

92. For the HMJ4 jars, see Greenhut and De Groot, *Salvage Excavations at Tel Moza*, fig. 3.18:1, 2. For the HMJ1 jars, see Greenhut and De Groot, *Salvage Excavations at Tel Moza*, fig. 3.18:3, 4.

93. Barkay, Fantalkin, and Tal, "Late Iron Age Fortress."

94. Greenhut and De Groot, *Salvage Excavations at Tel Moza*, 100–103.

95. For Stratum IV holemouth jars, see Greenhut and De Groot, *Salvage Excavations at Tel Moza*, fig. 3.20:14–18; for cooking pots and jugs, see Greenhut and De Groot, *Salvage Excavations at Tel Moza*, figs. 3.19:18, 3.20:2–5.

96. Mizrahi and Forestani, "Jerusalem, Ramot Alon, Preliminary Report."

97. For the neckless type, see Gitin, "Iron Age IIC," plate 3.3.3:6–8. For the outflaring type, see Gitin, "Iron Age IIC," plate 3.3.3:1–5.

5.3.1.12. Bet Ha-Kerem

Part of a building was excavated, revealing rims of the HMJ1 and HMJ5
holemouth-jar types, alongside late Iron IIC vessels and other vessels
defined as Babylonian.[98]

5.3.2. Distribution

It is of interest to determine whether there is some regional pattern of
distribution of the holemouth jars and, if so, how it correlates with the
chronological pattern. Many researchers, for example, have noted the connection between Ramat Raḥel and Emek Refaʾim, and have suggested that
Ramat Raḥel functioned as a center for collecting harvest produce from the
valley.[99] The holemouth jars are noteworthy in this context. Since they were
presumably used for storage and transportation of agriculture produce,
one may assume that sites yielding jars identical to the ones from Ramat
Raḥel are contemporaneous with it. Conversely, sites with holemouth-jar
types that are not common in Ramat Raḥel—if they are geographically
close and from the same general period—may be unconnected to Ramat
Raḥel. If, indeed, Ramat Raḥel served as a center for collection of agricultural produce, one may determine the sites from which produce was sent
to Ramat Raḥel on the basis of the holemouth-jar types. For example, the
holemouth jars from Building 3 at Khirbet er-Ras are mostly of the HMJ4
type, which although not common at Ramat Raḥel, can be found in the
first construction phase. In contrast, the holemouth jars from Building 5
at Khirbet er-Ras are mostly of the HMJ1 type, which are very common in
the second building phase. The holemouth jars uncovered in the Diplomat

---

98. Billig, "Jerusalem, Bet Ha-Kerem."
99. Oded Lipschits and Yuval Gadot, "Ramat Rahel and the Emeq Rephaim Sites:
Links and Interpretations" [Hebrew], in vol. 2 of *New Studies in the Archaeology of
Jerusalem and Its Region: Collected Papers*, ed. David Amit and Guy Stiebel (Jerusalem,
2008), 88–96; Avraham Faust, "Jerusalem's Countryside during the Iron Age II–Persian Period Transition" [Hebrew], in *New Studies on Jerusalem 7*, ed. Avraham Faust
and Eyal Baruch (Ramat Gan: Bar-Ilan University, 2001), 83–89; Raphael Greenberg
and Gilad Cinamon, "Stamped and Incised Jar Handles from Rogem Ganim, and
Their Implications for the Political Economy of Jerusalem, Late Eighth–Early Fourth
Centuries BCE," *TA* 33 (2006): 233–35; Greenberg and Cinamon, "Rock-Cut Installations from the Iron Age, Persian and Roman Periods," *Atiqot* 66 (2011): 79–106.

Hotel are also identical to the HMJ1 type, very common at Ramat Raḥel.[100] Unlike the above-mentioned types, the HMJ5 vessels from Bet Ha-Kerem, Givʿat Shaʾul, Ras el-ʿAmud, and Ramot Alon (in large quantities there) are not at all common in Ramat Raḥel, probably because those sites supplied produce to a different center, such as the City of David, where they were found at Mazar excavations at the summit of the City of David.

5.3.3. The Prevalence of Holemouth Jars Compared to Other Vessel Types during the Iron Age IIB–C

The growing popularity of holemouth jars in Judah at the end of the Iron IIB and during the Iron IIC is well known. To understand this phenomenon, one should compare the prevalence of holemouth jars to the quantities of other large storage vessels uncovered.

Table 5.2 presents the number of holemouth jars uncovered in each site, broken down into types, compared to other jar types found in the same assemblages. In the first construction phase at Ramat Raḥel, the most common jars were the *lmlk*- and the bag-shaped jars, while holemouth jars were less popular. In the first part of the second construction phase, the assemblages consist mainly of holemouth jars, with very few other jars.[101]

The most common holemouth jars found in large quantities are HMJ1, HMJ4, and HMJ5. Khirbet er-Ras and Ramot Alon demonstrated holemouth-jar types such as HMJ4 (both subtypes), which can already be found in the City of David Stratum 12. At Khirbet er-Ras most of these were uncovered in Building 3, which contained mainly holemouth jars. In Buildings 1, 2, and 5, the most common vessel is the HMJ1 type, while other types of storage jars were hardly found.

As table 5.3 demonstrates, the main types that appeared at Bet Ha-Kerem, Givʿat Ḥoma, and Ras el-ʿAmud were HMJ1 and HMJ5 rims, with a few HMJ4 rims. The process whereby the large storage jars were replaced by others at the end of the period is clearly evidenced in the

---

100. Vitto, "First Century CE Mint"; and personal communication.

101. The number of rosette-stamped impressions found on the floor is much smaller than that of the *lmlk* stamps found beneath it. One might theoretically assume that the use of this jar type decreased in comparison to the *lmlk*-type jars that preceded it, unless the timespan for each jar type is taken into account (Koch and Lipschits, "Rosette Stamped Jar Handle System and the Kingdom of Judah," 62–63; Lipschits, Sergi, and Koch, "Royal Judahite Jar Handles," 17–21).

Table 5.2: Comparison of the Number of Holemouth Jars and Other Storage Jars in Sites Where Holemouth Assemblages Were Found (the Total Minimum Number Based on One-Eighth Rim Count Is Given in Parentheses)

Site	Period	Holemouth-jar rims	*lmlk*- and rosette-stamped jar rims	Rims of bag-shaped jars	Pithos rims
Ramat Raḥel, square D-86-87, under floor of Courtyard 380, first building phase, few holemouth jars	End of eighth–seventh century BCE	17 (7 HMJ1, 10 other types)	37	10	2
Ramat Raḥel, holemouth concentration, second building phase	End of seventh–beginning of sixth century BCE	13 complete, ca. 20 additional sherds	–	2	–
Ramot Alon, storage building (number painted for publication)	End of seventh–beginning of sixth century BCE	HMJ1 20 (34) HMJ5 8 (34) HMJ4a (11) HMJ4b (7)	1 (+ a few sherds)	1 (+ a few sherds)	2 (+ a few sherds)
Khirbet er-Ras, Building 2, Room 422 (number painted for publication)	First half of seventh century BCE	HMJ1 24 (335) HMJ4a 12 (85) HMJ4b 3 (19)	1	2	

Site	Period	Holemouth-jar rims	lmlk- and rosette-stamped jar rims	Rims of bag-shaped jars	Pithos rims
Khirbet er-Ras, Building 5, loci 701, 702 (number painted for publication)	End of eighth–mid-seventh century BCE	HMJ1 8 (21) HMJ4a 7 (19) HMJ4b 15 (75) HMJ2 1 (3) HMJ3 (2)	–	–	1
Khirbet er-Ras, Building 1	End of eighth–mid-seventh century BCE	HMJ1 4 HMJ4 4			3
Khirbet er-Ras, Building 3 (8 out of 300 were painted)	End of eighth–mid-seventh century BCE	HMJ4 (300) HMJ4a - 4 HMJ4b - 4		4	2

Table 5.3: Comparison of the Number of Holemouth Jars and Other Jars at Sites Where Only a Few Holemouth Jars Were Uncovered

Site	Date	Holemouth-jar rims	lmlk- and rosette-stamped jar rims	Rims of bag-shaped jars	Pithos rims
Bet Ha-Kerem, loci 64, 66 (Billig, "Jerusalem, Bet Ha-Kerem")	End of seventh–sixth century BCE	HMJ1: 1 HMJ5: 5	SJ1-5	SJ2-2	2
Givʿat Ḥoma (May, "Givʿat Ḥoma")	End of seventh–sixth century BCE	HMJ1: 2 HMJ2: 1 HMJ4: 1	3	5	——
Ras el-ʿAmud, water cistern (ʿAdawi, "Jerusalem, Ras el-ʿAmud")*	End of seventh–sixth century BCE	HMJ1: 3 HMJ4: 1	1	1	
Ras el-ʿAmud, fills (Nagorski and Greenhut, "Ras el-ʿAmud")	End of seventh–beginning of sixth century BCE	HMJ1/5: 10 HMJ4b: 1	1		
Summit of City of David, Layer 10-4 (Yezerski and Mazar, "Iron Age III Pottery")	Seventh century BCE	18	26		

Site	Date	Holemouth-jar rims	*lmlk*- and rosette-stamped jar rims	Rims of bag-shaped jars	Pithos rims
Summit of City of David, Layer 10-3 (Yezerski and Mazar, "Iron Age III Pottery")	Seventh century BCE	13	20		
Summit of City of David, Layer 10-2 (Yezerski and Mazar, "Iron Age III Pottery")	Seventh–beginning of sixth century BCE	72	95		
Summit of City of David, Layer 10-1 (Yezerski and Mazar, "Iron Age III Pottery")	Beginning of sixth century BCE	68	36		
Summit of City of David, Layer 9/10 (Mazar, Summit of the City of David)	Sixth century BCE	80	39		

Note:
* Zubair ʿAdawi, "Jerusalem, Ras el-ʿAmud (A)," *HA* 125 (2013): https://tinyurl.com/SBL2643a.

stratified fills from the summit of the City of David.[102] As shown in table 5.3, the number of holemouth jars in the upper layers, dated to the end of the Iron IIC, significantly increases compared to other jars, whereas in the early layers of Stratum 10 (10-3, 10-4), storage jars predominate. In Layer 10-1, the holemouth jars are dominant. In Layer 9/10 from the Babylonian period, the number of holemouth-jar rims is twice that of the rims of other storage jars. Indeed, Franken, who studied the same fills from Kenyon's excavations, already pointed out that the quantity of holemouth jars was significantly higher at the end of the Iron Age IIC.[103] This phenomenon is typical mainly of Judean sites in the Jerusalem vicinity.[104]

One may conclude that the number of holemouth jars increased at the end of the seventh century at the sites in the vicinity of Jerusalem. This growth directly corresponds with the decline in numbers of the other large storage jars, such as the rosette-stamped and the bag-shaped jars. During the sixth century BCE use of the holemouth jar declined, and it was replaced by the typical Persian-period holemouth krater.[105] Toward the end of the sixth century BCE, the large storage jars increased in popularity, and the four-handled oval jar and bag-shaped jar became once again the most common ones in the Jerusalem area. The four-handled jar continues the Judean tradition of the *lmlk-* and rosette-stamped jars, impressed with

---

102. Yezerski and Mazar, "Iron Age III Pottery," tables 5.1–5.5.

103. Franken, *History of Pottery and Potters*, 65–66; Franken and Steiner, *Excavation in Jerusalem*, 112.

104. In the Shephelah, e.g., holemouth jars were found in large quantities, but were not the main jar. At Tel Batash, the number of holemouth jars increased from 24 percent of all the jars in Stratum III to 29 percent in Stratum II (Mazar and Panitz-Cohen, *Timnah [Tel Batash] II*, 91). Beth Shemesh and Tel Ḥamid are exceptional in this respect: many holemouth jars were uncovered at Beth Shemesh, especially in the water reservoir from the second half of the seventh century BCE and in a pit dated to Stratum 2 (Shlomo Bunimovitz and Zvi Lederman, eds., *Tel Beth-Shemesh: A Border Community in Judah; Renewed Excavations 1990–2000; The Iron Age*, vol. 2, Sonia and Marco Nadler Institute of Archaeology Monograph Series 34 [Winona Lake, IN: Eisenbrauns, 2016], figs. 5.72, 12.37 HM); at Tel Ḥamid, many holemouth jars from the eighth century BCE were found (Sam Wolff and Alon Shavit, "Tel Ḥamid," *HA* 109 [1999]: 68*–70*).

105. Ephraim Stern, "Persian Period," in vol.2 of *The Ancient Pottery of Israel and Its Neighbors from the Iron Age through the Hellenistic Period*, ed. Seymour Gitin (Jerusalem: Israel Exploration Society, 2015), plate 5.1.26:5, 6.

the lion stamp of the sixth century BCE and then with the various Yehud stamps in the Persian period.[106]

The temporary growth in the number of holemouth jars coupled with the decline in other jar types reflects, in my opinion, a more extensive process. The holemouth jar is known as early as the Iron Age I, but was never so mass-produced. The increase in production may be linked to the tremendous population growth at that time in the vicinity of Jerusalem and the need to provide agricultural products for marketing or tax purposes.[107] However, this population growth does not suffice to explain why this small heavy vessel became a favorite over the bag-shaped or rosette-stamped storage jars; nor does it explain why the phenomenon was restricted to the Jerusalem area and did not occur in the Negev, which witnessed a large population growth at the same time. One possible explanation might pertain to the place of production of the jars. Many of the holemouth jars were made in pottery workshops in the Jerusalem area (most of them produced of Moza clay, which was also used to make the large pithoi in the Iron Age IIB–C, and some of local terra rossa), and many of the jars related to the administrative system, such as the stamped *lmlk* and rosette jars, were made in the Shephelah from terra rossa clay.[108] Small vessels of the Jerusalem area were made out of terra rossa and local rendzina clay.[109] It appears that during the Iron IIC, most of the holemouth jars were made of a different type of clay than the other storage jars and vessels. This situation was probably due to pottery workshops operating in different locations. The decline in the numbers of large storage vessels produced in the area at the end of the Iron IIC may suggest that the pottery industry in the Shephelah

---

106. Oded Lipschits and David S. Vanderhooft, *Yehud Stamp Impressions: A Corpus of Inscribed Stamp Impressions from the Persian and Hellenistic Period in Judah* (Winona Lake, IN: Eisenbrauns, 2011).

107. Gadot, "In the Valley of the King," 3, see references therein; Na'aman, "When and How Did Jerusalem Become a Great City"; Feig, "Agricultural Settlement"; Alon De Groot and Zvi Greenhut, "Moza—A Judahite Administrative Center near Jerusalem" [Hebrew], in *New Studies on Jerusalem 8*, ed. Eyal Baruch and Avraham Faust (Ramat Gan: Bar-Ilan University, 2002), 7–14, with English summary.

108. Joseph Yellin and Jane M. Cahill, "Rosette-Stamped Handles: Instrumental Neutron Activation Analysis," *IEJ* 54 (2004): 191–213; Yuval Goren, "Excursus: Petrographic Analysis of the *lmlk* and Official Sealed Jar Handles from the Renewed Excavations," in Bunimovitz and Lederman, *Tel Beth-Shemesh*, 502–4; Lipschits et al., *What Are the Stones Whispering*, 88.

109. Boness and Goren, "Petrographic Study."

suffered some disaster or simply could not meet the growing demand. Perhaps the pottery workshops producing the holemouth jars and the great pithoi in the Jerusalem area began mass production of the holemouth jars as compensation for the lack of other storage vessels. The reasons could be geographical, technological, administrative, or political, since the vessels made of terra rossa (bowls, kraters, and red-burnished decanters) in the Jerusalem area gradually disappeared as well, with other vessels taking their place. The process was completed when almost all the production, with the exception of cooking pots, transitioned over to Moza clay, as demonstrated by the Persian period pottery and by the four-handled, oval, lion- and Yahud-stamped jars made of Moza clay.[110]

5.4. Summary

Many holemouth jars have been uncovered over the past few years in the renewed excavations at Ramat Raḥel, as well as at Khirbet er-Ras, the summit of the City of David, Ramot Alon, and other sites. Their classification into types and their comparison to well-dated assemblages have yielded several conclusions bearing chronological significance.

(1) The HMJ4 type holemouth jar (both subtypes) was common in late eighth- and early seventh-century BCE assemblages. In this we concur with some of the researchers on the subject, such as Barkay, Fantalkin, and Tal, who claimed that toward the end of the eighth century the bulbous type with triangular section, HMJ4b, was replaced by the smooth-rimmed HMJ4a type.[111] These types existed simultaneously for a certain period of time and were found together at sites such as Khirbet er-Ras and Ramot Alon. These holemouth jars often appear in destruction layers of the end of the Iron Age IIC, but it seems that they simply survived over the years and were used and found, in small quantities, alongside the more numerous HMJ1 or HMJ5 jars.

(2) The HMJ1 type is common in assemblages from the mid-seventh and early sixth century BCE and perhaps even later in places with settlement continuity, such as Bet Ha-Kerem. In the large concentration of holemouth jars uncovered at Ramat Raḥel, the more common type was HMJ1, with all forms of the elongated rim exemplified.

---

110. Gorzalczany, "Appendix"; Boness and Goren, "Petrographic Study."
111. Barkay, Fantalkin, and Tal, "Late Iron Age Fortress," 64.

(3) The HMJ2, HMJ3, and HMJ4 types were found in small quantities beneath the courtyard floor, along with a few HMJ1 specimens. If we accept the assumption that HMJ1 replaced HMJ4, and that HMJ2 makes its first appearance in the seventh century BCE, it seems that the many HMJ1 jars from Ramat Raḥel must be dated to later than the mid-seventh century BCE.

(4) The HMJ5 type appears mostly in assemblages close to the destruction of the first temple or immediately following it, in the first half of the sixth century BCE, as in Ramot Alon, at the summit of the City of David, and in Bet Ha-Kerem. This is the latest type of holemouth jar. It appeared in many sites where Iron IIC pottery types were found alongside additional types produced in the tradition of the Iron Age, but differing slightly from them in clay type and decoration. In these sites there is settlement continuity from the end of the Iron Age to the Babylonian period.[112]

(5) HMJ2 is probably a version of the holemouth-rim jar, known in eighth- and seventh-century BCE strata.[113] From the seventh century onward, the finds were mainly restricted to sherds, and it is therefore difficult to classify this type. In addition, it is found only in small quantities and apparently was not mass-produced.

(6) HMJ3 is not common in the Jerusalem area; consequently, it is difficult to draw chronological conclusions about it.

(7) The growth in the quantity of holemouth jars occurred concurrently with the decline in the number of large storage jars toward the end of the seventh and the beginning of the sixth century BCE.

(8) Sites with large quantities of holemouth jars are considered to be administrative sites, such as Ramat Raḥel (also because of the many stamp impressions found in it) or Moza (where large silos were found). In addition, there are hardly any rural sites in the Jerusalem area, no matter how small, that were settled at the end of the eighth and during the seventh century BCE and did not contain holemouth jars. In some, only a few items were found, but most revealed large accumulations. The differences might stem from the different agricultural products stored or processed in these jars, or might be due to random seasonal differences. It is possible that large amounts were collected for harvesting or for the storage of produce that ultimately was not used. Nor can we rule out the possibility that the holemouth jars arrived as containers full of supplies.

---

112. Bocher and Freud, "Persian Period Settlement," 155.
113. Gitin, "Iron Age IIC," 348, pl. 3.3.4:3–5.

Fig. 5.2. Chronological distribution of the various holemouth jar types. Prepared by I. Koch.

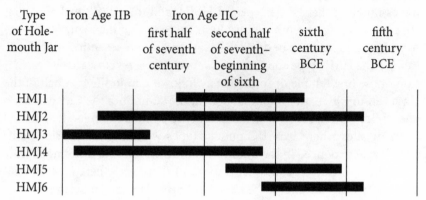

Part 3
Iconography, Cult, and Cultural Interaction

Pictorial Novelties in Context: Assyrian Iconography in Judah

Ido Koch

6.1. Introduction

The Assyrian hegemony in the southern Levant lasted one hundred years, beginning with the capitulation of Damascus and Samaria to Tiglath-pileser III and Sargon II and ending in the final decade of Assurbanipal or the short reign of one of his successors.[1] From its onset, Assyrian colonialism had a multifaceted impact on the local landscape. Local political centers were conquered, some, mostly the strongest in their region, were transformed into Assyrian hubs.[2] The inhabitants of these hubs, mainly the elite, were deported and replaced by newcomers that were forced to leave their homes from distant parts of the empire.[3] Local rulers were also integrated into the imperial network—took an oath of loyalty to the king and forced to send labor and tributes of raw materials and finished products to the court and to its agents that were based in the neighboring hubs.[4]

---

1. Ariel M. Bagg, *Die Assyrer und das Westland: Studien zur historischen Geographie und Herrschaftspraxis in der Levante im 1. Jt. v.u.Z.*, OLA 216 (Leuven: Peeters, 2011); Bagg, "Assyria and the West: Syria and the Levant," in *A Companion to Assyria*, ed. Eckart Frahm, BCAW (Hoboken, NJ: Wiley & Sons, 2017), 268–84.

2. Karen Radner, "Provinz. C. Assyrien," *RlA* 11:42–68.

3. Bustenay Oded, *Mass Deportations and Deportees in the Neo-Assyrian Empire* (Wiesbaden: Reichert, 1979); Nadav Na'aman, "Population Changes in Palestine Following the Assyrian Deportations," *TA* 20 (1993): 104–24; Karen Radner, "Economy, Society, and Daily Life in the Neo-Assyrian Period," in Frahm, *Companion to Assyria*, 209–12.

4. Eckart Frahm, "Revolts in the Assyrian Empire: A Preliminary Discourse Analysis," in *Revolt and Resistance in the Ancient Classical World and the Near East: In the*

The forced integration into the Assyrian network had several major effects evident in the archaeological record. A well-discussed issue is the Assyrian demands and the economic pressure felt by the local rulers coupled with the prosperity of interregional trade, which included the integration of a Phoenician trade network and the flow of commodities from Arabia. The common reaction was a search for new sources of capital and thus investment of existing capital in new economic enterprises such as large-scale olive oil production and wool production and weaving.[5] As the Assyrian pressure grew, demanding more tribute and further integrating into the local economic matrix, these local rulers actively resisted—a desperate move that was always answered by a fatal blow.[6]

Another major impact was the exposure of the local rulers and a wider audience of the elite to the Assyrian royal and elite ideology and to other elites in the southern Levant. The archaeological record from the region vividly reflects this exposure with various innovations in elite architecture, consumption, and iconography. Consequently, common wisdom would explain such processes as the Assyrianization of the local elite. Nevertheless, the growing influence of postcolonial critique in historical and archaeological discourse has led, in recent years, to the abandonment of Assyrianization, a term emphasizing acculturation (such as Hellenization or Romanization), and to the preference of an alternative term, such as transculturation, which emphasizes the initiative of each party in the cultural exchange, the reciprocal influence of two or more parties in contact zones, and the complex character of the act of appropriation.[7]

Crucible of Empire, ed. John J. Collins and J. G. Manning, CHANE 85 (Leiden: Brill, 2016), 76–89.

5. Ido Koch and Lidar Sapir-Hen, "Beersheba–Arad Valley during the Assyrian Period," *Sem* 60 (2018): 427–52; Oded Lipschits, *The Age of Empires: History and Administration in Judah in Light of the Stamped Jar Handles* [Hebrew] (Jerusalem: Yad Ben Zvi, 2018).

6. Nadav Na'aman, "An Assyrian Residence at Ramat Rahel?," *TA* 28 (2001): 260–80; Karen Radner, "Revolts in the Assyrian Empire: Succession Wars, Rebellions Against a False King and Independence Movements," in Collins and Manning, *Revolt and Resistance*, 41–54.

7. Angelika Berlejung, "The Assyrians in the West: Assyrianization, Colonialism, Indifference, or Development Policy?," in *Congress Volume Helsinki 2010*, ed. Martti Nissinen, VTSup 148 (Leiden: Brill, 2012), 21–60; Ariel M. Bagg, "Palestine under Assyrian Rule: A New Look at the Assyrian Imperial Policy in the West," *JAOS* 133 (2013): 119–44. For transculturation, see Mary Louise Pratt, *Imperial Eyes: Travel*

In what follows I would like to present two cases of appropriation of Assyrian imperial pictorial language in late Iron Age Judah that exemplify the complexity of such cultural interaction: the rosette icon and the iconography of the Moon God of Harran.

6.2. The Rosette

The most common motif in Iron IIC Judah was the rosette. Twenty-four now-lost seals, grouped into four stylistic families, were used to mark over two hundred storage jars (fig. 6.1).[8] Intact jars belonging to this system were unearthed in the destruction levels of Jerusalem (City of David Stratum 10B), Lachish (Level II), Tel Malḥata (Stratum IIIA), and Tel ʿIra (Stratum VI), associated with the Babylonian campaign(s) in the early sixth century BCE. Numerous stamped handles were also found at these and many other sites, some 70 percent of them in the Judahite heartland. The uniform morphology of the jars and their provenance attest to their production at a single workshop located somewhere in the eastern Shephelah and to their use in a single system for monitoring the collection and distribution of agricultural commodities, most probably olive oil and wine.

This was a development of a previous system that employed similar means to mark storage jars from the last third of the eighth century BCE.[9] Back then the marking included inscriptions ("belonging to the king" and the name of a royal estate) and one of two icons: a winged disk (fig. 6.2) and a four-winged beetle. Although it might be conceived as an Egyptian solar symbol by the modern beholder, the winged disk was a Levantine concept from the second millennium BCE onward, symbolizing celestial beings and not only sun deities.[10] The winged disk is known from late Iron IIA–early Iron IIB bullae found at the City of David in Jerusalem, and it

Writing and Transculturation, 2nd ed. (London: Routledge, 2008); Bill Ashcroft, Gareth Griffiths, and Helen Tiffin, *Post-colonial Studies: The Key Concepts* (London: Routledge, 2013), 213–14.

8. Ido Koch and Oded Lipschits, "The Rosette Stamped Jar Handle System and the Kingdom of Judah at the End of the First Temple Period," *ZDPV* 129 (2013): 55–78.

9. Oded Lipschits, Omer Sergi, and Ido Koch, "Judahite Stamped and Incised Jar Handles: A Tool for the Study of the History of Late Monarchic Judah," *TA* 38 (2011): 5–41; Lipschits, *Age of Empires*.

10. Tallay Ornan, "The Complex System of Religious Symbols: The Case of the Winged Disc in Ancient Near Eastern Imagery of the First Millennium BCE," in *Crafts and Images in Contact: Studies on Eastern Mediterranean Art of the First Millennium*

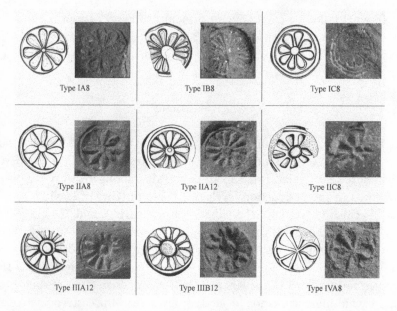

Fig. 6.1. Rosette-stamped handle typology based on the finds from Ramat Raḥel.
Photographs by P. Shargo; drawings by R. Pinchas.

was a royal symbol at least by the reign of King Hezekiah.[11] The winged
beetle was rarer, and its attestations in the Iron II southern Levant are limited; several bullae from Iron IIB Samaria show that it was not unknown
in the royal milieu of the region prior to its appearance on Judahite seals;
there it was either a subliminal heritage of second-millennium iconography or a more recent (Iron IIA) localization of Egyptian iconography,
perhaps through Phoenician mediation.[12]

BCE, ed. Claudia E. Suter and Christoph Uehlinger, OBO 210 (Fribourg: Academic
Press; Göttingen: Vandenhoeck & Ruprecht, 2005), 207–27.

    11. For late Iron IIA–early Iron IIB, see Othmar Keel, *Von Tel el-ʿIdham bis Tel
Kitan*, vol. 5 of *Corpus der Stempelsiegel-Amulette aus Palästina/Israel: Von den Anfängen bis zur Perserzeit*, OBO.SA 35 (Fribourg: Academic Press; Göttingen: Vandenhoeck & Ruprecht, 2017), 376–77 no. 215; 406–7 nos. 283 and 284; 408–9 no. 286. For
King Hezekiah, see the preliminary publication of a bulla found in the Ophel Excavations directed by Eilat Mazar: https://tinyurl.com/SBL26431.

    12. For Samaria, see John Winter Crowfoot, Grace M. Crowfoot, and Kathleen
M. Kenyon, *The Objects from Samaria*, Samaria-Sebaste 3 (London: Palestine Explo-
ration Fund, 1957), 88, pl. 15:29. For Judah, see, e.g., Keel, *Von Tel el-ʿIdham bis Tel
Kitan*, 410–411, nos. 288–289. For Phoenicia, see, e.g., the occurrences of the winged

Fig. 6.2. *lmlk*-stamped handle from Ramat Raḥel. Courtesy of Oded Lipschits.

One notable change in the stamped-jar system during the Iron IIC was the abandonment of the inscription designating the jars as belonging to the king (although its connection to the court is beyond doubt; see above). Another change is the adoption of the symbol of the rosette, which, although known in the Levantine pictorial repertoire, rarely appeared in Levantine glyptics and is yet to be found on seals from Jerusalem prior to the Iron IIC.[13] Indeed, since the days of William F. Albright, the rosette in Judah has been interpreted as the result of Assyrian influence, because of its long history as a symbol of Ishtar employed in royal iconography during the Neo-Assyrian era, adorning the crowns and clothes of the

---

beetle on metal bowls ascribed to Phoenician workshops (Glenn Markoe, *Phoenician Bronze and Silver Bowls from Cyprus and the Mediterranean* [Berkeley: University of California Press, 1985]).

13. Among the few Iron IIB occurrences, see a stamped handle from Tel Hazor Stratum VA (Othmar Keel, *Von Tel Gamma bis Chirbet Husche*, vol. 4 of *Corpus der Stempelsiegel-Amulette aus Palästina/Israel: Von den Anfängen bis zur Perserzeit*, OBO.SA 33 [Fribourg: Academic Press; Göttingen: Vandenhoeck & Ruprecht, 2013], 612–13 no. 72).

king and of the heir apparent and decorating royal monuments.[14] Such an interpretation found support in the excavations of Tel Miqne, the site of Ekron, Judah's western neighbor. There, in the heart of the city, Achish the son of Padi the ruler of Ekron built, in the first half of the seventh century BCE, a monumental complex that incorporates local architecture with an Assyrian-style ground plan.[15] The central room of the complex featured the famous inscription placed by Achish, dedicating the shrine to his patron goddess. A large stone slab from that room was engraved with a rosette icon associated by the excavators with the patron goddess and interpreted as reflecting Assyrian influence.[16]

The cultural influence of Assyria on Judah can be traced in additional aspects, the most conspicuous of which is the integration of imperial language in the Hebrew Bible and predominantly in the book of Deuteronomy.[17] It was the result of the preoccupation of the Neo-Assyrian kings with the danger of revolts, which is emphasized in the "calculated frightfulness" against their enemies at home and abroad, exhaustively described in royal inscriptions and depicted in royal monuments, and in the importance of loyalty oaths, aimed at the capitulation of every member of the state and its clients.[18] Such documents were known from the Assyrian capitals, and a

---

14. William F. Albright in Isaac Mendelsohn, "Guilds in Ancient Palestine," *BASOR* 80 (1940): 21 n. 51; Jane M. Cahill, "Royal Rosettes Fit for a King," *BAR* 23.5 (1997): 48–57, 68–69.

15. Seymour Gitin, "Temple Complex 650 at Ekron: The Impact of Multi-Cultural Influences on Philistine Cult in the Late Iron Age," in *Temple Building and Temple Cult: Architecture and Cultic Paraphernalia of Temples in the Levant (2.–1. Mill. B.C.E.)*, ed. Jens Kamlah, ADPV 41 (Wiesbaden: Harrassowitz, 2012), 223–56.

16. Gitin, "Temple Complex 650," 233 and pl. 52A. See also a silver medallion depicting a scene of a worshiper facing a goddess featuring Assyrian iconographic elements of Ishtar encircled with stars (Tallay Ornan, "Ištar as Depicted on Finds from Israel," in *Studies in the Archaeology of the Iron Age in Israel and Jordan*, ed. Amihai Mazar, JSOTSup 331 [Sheffield: Sheffield Academic, 2001], 246–49).

17. In the words of Frahm, "Revolts in the Neo-Assyrian Empire," 89: "From a world-historical perspective, the metamorphosis of the offence of revolting against the political autocrat into the sin of revolting against the one god is certainly the most significance legacy of the discourses that develop in the Neo-Assyrian time."

18. For the danger of revolts, see Radner, "Revolts in the Assyrian Empire." For the royal inscriptions and monuments, see Giovanni B. Lanfranchi, "Greek Historians and the Memory of the Assyrian Court," in *Der Achämenidenhof/The Achaemenid Court: Akten des 2. Internationalen Kolloquiums zum Thema "Vorderasien im Spannungsfeld klassischer und altorientalischer Überlieferungen" Landgut Castelen bei*

recent finding of such a treaty at a seventh-century BCE temple at Tell Tayinat hints at the possibility that a similar treaty was housed in the temple of
Jerusalem and was accessible to the authors of the "Ur-Deuteronomium."[19]

The innovations in the Judahite royal ideology appeared during the
zenith of Assyrian power and/or the chaotic decades of its rapid downfall.[20]
If the process began during the earlier part of the seventh century BCE,
contemporaneous with the construction of the palatial compound at Tel
Miqne/Ekron, both can be considered acts of usurpation. Usurpation in
postcolonial discourse is the localization of the language of the ruler by
the colonized as a means of resistance to colonial domination and its cultural influence. A prime example is the appropriation of the language of
the ruler by the colonized and its manipulation to promote a message, usually subversive in character, regarding the colonial arena.[21] Looking back
at seventh-century Judah, the usurpation of the imperial language by the
Jerusalemite court can be seen, for example, in the appropriation of the
loyalty oath in a manner that included the removal of the Assyrian king and
his replacement by the patron deity. Conversely, the appropriation of the
rosette can be dated to the final years of the Assyrian Empire or, most probably, to the days after its collapse. If that was the case, it can be explained as
the usurpation of the imperial *pictorial* language—the transformation of a
symbol well known for its association with the Assyrian king to a symbol of
the king of Judah, who became the sole ruler of the kingdom.

6.3. The Iconography of the Moon God of Harran

Imported Assyrian, Babylonian, and north Levantine seals were distributed across the southern Levant from the seventh century BCE onward

---

Basel, 23.–25. Mai 2007, ed. Bruno Jacobs and Robert Rollinger, Classica et Orientalia
2 (Wiesbaden: Harrassowitz, 2010), 40–42. For the loyalty oaths, see Frahm, "Revolts
in the Neo-Assyrian Empire," 84.

19. Bernard M. Levinson and Jeffrey Stackert, "Between the Covenant Code and
Esarhaddon's Succession Treaty: Deuteronomy 13 and the Composition of Deuter-
onomy," *JAJ* 3 (2012): 123–40; Hans U. Steymans, "Deuteronomy 28 and Tell Tayinat,"
VeEc 34 (2013): 1–13.

20. For a historical synopsis of the twilight period of the Neo-Assyrian Empire,
see Eckart Frahm, "The Neo-Assyrian Period (ca. 1000–609)," in Frahm, *Companion
to Assyria*, 191–93 with earlier literature.

21. Bill Ashcroft, Gareth Griffiths, and Helen Tiffin, *The Empire Writes Back:
Theory and Practice in Post-colonial Literatures*, 2nd ed. (London: Routledge, 2004).

and were most probably the main channel through which pictorial innovations appeared in local glyptics. The largest concentrations were found
in sites that served as imperial centers, such as Samaria and Megiddo, sites
affiliated with their administrative systems, such as Gezer, or other nodes
in the imperial network, such as Tell Jemmeh; there one finds a variety of
styles and icons and the most substantial evidence for their localization.[22]

The most prominent pictorial assemblage that was spread and localized in the southern Levant beyond the Assyrian provinces was lunar
imagery, and specifically, the iconography of the Moon God of Harran.
The temple at Harran was embraced by Assyrian kings as early as Adad-
nirari III, and its cult was employed in the service of imperial ideology
during the days of the Sargonids.[23] Considering the diffusion of Assyrian and Aramean practices in the imperial heartland at that time and the
service of Aramaic-speaking individuals in the imperial administration,
scholars consider the spread of lunar imagery to reflect an intensification
of Assyrian activity during the seventh century BCE across the southern
Levant. Furthermore, the scholarly discourse on the relations between
images depicted on seals and amulets and the biblical texts embraced this
specific pictorial assemblage and its imperial association to argue for an
Assyrian impact on the religion of the southern Levant.[24]

---

22. Tallay Ornan, "The Mesopotamian Influence on West Semitic Inscribed Seals:
A Preference for the Depiction of Mortals," in *Studies in the Iconography of Northwest
Semitic Inscribed Seals*, ed. Benjamin Sass and Christoph Uehlinger, OBO 125 (Fri-
bourg: Academic Press; Göttingen: Vandenhoeck & Ruprecht, 1993), 52–73; Ornan,
"Mesopotamian Influence on the Glyptic of Israel and Jordan in the First Millennium
B.C." (PhD diss., Tel Aviv University, 1997); Othmar Keel and Christoph Uehlinger,
Gods, Goddesses, and Images of God in Ancient Israel (Minneapolis: Fortress, 1998),
288–92.

23. Steven Winford Holloway, "Harran: Cultic Geography in the Neo-Assyrian
Empire and Its Implications for Sennacherib's Letter to Hezekiah in 2 Kings," in *The
Pitcher Is Broken: Memorial Essays for Gösta Ahlström*, ed. Steven Winford Holloway
and Lowell K. Handy, JSOTSup 190 (Sheffield: Sheffield Academic, 1995), 276–314;
Melanie Groß, "Ḥarrān als kulturelles Zentrum in der altorientalischen Geschichte
und sein Weiterleben," in *Kulturelle Schnittstelle: Mesopotamien, Anatolien, Kurdistan;
Geschichte; Sprachen; Gegenwart*, ed. Lea Müller-Funk et al. (Vienna: Instituts für Orientalistik der Universität Wien, 2014), 139–54.

24. Othmar Keel, *Goddesses and Trees, New Moon and Yahweh: Ancient Near
Eastern Art and the Hebrew Bible*, JSOTSup 261 (Sheffield: Sheffield Academic, 1998),
60–109.

Fig. 6.3. Moon god and iconography and related depictions: 1. Mamilla, tomb 7;[25] 2. City of David Stratum 10;[26] 3. Ḥorvat ʿUza;[27] 4. Tel Malḥata Stratum IIIA;[28] 5. Tel Arad Stratum IX;[29] 6. Tel Arad Stratum IX;[30] 7. Tel Arad Stratum XI.[31]

Doubts regarding a direct Assyrian religious influence upon Judah (in contrast to the indirect influence through usurpation, mentioned above) have been elaborated in past scholarship.[32] My focus will therefore be the context of the finds employed in this discourse.

25. After Keel, *Von Tel el-ʿIdham bis Tel Kitan*, 337 no. 131.

26. After Keel, *Von Tel el-ʿIdham bis Tel Kitan*, 323 no. 100.

27. After Pirhiya Beck, "A Neo-Assyrian Bulla," in *Ḥorvat ʿUza and Ḥorvat Radum: Two Fortresses in the Biblical Negev*, ed. Itzhaq Beit-Arieh, Sonia and Marco Nadler Institute of Archaeology Monograph Series 25 (Tel Aviv: Emery and Claire Yass Publications in Archaeology, 2007), fig. 6.1.

28. Irit Ziffer, "Iron Age Stamp Seals, A Cylinder Seal, and Impressions," in *Tel Malḥata: A Central City in the Biblical Negev*, ed. Itzhaq Beit-Arieh and Liora Freud, Sonia and Marco Nadler Institute of Archaeology Monograph Series 32 (Winona Lake, IN: Eisenbrauns, 2015), 520 fig. 6.5.

29. Miriam Aharoni, "An Iron Age Cylinder Seal," *IEJ* 46 (1996): fig. 1.

30. Othmar Keel, *Von Tell Abu Farağ bis ʾAtlit*, vol. 1 of *Corpus der Stempelsiegel-Amulette aus Palästina/Israel: Von den Anfängen bis zur Perserzeit*, OBO.SA 13 (Fribourg: Academic Press; Göttingen: Vandenhoeck & Ruprecht, 1997), 655 no. 24.

31. After Keel, *Von Tell Abu Farağ bis ʾAtlit*, 657 no. 31.

32. Jeffrey L. Cooley, "Astral Religion in Ugarit and Ancient Israel," *JNES* 70 (2011): 286–87 with literature.

Of the many exemplars mentioned in the scholarly literature, only three items featuring the Moon God of Harran iconography are known from stratified Iron IIC assemblages in Judah. One is a seal (fig. 6.3:1) from a burial at Mamilla, west of the Old City of Jerusalem, depicting a worshiper facing a crescent that might be considered a local product influenced by north-Levantine tradition.[33] Another is a bulla from the southeastern hill of Jerusalem (fig. 6.3:2), identified by Baruch Brandl as impressed by an Assyrian import.[34] The third is a bulla from Ḥorvat ʿUza (fig. 6.3:3), a fortress located southeast of Tel Arad. The original seal features a well-known Levantine variant of the Moon God of Harran iconography, depicting the crescent-on-a-pole symbol with two tassels and a standard with a rectangle base and two short legs.[35]

All other items from Jerusalem and its vicinity were found in mixed, later, or unstratified contexts, and thus the timespan of their use cannot be determined.[36] The many scenarios for reconstructing the biography of these artifacts should be considered, just like the possible circumstances that led to their appearance in the southern Levant. After all, even if manufactured in Sargonid Assyria, the continuous Levantine–Mesopotamian interaction that characterizes the post-Assyrian era under the Neo-Babylonian and Achaemenid Empires provides ample paths for such importation.[37] The

---

33. Ornan, "Mesopotamian Influence on the Glyptic of Israel," 307–8 no. 38; Keel, *Von Tel el-ʿIdham bis Tel Kitan*, 336–37 no. 131.

34. Baruch Brandl, "Bullae with Figurative Decoration," in *Inscriptions*, vol. 6 of *Excavations at the City of David 1978–1984 Directed by Yigael Shiloh*, ed. Donald T. Ariel, Qedem 41 (Jerusalem: Institute of Archaeology of the Hebrew University of Jerusalem, 2000), 63–65 no. B 48, figs. 10 and 11.

35. Beck, "A Neo-Assyrian Bulla," 194–96.

36. These include a seal and two bullae from the eastern slope dump in the City of David at Jerusalem (Ariel Winderbaum, "The Iconic Seals and Bullae of the Iron Age," in vol. 1 of *The Summit of the City of David Excavations 2005–2008: Final Reports*, ed. Eilat Mazar [Jerusalem: Shoham Academic Research and Publications, 2015], 366–68 no. 2 and fig.7.2, 385–87 no. 7 fig. 7.13 and no. 8 fig. 7.15), a seal from Tell en-Nasbeh Stratum I (dated to 750–350 BCE) (Chester Charlton McCown, *Tell en-Nasbeh I: Excavated under the Direction of the Late William Frederic Bade* [New Haven: American Schools of Oriental Research, 1947], 206 no. 51 and pl. 54:51), and a rectangle plaque from a Persian–Hellenistic context at Khirbet Tubeiqa (Ovid R. Sellers, *The Citadel of Beth-Zur* [Philadelphia: Westminster, 1933], 59 fig. 50.5).

37. Noteworthy in this regard is the special connection between King Nabonidus of Babylonia and the city of Harran and the moon god; see Groß, "Ḥarrān als kulturelles Zentrum," 145–47. This importation continued even later, during the Hellenis-

limited evidence from Jerusalem, consisting of a seal and a bulla of yet-to-be-determined provenance, coupled with the insecure or late stratigraphic contexts of all other artifacts, should deter scholars from suggesting widespread Assyrian impact on the Judahite religion.

Clearly, there could have been individuals in Jerusalem who were fascinated by the Moon God of Harran and worshiped him, but at the same time this iconography could have served local moon deities. The worship of such deities is most visible through glyptics found in the desert fringe: The bulla from Ḥorvat ʿUza is joined by a composite-material cylinder seal from Tel Malḥata Stratum IIIA (fig. 6.3:4) featuring a uraeus and a plant on a double groundline, a composition that echoes a scene consisting of a crescent-on-a-pole, a uraeus, and a tree.[38] These images were preceded by a cylinder seal (fig. 6.3:5) depicting an anthropomorphic figure, an ostrich, a rhomb, the Pleiades, and a crescent and a scaraboid (fig. 6.3:6) depicting a crescent, above which there seems to be a standard, both from the Iron IIB fortress at Tel Arad Stratum IX.[39] An earlier piece from late Iron IIA Tel Arad Stratum XI should be considered as well (fig. 6.3:7): a limestone plaque depicting a linear engraving of a T-shaped object, crossed by two additional horizontal lines and crowned by two small semicircles, is flanked by two large semicircles to the right and two circles to the left—a composition that might depict a tree flanked by celestial beings.[40]

In light of this, it may be concluded that the appearance of the iconography of the Moon God of Harran in Iron IIC Judah, as far as testified by stratified artifacts, is restricted to a handful of artifacts. These, especially from the desert fringe, should be understood against the background of the earlier appearance of similar icons in the same region and beyond.[41]

---

tic period. See, e.g., a second-millennium cylinder seal with an eighth-century BCE inscription found at a second-century BCE temple at Tel Beer-sheva (Ornan, Tallay, "On the Dating of Some Middle Assyrian Cylinder Seals," *NABU* 3 [2003]: 72).

38. Ziffer, "Iron Age Stamp Seals," 519 no. 5 and fig. 6.5.

39. For the cylinder seal, see Aharoni, "Iron Age Cylinder Seal," 52–54; Ornan, "Mesopotamian Influence on the Glyptic of Israel," 345 no. 125; Ziffer, "Iron Age Stamp Seals," 516–17. For the scaraboid, see Keel, *Von Tell Abu Farağ bis ʾAtlit*, 654–55 no. 24; Ornan, "Mesopotamian Influence on the Glyptic of Israel," 323–24, no. 63.

40. Keel, *Von Tell Abu Farağ bis ʾAtlit*, 656–57, no. 31.

41. See stamped handles from Tel Hazor Stratum X (Keel, *Von Tel Gamma bis Chirbet Husche*, 590–91 no. 23) and from Tell el-Farʿah (N) Stratum VIIB (Othmar Keel, *Von Tell el-Farʿa-Nord bis Tell el-Fir*, vol. 3 of *Corpus der Stempelsiegel-Amulette aus Palästina/Israel: Von den Anfängen bis zur Perserzeit*, OBO.SA 31 [Fribourg: Aca-

The impact of the Moon God of Harran lay therefore less in the shape of direct religious changes that included the embracing of new icons and new religious concepts and was rather an appropriation of imperial iconography for the local lunar deity (or deities).

6.4. Concluding Remarks

In summation, this short contribution aimed at exploring the various faces of icon localization in colonial situation.[42] The first is the rosette, a dominant icon in imperial pictorial language that became the icon of the Jerusalemite court in an act of usurpation: the Assyrian symbol was transformed to represent the reclaimed Judahite sovereignty following the collapse of the empire. The second case is the iconography of the Moon God of Harran, the chief Assyrian deity in the West: icons and complete scenes were localized in the southern Levant, updating in most cases an already existing iconography of local lunar deities.

In addition, these two cases emphasize the complexity of the encounters between the many agents active in the southern Levant during the days of Assyrian colonialism. While the local elite had contact with Assyrian officials (and even the court itself), they and other people interacted with additional individuals and groups that arrived from the Assyrian heartland and elsewhere, coming from diverse social roles and backgrounds, and it would be a mistake to present each newcomer as influencing the local population. The many nodes of the Assyrian network, whether they were imperial centers, trading stations, local centers, or other means, were diversely interrelated and manned by various kinds of agents, as there were constant movements of soldiers, deportees dislocated from other parts of the empire, alongside merchants, immigrants, and other individuals and groups, each with their own personality, past, status, and aim.

In other words, the variability of encounters precludes the formulation of any generalized reconstruction as to why and how a specific artifact was brought to its final deposition and why some icons and scenes were accepted and added to the local repertoire, while others were not. The individual appropriation of any practice or idea is contextualized in

---

demic Press; Göttingen: Vandenhoeck & Ruprecht, 2010], 6–7 no. 9). See also a seal from Cemetery 100 at Tell el-Farʿah (S) (Keel, *Von Tell el-Farʿa-Nord bis Tell el-Fir*, 110–11 no. 193).

42. See, already, Keel and Uehlinger, *Gods, Goddesses, and Images of God*, 286–87.

frequently changing societal circumstances, mechanisms that determine what is attractive, luxurious, and symbolic, and the way one group perceives the other. It is the fortunate mission of scholars to untangle the theoretical and material meshwork that would shed some light on the complex colonial encounters during these formative years in the history of the southern Levant.

Hezekiah's Cultic Reforms according to the Archaeological Evidence

David Rafael Moulis

Religious reforms during King Hezekiah's reign, based on archaeological records from the various Iron Age II Judean sites, such as Tel Arad, Beer-sheba, Lachish, and others, reveal cultic changes from a new point of view. At these sites, remains of the Iron Age II cultic places were discovered. Among them the altars, incense burners, standing stones, shrines, and more findings were found during the last few decades. No later than the end of the eighth century BCE, shrines were dismantled and destroyed under the influence of only one reform—probably Hezekiah's religious, military, and economic centralization. Nevertheless, events at Lachish occurred earlier than the end of the eighth century BCE. This could be considered a long-term process that might have been finished before Assyria's campaign against Judah in 701 BCE. However, the performance took different forms at every site, which shows that the command from Jerusalem required eliminating cultic activity outside the capital. How to realize reforms was not clearly defined and it probably depended on the local authority.

7.1. Introduction

The most important cultic events of the late eighth century BCE took place during the reign of King Hezekiah. According to the biblical text it is possible to classify him as an archetype of King David (2 Kgs 18:3). He achieved fame for his reforms (not only cultic reformation) and for now this fact is the most significant. We read in 2 Kings and 2 Chronicles the following descriptions about his activities:

> He removed the high places, broke down the pillars, and cut down the sacred pole. He broke in pieces the bronze serpent that Moses had made,

for until those days the people of Israel had made offerings to it; it was called Nehushtan. (2 Kgs 18:4 NRSV)

Now when all this was finished, all Israel who were present went out to the cities of Judah and broke down the pillars, hewed down the sacred poles, and pulled down the high places and the altars throughout all Judah and Benjamin, and in Ephraim and Manasseh, until they had destroyed them all. Then all the people of Israel returned to their cities, all to their individual properties. (2 Chr 31:1 NRSV)

The biblical text does not give the details of the destruction of cultic places, images, and high places. We do not know when, where, and exactly how it happened. For more details, it is necessary to focus on archaeological records. It is clear, according to the archaeological evidence, that in the eighth century BCE official cultic places existed in Judah. It is believed that these places (e.g., Tel Arad, Beersheba, Moza, and likely Tel Lachish) were dismantled in the same century. Two Judahite shrines of the First Temple period were discovered at Tel Arad (in 1963) and Tel Moza (in 2012). Besides this, archaeologists unearthed a large, dismantled incense altar at Beersheba and cultic rooms at Lachish and Tel Halif. All of these sites, with the exception of Tel Halif, were characteristically part of the official Judahite cult under royal control.

7.2. Tel Moza Temple

On the western periphery of modern Jerusalem sits the site of Tel Moza. In 2012, a most fascinating building was excavated—an Iron Age II temple. This temple is the second Judahite temple ever uncovered in Israel up to now. Archaeologists initially thought that they had found two strata of a comparable composition that looked similar to two historical phases known from the Arad temple. The first stratum of Building 500 was identified as a temple complex and was dated by Shua Kisilevitz to the early Iron Age II period, tenth–ninth century BCE. Due to unclear evidence for the continuation of the building in its second phase as a temple, it is called the monumental public "Building 500" and is dated to the seventh or the early sixth century BCE.[1] Originally the sanctuary consisted of the main hall, a

---

1. Shua Kisilevitz, "The Iron IIA Judahite Temple at Tel Moza," *TA* 42 (2015): 148–50.

courtyard with an altar, and five standing stones (cultic stelae). Later, when the building was rebuilt, the same situation occurred as at Arad. The floor level was filled and raised with a thick layer of fill and clusters of plaster. Building 500 was built up over the new level and cultic artifacts (such as lower levels of the temple walls, altar, refuse pit, and podium) were buried under the late Iron Age II walls.[2] Close to the sacrificial altar were bones of cultic animals, cultic objects, and also pottery that was found in a pit covered with a layer of ash. Some of these objects had a cultic character. Near this pit, the fragments of pottery figurines and the lower part of an incense burner with petals were found. A similar type is known from Tel Arad. All cultic objects were deliberately damaged and covered by a layer of ash.

This cultic place is the first evidence of changes in the religion during the Iron Age II of Judah, specifically a Judahite temple. The main altar and temple were covered with a layer of earth during the eighth century BCE.[3] It is impossible to date it better due to the unclear relations between two strata of the temple and Building 500. The cultic site at Moza ended in a similar way to the Arad temple, however, more than one hundred years later. Although we presume that Building 500 did not serve as a temple any longer, the reform happened sometime during the eighth century BCE. Moza could be the earliest sign of the long-term process or natural development of the official Judahite religion. The temple itself is the earliest Iron Age II shrine ever found in Judah. The cultic changes could be dated before the reign of King Hezekiah, but likely to the time of his rule over the kingdom of Judah as another Judahite site with cultic remains.

7.3. Tel Arad Temple

Tel Arad was one of the largest Canaanite city-states and was abandoned at the end of the Early Bronze Age II. It was occupied again after more than

---

2. Kisilevitz, "Iron IIA Judahite Temple," 156.

3. Shua Kisilevitz, "Cultic Finds from the Iron Age in the Excavations at Moza," *New Studies in the Archaeology of Jerusalem and Its Region: Collected Papers*, ed. Guy D. Stiebel et al., vol. 7 (Jerusalem: Israel Antiquities Authority; The Hebrew University of Jerusalem; The Jerusalem Development Authority, 2014), 38–43; and Zvi Greenhut and Alon De Groot, *Salvage Excavations at Tel Moza: The Bronze and Iron Age Settlements and Later Occupations*, IAAR 39 (Jerusalem: Israel Antiquities Authority, 2009), 50–54, 219–27.

1,500 years during the eleventh century BCE. A small open village (Stratum XII) was built on the southeastern ridge of Canaanite Arad. According to Yohanan Aharoni, the village was transformed into a fortress in the tenth century BCE (Stratum XI).[4] From the same period, the Israelite shrine and a square sacrificial altar were discovered in the northern corner of the fortress.[5] The sanctuary was partly enlarged in Stratum X after demolition. Furthermore, the altar was abolished in the late eighth century BCE (Stratum VIII) by Hezekiah, but the shrine was used until the end of the seventh century BCE (Stratum VII). The last chance to see the complete temple was in the next Stratum (VI). In Stratum VI the casemate wall was cut into the temple, which supported Aharoni's idea that the sanctuary was not functioning at that time. Aharoni came to the conclusion that this was evidence of two phases of the cultic centralization under Hezekiah and Josiah, as is written in the Old Testament. The first step was Hezekiah's prohibition of sacrifice, while the second step was the centralization of worship in Jerusalem during the time of Josiah.[6] The Arad researchers later moved the decommissioned temple and the altar to the same time as Stratum VIII at around 715 BCE in the first year of Hezekiah's reign.[7] Ze'ev Herzog, after his revision, claimed that the sanctuary and the offering altar existed in only two layers (Strata X and IX) that he postdated to the middle and the second half of the eighth century BCE.[8] The temple complex was already buried in Strata VIII and VII. There is no connection between the abolishment of the temple and Stratum VI because the casemate wall that Aharoni dated to this stratum belonged to the later Hellenistic period.[9] Inside the temple area, it is possible to distinguish only two floors (the lower floor is from Stratum X and above it is the floor from Stratum IX). According to Herzog, the abolishment of the sanctuary is stratigraphi-

---

4. Yohanan Aharoni, "Arad: Its Inscriptions and Temple," *BA* 31 (1968): 4–5.

5. Aharoni, "Arad: Its Inscriptions and Temple," 6, 18–19.

6. Aharoni, "Arad: Its Inscriptions and Temple," 26.

7. Yohanan Aharoni, "Arad," in *Encyclopaedia of Archaeological Excavations in the Holy Land*, ed. Michael Avi-Yonah (Englewood Cliffs: Prentice-Hall, 1978), 76; Ze'ev Herzog et al., "The Israelite Fortress at Arad," *BASOR* 254 (1984): 19–22.

8. Ze'ev Herzog, "The Fortress Mound at Arad: An Interim Report," *TA* 29 (2002): 14, 50.

9. Ze'ev Herzog, "Perspectives on Southern Israel's Cult Centralization: Arad and Beer-sheba," in *One God–One Cult–One Nation: Archaeological and Biblical Perspectives, ed. Reinhard G. Kratz and Hermann Spieckermann, BZAW 405 (Berlin: de Gruyter, 2010), 169, 172.

cally clear because the floor of Stratum VIII covered all parts of the temple walls, the height of which was reduced before Stratum VIII.[10]

Some scholars disagree with the conclusions of the Arad team and they suggest that the shrine was used until after the end of Stratum IX when the city was destroyed by Sennacherib in 701 BCE (e.g., Nadav Na'aman).[11] Diana Edelman suggests that the end of the shrine was under the influence of new occupiers in Stratum VII.[12] The new political regime controlled the Arad fortress and it closed the temple that had been dedicated to the defeated deity—YHWH. The new inhabitants respected the sanctity of the fallen god. They buried his cultic objects such as altars and *masseboth* (standing stones). They did not need to rebuild a sanctuary for their deity over the previous holy site. The stratigraphy of many loci is unclear, and it is impossible to determine if there was any destruction between Strata IX and VIII. Arad was probably not destroyed by Sennacherib, but rather Hezekiah surrendered it and Stratum VIII may have been controlled by the Arab leader Asuhili. This possibility is plausible, because there is no proof that the city was destroyed during Sennacherib's campaign.[13]

The temple area (a main room [*hekal*], a broad room and a holy of holies [*debir*], standing stones, two incense altars, a square stone altar, and a courtyard with side rooms) was well preserved (figs. 7.1 and 7.2). This could be a sign that it was preventively saved and buried from the enemy's eyes so that later it could be restored and reused. Such a practice protected holy places and ritual objects in ancient times before attackers defiled them. Usually sacred places were buried after destruction and it had a fate similar to human burial—burial forever. According to Herzog's revision, the Arad sanctuary and its altar were covered by dirt by order of Hezekiah before Sennacherib's campaign through Judah. The altars and *massebah* were buried in a pit above the steps. The pit was dug into

---

10. It is impossible to imagine that the courtyard with the altar and surrounding area filled with approximately 0.9–1.3 m thick layer of soil that the main hall was still in use. The difference in elevation between these two parts of the temple made it unapproachable, and, moreover, no stairs were found there. See Herzog, "Perspectives on Southern Israel's Cult Centralization," 173–74.

11. Nadav Na'aman, "The Abandonment of Cult Places in the Kingdoms of Israel and Judah as Acts of Cult Reform," *UF* 34 (2002): 589–92.

12. Diana Edelman, "Hezekiah's Alleged Cultic Centralization," *JSOT* 32 (2008): 407.

13. Edelman, "Hezekiah's Alleged Cultic Centralization," 410.

the floor of Stratum X.[14] It is very difficult to determine why and when this change occurred, but most scholars agree that it was abandoned in the second half of the eighth century BCE. Despite the fact that the fortress of Stratum IX indicated evidence of destruction, inside the temple itself nothing was found to be reminiscent of destruction or burning. This means that the sanctuary and its cultic objects were abolished and buried before the Arad fortress was attacked and destroyed by the Assyrian army after only a short period of existence of fifty to eighty years.[15] At Arad we have an accurate example of controlled decommissioning and the burying ritual typical of cultic objects across the ancient Near East. This style of burying and sealing parts of the sacred architecture and equipment is characteristic of other places, however every site is characterized by different ritual customs (see below).

7.4. Beersheba Altar

The large horned burning altar from the ninth century BCE (Stratum III) was discovered at Beersheba in 1973. It was not found pillared, but it was dismantled, and its ashlar stones were reused for a public storehouse (also known as the "pillared house") in the eighth century BCE (Stratum II). Three of the four horns were discovered intact in the wall and the fourth horn was removed. Other stones were found in the same wall and others lay in the fill of the rampart on the slope outside the gate.[16] The secondary use of these stones for public buildings and the removal of the single horn indicate that they were not meant for inhabitants because they did not have sacred importance.[17] Aharoni concluded that the horned altar was dismantled during Hezekiah's reign (fig. 7.3). At the same time the storehouse was built as a new project associated with guarding and protecting one of the strategic sites when the Assyrians threatened Judah. The public storehouse was finally destroyed by the Assyrian army under Sennacherib in 701 BCE.[18]

---

14. The same remains of plaster were discovered on the altars and close to the wall where they were standing originally. Herzog, "Perspectives on Southern Israel's Cult Centralization," 169, 174.

15. Herzog, "Perspectives on Southern Israel's Cult Centralization," 175.

16. Yohanan Aharoni, "The Horned Altar of Beer-sheba," *BA* 37 (1974): 2–3.

17. Herzog, "Perspectives on Southern Israel's Cult Centralization," 176.

18. Aharoni, "Horned Altar of Beer-sheba," 6.

Fig. 7.1. Tel Arad, holy of holies.
Photograph by author.

Fig. 7.2. Tel Arad, offering altar (reconstruction at the site). Photograph by author.

Fig. 7.3. Reconstruction of the Beersheba altar. Drawing by author.

Other later theories questioned some of the conclusions. For example, dating the end of Stratum II (701 BCE) is problematic; the location of the altar and the possible sanctuary that was never discovered is highly debated (fig. 7.4).[19] There is no destruction layer between Strata II and III that would help to distinguish two different levels. According to Aharoni, two different phases were identified at some structures. These two phases of the same city existed almost two hundred years.[20] During these years the altar was dismantled, and its stones were transferred for secondary use. Although one of the altar's stones was discovered in the retaining wall that is dated to Stratum III, this wall could have fallen, and therefore it was fixed with later material from Stratum II.[21] The storehouse was used in Stratum III and II and Aharoni claimed that it was difficult to see the differences between these strata. For example, the line of the wall of Stratum II has a different position than the previous one. This is a significant fact as to the separation of the two different strata.[22] Although there is no direct archaeological evidence about the existence of the temple at Beersheba during the Iron Age IIA period, it is very difficult to imagine such an urbanist city without a legitimate sanctuary. Instead of the main cultic object (the altar), in Beer-sheba an Iron Age krater was discovered with an inscription of three Hebrew letters *q-d-sh* meaning *qodesh* (*holiness* or *holy*).[23] The inscription means

---

19. Robb Andrew Young, *Hezekiah in History and Tradition*, VTSup 155 (Leiden: Brill, 2012), 96.

20. Yohanan Aharoni, "Stratification of the Site," in *Beer-Sheba I: Excavations at Tel Beer-Sheba, 1969–1971 Seasons*, ed. Yohanan Aharoni, Publications of the Institute of Archaeology 2 (Tel Aviv: Tel Aviv University, Institute of Archaeology, 1973), 5.

21. Young, *Hezekiah in History and Tradition*, 97.

22. Herzog, "Perspectives on Southern Israel's Cult Centralization," 176.

23. Yohanan Aharoni, "Excavations at Tel Beer-sheba," *BA* 35 (1972): 126.

that the object belonged to or was dedicated to the temple. Usually it was used by a priest in a cultic ceremony. Similar inscriptions were found on two identical ceramic bowls from Arad Stratum X. The second interpretation means *kodesh kohanim* (*holy to the priests*—letters *qoph* and *kaph* rather than *qoph* and *shin*).[24] If this is correct the first or the second interpretation of the letters both had very close relation with cult or temple staff.

Fig. 7.4. Beersheba, possible place where the altar and shrine were located. Photograph by author.

Changes in the Beersheba cult could evince similarities with Arad. Some parts of the sacrifice altar were buried, but were not sealed, but rather were used for secular public construction. More significant is that everything was completely dismantled without any visible remembrance of the holiness of the objects (compared to Arad and Moza).

---

24. Herzog, "Fortress Mound at Tel Arad," 56.

7.5. Lachish Cultic Assemblages and the "Gate-Shrine"

Lachish was the second most important city in Judah after Jerusalem. It was a military and administrative center in the Shephelah. We know almost nothing about the Iron Age official cult that was in the Lachish stronghold. Since the city was besieged and destroyed by the Assyrians in 701 BCE and we also have extrabiblical sources (the relief at the royal palace at Nineveh and annals), it is easier to work with archaeological data from this site. The question is what was depicted on the relief at Nineveh. There is no doubt that Lachish is really mentioned on the relief because a cuneiform text states the name of the city as Lachish. Depicted on the relief, Assyrian soldiers are carrying an incense burner. Where was the incense burner originally stored? We also do not know if this was only a symbolic act or if the army really plundered some cultic place; from the relief it is impossible to say something specific about the supposed existence of a Judahite sanctuary. Aharoni claimed that he found a Judahite sanctuary (cult room 49) and a high place in Stratum V. Stratum V was the first Iron Age settlement that was transformed into the fortified city of Stratum IV. Both Strata V and IV are dated to the Iron Age IIA. Stratum IV was probably destroyed by an earthquake in 760 BCE.[25] According to Aharoni this small broad room was a sanctuary with benches along the walls. A raised platform (*bamah*) was found in the corner. Furthermore, a broken stele (*massebah*), a limestone altar, pottery vessels, chalices, incense burners, lamps, and more ceramic equipment were uncovered among cultic objects in the area of a later Hellenistic temple.[26] Close to the *bamah* a black ash-dump was identified by Aharoni as an olive tree—*asherah*.[27] Revision of the sanctuary leads to the conclusion that this structure consisted of several structures of different strata (at least four phases). The *bamah* was probably part of the mud-brick wall. From the original photographs there is no clear evidence of destruction. Moreover, the cultic objects were buried in a circle at different elevations. Some

25. David Ussishkin, "Synopsis of Stratigraphical, Chronological, and Historical Issues," in *The Renewed Archaeological Excavations at Lachish (1973–1994)*, ed. David Ussishkin, 4 vols., Sonia and Marco Nadler Institute of Archaeology Monograph Series 22 (Tel Aviv: Emery and Claire Yass Publications in Archaeology, 2004), 1:76.

26. Yohanan Aharoni, "The Sanctuary and High Place," in *Investigation at Lachish? The Sanctuary and the Residency (Lachish V)*, Publications of the Institute of Archaeology 4 (Tel Aviv: Gateway, 1975), 26–28.

27. Aharoni, "Sanctuary and High Place," 30.

of them mimicked the shape of the edge of the rounded pit. The collection of vessels is very unique; therefore, it is impossible to assign it to a specific stratum. It seems that it was deposited into a pit not later than the beginning of Stratum III, when palace C was erected.[28] Ussishkin claimed that the sanctuary was part of the palace-fort courtyard and its cultic vessels, altar, and standing stone were all buried in the pit sometime in Stratum IV (IA IIB). At this time, it is believed that the cult room was not being used.[29] When the cultic objects were buried is still up for discussion, nevertheless it could have been during the reign of King Hezekiah as a "prelude" to other cultic changes. Robb Young states that it is unverifiable because there is no evidence of destruction by fire and Stratum IV is dated before Hezekiah's reign.[30] When we focus on the incense burner that is portrayed in the Lachish relief, it suggests the theory that it would have been an approved cultic object outside the official Solomon's temple in Jerusalem because at Arad the incense burners were found covered with fill. We are able to verify that the burner from Lachish was not an object from the temple, but it may have been confiscated by Assyrians from the palace.[31]

Another cultic structure was excavated in the area of the gate in 2016. This gate-shrine served as a small cultic room inside one of the chambers of the six-chamber gate. Excavators under the direction of Sa'ar Ganor and Yosef Garfinkel unearthed pottery bowls, oil lamps, and two small altars, originally with horns in their corners but later cut off as a result of cultic reforms. The shrine consists of benches and the holy of holies. Stamp impressions (*lmlk* and *lnhm avadi*) found helped to date the structure to the eighth century BCE, when King Hezekiah ruled over Judah.[32] A different style of desecration is evident on two altars without former horns and a toilet placed over the shrine. This form of desecration is also known from the Old Testament and is described as an act of King Jehu (ninth century BCE) from the Northern Kingdom: "Then they demolished the pillar of

---

28. Ussishkin, "Synopsis of Stratigraphical, Chronological, and Historical Issues," 105 and 107. Stratum III was destroyed by Sennacherib in 701 BCE, p. 76.

29. Ussishkin, "Synopsis of Stratigraphical, Chronological, and Historical Issues," 109.

30. Young, *Hezekiah in History and Tradition*, 98.

31. Young, *Hezekiah in History and Tradition*, 99–100.

32. Israel Antiquities Authority, "A Gate-Shrine Dating to the First Temple Period Was Exposed in Excavations of the Israel Antiquities Authority in the Tel Lachish National Park," https://tinyurl.com/SBL2643e.

Baal, and destroyed the temple of Baal, and made it a latrine to this day. Thus Jehu wiped out Baal from Israel" (2 Kgs 10:27–28 NRSV).

A completely new scenario of cultic reforms was uncovered at Lachish. The cultic objects, which were buried under the palace much earlier than the gate-shrine, were abandoned. Due to this, it is not possible to see some connection between these two remains of cultic life. If an official temple existed at Lachish, then, on the one hand, the cultic assemblages from the area of cultic room 49 had their origin in this shrine. The conclusion would be warranted that they were just buried in the rounded pit as cultic artifacts at Moza and Arad. On the other hand, another convincing deduction is that the gate-shrine was abandoned later, and it had its own cultic objects, which were uncovered in 2016. Thus we have two events in different years but in the same century having occurred again as a longer process of cultic reforms and its centralization.

7.6. Tel Halif Private Shrine

This archaeological site to the south of Lachish is positioned very close to Tel Arad and Beersheba. In 1992, the shrine room was discovered in Stratum VIB in one of the typical Iron Age four-room houses as part of a casemate wall. It was originally a domestic house, but later in the second phase it was remodeled into a shrine. A doorway was moved to the south side, more walls were added, and benches were likely built on the walls. The room contained pottery vessels, such as jars, a bowl, juglets and cooking pots, bone implements, pieces of pumice, and arrowheads as military objects from the time when Stratum VIB was destroyed. Other organic materials that were discovered included carbonized grape pips, cereals, legumes, and fish bones. The remains from the food lead us to the conclusion that everything was consumed or used in cultic rituals. As cultic artifacts it is possible to identify a white painted head of a female figurine (Judean/Judahite pillar figurine), a pottery stand from an incense altar, two flat stones with signs of fire (offering tables), and two limestone blocks. They could have served as standing stones or as a stand for cultic vessels.

The small shrine as a part of the private house was controlled and operated by women during the late eighth century BCE. It was destroyed with other Judahite sites by Sennacherib, at the same time.[33]

---

33. Oded Borowski, "Hezekiah's Reforms and the Revolt against Assyria," *BA* 58 (1995): 151.

How is it possible that this shrine was active later than other cultic sites in Judah? There are two possible answers. The first answer is that King Hezekiah reformed predominantly official state shrines and that he did not care about household cults. The second answer is that Hezekiah tolerated incense burning at the places where there were no sacrificial altars. This theory is supported by the Lachish reliefs from the Sennacherib palace at Nineveh.[34] We can see on the relief how the Assyrian army confiscated important objects of the kingdom (i.e., a king's throne) and cultic objects (incense burners). This scenery shows us that it occurred after 701 BCE at the time when we do not expect official shrines.

It is assumed that we have two archaeological sites (Tel Halif and Lachish) where the cults were not absolutely abolished. It is possible that at Tel Halif the cult was outside of the king's control and the reform did not affect its local private shrine.

7.7. Summary

Archaeological evidence of Hezekiah's reform had four potential sites: Tel Arad, Beersheba, Lachish, and Tel Moza. At Arad, Moza, and Lachish a similar situation was unearthed, the remains of the sanctuaries were discovered at these sites. They were partly dismantled at the end of their use and cultic objects, as well as altars, were carefully covered by earth (at Lachish by a stone object—a toilet was put over the sanctuary). This poses a question as to the style and how the cultic reform was practiced. The holy sites were abolished and desacralized but not dishonored or completely removed as in Beersheba and Lachish. For an overview of the cultic background, it is possible to use archaeological data from another Judahite site (Tel Halif) that indicates a different situation—the cult continued until Sennacherib's destruction in 701 BCE. We are able to identify four types of cultic changes or reforms according to archaeology in the kingdom of Judah. First, some sanctuaries were partly dismantled, and they were then buried with their components with respect to the holiness of these sites. This occurred at Arad and Moza. Second, some cultic objects (the altar at Beersheba and also shrines at Beersheba and Lachish—if we assume their existence in royal cities) were completely removed. Third, the sanctuary was strongly desecrated in the gate-shrine at Lachish. Fourth, at Tel Halif,

---

34. Borowski, "Hezekiah's Reforms and the Revolt against Assyria," 152.

we have something that was described as a household cult. According to finds from this site it is clear that this place was tolerated by authorities—the king—because nothing more "dangerous" than incense was sacrificed at this location. The best candidate for most of these cultic eliminations is King Hezekiah. He probably issued an order for the abolishment of all official cultic sites and also sites where various gods were worshiped by burning offerings, except for the Jerusalem temple and small household private shrines. Apparently, the king did not specify how to abolish them. Therefore, we have two close sites at Tel Arad and Beersheba where we have a totally different method of termination and removal of cultic installations. Hezekiah's cultic centralization had many aspects. Many of them are debatable and some direct connections are missing. First of all, the centralization had political and economic aims. During the end of the eighth century BCE it was necessary for King Hezekiah to centralize the government, military and religion to the capital city of Jerusalem.[35] Hezekiah prepared the kingdom of Judah for the Assyrian attack and, as it had been associated with control over the economy, to gather taxes and revenues from the cultic activity (pilgrims coming from across the country to worship in Jerusalem). He began new urbanism projects for the protection of Jerusalem (he fortified the Western Hill and the Siloam pool; he probably built a new tunnel from the Gihon Spring), he built new storehouses (Lachish), and others. He needed enough money, which the centralization was able to provide. For this paper it is not important if Hezekiah tried to organize the revolt against Assyria. It is without doubt that Assyria as an enemy of Judah had its role in Hezekiah's cultic reforms. Indeed, some cultic changes also happened before Hezekiah became the king of Judah (Lachish and Moza) and it may open a new question about the Judahite cult and its development. No doubt it is possible to claim that archaeological evidence uncovered a long-term process of the decline of official cultic places. To complete a mosaic of cultic changes and reforms, it will be necessary to find more "pieces of glass" to understand better what really happened in religion during the Judean kingdom from the tenth century BCE to the end of the eighth century BCE.

---

35. Herzog, "Perspectives on Southern Israel's Cult Centralization," 197.

Through a Glass Darkly:
Figurines as a Window on the Past

Josef Mario Briffa, SJ

The Iron Age figurines of the southern Levant are hardly a new topic, and any attempt to say something new may appear futile. The figurines are well known, particularly the so-called Asherahs, or Judean pillar figurines, and their understanding as cultic seems well established. A more careful look at the available literature, however, shows that there is plenty of room for further exploration. Better still, there is room to work at a more solid theoretical underpinning for the interpretation of the entire discourse on figurines.

This paper questions the current interpretative paradigms for the figurines of Judah and suggests that the figurines offered a means of representation and construction of social meanings, values, and concerns, in our case of Judah in the late Iron Age, a sort of window on the past that allows us to look "through a glass darkly," to borrow the New Testament reference (1 Cor 13:12) picked up powerfully in cinema and literature.[1]

8.1. The Prevailing Paradigm

A necessary first step in the process is to understand, and where necessary deconstruct, the prevailing paradigms, what questions are being asked, what is conditioning current readings. The questions asked necessarily condition the answers, with the risk getting stuck in a rut, either by asking questions which cannot really be answered, or missing out on the ones that can be.

---

1. Such as Ingmar Bergman's 1961 film by the same name, as well as several novels including ones by Jostein Gaarder (*I et speil, i en gåte* [Oslo: Aschehoug, 1993]) and Karleen Koen (*Through a Glass Darkly* [New York: Doubleday, 1986]).

Despite the abundant literature on the figurines of Judah, a review is surprisingly straightforward, with many of the question repeated, and theoretical underpinnings limited.[2] Most of the research has strongly focused on the Judean pillar figurines and reads them as relating to female and household religion. The major exponent of this in recent years has been Raz Kletter, who has proposed reading these figurines as representations of Asherah.[3] Kletter was not particularly original in this proposal and follows in a long line of interpretation—for example, William F. Albright and James Pritchard—that looked at the female figurines and linked them with female deities and female concerns.[4]

Kletter's doctoral work makes an interesting contribution but has tended now to be misdirected. The original project was, actually, not about the figurines and their interpretation, but rather about material culture that could help discuss and define the borders of Judah.[5] Kletter convincingly shows how the prevalence of the female figurine type with breasts, and a molded or pinched head is typical of Judahite contexts.[6] Unfortunately, the interpretation regarding their meaning, very tentative in the monograph itself, has become in some circles, and in Kletter's later papers and chapters, almost an established dogma, presumed correct and hardly discussed, if at all.[7]

---

2. See literature reviews in Raz Kletter, *The Judean Pillar-Figurines and the Archaeology of Asherah* (Oxford: Tempus Reparatum, 1996), 10–24; Erin Darby, *Interpreting Judean Pillar Figurines: Gender and Empire in Judean Apotropaic Ritual*, FAT 2/69 (Tübingen: Mohr Seibeck, 2014), 34–60; Josef M. Briffa, "The Figural World of the Southern Levant during the Late Iron Age" (PhD diss., UCL Institute of Archaeology, 2017), 28–49.

3. Kletter, *Judean Pillar-Figurines*, 81.

4. William F. Albright, "Astarte Plaques and Figurines from Tel Beit Mirsim," in *Mélanges syriens offerts à monsieur René Dussaud*, ed. Académie des inscriptions & belles-lettres (Paris: Geutner, 1939), 107–20; James B. Pritchard, *Palestinian Figurines in Relation to Certain Goddesses Known through Literature*, AOS 24 (New Haven: American Oriental Society, 1943).

5. Raz Kletter, "Selected Material Remains of Judah at the End of the Iron Age in Relation to its Political Borders" (PhD diss., Tel Aviv University, 1995). A summary was published as Kletter, "Pots and Polities: Material Remains of Late Iron Age Judah in Relation to Its Political Borders," *BASOR* 314 (1999): 19–54.

6. Kletter, *Judean Pillar-Figurines*, 43–48.

7. "[It] is not proven and should be taken for granted." Kletter, *Judean Pillar-Figurines*, 81. For later interpretations, see, e.g., John Day, *Yahweh and the Gods and Goddesses of Canaan*, JSOTSup 265 (Sheffield: Sheffield Academic, 2000), 227; William G.

Established dogmas in academia need to be questioned; often the premise on which they are based can be faulty. In the case of Judean pillar figurines, the premises seem rather clear: first, the Judean pillar figurines are read in isolation from the rest of the repertoire; second, in line with earlier authors like Pritchard and Albright, there is an underlying presumption of continuity between the plaque figurines of the Bronze Age, which were exclusively female, and the pillar figurines; third, a rather simplistic process of interpretation: breasts > female > fertility > goddess; fourth, in Kletter's sense, there is the assumption that we can therefore link female figurines to a female goddess, and therefore, in Judah's case, Asherah.[8] While it is likely, on both biblical and archaeological grounds, that Asherah was considered YHWH's consort in late Iron Age Judah, as would have been typical for the ancient Near East, and that the concept of monotheism only developed later, there is no necessary connection between a female figurine and a female divinity.[9]

Kletter's secondary suggestion was also that the figurines had some sort of apotropaic use. His argumentation in this respect is, unfortunately, rather weak: Kletter links the figurines with good/white magic because of " 'good' outward shape (smile, full face, 'offering' the breasts)."[10] It is rather a pity that Kletter strayed from his more secure archaeological grounds.

A more interesting work on the potential apotropaic use of the figurines comes from a more recent doctoral dissertation by Erin Darby. Besides studying the archaeological contexts, Darby provided a detailed study of figurine rituals from Assyria, which shed light on *potential* use of

---

Dever, *Did God Have a Wife? Archaeology and Folk Religion in Ancient Israel* (Grand Rapids: Eerdmans, 1995), 194; Raz Kletter and Katri Saarelainen, "Horses and Rider and Riders and Horses," in *Family and Household Religion: Toward a Synthesis of Old Testament Studies, Archaeology, Epigraphy, and Cultural Studies*, ed. Rainer Albertz et al. (Winona Lake, IN: Eisenbrauns, 2014), 216.

8. Both Pritchard and Albright include the figurines from both periods in their studies, cited above, with a focus on the Bronze rather than the Iron Age.

9. Second Kings (21:7; 23:6) places the Asherah in YHWH's temple in Jerusalem; and the well-known inscriptions from Kuntillet ʿAjrud and Khirbet el-Qôm both invoke YHWH and his Asherah (Shmuel Aḥituv, Esther Eshel, and Zeʾev Meshel, "The Inscriptions," in *Kuntillet ʿAjrud [Ḥorvat Teman]: An Iron Age II Religious Site on the Judah-Sinai Border*, ed. Zeʾev Meshel and Liora Freud [Jerusalem: Israel Exploration Society, 2012], 87–91, 95–100, 105–7; André Lemaire, "Les inscriptions de Khirbet el-Qôm et l'Asherah de Yhwh," *RB* 84 (1977): 595–608.

10. Kletter, *Judean Pillar-Figurines*, 77.

the figurines.[11] The study itself is very interesting, but the very different type of figurines—including the fact that the Assyrian ones seem to have been only ephemeral items, made for the one occasion, and completely destroyed afterward—indicate that the phenomenon we see in Judah is actually rather different.

A third possible interpretation that has been proposed, and especially so for the animal figurines, has been as playthings, as toys.[12] This label was often meant more as a means of dismissing their significance. Here P. R. S. Moorey is correct "that a terracotta might have been a children's toy is arguably the least interesting which might be said of it and no justification for then dismissing it out-of-hand as a cultural signifier within the society where it was made."[13]

Where each possibility has some merit and every answer can be equally true, with no way to differentiate between the various options, the truth is there is no answer at all but merely plausible hypotheses. At such a stage, it is important to go back to the drawing board and think again.

8.2. Theoretical Underpinnings:
Semiotics, Scottish Toilets, and Bletchley Park

One route that has not been sufficiently explored for the figurines is that of semiotics: how meaning is constructed, and how things can be interpreted. Rather tongue-in-cheek, a good starting point could be the problem of the Scottish toilets (see fig. 8.1). The figure, and the humor behind it, serves well its purpose here, whether the joke is understood immediately or not. Such humor can only work where a common (visual) language, and a common cultural register are shared. This simple

Fig. 8.1. The problem of Scottish toilets.

---

11. Darby, *Interpreting Judean Pillar Figurines*, 61–97.

12. E.g., William F. Albright, James L. Kelso, and J. Palin Thorley, *The Iron Age*, vol. 3 of *The Excavation of Tel Beit Mirsim*, AASOR 21–22 (New Haven: American Schools of Oriental Research, 1943), 82, 142.

13. Peter Roger Stuart Moorey, *Idols of the People: Miniature Images of Clay in the Ancient Near East*, Schweich Lectures (Oxford: Oxford University Press, 2003), 8.

joke is underpinned by a number of shared assumptions: (1) the difference in standard signage between toilets designated for men/women, (2) the understanding that the standard sign refers to gender rather than dress, such that a woman wearing trousers or a man wearing a kilt or cassock should know where to go anyway, (3) a knowledge that Scotsmen wear a kilt and that wearing a kilt does not make them question gender or orientation. While it is clear to us that such baggage is required to understand a simple joke, it is often presumed that Iron Age figurines can be read easily, even naively. Since the cultural register is generally lost, is there any hope to understand the figurines?

Rather than resign oneself to the impossibility of cracking the code, more recent history may suggest some solution. What lessons may be learned from places like Bletchey Park, the cypher school so instrumental in decoding encrypted German messages to provide the Allied Forces with precious intelligence? We may ask what can Bletchley (and semiotics) teach us in deciphering the figurines, if you allow me the term? First, *context*: it is far easier to decipher the single term within a wider context. Second, *repetition*: a message that is repeated, and one that is repeated with slight variations is easier to crack (often the predictability of certain messages made them possible to decipher). Third, *traffic analysis*: where the messaging is coming from, where it is directed to. Discussion on language and meaning is, of course, not new, and plenty has been written on the subject of semiotics, with important models for the understanding of the complex relation between signs/symbols and meaning, between signifier and signified, presented by Ferdinand de Saussure, Charles Peirce, and Umberto Eco (see fig. 8.2).[14] But what about the figurines? Can we apply the lesson of Bletchley, and those of semiotics to a better understanding of the figurines?

This study identified a number of essential criteria. First, the need to look at context: (1) context within the repertoire itself, since individual figurines do not stand in isolation, but form part of a repertoire, and (2) archaeological context, within a site and within the region, including the

---

14. For semiotics, see Daniel Chandler, *Semiotics: The Basics*, 2nd ed. (London: Routledge, 2007). Ferdinand de Saussure, *Course in General Linguistics*, ed. C. Bally and A. Sechehaye, trans. R. Harris (London: Duckworth, 1983), 66–68; Charles S. Peirce, *Principles of Philosophy*, vol. 1 of *Collected Papers of Charles Sanders Peirce*, ed. C. Hartshorne and P. Weiss (Cambridge: Harvard University Press, 1931), §339; Umberto Eco, *A Theory of Semiotics* (Bloomington: Indiana University Press, 1976), 71.

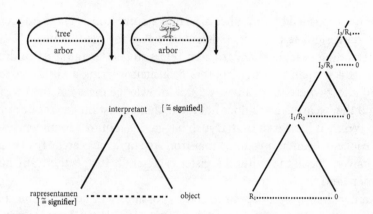

Fig. 8.2. Models of semiotics. Top left: Saussure's model of the signifier and signified; bottom left: Peirce's model of the sign; right: Eco's model of infinite semiosis.

attempt to differentiate between primary and secondary archaeological contexts. Second, as to the figurines themselves: (1) repetition and variation, since the figurines clearly fall within a predetermined set of types, yet have considerable variation, such that considering the different variables it may be possible to determine what is meaningful within the code and what may simply be accidental; (2) performative value of the figurines, not looking at the figurines as merely static objects.

8.3. Figurines in Jerusalem

Shifting focus from the theoretical to the more concrete, the figurines of Jerusalem will be considered as a case study.[15] After taking briefly into account the figurines as a repertoire, the paper will focus on two levels. First, on a site level, it will present the results of a detailed distribution study with a resolution on a locus level. Second, widening the view to a regional level, the figurines of Jerusalem can be placed in the context of the southern Levant.

---

15. Full details of the case study are in Briffa, "Figural World of the Southern Levant," 126–84.

8.3.1. Figurines as a Repertoire

As noted, it is important to remember that the figurines form a repertoire, often a rather limited set of types (see fig. 8.3), presented here in the form of a tag cloud. It is preferable to present them in such a nonstructured format, avoiding the usual discourse that tends to subordinate one type to another. If they are considered a repertoire, then it follows that it is more likely to understand their meaning if they are considered together. Moorey's observation is, in this regarded, very apt: "[The figurines] are like chessmen scattered randomly without either surviving boards to give them coherent relationships or guidelines for acting them out in ritualized play."[16]

quadrupeds   wild hoofed animals

wheels   **horses and rider**   couch/chair

birds   bovines   **female pillar figurines**

drummer   figurines holding a child

Fig. 8.3. Examples of figurine types from Jerusalem, presented as a tag cloud.

The figurine types from Jerusalem are as expected. Anthropomorphic types with molded or pinched heads, generally with breasts, occasionally holding an object. Sometimes a rider or other anthropomorphic type not more clearly defined. It should be noted that most figurines are found in a very fragmentary fashion, which makes it harder to compare like with like. Among other types are horses with or without rider, and other quadrupeds, often with hardly any detail. Some zoomorphic figures were clearly spouted and formed part of vessels. Occasionally, there are other types: birds, couches, and very rarely a shrine.[17]

The study of Jerusalem presented here was based on 729 figurine fragments (see fig. 8.4) that could be stratigraphically dated to the late Iron Age in Jerusalem, from the excavations of Yigal Shiloh and Kathleen Kenyon on the southeastern hill, Nachman Avigad in the Jewish Quarter, and the Eilat and Benjamin Mazar below the Temple Mount.[18] Adopting such a

---

16. Moorey, *Idols of the People*, 21.

17. Briffa, "Figural World of the Southern Levant," 130–33.

18. For Shiloh's excavations, see Diana Gilbert-Peretz, "Ceramic Figurines," in *Various Reports*, vol. 4 of *Excavations at the City of David, 1978–1985 Directed by Yigal Shiloh*, ed. Donald T. Ariel and Alon De Groot, Qedem 35 (Jerusalem: Institute of Archaeology, Hebrew University of Jerusalem, 1996); Kenyon's figurines have yet to be systematically published. The dataset is based primarily on Thomas A. Holland,

Description	Avigad	%	Kenyon	%	E. & B. Mazar	%	Shiloh Area B	%	Shiloh Area D	%	Shiloh Area E	%	Shiloh Area G	%	Total sample	%
Human head handmade			26	9	1	6			5	9	13	6	6	4	51	7
Human head moulded			8	3					1	2	3	1	3	2	15	2
Pillar figurine (with breasts)	1	6	35	12	1	6				0	6	3	5	4	48	7
Pillar figurine (with object)											2	1	2	1	4	1
Pillar? figurine (no breasts)											1	<1	1	1	2	<1
Human female torso moulded			1	<1											1	<1
Pillar figurine base			6	2					1	2	24	11	10	7	41	6
Human? other			2	1					1	2					3	<1
Rider			2	1											2	<1
Total Anthropomorphic	1	6	80	28	2	12	0	0	8	14	49	23	27	20	167	23
Horse-and-rider			11	4					1	2	10	5	5	4	27	4
Horse complete			8	3											8	1
Horse head			1	<1	2	12	.		5	9	31	14	13	10	52	7
Animal head	4	24	51	18	3	18					3	1	9	7	70	10
Animal body	8	47	87	31	9	53			21	38	42	20	34	25	201	28
Animal leg	3	18	22	8			2	50	14	25	56	26	34	25	131	18
Bird			8	3					2	4	2	1	1	1	13	2
Animal vessel spout			2	1	1	6									3	<1
Animal vessel									1	2					1	<1
Total Zoomorphic	15	88	190	69	15	88	2	50	44	79	144	67	96	71	506	69
Model couch			7	2			1	25			4	2	6	4	18	2
Model shrine			1												1	<1
Model wheel			1												1	<1
Fragment	1	6	6	2			1	25	4	7	17	8	7	5	36	5
Grand Total (=100%)	17		285		17		4		56		214		136		729	

Fig. 8.4. A statistical study of figurine types from Jerusalem.

"A Typological and Archaeological Study of Human and Animal Representations in the Plastic Art of Palestine" (PhD diss., Oxford University, 1975), Holland, "A Study of Palestinian Iron Age Baked Clay Figurines, with Special Reference to Jerusalem Cave 1," *Levant* 9 (1977): 121–55; and the finds registered in Kenyon's Jerusalem excavation archive in Manchester. For Avigad's excavations, see Irit Yezerski and Hillel Geva, "Iron Age II Clay Figurines," in *The Finds from Areas A, W and X-2*, vol. 2 of *Jewish Quarter Excavations in the Old City of Jerusalem*, ed. Hillel Geva (Jerusalem: Israel Exploration Society, 2003), 63–84. For the excavations by the Mazars, see Yonatan Nadelman, "Iron Age II Clay Figurine Fragments from the Excavations," in *Excavations in the South of the Temple Mount: The Ophel of Biblical Jerusalem*, ed. Eilat Mazar and Benjamin Mazar, Qedem 29 (Jerusalem: Institute of Archaeology, Hebrew University of Jerusalem, 1989), 123–27.

stratigraphic criterion was important methodologically: if any statistical comparison is to be attempted at all, it is necessary to provide some level of context.

Second, a quick glance also shows that the zoomorphic figurines, which essentially are horses or generic quadrupeds outnumber the anthropomorphic types by 69 percent to 23 percent. Since, as will be noted, there is no way of separating the types by archaeological context, any discourse that isolates the female anthropomorphic figurines from the rest is methodological vitiated. To follow the chess analogy, it would be like trying to figure out the rules of chess ignoring all the pawns.

8.3.2. Archaeological Contexts within the Site

The paper will now focus on two smaller areas of the southeastern hill of Jerusalem, taking a closer look at the archaeological context where such figurines were found. Two areas will be considered. First, since so much has been written about Cave I of Kenyon's excavation, it is important to return there. Second, Area E of Shiloh's excavation will be considered briefly, as it can provide a relatively wide area of excavation datable to Stratum 12, or the eighth century.

8.3.3. Jerusalem: Cave I

Any discussion on figurines needs to start with Cave I (see fig. 8.5): the number of figurines found in a single context had an important impact on figurine studies.[19] One of the rules of field archaeology is that the more interesting contexts are likely to turn up at the end of an excavation, and when time and funds are about to run out. Cave I of Kenyon's excavation is no exception.[20]

Kenyon interpreted Cave I as a *favissa*, a dump for ritual material relating to some sanctuary. She also understood Cave II and the surrounding complex, only a few meters to the southeast of Cave I as a sanctuary of some sort, with Cave II as a *favissa*, an altar-type installation in Area S, and two pillars understood as *massebot* in Area N.[21] Critics have long disputed her reading. The two pillars can be simply pillars to help support

---

19. Holland, "Study of Palestinian Iron Age Baked Clay Figurines."

20. Kathleen Kenyon, "Excavation in Jerusalem 1967," *PEQ* 100 (1968): 108.

21. Kenyon, "Excavation in Jerusalem 1967," 106–8.

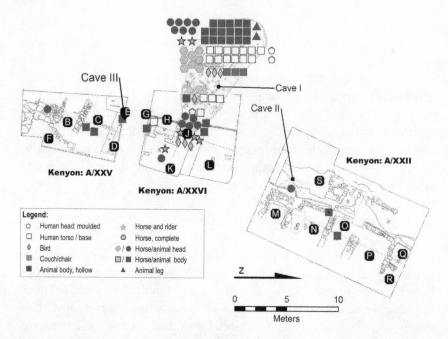

Fig. 8.5. Distribution of figurine types in Cave I area (Stratum 2 and Stratum 4). Composite plan showing Kenyon's A/XXII phase 2C (Franken and Steiner, *Excavations in Jerusalem*, 23, fig. 2.17), A/XXV–XXVI phase 4 (Franken and Steiner, *Excavations in Jerusalem*, 31, fig. 2.22), Cave I (Holland, "Study of Palestinian Iron Age Baked Clay Figurines," 135). Reproduced by the permission of the Council for British Research in the Levant, London.

a roof, and the installation on the upper ledge may well have served a more mundane purpose.[22] Other readings have been offered for the cave. Margreet Steiner has suggested that Cave I was a popular cult center (similar to the equally problematic Locus E207 in Samaria), surrounded by a guesthouse.[23] More recently, Darby has suggested that the cave may be linked

---

22. For the pillars, see Carl F. Graesser, "Standing Stones in Ancient Palestine," *BA* 35.2 (1972): 33–63. For the upper ledge, see Itzhak Eshel and Kay Prag, eds., *The Iron Age Cave Deposits on the South-East Hill and Isolated Burials and Cemeteries Elsewhere*, vol. 4 of *Excavations by K. M. Kenyon in Jerusalem 1961–1967* (Oxford: Oxford University Press, 1995), 216.

23. Henry J. Franken and Margreet L. Steiner, eds., *The Iron Age Extramural Quarter on the South-East Hill*, vol. 2 of *Excavations by K. M. Kenyon in Jerusalem 1961–1967* (Oxford: Oxford University Press, 1990), 49; Steiner, "Two Popular Cult

with pottery production; however, while the idea sounds interesting, none of the items that would generally be associated with pottery production—wasters, basalt wheels, slag, or ochre—have been found.[24]

Why all the excitement about Cave I? The answer lies in the sheer number of figurines. Figurines of all the various types were found in Cave I: Judean pillar figurines and other anthropomorphic types, horses and riders, bird, other wild animals, as well as other types of models and cultic material such as a model couch, a model shrine, a fenestrated stand, and more.[25]

Taking all data into consideration, what can really be concluded about the cave? The simplest and, alas, the least interesting answer may be the right one. First, considering the joins between the fragments, the figurines were broken *before* being dumped in Cave I, as some figurine fragments join with others in rooms close by.[26] Second, the pictures of the cave as found show how material in the cave was in a total mess, suggesting dumping.[27] The trench supervisor's observation in the field notebook is, therefore, rather pertinent: "There appear to be many more vessels closer to the entrance than further in. Does this fact coupled with their haphazard grouping suggest that they were cast in from the entrance, rather than carried in and carefully placed?"[28]

An objection may be raised, of course, that it may well be a dump, but a special ritual one, considering the number of figurine fragments. After all, Kenyon's description of the context as a *favissa* meant that she understood as a dump, albeit a cultic one. Within Kenyon's Area A itself, this view may seem justified, as figurine fragments were present elsewhere, but rather few. The picture changes, however, once other areas are included in the discussion.

Sites of Ancient Palestine: Cave 1 in Jerusalem and E 207 in Samaria," *SJOT* 11 (1997): 16–28.

24. Darby, *Interpreting Judean Pillar Figurines*, 131–35.

25. Holland, "Study of Palestinian Iron Age Baked Clay Figurines."

26. Fragments 7450 (A.965.35, Room G) and C.778 (Cave I); 7372 (A.965.20, Room H, Stratum 5) and C.374 (Cave I). See Briffa, "Figural World of the Southern Levant," 145–46.

27. Eshel and Prag, *Excavations by K. M. Kenyon*, 12–13.

28. Kenyon Archive, "Notebook 24," 67 (unpublished).

8.3.4. Jerusalem: Area E

Area E of Shiloh's excavation provides an important measure for comparison.[29] Even a cursory glance at a distribution map of the figurines (see fig. 8.6) is rather telling. The sheer number of figurine fragments found all over the area is striking, and these cannot be immediately associated with one structure as opposed to another. Equally striking is the general spread, such that it is hard to pin down one particular type to one particular building, but rather the repertoire is spread all over the site.[30] Taking into account this wider context, Cave I suddenly is less surprising and less particular.

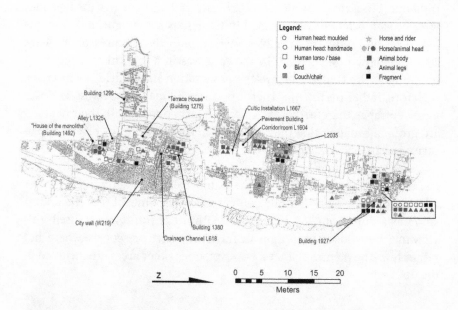

Fig. 8.6. Distribution of figurine types in Jerusalem Area E, Stratum 12. After De Groot and Bernick-Greenberg, *Excavations at the City of David*, plan 11, 32b, 47a, 47b. Reproduced with the permission of the Institute of Archaeology, The Hebrew University of Jerusalem.

---

29. Alon De Groot and Hannah Bernick-Greenberg, eds., *Area E; Stratigraphy and Architecture*, vol. 7A of *Excavations at the City of David 1978–1985 Directed by Yigal Shiloh*, Qedem 53 (Jerusalem: Institute of Archaeology, Hebrew University of Jerusalem, 2012).

30. See the detailed locus-by-locus study in Briffa, "Figural World of the Southern Levant," 160–69.

If one wanted to argue for an immediate cult connection, a potential shrine may be identified in Locus L1667. Ironically, however, only animal figurine fragments were found in the same room, rather than anthropomorphic ones, contrary to the received wisdom where the anthropomorphic figurines are more likely to be considered cultic.[31] Considering, however, how generally ubiquitous the animal figurines are, there is hardly any basis for a solid argument.

8.4. Regional Context

Expanding the perspective from Jerusalem is fundamental to place the discourse on the figurines within the wider regional context.[32] It must be said, for example, that while the Judean pillar figurine, as identified by Kletter, is typically Judahite as a stylistic type, the figurine repertoire fits well with the general set of types that are common throughout the southern Levant: female figurine, musicians (especially holding a hand-drum), horses and riders, and so on, with occasional types being restricted to some subregions, such as the boats, unsurprisingly found in Achziv and Tell Keisan, both on the Mediterranean coastal plain in the Galilee.

It is, therefore, important not to isolate the Judahite figurine phenomenon from the rest of the southern Levant, as what was happening in Judah and Jerusalem did not happen in isolation, but forms part of a wider picture. Unfortunately, a close study of the material shows the difficulty in comparing material statistically: before we can start comparing material and numbers, we need to set a level playing field. Any statistical comparison needs to narrow down on dates from a stratigraphic rather than stylistic point of view, with sufficient material that was adequately published. In many cases, this is lacking, and therefore the results are, by definition, rather limited.

This study, therefore, opted to consider three sites—Jerusalem, Lachish, and Megiddo—for a site-level analysis, and twenty sites, spread across the southern Levant, for a more regional study (see fig. 8.7). This provides a total dataset of 3099 fragments that could be stratigraphically dated to

---

31. Contra De Groot and Bernick-Greenberg, *Excavations*, 170. The numerous figurines they cite come from an adjacent room, from Locus L1604 classified as a fill in the locus register (De Groot and Bernick-Greenberg, *Excavations at the City of David*, 206).

32. Briffa, "Figural World of the Southern Levant," 276–380.

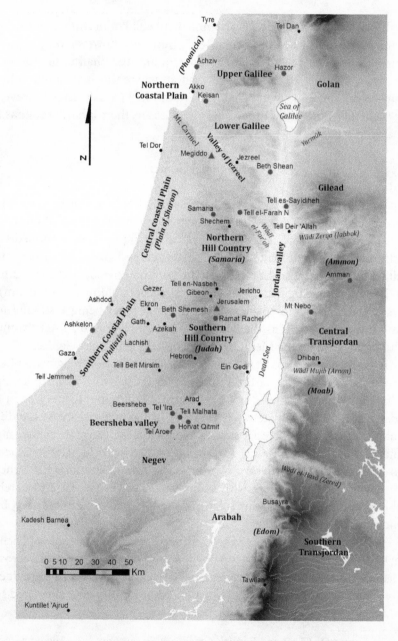

Fig. 8.7. Map of region with sites chosen for case study indicated with larger dots; triangles mark the three sites included both in the regional case study and the site-level case studies. Smaller dots mark a number of other significant sites in the region; map by author, using ArcGIS.

the late Iron Age.[33] Three aspects will be discussed here: manufacture, gender, and performative potential.

8.4.1. Manufacture

One first aspect that was looked into for regional analysis was the type of manufacture used in the figurines: solid pillar figurines, hollow pillar figurines, other solid types, high-relief plaques. Statistical tools were applied to the dataset, including correspondence analysis (see fig. 8.8), providing results that are interesting, if not unexpected. What appears particularly characteristic of different geographical areas were the type of manufacture: solid pillar figurines are typical of the southern hill country and the Shephelah, both of which can be identified as Judahite territory; hollow pillar types and high-relief plaques are typical in the southern coastal plain, northern hill country, the Galilee, and Jordan Valley.

8.4.2. Gender

Since past figurine studies have often focused on the figurines as female, it was also interesting to consider how gender is constructed in the figurines. As far as the contexts could be dated, there seems to be a shift from figurines that are more explicitly marked as female (showing both breasts and genitalia), to ones where gender is decreasingly biologically marked (only breasts represented), and finally to ones where biological markers are absent. It is interesting to ask, therefore, whether figurines that are not immediately gender marked (such as the drummer figurines from Achziv) were understood as female, in which case now gender is expressed socially/culturally rather than biologically, and whether it made any difference in the first place to the people who made and used these figurines.

From a theoretical standpoint, it is also important to go beyond the type of dichotomies proposed by scholars such as William Dever, who seems to divide the world rather rigidly in two—male/female, official/popular, and so on.[34] In this respect, contemporary gender theory is rather refreshing: while it important not to impose a twenty-first century

---

33. Briffa, "Figural World of the Southern Levant," 278.
34. Dever, *Did God have a Wife*, 5.

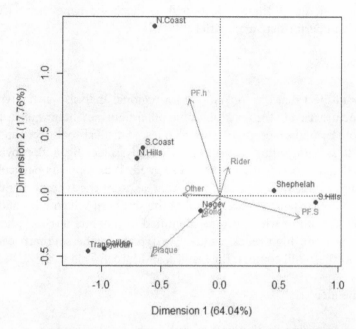

Fig. 8.8. Correspondence analysis plot of major manufacturing types across the different subregions (n=495).

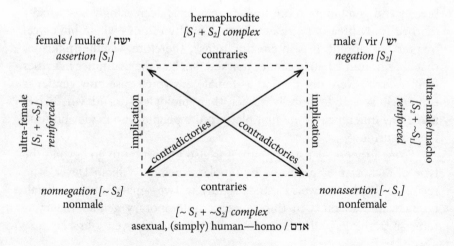

Fig. 8.9. Greimas's semiotic square applied to gender.

view of the world on ancient societies, it can help remind us how gender is very strongly culturally constructed. Applying Algirdas Greimas's semiotic square to explore the possible variety of gender representation may provide an interesting route beyond the male/female binary (see fig. 8.9).[35] In particular, it is interesting to note that in all the figurine fragments, male sexuality is hardly, if ever, marked. Yet, it seems clear that not every nonfemale figurine was necessarily intended as male. Which, once more highlights how gender, in the figurines, is increasingly a cultural construct.

8.4.3. Performance

A third aspect that may provide a further avenue for research is the *performative* potential of the figurines. In this, the figurines themselves can physically provide a useful indicator: some figurines can stand on their own feet, while others clearly need to be held in some way or other, and others (such as some zoomorphic figurines) can be used for pouring (see fig. 8.10). These characteristics provide some indication of potential use of the different elements of the repertoire as part of a performance of some sort.

Read in this light the apparent shift away from the high-relief plaque toward the pillar types (see fig. 8.11) may reflect a shift from a figurine

Type	Characteristic	Performative potential
Appliques to stands, etc.	Fixed	Static
Hollow and solid pillar figurines	Free standing	Handled or placed
Horses-and-riders		
Solid zoomorphic figurines		
Model couches, chariots, boats		
Plaque figurines in high relief	Nonfreestanding	Handled
Peg figurines		
Anthropomorphic vessels	Vessel	Receiving or pouring of liquids
Zoomorphic vessels		
Architectural models	Container	Receiving an image (?)

Fig. 8.10. Performative potential of figurines.

---

35. Algirdas J. Greimas, "La structure élémentaire de la signification en linguistique," *L'Homme* 3.3 (1964): 5–17.

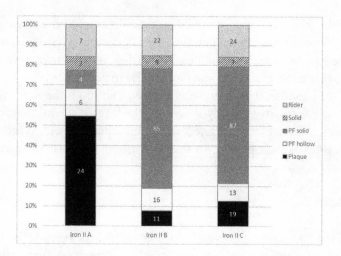

Fig. 8.11. Bar graph comparing the distribution of the main figurine types across the various periods (n=395).

practice where figurines were meant to be handheld to one where they are rather placed.

Unfortunately, the study was only able to touch the tip of the iceberg in this regard, and there is potential for further study. A major limitation is often the quality of the dataset that is currently available, which depends highly on the quality of excavation and publication. As excavations undertaken a few decades ago slowly come to publication, such as Ramat Raḥel and Beersheba, to mention but two, there is hope that more detailed contextual study will indeed be possible.[36]

8.5. Conclusions

Finally, we can draw some conclusions.

First, the figurines always need to be discussed as part of a repertoire of figurines: no single type can and should be isolated to make any sense

---

36. Oded Lipschits, Yuval Gadot, and Liora Freud, *Ramat Raḥel III: Final Publication of Yohanan Aharoni's Excavations (1954, 1959–1962)*, Sonia and Marco Nadler Institute of Archaeology Monograph Series 35 (Winona Lake, IN: Eisenbrauns, 2016); Ze'ev Herzog and Lily Singer-Avitz, eds., *Beer-Sheba III: The Early Iron IIA Enclosed Settlement and the Late Iron IIA–Iron IIB Cities*, Sonia and Marco Nadler Institute of Archaeology Monograph Series 33 (Winona Lake, IN: Eisenbrauns, 2016).

as a system/code, and regional variations can and should be noted but not isolation.

Second, detailed study of contexts confirms that they are found in domestic (and some funerary) contexts, suggesting a link with daily life (and, perhaps, daily afterlife?), but there is no clear indication that they are cultic, without any possibility of isolating specific types for specific contexts.

Finally, it is best to read the figurines as a miniature world, therefore asking a new set of questions. What were they choosing to represent, and why? There is a need to look more at social identities and values (looking also at texts, not to see figurines, but identities and values). Such a miniature world may offer a window on the real one, even if only "looking through a glass darkly" (1 Cor 13:12). Looking ahead, it will also be important to look at the texts—including the Hebrew scriptures—to help tease out the potential social meanings of the figurines. Research in this respect has so far only attempted to find traces of figurine use, rather than a sense of what the biblical text can tell us about the social meaning of horses, riders, chariots, motherhood, couches, boats, and music in late Iron Age Judah.

It is unlikely that we will ever really know what the figurines were used for: whether they had a strong religious significance, or whether their use was more mundane. However, whatever the immediate use of the figurines, they remain a precious window on the past in the very choice of what was represented in the figural world and how. Through the centuries they remain powerful, if enigmatic, conveyors of meaning.

Part 4
Judah in the Seventh Century BCE,
Reflected Not Only in Biblical Texts

Prophetic Books as a Historical Source for the Monarchic Period: The Problem of Historical Reliability

Adam Mackerle

The preexilic prophetic books, such as Hosea, Amos, Micah, Zephaniah, and Isaiah are clearly and explicitly set in a concrete historical setting, and they—sometimes very vividly—describe the concrete social, religious, economic, and political situations of Israel and Judah in the eighth and seventh centuries BCE. Thus, they seem to offer themselves as a supportive historical source and help us complete our image of Israel and Judah of that time and of the historical panorama of these kingdoms, and they are often used in this way.

A number of arguments have been raised against and in favor of such historical reading of the prophetic books, and I do not want to repeat them here.[1] In this instance, I would like to focus just on a twofold serious problem with using these books as a historical source. First, by using the prophetic texts as a historical source, we presuppose that the books are historically reliable; second, we assert that we understand these books, what they tell us, and all (or at least the major part of) the historical, social, economic, and so on, references contained in the books. But neither of these presuppositions is free from serious doubts.

---

1. See, e.g., Megan Bishop Moore, "Writing Israel's History Using the Prophetic Books," in *Israel's Prophets and Israel's Past: Essays on the Relationship of Prophetic Texts and Israelite History in Honor of John H. Hayes*, ed. Brad E. Kelle and Megan B. Moore (London: T&T Clark, 2006), 23–36.

9.1. The Issue of Historical Reliability

Let us begin with considering the problem of the historical reliability of the books, and, more specifically, with focusing on the problem of the dating of their origin and its impact on their reliability.

9.1.1. Defining the Issue

The date of origin of a book is defined by two extreme points: by its *terminus a quo* and *terminus ad quem*. The *terminus a quo* is dictated generally by the content of the book. The book could not have been written before the events and people it recounts. In this case, the books could not have been written before the middle of the eighth or seventh century BCE. Nevertheless, the same applies for any single part of the book, which may be older than the book as a whole but still cannot be older than the events it is reporting.

On the other hand, the *terminus ad quem* is normally determined by the oldest extant exemplar of the text or the oldest known explicit mention of its existence (provided we are sure that it really mentions the same text in the same form as we have it today). In our case, it is the Qumran caves that gave us the oldest manuscripts.[2] We must also add to this Qumranic evidence the existence of more and slightly divergent textual versions. This leads to the conclusion that the Qumranic texts are not originals and that they must have had been in use already for some period of time before the second century BCE. Still, this does not have to be more than a few decades.[3]

---

2. There are several scrolls containing the Minor Prophets: 4Q76–82 (4QXII[a–g]) and 5Q4 (5QAmos); see Eugene Ulrich, *The Biblical Qumran Scrolls: Transcriptions and Textual Variants*, VTSup 134 (Leiden: Brill, 2010). The text of the books in these manuscripts is not complete; however, from the extant evidence it is highly probable that the books retrieved in the caves were the same books as we have them now. The differences are classifiable as normal divergences between diverse versions of a text that is considered to be basically the same.

3. Cf. Robert P. Carroll, "Jewgreek and Greekjew: The Hebrew Bible Is All Greek to Me; Reflections on the Problematics of Dating the Origins of the Bible in Relation to Contemporary Discussion of Biblical Historiography," in *Did Moses Speak Attic? Jewish Historiography and Scripture in the Hellenistic Period*, ed. Lester L. Grabbe, JSOTSup 317 (Sheffield: Sheffield Academic, 2001), 93–95.

The date of origin of a book is to be found somewhere in between those two *termini*. Exactly where is a question of higher or lower probability. Still more precisely, and considering the composite nature of the prophetic books, talking about an "origin of the book" might be problematic. It is better to talk about a process of the origin of a book. The period of this process might have extended over several centuries. At the end of such a process is the book as we have it today. Since there might have been other versions of the book that have originated throughout the process and have gone their own path, the determination of the end of the process depends on the nature or on the version of the text in which we are interested. While the determination of what we mean by the "end" is rather clear, the beginning of the process is more vague. In the case of a prophetic book, there might have been a prophet with that name, although he might have nothing to do with the text bearing his name (like Jonah); there might have been the writing down of the first of the oracles contained in the book, and so on.

Be that as it may, there are some clues that lead to the conclusion that the content of the books, that is, the oracles of which they consist, are older than the books themselves.

First, from the shape of the books it is clear that they are composed of various layers and that they developed gradually through time. Thus, although the final shape of the book might be rather young, the individual passages are probably older.

Second, some of ancient texts also present in Qumran mention or quote some verses of these books as authoritative.[4] While we cannot be sure that the authors had at their disposal the books as we have them today, they at least knew the tradition the books are built upon. Consequently, if

---

4. E.g., Tobit (2:6) quoting Amos (8:10); Jeremiah (26:18) quoting Micah (3:12); Sirach (49:10) mentioning "the bones of the Twelve." Some of the books are also quoted in other Qumranic literature. E.g., Amos in Damascus Document (4Q266 [4QD^a] 7:14–16), in Florilegium (4Q174 [4QFlor] 1:12) and in the Apocryphon of Jeremiah C (4Q387 3:8–9). In these instances, we face the problem that we have only some verses, and we are not sure whether the author knew or had at his disposal the whole book as we have it today; the fact that Sir 51:13–20, 30b was contained in a scroll with Psalms (11Q5 [11QPs^a]) clearly shows that not every fragment of a book is a proof of the existence of the book as a whole as we know it. Similarly, we do not know whether Sirach (49:10) is referring to the prophets as persons, or to the writings that bear their names, and if so, whether those writings were the same as we have them today.

this tradition and at least some portions of the texts were known and held as authoritative, they must come from yet an older time.

Third and finally, if we compare the preexilic prophets, we realize that although the genre is definitely the same: that is, all four books are formally collections of oracles, almost all focused on the relations between sin and punishment, or on the restoration of Israel or Judah (or both, sometimes of other nations, too), there are rather large differences among them. They use a different vocabulary, they have a different structure, the logic of arguments is different, and so on. While the books share the genre, there are a large number of differences within the genre. Moreover, some books quote others: for example, the content of Obadiah is partly contained in Jeremiah, Jeremiah quotes Micah, Micah contains a text very similar to a passage from Isaiah, Amos and Hosea contain short, but strangely similar expressions.[5] All of this requires a longer existence of the genre, and thus of the books that form the genre, especially if the genre is a typical literary phenomenon native to Israel, that is, present exclusively in the Old Testament and nowhere else in the ancient Near East.

All of this points to what Horacio Simian-Yofre says about the date of origin and the composition of the book of Amos. He calls the book of Amos "Amos's prophecy according to an unnamed redactor" who was active somewhere before the second century BCE and who collected and put together what he knew about Amos and his words from tradition. How old the tradition was, we cannot say.[6] Thus, the only thing we know is that the books (as we have them today) probably existed and were read in postexilic Judah.

---

5. E.g., in Jer 17:27; 21:14; 49:27; 50:32 we find the verb יצת hiphil ("to kindle"), as in Amos 1:14 (a strange and unexpected deviation from the constant schema in Amos's oracles against the nations); Hos 8:14 contains a rather unusual verb שלח piel ("to send"), like Amos 1:4, 7, 10, 12; 2:5. In Amos, there is a strange expression "I will kindle a fire in the wall of Rabbah, and it shall devour her strongholds." It might be one of the signs of a common redaction or at least a mutual contact in the redaction process; cf. Aaron Schart, Die Entstehung des Zwölfprophetenbuchs: Neubearbeitungen von Amos im Rahmen schriftenübergreifender Redaktionsprozesse, BZAW 260 (Berlin: de Gruyter, 1998), 154.

6. Horacio Simian-Yofre, Amos: Nuova versione, introduzione e commento (Milano: Paoline, 2002), 22. Jean Louis Ska presents a similar view for the nature of the Pentateuch, Introduzione alla lettura del Pentateuco: Chiavi per l'interpretazione dei primi cinque libri della Bibbia (Bologna: Dehoniane, 1998), 211–12.

Therefore, it is much more secure to read the books and their parts against the background of postexilic Judah (i.e., to treat them as a product of that time, although it does not have to mean the same). Unfortunately, the scholars that read these books in this way are rather few.[7] On the other hand, to try to separate some "more authentic," that is, more ancient parts, and to attribute them to the prophet himself or to his disciples is to push our ambition too far. Ultimately, the only argument for that will be nothing other than the presumption of historical authenticity.

We are sure that the books in the form we have today were read during the third century BCE. It is probable that they were read also some time before that. But the more deeply we proceed against the flow of time, the lesser the probability of authenticity. From this point of view, to consider the very *terminus a quo* as the date of origin of the book is the less probable option. A lot of authors, when speaking about the preexilic Minor Prophets, consider their date of origin or the date of origin of some parts of them to be actually equivalent to their *terminus a quo*. Sometimes, and quite often, the argument is based on the presumption of historical reliability; the text is to be held historically authentic until it is proven false.[8] The burden of proof, then, lies on those who question the authenticity. If, it is said, it turns out that we cannot say that the book as a whole is authentic, we can find at least some (or a good number of) passages in it, that are authentic.[9] The historical authenticity is then used as an important

---

7. Among them Simian-Yofre, *Amos*; Ehud Ben Zvi, *A Historical-Critical Study of the Book of Zephaniah*, BZAW 198 (Berlin: de Gruyter, 1991); Ben Zvi, *Micah*, FOTL 21B (Grand Rapids: Eerdmans, 2000); Richard J. Coggins, *Joel and Amos*, NCB (Sheffield: Sheffield Academic, 2000).

8. Examples are not lacking. If we limit ourselves to the book of Amos, we can mention a general statement by Aaron W. Park: "Since the final form of a prophetic book claims that the present is the work of the prophet, we must begin with that point. If and only if we can refute its claim based on our experience and perception according to the law of literature, we can challenge the final redactor's claim and seek for an alternative" (*The Book of Amos as Composed and Read in Antiquity*, StBibLit 37 [New York: Lang, 2004]), 36; Douglas Stuart on Amos 9:11–15: "Thus nothing in Amos 9:14–15 need be seen as reflecting a later or a southern origin. Moreover, nothing in the oracle hints at the place or time of its initial delivery" (*Hosea–Jonah*, WBC 31 [Waco, TX: Word, 1987], 397); or Shalom Paul on Amos 2:4–5: "Thus there is no compelling reason to deny this expression to the prophet" (*Amos: A Commentary on the Book of Amos*, Hermeneia [Minneapolis: Fortress, 1991], 75).

9. This leads to a stratification of a prophetic book into various redactional layers. Somewhat extreme examples of such an approach to the book of Amos are, e.g.,

argument when using these texts for reconstructing the social, political, historical, economic, religious, milieu of the preexilic kingdoms. However, there is nothing that justifies such a presumption.[10]

Needless to say, it is not the same as saying that the books or their parts are historically not authentic; it is just to say that we are not—and we cannot be—sure, and thus any historical reconstruction based on these texts will suffer heavily from this uncertainty, and may be more or less naive.

9.1.2. Examples of How It Works

I will offer some examples of how the whole problem works, taken from three historical reconstructions of the Israelite and Judahite society written by Gunther Fleischer, Rainer Kessler, and Devadasan Premnath.[11] What I want to do is to point out, by the example of these works, some methodological problems any historical reconstruction must deal with, and the fact that these problems are sometimes unsurmountable and remain tacitly passed by.

All of these authors are aware of the importance of the historical reliability of the prophetic texts used for historical reconstruction, that is, that if they want to use the selected prophetic texts for historical reconstruction, they must prove that the texts originate from that period. Kessler rightly observes that we are not digging and searching the text for the

---

Theodor Lescow, distinguishing five layers: Amos, two preexilic, and two postexilic ("Das vorexilische Amosbuch: Erwägungen zu seiner Kompositionsgeschichte," *BN* 93 [1998]: 23–55), or Dirk U. Rottzoll, finding even twelve layers (*Studien zur Redaktion und Komposition des Amosbuches*, BZAW 243 [Berlin: de Gruyter, 1996]). The stratification of the book into layers relies on our presumed reliable knowledge of the social, political, religious, and economic history of Israel and Judah—indeed, the various texts are attributed to various periods according to their aptness to them; the fact that we use these books to reconstruct the history shows a vicious circle.

10. For a similar view, see, e.g., Mark Zvi Brettler, "Redaction, History, and Redaction-History of Amos in Recent Scholarship," in Kelle and Moore, *Israel's Prophets and Israel's Past*, 103–12.

11. Gunther Fleischer, *Von Menschenverkäufern, Baschankühen und Rechtsverkehren: Die Sozialkritik des Amosbuches in historisch-kritischer, sozialgeschichtlicher und archäologischer Perspektive*, BBB 74 (Frankfurt: Athenäum, 1989); Rainer Kessler, *Staat und Gesellschaft im vorexilischen Juda: Vom 8. Jahrhundert bis zum Exil*, VTSup 47 (Leiden: Brill, 1992); Devadasan N. Premnath, *Eighth Century Prophets: A Social Analysis* (Saint Louis: Chalice, 2003).

ipsissima verba of the prophets, but we are interested in the social and economic background (*Sachwelt*), which has nothing to do with the prophetic authorship.[12] Thus, as he says, he works with the model of "developing text" (*Fortschreibungsmodell*) and "discipleship" (*Schülerkreis*), that is, of a circle around the prophet who wrote down his message; it is the—presupposed—close factual and temporal relation that guarantees the historical reliability.[13] Although the whole argument relies on the historical reliability of the texts, and the reliability relies on one model of the origin of the books, it is given just one paragraph of space with no further explanation or defense.

Fleischer works with the same model as Kessler. What makes his work different is that he tries, text after text, to identify the place of the segments of the book of Amos in its redaction history and to attribute the separate units to Amos or to later redactional layers.[14]

Fleischer's work suffers, in my view, from three weak points. The first weakness is the model itself. It is based on a conviction that whatever redactional history the text has undergone, the oldest layer is that of Amos. In this sense it is yet another example of the a priori pushing the date of origin to the very *terminus a quo*. The procedure is simple: what has been identified as the oldest layer is attributed to Amos; what is thought to be incompatible with that must be a work of a later redactor.[15]

The second weakness is the criteria for separating individual textual units. Whenever the text is incoherent, whenever it stands in contradiction to what precedes or follows, Fleischer interprets it as a sign of redactional activity. Thus, Fleischer's starting point seems to be the fact that the book in its final form does not make sense, is full of incoherencies and contradictions, and cannot be work of a single author. It compels us to see the

---

12. Kessler, *Staat und Gesellschaft*, 22. Premnath, for the sake of completeness, says basically the same when he asserts that we are interested not in the authorship, but in the "systemic reality" described by the book (*Eighth Century Prophets*, 178–79).

13. See Kessler, *Staat und Gesellschaft*, 21. Unless otherwise noted, all translations are mine.

14. See the overview table in Fleischer, *Von Menschenverkäufern*, 254–58. The layers are respectively: Amos (ca. 740)—733/722—Judah redaction—Deuteronomistic—postexilic—apocalyptic. For a description of his methodology, see pp. 15–17.

15. A good example is offered by the text Amos 4:1–3 (dealt with on pp. 80–93). Since Fleischer considers the text as almost completely coherent, in his view it comes from one single layer and is attributed to Amos. Fleischer would obviously also consider another criterion, that of Amos's style; for this see below.

book as a composite text in the need to be split into several separate units in order to be fully understandable. Besides the fact that a lot of scholars would disagree with this view of the book, there is at least one other model—the book as a product of a redactor who had collected several materials from different sources and put them together. In this case, there would not be any gradual development of textual layers, and more of the sources (or none of them) could come in some way from Amos.

Besides the criterion of (in)coherence, there are also other criteria, for example, that of Amos's style. Amos's style, that is, his way of expressing himself and his thought and also the dominant themes of his preaching, is excerpted from those passages that are certainly attributed to him; whatever is different, can be judged as not genuine.[16] But the logic is wrong. It may work in the opposite direction: if some text shares the style of the oracles attributed to Amos, it may be from him. But the conclusion cannot be that if it does not share his style, it is not genuine.

The third weakness consists in the attribution of individual layers to concrete historical situations. First, as I have already said, the attribution of the first layer to Amos has no real foundation. Second, if we want to attribute individual layers and texts to concrete historical situations, we presuppose a fairly good knowledge of it. Without such a good knowledge an attribution of individual, small literary units to specific periods (distant from each other sometimes by only a few decades) would be impossible. For instance, the text Amos 8:5 is attributed to the Judahite redaction on the basis of a study by Gnana Robinson that analyzes the term "new moon" in relation to "Shabbat."[17] That means that the attribution of the text to a specific redactional layer depends on just one (albeit comprehensive) study. Third, we presuppose that the text reflects all historical changes we think we know about. All of this is in my view too dubious.

Finally, Premnath seems to be as aware of the need for proving the historical reliability as Fleischer, and thus of the importance of an early date of origin of the respective passages. Every time he commences treating a new piece of prophetic text, he gives proofs for its early date of origin. Still, some questions arise when we consider more deeply the arguments in favor of historicity. If we now consider the examples from Amos and

---

16. See, e.g., Fleischer's argumentation at Amos 3:9–11 (*Von Menschenverkäufern*, 206–7).

17. Gnana Robinson, "The Origin and Development of the Old Testament Sabbath: A Comprehensive Exegetical Approach" (PhD diss., Hamburg, 1975).

Micah, eleven texts are accepted as historically reliable on the basis that they "are generally not disputed." Since the main argument is the prevalent scholarly consensus of authorities, we can go a step further and verify the arguments the quoted authorities offer for the authenticity of respective texts.[18] We have already seen that, for instance, Wilhelm Rudolph presupposes the historicity without any positive argumentation in favor of it; for him, it is enough to say that "our knowledge of the timespan in which Micah was active, is too limited to declare that there could not have existed such conditions; there are even no other clues, such as, for instance, the use of language that could be brought against Micah's authorship."[19] Hans Walter Wolff, on the other hand, does not hesitate to judge some texts to be written later, but he builds—not unlike Kessler and Fleischer—upon the model of an originally Micahean text rewritten in later times. This model works with the presupposition of basic Micahean authorship of the core of the book (with no positive argument in favor) and with a rather good knowledge of the historical situation, because this is the criteria for determining the dating of concrete passages.[20]

Whenever the scholarly consensus is missing, Premnath finds arguments for the historicity elsewhere. For example, when dealing with Mic 5:9–10, he relies on the argument proposed by John Willis against the consensus. However, the only thing Willis's arguments do is to call into question the necessity of denying the Micahean origin of Mic 4–5, and not vice versa, in other words, they do not give any positive valid argument for attributing the oracles to Micah (or to his time).[21]

---

18. The most quoted scholars are Hans Walter Wolff, Wilhelm Rudolph, Francis I. Andersen and David Noel Freedman, Robert B. Coote, Shalom Paul, James Luther Mays, Marvin A. Sweeney, Otto Kaiser, Ronald E. Clements, and Hans Wildberger.

19. Wilhelm Rudolph, *Micha–Nahum–Habakuk–Zephanja*, KAT 13.3 (Berlin: Evangelische Verlaganstalt, 1977), 126, pondering the historical setting and authorship of Mic 7:1–7.

20. See his model of the development of the book of Micah in Hans Walter Wolff, *Dodekapropheton 4: Micha*, BKAT 4 (Neukirchen-Vluyn: Neukircher Verlag, 1982), ix–xiii; a similar model for the book of Amos is in Wolff, *Dodekapropheton 2: Joel und Amos*, BKAT 2 (Neukirchen-Vluyn: Neukircher Verlag, 1985), 129–38.

21. John T. Willis, "Structure of Micah 3–5 and the Function of Micah 5:9–14 in the Book," *ZAW* 81 (1969): 191–214. Premnath himself admits the limitation of Willis's argument, when he says, "it would not preclude the possibility of a later editor taking earlier material and arranging it for his/her purposes" (*Eighth Century Prophets*, 121).

In the case of Amos 5:7–10 he copes with the problem by saying that since the content corresponds to the eighth century BCE, it is possible that it comes from that period. In the case of Mic 7:2–3, he affirms that since the systemic reality found in the text is that of the eighth century BCE, it is interpretable against that background. In both cases, Premnath starts the argumentation with knowing what was going on in the eighth century and thus violates the basic rule I am going to mention below: if we want to reconstruct the historical reality from the texts, we cannot interpret the texts according the presupposed knowledge of the period, which is still to be proven.[22] Second, he does not prove that the systemic reality found in the text is specific to the eighth century BCE so that it could not have originated from another period. If that were so, that is, if it could have originated from another period, it might say nothing at all about eighth-century Judah. The same happens when Premnath deals with the text of Mic 6:9–19. In this case he talks about a *possibility* that the text might have originated in the eighth century; once more, such a *possibility* does not provide a reliable basis for any historical reconstruction. The same applies to Fleischer's arguments. His attribution of the texts to individual redactional layers means that the supposed textual units are understandable with that historical background, but it does not exclude other possibilities at all. Moreover, he talks about a lot of editorial history, so that we must rearrange the text in order to make it understandable. If there could have been such an editorial history that has made the text unintelligible, how can we be sure that the description of the systemic reality in the text has been preserved unaltered?[23] Moreover, if we interpret a text we have previously reconstructed, the text will yield the meaning we have given it.

Summed up, the above-mentioned arguments for historicity (adduced by Premnath and Fleischer) are arguments saying that the historical reading of the selected passages is *possible*, not the *only possible* or *necessarily*

---

22. I remind the reader of Rudolph's argument quoted above, that "our knowledge of the timespan in which Micah was active, is too limited to declare that there could not have existed such conditions" (*Micha–Nahum–Habakuk–Zephanja*, 126). There, to prove the same, i.e., the possibility of Micah's authorship, the very lack of our knowledge of that period was used.

23. I remind the reader of the Kessler's argument mentioned above, that the text written down by the prophet's discipleship is—in factual and temporal aspect—so close to the prophet, that it guarantees the historical reliability of the text (*Staat und Gesellschaft*, 22).

preferable reading. The very fact that Premnath relies on consensus, and when missing finds arguments elsewhere, points to the same conclusion: if the historical reading is possible, then he will read the text that way.

The main problem with dating is that the text may not provide a reliable historical picture but instead create a historical fiction or distort the original texts in order to use them as an appropriate response for the author's (redactor's) own time and audience.

The first example of such a possible procedure is hinted at by Kessler himself. Kessler identifies indebtedness as the main problem of monarchical Judah. But he admits that indebtedness also went on in postexilic times and culminated in a debt crisis under Nehemiah.[24] If this is so, then the texts talking of indebtedness might be a product of a postexilic interest, projected onto preexilic times. I definitely do not argue that there was no preexilic prophetic tradition containing allusions to the problems of indebtedness. However, such a tradition might have only facilitated the stress on indebtedness as *the* problem of the preexilic monarchy, just because it was *the* problem of the postexilic community. Therefore, it might be that the social and economic problems described in the preexilic prophetic books are neither typical problems of that period, nor a witness to a specific stage of development of the society in that period, but rather an omnipresent problem of all societies of that kind, stressed because it was a cogent problem of the author's (redactor's) community. If we want to remain sober, the maximum we can say is to affirm with Walter Houston that "the processes of class formation and exploitation … covered centuries. Everyone involved in the editing and transmission of the prophetic books knew what was meant by the oppression of the poor."[25]

The anti-Edomite oracles might provide another example of such a technique in general and by the book of Obadiah in particular. Usually, the anti-Edomite oracles are interpreted as oracles originating from the period of Babylonian conquest of Judah. They are supposed to reflect and to describe the attitude of Edom toward Jews and their taking part in the looting of Jerusalem. All of these oracles seem to talk of the same events, and thus to furnish an unambiguous historical reference. However, there are scholars who question these conclusions, that is, that there

---

24. See Neh 5:1–13; cf. 10:32. See Kessler, *Staat und Gesellschaft*, 121–24. See also Walter J. Houston, *Contending for Justice: Ideologies and Theologies of Social Justice in the Old Testament* (New York: T&T Clark, 2006), 18–19.

25. Houston, *Contending for Justice*, 52.

would have been an Edomite participation in the conquest of Jerusalem.[26] The almost unanimous voice throughout the Old Testament that attributes to the Edomites a hostile attitude against Jerusalem in the day of its distress might be nothing other than a later tradition projecting on the past some present (exilic or shortly postexilic) motives. If this is so, it is a good example of how later texts can literally create history; if they are taken for a reliable historical source, they might decisively influence our view of the past.

In my view, the only valid argument that might attenuate the general negative judgment of historical reliability of the preexilic prophetic books might be the cumulative argument. All of those books, despite their different vocabulary, structure, and accents, mention some common thematic features, such as, for instance, the social problems connected with exploitation, oppression, land accumulation. Therefore, it might be that there was such a problem at that time in Israel and Judah. But it is impossible to determine the extent to which the individual texts, upon which our eventual reconstruction is based, are historically reliable.[27]

9.2. The Issue of Our Understanding the Texts

The second problem is whether and to what extent we understand the prophetic texts we use for historical reconstruction. Let us begin with a simple scheme:

---

26. E.g., John R. Bartlett, *Edom and the Edomites*, JSOTSup 77 (Sheffield: Sheffield Academic, 1989); Juan Manuel Tebes, "The Edomite Involvement in the Destruction of the First Temple: A Case of Stab-in-the-Back Tradition?," *JSOT* 36 (2011): 219–55; Adam Mackerle, "Kniha Abdijáš: Co má Starý zákon proti Edómu? (Abd 1,1–21)," in *Obtížné oddíly Zadních proroků*, ed. M. Prudký (Kostelní Vydří: Karmelitánské nakladatelství, 2016), 193–205; Bob Becking, "The Betrayal of Edom: Remarks on a Claimed Tradition," *HTS* 72 (2016): 1–4.

27. John P. Meier talks about a similar paradox in his volume on Jesus as a miracle worker: on the one hand, "the statement that Jesus acted as and was viewed as an exorcist and healer during his public ministry has as much historical corroboration as almost any other statement we can make about the Jesus of history," but, on the other hand, what happens "if each miracle story in turn—or the sum total of miracle stories taken together—is judged to have no basis in the life of the historical Jesus?" (*Mentor, Message, and Miracles*, vol. 2 of *A Marginal Jew: Rethinking the Historical Jesus*, ABRL [New York: Doubleday, 1994], 970 and 968).

Text [↔] Historical Reality

The arrows are wrong—they can go in only one direction. Either we know the historical reality in which the text was written and based on this knowledge we can understand what the text says, or we understand what the text says—we know its genre, purpose, and so on—and based on this we can reconstruct the historical reality behind the text. But, in either case, we must begin with knowing and understanding either the historical situation or the text itself. The problem with the preexilic Minor Prophets when used for reconstructing the historical situation of Israel and Judah is that we do not understand either of them. In other words, reconstructing the historical reality in the light of the texts presupposes our good knowledge of the texts. If it is not so, it means that we presuppose that we understand the book, then—on that basis—we reconstruct the historical reality, and then we turn back and—finally knowing the historical situation—interpret the book. In this way we fall into an exemplary vicious circle.

I will illustrate what I have just said with an example that regards the religious milieu of Israel. The book of Hosea contains a number of oracles mentioning בעלים or מאהבים, especially in chapters 1–3. Usually, the בעלים are understood and interpreted as referring to some pagan deities, venerated in Israel. Thus, Hosea is criticizing religious infidelity of Israelites of his time, described as harlotry. Sometimes the harlotry is interpreted in its literal meaning, pointing to pagan sexual rites connected with cult (such as sacral prostitution, ritual deflowering of virgins, etc.).[28] If we focus on a similar text, Mic 1:7, to interpret the consequence literally, that is, that the wages of a harlot will become once more the wages of a harlot in a literal sense, we are pushing the sexual interpretation to its extremes.[29] Still, it means that we think we understand the text, and based on this we create our conviction of how that society looked in that period. Nonetheless, at the beginning there is a specific understanding of a text that helps us create our own view of Israelite society.

---

28. E.g., Artur Weiser, *Die Propheten Hosea, Joel, Amos, Obadja, Jona, Micha*, vol. 1 of *Das Buch der zwölf kleinen Propheten*, ATD 24 (Göttingen: Vanderhoeck & Rupre-cht, 1974), 238; Rudolph, *Micha–Nahum–Habakuk–Zephanja*, 42.

29. See, e.g., Elizabeth Achtemeier, *Minor Prophets I* (Grand Rapids: Baker, 2012), 299; Weiser, *Propheten*, 238; Bruce K. Waltke, *A Commentary on Micah* (Grand Rapids: Eerdmans, 2007), 54; Manfred Dreytza, *Buch Micha* (Witten: Brockhaus, 2009), 99.

Recently, some studies have questioned such an interpretation.[30] They start negatively by pointing to the scant—if any—evidence for sacral prostitution in Canaan at that time. According to Alice Keefe and Brad Kelle, it is much more probable that the prophet has in mind rather political and economic prostitution, which is intrinsically connected to religious promiscuity and is regarded as a kind of infidelity to the Lord: Israel is looking for safety and prosperity outside its relationship with the Lord.[31] Also the (not only sexual) violence of the husband against the woman is a literary topos for describing the destruction of a city; it does not need to have anything to do with sexuality at all. The religious and political aspects are not strictly separated. This can be seen clearly in the assertion by Keefe that the two basic means for establishing international political relations are marriages and sponsoring the cult of the deity of the other party.[32] Such a practice is well illustrated by the policy of Ahab. Francis Andersen and David Noel Freedman put it in these words: "The religious components in such relationships arose from political treaties or trade agreements that required acknowledgment of foreign gods or even the installation of their images as concessions to merchant colonies or through cosmopolitan syncretism."[33]

Another example can be found in Amos 4:1–3. The nature of transgression described in 4:1 depends on our understanding of the terms "cows" (פרות), their "lords" or "lord" (אדניהם), and the pronominal suffix in the same word (referring to the cows, or to their victims?). The various interpretations lead to several and quite different conclusions: the addressees are the rich women of Samaria; the addressees are the (male or both) Israelites described as cows; the "lord" is a pagan deity, and thus the transgression is religious in nature; the "lords" are the landholders, and thus the transgression consists in economic oppression; the "lords" are the

---

30. Alice A. Keefe, *Woman's Body and the Social Body in Hosea*, JSOTSup 338 (Sheffield: Sheffield Academic, 2001); Brad E. Kelle, *Hosea 2: Metaphor and Rhetoric in Historical Perspective*, AcBib 20 (Atlanta: Society of Biblical Literature, 2005). The same example is also adduced by Moore, "Writing Israel's History Using the Prophetic Books," 28–29.

31. Cf. Miroslav Varšo, *Abdiáš, Jonáš, Micheáš*, Komentáre k Starému zákonu 2 (Trnava: Dobrá kniha, 2010), 192.

32. Keefe, *Woman's Body*, 127–28.

33. Francis I. Andersen and David Noel Freedman, *Micah: A New Translation with Introduction and Commentary*, AB 24E (New York: Doubleday, 2000), 184.

husbands of the cows, Israelite rich women; and so on.[34] The interpretation of the text then may determine our understanding of the religious or social history of Israel.

From these examples it is evident that different interpretations of the same text, based not on new historical evidence but on just another interpretation of terms and images, lead to different interpretations of the meaning of the text, and consequently—if the text is used for a historical reconstruction—to a completely different view of the religious milieu of Israel in the eighth and seventh century BCE.

9.3. Conclusion

From what has been said so far, it is clear that to use the prophetic texts as an a priori reliable historical source is dangerous. First, we are sure neither about the date of origin of the books nor about their actual relation to the period they talk about. Second, we often do not understand the highly metaphorical language and the images they use. Therefore, the prophetic texts cannot be used as a direct and unambiguous source for historical reconstruction.

The first issue remains an insurmountable obstacle. It puts an implicit and relativizing question mark at the end of all conclusions. All historical reconstructions based on the (prophetic) texts presuppose the historical reliability of the texts, even if it is not explicitly announced and admitted by the author.

The second issue prevents us from using the (prophetic) texts as a historical source, because their very interpretation depends on knowing its historical background. On the other hand, and unlike in the first case, they can become a probing stone of different theories and hypotheses. If there is a theory of how the society looked or of what might have happened at a specific period, the prophetic texts can be interpreted using that background (still provided they are historically reliable). This is exactly how

---

34. I have dealt with the interpretation of this passage several times; Adam Mackerle, "Možnosti a úskalí práce s hebrejským textem," in *Jednota v mnohosti: Zborník z Teologickej konferencie mladých vedeckých pracovníkov*, ed. A. Biela, R. Schön, and J. Badura (Bratislava: Univerzita Komenského v Bratislave, 2012), 30–48; more recently in my commentary on Amos: Mackerle, *Ámos: Když Bůh musí řvát jako lev* (Prague: Česká biblická společnost, 2017), 117–24. The reader can consult any detailed commentary on Amos to obtain an understanding of the problematic nature of the text.

Premnath uses them. In the first part of his study, Premnath expounds a theory of social development and of the transition of a society from a natural, subsistence economy to a market economy. Then he applies the model to monarchic Israel and Judah, and then, finally, he proposes a way of understanding the content of prophetic oracles as a witness to such a social change. By doing this, he shows what they mean, if understood in this way. He says it explicitly and appropriately at the beginning of chapters 3 and 4; chapter 3 delineates a "working hypothesis regarding the systemic reality of the eighth-century Israel and Judah to be tested against the prophetic texts," while chapter 4 is devoted to "testing extensively the hypothetical reconstruction of the systemic reality of eighth-century Israel and Judah proposed in the previous chapter against the data in the prophetic oracles."[35] To work in the opposite direction, that is, to start with an interpretation of the texts and on that basis to try to reconstruct the social reality (like Fleischer and Kessler), is insecure.

What Premnath's study basically says is that if we assume the historical reliability of the prophetic texts, we can say that the theory of transition from subsistence to market economy, as far as witnessed by the prophetic texts, makes sense, that is, that the prophetic texts are interpretable in this way. If any historical reconstruction is to be carried out upon these conclusions, it will depend on the premises of (1) the historical reliability of the prophetic texts, and of (2) the correctness of the working hypothesis that is being tested, which—as such—is not proven by the study. These premises present insurmountable limitations to any historical reconstruction of ours. If there is an unsolvable limitation to our work and knowledge, it is in my opinion good to—at least—be aware of it.

---

35. Premnath, *Eighth Century Prophets*, 43 and 99.

The Seventh Century in the Book of Kings
and the Question of Its First Edition

Jan Rückl

10.1. Introduction

No matter when the book of Kings was first created, it no doubt is based on documents and memories stemming from the time of the Israelite and Judahite monarchies. As such, Kings represents a valuable source for the history of these states. Therefore, a historian searching for material concerning the kingdoms of Israel and Judah may leave the problem of the book's origin to some degree open. However, for the philological question of how the text is to be understood according to its intention in the time of its first publication, the work's date of origin seems essential. The importance of the link between a work's interpretation and the date of origin ascribed to it transpires, for example, in the difference between the evaluations of the so-called Deuteronomistic History suggested by Martin Noth and Frank Moore Cross, with both authors basing their interpretations to a large degree on Kings as the most Deuteronomistic book of the Former Prophets. While for Noth, who situated the origins of the Deuteronomistic History to the exilic period, the Deuteronomist composed his work more or less for his personal needs, in order to explain to himself the catastrophe that had befallen his people for whom he did not see any future, Cross considered the Deuteronomistic History to be triumphalist propaganda that proclaimed Israel's salvation under the reign of Josiah depicted as a new David.[1]

---

1. Martin Noth, *The Deuteronomistic History*, 2nd ed., JSOTSup 15 (Sheffield: Sheffield Academic, 1991), 142–45; Frank Moore Cross, *Canaanite Myth and Hebrew Epic: Essays in the History of the Religion of Israel* (Cambridge: Harvard University Press, 1973), 274–89.

Yet, what do we mean by the book of Kings when we speak about its first composition? Kings is clearly based on various sources, of which the most important were perhaps the lists of Judahite and Israelite kings.[2] These lists, kept separately for the two kingdoms, cannot be considered to constitute the first editions of Kings. The first edition of Kings was only created when these lists (which probably also contained concise notes concerning the events pertaining to the reigns of individual kings) had been combined into a synchronistic history of Israel *and* Judah. One of the fundamental questions of the research on the book is the time of its emergence in this basic form.

In past decades, numerous redactional models of Kings were suggested, very often in the frame of various forms of the Deuteronomistic History hypothesis.[3] According to some scholars, the first version of Kings appeared very early. André Lemaire, for instance, believes that the first edition of the synchronistic history of Israel and Judah was already compiled during the reign of Jehoshaphat around 850 BCE and that this work then passed through several stages of development until the exilic period.[4] Other scholars are of the opinion that the first edition of the book culminated in Hezekiah's reform and was written either during his or Manasseh's

---

2. Shoshana R. Bin-Nun, "Formulas from Royal Records of Israel and of Judah," *VT* 18 (1968): 414–32; John Van Seters, *In Search of History: Historiography in the Ancient World and the Origins of Biblical History* (New Haven: Yale University Press, 1983), 297–98, who believes that these two royal lists were in the first stage expanded into the "chronicles of the kings of Israel" and the "chronicles of the kings of Judah," and these were later used by the author of Kings (i.e., the Deuteronomist); Erik Eynikel, *The Reform of King Josiah and the Composition of the Deuteronomistic History*, OTS 33 (Leiden: Brill, 1996), 122–29; Nadav Na'aman, "The Temple Library of Jerusalem and the Composition of the Book of Kings," in *Congress Volume Leiden 2004*, VTSup 109, ed. André Lemaire (Leiden: Brill, 2006), 134–35; Benjamin D. Thomas, *Hezekiah and the Compositional History of the Book of Kings*, FAT 2/63 (Tübingen: Mohr Siebeck, 2014), 62–68, 122–23; Jan Rückl, "Aspects of Prologue Formulae in Kings," in *A King Like All the Nations: Kingdoms of Israel and Judah in the Bible and History*, ed. Manfred Oeming and Petr Sláma, BVB 28 (Münster: LIT, 2015), 159–74.

3. For overviews of the research, see Gary N. Knoppers, "Theories of the Redaction(s) of Kings," in *The Books of Kings: Sources, Composition, Historiography and Reception*, ed. André Lemaire and Baruch Halpern, VTSup 129 (Leiden: Brill, 2010), 69–88; Baruch Halpern and André Lemaire, "The Composition of Kings," in Lemaire and Halpern, *Books of Kings*, 123–53.

4. André Lemaire, "Vers l'Histoire de la Rédaction des Livres des Rois," *ZAW* 98 (1986): 221–36; cf. also Halpern and Lemaire, "Composition of Kings."

reign or at the beginning of Josiah's reign, but without including the kings after Hezekiah.[5] However, most current scholars advocate one of two positions that may be approximately described as follows: many believe that Kings climaxes with the depiction of Josiah's reign, which also is the time when it was written; others are of the opinion that the book was only composed in the exilic or Persian period.[6]

The seventh-century date of origin for Kings is defended by the adherents of the so-called Cross school, and in more recent times, it has gained support in the compromise model suggested by Thomas Römer.[7] Baruch Halpern and Lemaire wrote in 2010 that the idea of a Josianic redaction represents a consensus.[8] This, however, seems overstated. In the past decades, the exilic origin of the first edition of the Deuteronomistic History encompassing Kings was defended by scholars who have developed the legacy of the so-called Göttingen school, as well as by the so-called neo-Nothians.[9] Recently, Felipe Blanco Wissmann, having carried out a detailed study of texts in Kings that evaluate either the kings or the people,

---

5. E.g., Ian W. Provan, *Hezekiah and the Books of Kings: A Contribution to the Debate about the Composition of the Deuteronomistic History*, BZAW 172 (Berlin: de Gruyter, 1988); Thomas, *Hezekiah and the Compositional History of the Book of Kings*.

6. In this case, the conventional term *exilic* seems better than *Neo-Babylonian*, since the point is that the book would be written after the last events it depicts, and not during the reigns of the last monarchs who were Babylonian vassals. I use the term *exilic period* rather conventionally to describe the time between the fall of Jerusalem under Zedekiah and the conquest of Babylon by Cyrus.

7. For the Cross school, see Cross, *Canaanite Myth and Hebrew Epic*, 274–89; Richard D. Nelson, *The Double Redaction of the Deuteronomistic History*, JSOTSup 18 (Sheffield: JSOT Press, 1981); Andrew D. H. Mayes, *The Story of Israel between Settlement and Exile: A Redactional Study of the Deuteronomistic History* (London: SCM, 1983). For the compromise model, see Thomas Römer, *The So-Called Deuteronomistic History: A Sociological, Historical and Literary Introduction* (New York: T&T Clark, 2005).

8. Halpern and Lemaire, "Composition of Kings," 149.

9. For the Göttingen school, see, e.g., Rudolph Smend, *Die Entstehung des Alten Testaments*, ThW 1 (Stuttgart: Kohlhammer, 1978), 111–25; Timo Veijola, *Die Ewige Dynastie: David und die Entstehung seiner Dynastie nach der deuteronomistischen Darstellung* (Helsinki: Suomalainen Tiedakatemia, 1975); Walter Dietrich, *Prophetie und Geschichte: Eine Redaktionsgeschichtliche Untersuchung zum deuteronomistischen Geschichtswerk*, FRLANT 108 (Göttingen: Vandenhoeck & Ruprecht, 1972). For the neo-Nothians, see, e.g., Van Seters, *In Search of History*; Van Seters, *The Biblical Saga of King David* (Winona Lake, IN: Eisenbrauns, 2009); Steven L. McKenzie, "The Trouble with Kingship," in *Israel Constructs Its History: Deuteronomistic Historiography in*

including the religious judgment formulas in the prologues to the reigns of individual kings and the prophetic oracles against the northern dynasties, concluded that the first redaction of the book was prepared in the time of Nabonidus's rule or later, most likely between 550–520 BCE.[10] I myself have argued for the exilic or even Persian period origin of Samuel–Kings on the basis of a study regarding the motif of the dynastic promise to David in these books.[11]

Cross believed that two main themes of Kings, that is, the (non)centralized cult and the Davidic dynasty promised by YHWH to reign forever, meet and climax in the depiction of Josiah's reign. If so, the whole history of kingship in Israel would have been envisioned from a "Josianic perspective," and it would seem pertinent to look for the author of the work on Josiah's court. The portrayal of Josiah's acts in 1 Kgs 22–23 thus was used by Cross and others as an argument for the book's composition in the seventh century. Now, if the book were indeed created under Josiah, this fact should perhaps also be somehow reflected in the accounts of his two predecessors. However, the depictions of Manasseh's and Amon's reigns did not play any important role in the argumentation for the book's composition in the seventh century. In the present article, I will review the section of Kings dedicated to the seventh century until Josiah's reign, with the sole question in mind of whether the wording of the accounts of individual reigns suggests a Josianic or rather an exilic (or even Persian period) context of emergence. I leave aside Hezekiah's account for a mixture of conventional and pragmatic reasons: most of his reign falls into the eighth century, the treatment of his account would demand a lot of space, and it would be necessary to address the question of the first redaction culminating with his reign.

10.2. Manasseh (2 Kings 21:1–18)

In its current form, the account of Manasseh's reign stems from the exilic or Persian period. This is especially clear in verses 10–15 where Manasseh

---

Recent Research, ed. Albert de Pury, Thomas Römer, and Jean-Daniel Macchi, JSOT-Sup 306 (Sheffield: Sheffield Academic, 2000), 286–314.

10. Felipe Blanco Wissmann, *"Er tat das Rechte...": Beurteilungskriterien und Deuteronomismus in 1Kön 12–2Kön 25*, ATANT 93 (Zürich: TVZ, 2008).

11. Jan Rückl, *A Sure House: Studies on the Dynastic Promise to David in the Books of Samuel and Kings*, OBO 281 (Fribourg: Academic Press; Göttingen: Vandenhoeck & Ruprecht, 2016).

is accused of being responsible for the disappearance of the Judahite kingdom, the destruction of Jerusalem, and the exile. The advocates of the preexilic edition of Kings thus have to suppose that in the first edition, the account had a different shape than it does today. While Cross ascribed the whole of 2 Kgs 21:2–15 to the exilic editor, so that from the work of the first Deuteronomist we would only have the frame of Manasseh's reign comprising the formulaic prologue and epilogue, others attempted to reconstruct a longer text stemming from the Josianic edition.[12] For instance, Richard Nelson believes that the first Deuteronomist is responsible for verses 1–3bα, 4a, 6a, (7a), 16–18.[13] A fairly maximalist reconstruction of Manasseh's preexilic account was suggested by Richard H. Lowery who defends the possibility that the whole passage, with the exception of verse 16, "took its definitive (though not final) shape in the pre-exilic period."[14] Lowery considers the oracle announcing Judah's destruction in verses 10–15 to be vague, which in his view is due to the fact that it is not a *vaticinium ex eventu*. Originally, Manasseh's wickedness did not serve to explain the Babylonian exile "but to be a foil for Josiah's reform."[15]

As far as verses 10–15 are concerned, Lowery's argumentation is desperate.[16] As to Nelson's reconstruction of the first Deuteronomistic version, to some extent it is a result of subtracting the sections of text that cannot be part of Kings' preexilic edition, and as such it might seem to be motivated by the pressure of the larger redactional model. However, the situation cannot be reduced to this, since even some of those scholars (including myself) who situate the book's first edition into later times will face some difficulties with reconstructing the basic layer of Manasseh's account. The text of 2 Kgs 21:1–18 is rather repetitive, and at least some of these repetitions may indicate the text's diachronic growth. More importantly, 2 Kgs 21:1–18 indeed contains many phraseological and thematic

---

12. Cross, *Canaanite Myth and Hebrew Epic*, 285–86.

13. Nelson, *Double Redaction of the Deuteronomistic History*, 65–69.

14. Richard H. Lowery, *The Reforming Kings: Cults and Society in First Temple Judah*, JSOTSup 120 (Sheffield: Sheffield Academic, 1991), 169–85 (quotation from p. 171).

15. Lowery, *Reforming Kings*, 185.

16. For arguments against Lowery's case, see Percy C. F. van Keulen, *Manasseh through the Eyes of the Deuteronomists: The Manasseh Account (2 Kings 21:1–18) and the Final Chapters of the Deuteronomistic History*, OTS 38 (Leiden: Brill, 1996), 192.

features that are generally considered to stem from a later author than the one responsible for the book's first edition.

Therefore, in what follows I will proceed in two steps. First, I will try to mark out passages that clearly presuppose the fall of Judah, asking whether they may be excised from a supposed basic text on other grounds than their post-586 BCE origin.[17] Second, if (some of) these passages prove to be secondary, it will still be necessary to ask whether the basic text fits better in a preexilic or a later edition of Kings.

The passage concerning the statue of Asherah (2 Kgs 21:7–9) clearly presupposes the exile in verses 8–9, which refer to YHWH's promise that he will not let Israel go from its land if they follow what he (and Moses) commanded them. These verses also contain other motifs that are usually considered to be late and that most likely presuppose the experience of exile, as, for example, the theology of YHWH's name.[18] Since verse 7 comes back to the theme of Asherah mentioned already in verse 3, and since verse 9, which states that the people did more evil than the nations, seems to develop an accusation already present in verse 2, it might be argued that the whole passage contained in verses 7–9 is secondary. Verses 7–9 or a part of them are considered to be secondary even by some of the scholars who do not believe there was a preexilic form of 2 Kgs 21*.[19] Blanco Wissmann observes, among other things, that in verse 8 the people are evaluated according to their obedience to the תורה, which is a criterion that, in his opinion, only appears in the Persian period.[20] Verses 7–8 seem to refer to 2 Sam 7 (above all to vv. 10, 13) and 1 Kgs 9:1–9 (mainly to vv. 3, 6–9).[21] While 2 Sam 7 with the unconditional dynastic promise probably constituted one of the key texts of the primitive edition of Samuel–Kings (in my view stemming from the exilic or Persian period, but this should be left aside for the moment), 1 Kgs 9:4–5 contains the

---

17. Van Keulen, *Manasseh through the Eyes of the Deuteronomists*, 50–51, formulates the basic question of his important monograph in a similar way. After a thorough examination of the text, he answers it in the negative.

18. Blanco Wissmann, *Er tat das Rechte*, 168–69.

19. E.g., Erik Aurelius, *Zukunft jenseits des Gerichts: Eine redaktionsgeschichtliche Studie zum Enneateuch*, BZAW 319 (Berlin: de Gruyter, 2003), 60–64; Blanco Wissmann, *Er tat das Rechte*, 169.

20. Blanco Wissmann, *Er tat das Rechte*, 169; for this criterion in Kings in general, see p. 139–44.

21. E.g., van Keulen, *Manasseh through the Eyes of the Deuteronomists*, 105–6, 113; Aurelius, *Zukunft jenseits des Gerichts*, 61–62.

later conditional form of the promise.[22] Theoretically, 1 Kgs 9:4–5 might be considered later than verses 3, 6–9, which are referred to by 2 Kgs 21:7–9. However, it also seems quite plausible that at least 1 Kgs 9:4–9 constitute a more or less unified whole (whose function is to accentuate that YHWH's favor, whether directed toward the dynasty or the people, is conditional), and that it is more or less the current form of 1 Kgs 9:3–9 that is referred to in 2 Kgs 21:7–9.[23] All in all, it seems reasonable to exclude 2 Kgs 21:7–9 from Kings' first edition, no matter when the latter was created.[24]

As already mentioned, the exile is also clearly alluded to in verses 10–15. Again, these verses are considered secondary even by some of the scholars that situate the first edition of Kings in the exilic period.[25] Yet, it is more difficult to argue for a secondary origin of this text, and it is only possible to do so by means of thematic and linguistic parallels with other texts that these scholars consider secondary. There are no formal literary-critical signs testifying for the excision of this text.

The content of these verses is important for our question. While in verses 7–9 Manasseh is accused of a sin that is specifically Judahite (because it consists in profaning the temple of Jerusalem that YHWH has chosen from all the tribes of Israel, and the northern kings thus could not have committed this kind of sin), verses 10–15 describe the guilt of Manasseh and the Judahites in a way that creates parallels on the one hand between Manasseh and the kings of Israel, and on the other hand between the people of Judah and the people of Israel. So, for instance, YHWH will stretch "over Jerusalem the measuring line of Samaria, and the plumb line of the house of Ahab" (v. 13) because Manasseh "has made Judah also [גם את יהודה] to sin with his idols" (v. 11).[26] The word "also" explicitly refers to the fact that before Judah, it was Israel that sinned with the idols, as is

---

22. For 2 Sam 7, see Rückl, *Sure House*, 17–191; for 1 Kgs 9:4–5, see Rückl, *Sure House*, 291–94 (with further references).

23. For 1 Kgs 9:4–9 as a unified whole, see Provan, *Hezekiah and the Books of Kings*, 110, and many others (see Provan's references). For 2 Kgs 21:7–9, see Provan, *Hezekiah and the Books of Kings*, 117.

24. According to van Keulen, *Manasseh through the Eyes of the Deuteronomists*, 169–71, only vv. 8–9aα are secondary. This difference is not very important for our purpose.

25. E.g., Aurelius, *Zukunft jenseits des Gerichts*, 64–65; Blanco Wissmann, *Er tat das Rechte*, 165, 168.

26. All translations are mine.

said in 2 Kgs 17:12 (cf. 1 Kgs 21:26, concerning Ahab). Perhaps even more importantly, the *hiphil* of the verb חטא, when not used with Manasseh, in Kings is always used with regard to the sins of a few northern monarchs who are said to have made Israel sin. It is used of Baasha (16:2), Baasha and Ela (16:13), and Ahab (21:22), but first and mostly of Jeroboam I, who made Israel sin by building the sanctuaries in Bethel and Dan (1 Kgs 14:16, etc.). The reference to Jeroboam's sin "which he made Israel sin" is a stereotypical part of the religious evaluations of the northern kings in the formulaic prologue to their reigns (1 Kgs 15:26, etc.), and as such it belongs to the most basic structure of the book's first edition. These sins of the northern kings serve as an explanation for the fall of the kingdom of Israel, and—as noted by Blanco Wissmann—if the reference to Manasseh's sin "that he made Judah sin" was part of the first edition of Kings, then this edition most probably included the fall of the kingdom of Judah.[27]

Apart from 2 Kgs 21:11, Manasseh's sin "that he made Judah sin" also appears in verse 16, and, finally, in the following verse, where Manasseh's sin that he committed (this time with the *qal* of חטא) is mentioned in the formulaic reference to the chronicle of the kings of Judah: "Now the rest of the acts of Manasseh and all that he did, and the sin that he committed [וחטאתו אשר חטא], are they not written in the book of the chronicles of the kings of Judah?" At first glance, it might seem surprising that the source to which the author of Kings refers, most likely an annotated king list, should contain a mention of Manasseh's sin.[28] However, in reality the source may have contained a brief note of the king's cultic activities that the author of Kings considered to be sinful (compare, in this connection, the use of *waw*-perfects in vv. 4a and 6a, which is sometimes considered to be characteristic of an annalistic style).[29] In respect to our question, it might be important to recall what Nadav Na'aman observed concerning the references to the chronicles of Judah or Israel: "Strangely, almost all the events mentioned in the final verses are known from the history of the said

---

27. Blanco Wissmann, *Er tat das Rechte*, 162. The following paragraph depends on Blanco Wissmann's argumentation on 166–73. For a detailed comparison of the use of the motif of making a nation sin with Jeroboam, Ahab, and Manasseh, see van Keulen, *Manasseh through the Eyes of the Deuteronomists*, 125–27.

28. This is why Aurelius, *Zukunft jenseits des Gerichts*, 59, considers וחטאתו אשר חטא in v. 17 to be an addition.

29. Nelson, *Double Redaction of the Deuteronomistic History*, 66; differently van Keulen, *Manasseh through the Eyes of the Deuteronomists*, 161–68.

kings" as it is told in Kings.[30] From this situation Na'aman deduces that "the author made the utmost use of the sources at his disposal."[31] Simultaneously, as noted by Blanco Wissmann, this means that Manasseh's sin most likely also appeared in the basic text of the middle corpus of the account of his reign, between the prologue and epilogue. Indeed, even if we would consider verses 10–15 as secondary, Manasseh's sin "that he made Judah sin" would still be present in verse 16, and the reference to Manasseh's sin in the formula in verse 17 may indicate that at least verse 16 was part of the oldest composition of the chapter.[32]

Theoretically, one might speculate that in the Josianic edition of Kings, Manasseh's cultic misdeeds were meant to contrast with Josiah's reform. It is true that at least in the text's current form, Josiah removes, among other things, the consequences of Manasseh's counterreform (cf., e.g., 21:4–5; and 23:12).[33] Nevertheless, as we saw, the concept and terminology of "making a nation sin" rather suggest that already at the text's most basic level, Manasseh not only constituted a contrast to Josiah, but above all a parallel with Israel's kings, especially Jeroboam and Ahab, which suggests the exilic or postexilic origin of this basic layer.

As described in detail by Percy van Keulen, the parallelizing of Manasseh especially with Ahab, but to a lesser degree also with Jeroboam, is omnipresent in Manasseh's account.[34] For instance, Manasseh is said to have erected altar(s) to Baal (2 Kgs 21:3), which was said of Ahab in 1 Kgs 16:32; van Keulen notes that in Kings, "prior to 2 Kgs. 21, Baal worship is exclusively linked with Ahab's house."[35] Moreover, according to 2 Kgs

---

30. Nadav Na'aman, "The Sources Available for the Author of the Book of Kings," in *Convegno Internazionale Recenti Tendenze nella Riccostruzione della Storia Antica d'Israele (Roma, 6–7 marzo 2003)*, ed. Mario Liverani, Contributi del Centro Linceo Interdisciplinare "Beniamino Segre" 110 (Roma: Accademia Nazionale dei Lincei, 2005), 110.

31. Na'aman, "Sources Available," 110.

32. So Blanco Wissmann, *Er tat das Rechte*, 166–73.

33. The links between Manasseh's account and Josiah's reform are emphasized by Hans-Detlef Hoffmann, *Reform und Reformen: Untersuchungen zu einem Grundthema der deuteronomischen Geschichtsschreibung*, ATANT 66 (Zürich: TVZ, 1980), 162–67.

34. See the summary in van Keulen, *Manasseh through the Eyes of the Deuteronomists*, 145–48.

35. Van Keulen, *Manasseh through the Eyes of the Deuteronomists*, 95. There is a textual difference concerning the number of altars in vv. 3–5. MT always reads the plural (in vv. 3 and 4 written *defective*, and in v. 5 written *plene*), LXX[B] always reads

21:3, Manasseh "made an Asherah, as Ahab king of Israel had done" (cf. 1 Kgs 16:33). The author's desire to create a parallel between Manasseh and Ahab transpires clearly from, on the one hand, its explicit character, and on the other hand from the fact that in this case, the comparison is somewhat reductive—it is true that Ahab is said to have made an Asherah, yet according to other information given in Kings, the veneration of Asherah was practiced in Judah before Manasseh (cf. 1 Kgs 14:23; 15:13; 2 Kgs 18:4).[36] The purpose of the comparison is explicit in 2 Kgs 21:13: because Manasseh acted similarly to Ahab, Jerusalem and Judah will suffer the fate of Samaria and the house of Ahab. No matter whether the oracle in verses 10–15 is secondary or not, it is most likely that the comparison of Manasseh to Ahab and Jeroboam served from the beginning to draw a parallel between the fall of Israel and Judah.[37]

Also of particular interest to our purpose is the formula of the religious evaluation in the prologue to Manasseh's account. According to this formula, Manasseh "did what was evil in the sight of YHWH, according to the abominations of the nations whom YHWH dispossessed [הוריש] before the people of Israel" (v. 2). The idea that Israel conquered the land of Canaan in a military way is no doubt influenced by Assyrian militaristic propaganda, and the first edition of the book of Joshua may indeed have been written in the seventh century BCE, at the time when this influence was particularly strong on the Jerusalem scribes.[38] Nevertheless, the notion that the autochthonous population was dispossessed of the land because of their wickedness reflects an idea of Israel's "unnatural" and problematized relationship to the land, most likely provoked by the experience of exile. Moreover, the verse may even be construed as implying that by committing these sins, Manasseh brought on Judah the same fate as that of the nations dispossessed before Israel, that is, as an allusion to

---

the singular, and LXX[L] reads the singular in vv. 3, 4, and the plural in v. 5. In v. 5, the plural seems necessary and is confirmed by 23:15. I tend to prefer the singular in v. 3, and consider MT's plural to be a result of assimilation to the plural in v. 5 (and 4?); the plural of הבמות in v. 3 might also have contributed to this assimilation. However, the difference is not essential, although the singular makes the parallel with Ahab in 1 Kgs 16:32 closer.

36. Van Keulen, *Manasseh through the Eyes of the Deuteronomists*, 95.

37. Hoffmann, *Reform und Reformen*, 162; van Keulen, *Manasseh through the Eyes of the Deuteronomists*, 193.

38. E.g., Römer, *So-Called Deuteronomistic History*, 81–90.

Judah's exile.[39] Again, this exilic/postexilic feature appears on the basic level of the prologue formula.

There has been a literary-critical discussion considering the comparison in verse 2b, as those who situate the first edition of Kings under Josiah are practically forced to consider the half-verse secondary.[40] The comparison of the king to pre-Israelite inhabitants of Canaan is not entirely exceptional in the religious judgment formulae. In 2 Kgs 16:2–3, Ahaz is compared to three entities: he did not do what was right as his father David had done, he walked in the way of the kings of Israel, and "he made his son pass through the fire according to the abominations of the nations whom YHWH dispossessed before the people of Israel." A similar comparison appears in Rehoboam's evaluation in 1 Kgs 14:24. Here, in MT and the majority text of LXX, acting according to the abominations of the nations is ascribed to the people, while LXX^L accuses the king himself. Outside of the formulaic prologue, a similar evaluation appears with Ahab in 1 Kgs 21:26 (cf. also 2 Kgs 17:8, 11, and, again concerning Manasseh, 21:9). Not surprisingly, some defendants of the Kings' preexilic edition (together with some other scholars) consider all these passages secondary.[41] It is impossible to enter here into a detailed redaction-critical discussion of all these passages. Nevertheless, it may be noted that in all three passages where the comparison to the pre-Israelite inhabitants of Canaan appears as part of a king's judgment formula (1 Kgs 14:24; 2 Kgs 16:3; 21:2), there are no convincing literary-critical indices for its excision from the text (separately or as a part of a longer section).[42]

---

39. So Provan, *Hezekiah and the Books of Kings*, 115; van Keulen, *Manasseh through the Eyes of the Deuteronomists*, 75.

40. So already Bernhard Stade, "Miscellen," *ZAW* 6 (1886): 186; similarly, e.g., Mark A. O'Brien, *The Deuteronomistic History Hypothesis: A Reassessment*, OBO 92 (Fribourg: Presses Universitaires; Göttingen: Vandenhoeck & Ruprecht, 1989), 227, 232. Verse 2b is also secondary according to Aurelius, *Zukunft jenseits des Gerichts*, 34–36; Blanco Wissmann, *Er tat das Rechte*, 170.

41. O'Brien, *Deuteronomistic History Hypothesis*, 203, 209–11; 214, 219, 278–79; Provan, *Hezekiah and the Books of Kings*, 70–77, 85–86, 163; Blanco Wissmann, *Er tat das Rechte*, 157–60 (2 Kgs 17:7–20), 236 (1 Kgs 14:24). Contrary to that, Nelson, *Double Redaction of the Deuteronomistic History*, 66–67, ascribes 1 Kgs 14:24; 21:26; 2 Kgs 16:3 to Dtr1.

42. As far as 2 Kgs 21:2 is concerned, Provan asserts that no seam is visible inside the verse and he assigns the whole verse—in fact the whole account of Manasseh—to an exilic hand (*Hezekiah and the Books of Kings*, 115; similarly van Keulen, *Manasseh*

In this connection, the question of the relation between 2 Kgs 21:2, 6 and Deut 18:9–12 may be of some importance. Manasseh's cultic misconducts listed in 2 Kgs 21:6 are (together with others) all forbidden in Deut 18:10–11. Moreover, in 18:9, 12, these practices are designated as abominations of the nations that YHWH is dispossessing before Israel, which corresponds to the fact that in 2 Kgs 21:2 Manasseh is accused of acting according to the abominations of these nations (cf. also 1 Kgs 21:3, 5; Deut 17:3–4). Consequently, scholars often believe that 2 Kgs 21:6 depicts Manasseh's wrongdoings with the help of the list of heterodox practices adduced in Deut 18.[43] Erik Aurelius tried to demonstrate this direction of influence on the ways Deut 18:9 and 2 Kgs 21:2b speak about the nations. While in the former passage, "those nations" (הגוים ההם) refers to the nations mentioned in 17:14, in the latter text the "nations that YHWH dispossessed before the children of Israel" comes from nowhere.[44] For some scholars, the dependence on Deut 18 constitutes another argument for seeing 2 Kgs 21:2b, 6 as late secondary additions.[45]

However, this majority view of the relationship of Deut 18:9–12 and 2 Kgs 21:2b, 6 is not without difficulties. In their immediate literary context, the words "those nations" in Deut 18:9 clearly refer to the nations mentioned in 17:14. The problem is, however, that the nations referred to in these two passages are different: in Deut 18, they are pre-Israelite inhabitants of Canaan, while in Deut 17:14 they are nations living *around* Israel. The incoherence of this identification may be due to relationships of the Deuteronomic laws of the king and prophet to other texts. As I have tried to show elsewhere, the reference to "all the nations around me" in

---

through the Eyes of the Deuteronomists, 175–76). In 1 Kgs 14:22–24 (Provan, *Hezekiah and the Books of Kings*, 74–77) and 2 Kgs 16:2–4 (pp. 85–86), however, Provan deems the comparison to the nations to be a part of a secondary reworking. As for the latter two passages, it seems to me that the moment we accept the possibility that the first edition of Kings was composed in the exilic or Persian period, Provan's arguments lose some of their weight. Note that in 2 Kgs 16:3b, the presence of the expression וגם is deemed to represent "further evidence of a break in the text at this point" (p. 86), while in 1 Kgs 14:22–24, v. 24a, beginning with וגם as well, it is considered to be original (p. 76).

43. E.g., van Keulen, *Manasseh through the Eyes of the Deuteronomists*, 90–92, 99–101, 122.

44. Aurelius, *Zukunft jenseits des Gerichts*, 60.

45. Aurelius, *Zukunft jenseits des Gerichts*, 60; Blanco Wissmann, *Er tat das Rechte*, 170.

Deut 17:14 is dependent on 1 Sam 18:5.[46] A similar relationship may exist between Deut 18:9–12 and 1 Kgs 21:2, 6. The depiction of Manasseh's transgressions as "abominations of the nations whom YHWH dispossessed before the people of Israel" is consistent with the fact that this king is viewed as responsible for the fall and exile of Judah. Contrary to that, no such strong motive for the reference to the dispossessed nations is present in Deut 18. A similar reflection can be made concerning the practice of making a child to pass through fire. In 2 Kgs 21, it has a good place as one of the cultic abominations perpetrated by Manasseh. Contrary to that, as it is not clear that the function of this practice was mainly divinatory, its appearance in Deut 18:10 is not self-evident at all, and it can, again, be due to the influence of Manasseh's account on the formulation of Deut 18:9–12.[47] Therefore, the dependence of 2 Kgs 21:2b, 6 on the Deuteronomic law of the prophet is unlikely, and it should not be used as an argument for the secondary character of these parts of Manasseh's account.

To conclude, two elements pointing to the exilic/Persian period emergence appear even inside the formulaic frame of Manasseh's account, that is, on the text's most basic layer. This observation makes any attempts at reconstructing a preexilic account of Manasseh's reign questionable.

Finally, it should also be noted that the account of Manasseh's reign is surprisingly brief and vague, especially if we consider that, according to the data in Kings, his reign of fifty-five years was the longest of all Judahite and Israelite kings.[48] No matter whether we reconstruct a shorter basic text inside this section or not, Manasseh's account comprises little more than a few pieces of information about the development of the cult during

---

46. Rückl, *Sure House*, esp. 304–5.

47. For a short discussion of this practice, with further references, see van Keulen, *Manasseh through the Eyes of the Deuteronomists*, 99. The dependence of Deut 18:9–14 on (among other texts) 2 Kgs 21:2, 6 is also defended by Matthias Köckert, "Zum literargeschichtlichen Ort des Prophetengesetzes Dtn 18 zwischen dem Jeremiabuch und Dtn 13," in *Liebe und Gebot: Studien zum Deuteronomium; Festschrift zum 70. Geburtstag von Lothar Perlitt*, ed. Reinhard Gregor Kratz and Hermann Spieckermann, FRLANT 190 (Göttingen: Vandenhoeck & Ruprecht, 2000), 95–96. Contrary to that, Aurelius, *Zukunft jenseits des Gerichts*, 60, recognizes that child sacrifice is better anchored in 2 Kgs 21:6, but considers it for that reason a secondary addition in Deut 18:10, based on Manasseh's account or on 2 Kgs 17:17. This kind of argumentation is rather arbitrary.

48. For more observations considering the narrative time of Manasseh's account, see van Keulen, *Manasseh through the Eyes of the Deuteronomists*, 84–86.

his reign. This information was developed into a conventional catalogue of sins, accompanied by a religious interpretation and evaluation of the king's rule. The proponents of Josianic history sometimes surmise that we should not look for written sources concerning Manasseh, Amon, and Josiah, since the historian wrote on the basis of his memories.[49] However, curiously enough, the historian had less to say about Manasseh's extremely long reign than about Ahab whose wickedness he illustrated by the story of Naboth's vineyard. This would be most peculiar if the first edition of the book were produced under Josiah, but seems quite understandable if the first edition was prepared in the exilic or Persian period, on the basis of sources that did not have much to say about Manasseh's rule.

10.3. Amon (2 Kings 21:19–25)

The observation made in the end of the preceding section holds true for Amon's reign as well. The author had no information concerning his reign except the one that he could always extract from the king list he had as a source: the king's age at the accession, the time of his reign, the name of his mother, perhaps the place of his burial and the unusual conditions of his death. The latter is described in a similar brief manner as with all the other kings for whom the information on the conspiracy is taken from the king lists, contrariwise to the vivid portrayal of Jehu's conspiracy for which the author no doubt also had another source. The religious evaluation of Amon simply follows up the evaluation of Manasseh. Again, all this does not testify in favor of a preexilic edition of Kings.

10.4. Josiah (2 Kings 22:1–23:30)

The account of Josiah's reign is one of the most debated texts in Kings, and it is impossible to address all aspects of the discussion in this paper. I will only present a few general observations in support of the view that the edition of Kings that contained the basic form of the account of Josiah's reform was written in the exilic or postexilic period.

Cross argued that two themes were omnipresent in Kings—the theme of the noncentralized cult (mainly the sin of Jeroboam), and the theme of the Davidic dynasty, promised unconditionally to rule in eternity. Because,

---

49. Na'aman, "Sources Available for the Author of the Book of Kings," 117.

in Cross's view, both of these themes meet in climax in the portrayal of Josiah's reign, it seems reasonable that the whole history was conceived from the viewpoint of this historical epoch.[50] Both themes identified by Cross no doubt play principle roles in Samuel and Kings, yet, as I have tried to show in detail elsewhere, the role they play in these books is essentially linked to the situation of the Davidic house in the exilic/postexilic period.[51] I will only note in passing here that the explicit unconditionality, guaranteed by God, of the king's right to the throne, as we find it in 2 Sam 7:14–15, does not belong among the main usual features of the royal ideologies attested in the ancient Near East. On the contrary, in many texts from the ancient Near East, there is a notion of the conditional character of the king's rule, since the ruling king often wished to legitimate his power on account of his being a good king, and thus also to present his blessed rule as merited. The king does not usually have an interest in such presentations of unconditional divine guarantee of his rule that would openly highlight his faults, as is the case in 2 Sam 7:14–15. In the Babylonian exile and in the Persian period, however, this unconditional character of the promise makes perfect sense: when the reality of the loss of power is regarded as a (temporal) punishment, the author of 2 Sam 7 affirms that the Davidides have a right to the throne in spite of their sins, because this right is based on their filial relationship with YHWH.[52]

In conformity with its function to assert the Davidides' right to rule despite their sins, the promise is completely absent from the account of the righteous king Josiah, although it is said of him in 2 Kgs 22:2 that he "walked in all the way of David his father." Therefore, while the theme of the promise is important for the composition of Samuel–Kings, it cannot be argued that it comes to its fulfillment in Josiah's reign.[53] Contrarily to Cross's thesis, Josiah's account does not constitute a point where the two themes developed across the book of Kings would meet in climax.

Another difficult point is the question of the end of the supposed Josianic edition of Kings. Cross and others after him situated it in 2 Kgs 23:25a(α), sometimes arguing that this final note would create an *inclusio* with Deut 6:5: "Before him there was no king like him, who turned to YHWH with all his heart and with all his soul and with all his might,

---

50. Cross, *Canaanite Myth and Hebrew Epic*, 278–85.
51. Rückl, *Sure House*.
52. For a more detailed argument, see Rückl, *Sure House*, 183–84.
53. Provan, *Hezekiah and the Books of Kings*, 28–29.

(according to all the Law of Moses)."[54] The problem is, however, that besides the pressure of the redactional model, there are no grounds for considering the next half-verse ("nor did any like him arise after him") or the whole of verses 25b–27 as stemming from another hand than the one of verse 25a(α).[55]

Mark O'Brien believes that the first edition of the Deuteronomistic History ended with the celebration of Passover under Josiah in 23:21–23.[56] Could Josiah's account ending in 23:23 be preexilic? Obviously not in its current shape, with Huldah's oracle that clearly announces the fall of Judah. Some scholars perceive a tension between Huldah's prediction that Josiah will be gathered to his grave in peace and his violent death, deducing from this alleged tension that at least the part of the prophecy dedicated to Josiah's fate is authentic.[57] Passing over the fact that in the real world, Huldah's prophecy would be a most unusual oracle of salvation addressed to a king, I would agree with those who do not see a contradiction between the oracle and Josiah's fate. Huldah does not promise Josiah that he will die in peace, but rather that he will be gathered to his fathers and buried in peace, without seeing the disaster of Jerusalem.[58] This prob-

---

54. Cross, *Canaanite Myth and Hebrew Epic*, 283, 286; Nelson, *Double Redaction of the Deuteronomistic History*, 83–84; Römer, *So-Called Deuteronomistic History*, 104.

55. This is acknowledged even by Nelson, *Double Redaction of the Deuteronomistic History*, 84, who situates the redactional break in this verse. Of course, the defendants of the Josianic edition adduce other arguments for the redactional break after Josiah's account, as, e.g., the rigidity of the evaluating formulas in the last chapters of Kings, but these arguments fall outside the scope of this paper. For a detailed case against the editorial break in 2 Kgs 23:25, see van Keulen, *Manasseh through the Eyes of the Deuteronomists*, 45–48.

56. O'Brien, *Deuteronomistic History Hypothesis*, 267–68.

57. E.g., John Priest, "Huldah's Oracle," *VT* 30 (1980): 366–68; O'Brien, *Deuteronomistic History Hypothesis*, 244–46; David Noel Freedman and Rebecca Frey, "False Prophecy Is True," in *Inspired Speech: Prophecy in the Ancient Near East; Essays in Honor of Herbert B. Huffmon*, ed. John Kaltner and Louis Stulman, JSOTSup 378 (London: T&T Clark, 2004), 82–87; Cf. also Tal Ilan, "Huldah, the Deuteronomic Prophetess of the Book of Kings," *Lectio Difficilior* 11 (2010): 3, https://tinyurl.com/SBL2643j.

58. So, e.g., Provan, *Hezekiah and the Books of Kings*, 147–49 (with further references); van Keulen, *Manasseh Through the Eyes of the Deuteronomists*, 45–46; Michael Pietsch, "Prophetess of Doom: Hermeneutical Reflections on the Huldah Oracle (2 Kings 22)," in *Soundings in Kings: Perspectives and Methods in Contemporary Scholarship*, ed. Mark Leuchter and Klaus-Peter Adam (Minneapolis: Fortress, 2010),

ably is meant to correspond to the notice in 23:30 that Josiah was buried in his grave. Therefore, no preexilic form of Huldah's oracle can be reconstructed, and, again, there are no formal signs permitting an excision of Huldah's oracle from its context.

According to some scholars, however, not only Huldah's oracle, but the whole theme of the finding of the book is secondary in 2 Kgs 22–23. For instance, Blanco Wissmann believes that it is possible to reconstruct a meaningful primitive text leading from the temple's renovation to its cultic purification. Therefore, in the first edition of Kings, Josiah would be presented as an exemplary king only because of his care for the kingdom's main sanctuary, not for being obedient to a discovered scroll. In Blanco Wissmann's view, the literary seam between the primitive text and a later redaction that added the narrative about the discovery of a book of law is visible in 22:10's repeated introduction of Shaphan's speech (which already was introduced in v. 9).[59] This does not seem convincing. Verse 9 in its current form can hardly follow after verses 3–7. In verses 3–7, Josiah gives Shaphan instructions to oversee the funding of the temple renovations. Verse 9, in its turn, begins with the sentence "And Shaphan the secretary came to the king" (ויבא שפן הספר אל המלך). This sequence would give a rather strange impression, and the text reads much better with verse 8, in which Shaphan meets Hilkiah who informs him about the discovered book.[60] Furthermore, verse 9, where Shaphan reports to the king that his order has been carried out, would also look peculiar without the verse that *follows*. What would be the use of displaying in such a dramatic fashion, that is, with the help of direct speech, Shaphan's informing the king that his orders have been carried out, if this subplot would end here? Contrary to that, in the current context the first part of Shaphan's speech to the king makes good sense, since it corresponds to an idea also observable in other biblical texts that an initiative taken before the monarch should be preceded by a manifestation of one's desire for the king's well-being, compliance to his will, and so on (cf., e.g., 2 Sam 24:3; Neh 2:3). This function of the first part of Shaphan's speech was well understood by the Chronicler. Josiah's temple renovations have a more important place in Chronicles than in Kings. While 2 Kgs 22:3–7 only contain the king's instructions

---

71–80. Contrary to Pietsch, I do not believe that there are safe grounds to consider the oracle an insertion.

59. Blanco Wissmann, *Er tat das Rechte*, 151–54.

60. Similarly O'Brien, *Deuteronomistic History Hypothesis*, 239.

to oversee the financing, with nothing being said about the actual repair of the temple, 2 Chr 34:8–13 presents a self-contained description in the third-person of how the works proceeded.[61] Quite significantly, however, Shaphan's report on the financing of the repair is not part of this account, and it only appears in verses 16–17, where it retains its function of introducing the report on the discovery of the book.

It thus seems difficult to link the introductory part on the financing of the temple renovations (vv. 22:3–7 + 9) directly with the cultic reform in 23:4–23*. As noted by Oded Lipschits, the instructions given by the king to Shaphan serve to set in motion the events that will lead to the discovery of the book and to the reform.[62] Without entering into a discussion on whether the king's instructions are based on a source used in the description of the financing of the temple repairs under Jehoash in 2 Kgs 12, or whether both texts come from the same author, it seems that in 2 Kgs 22 the system of financing the repairs was used mainly in order to bring on the scene the king's scribe and the high priest who according to 2 Kgs 12:11–16 were supposed to collaborate in the distribution of the silver collected in the box.[63]

Finally, I would like to suggest one more argument for the basic literary unity of the account contained in 2 Kgs 22:3–23:15 + 23:21–23. As demonstrated by Römer and others, there seems to be a link between 2 Kgs 22 and Jer 36. In both texts the king is presented with a book, and in both texts members of Shaphan's family play an important role. The kings' reactions to the words of the book are, however, different—while Josiah tears his clothes as a sign of contrition (22:11, 19), it is said of Jehoiakim and his servants that they did not tear their garments (Jer 36:24). For this reason, Josiah will be buried in peace (2 Kgs 22:20), while Jehoiakim will not be buried at all (Jer 36:30). Scholars disagree on the direction of the literary dependence between the two texts, but Römer suggested that "both

---

61. That the actual repair is unmentioned in 2 Kgs 22 is emphasized by Oded Lipschits, "On Cash-Boxes and Finding or Not Finding Books: Jehoash's and Josiah's Decisions to Repair the Temple," in *Essays on Ancient Israel in Its Near Eastern Context: A Tribute to Nadav Na'aman*, ed. Yairah Amit et al. (Winona Lake, IN: Eisenbrauns, 2006), 241, 250.

62. Lipschits, "On Cash-Boxes and Finding or Not Finding Books," 241, 251.

63. Lipschits believes both texts came from the same source, "On Cash-Boxes and Finding or Not Finding Books." For other suggestions, see the references he gives on 246–47.

texts emanate from the same dtr. circle and they are written as two poles corresponding to each other."[64] There is a formal feature in both texts that may testify in favor of this suggestion. In both texts, the kings are systematically designated only by the title "king," not by the name together with the title or the name alone. This procedure has an artistic effect. Both texts portray the kings' interactions with various functionaries, and this way of designating the monarchs evokes those circles where it is always clear which monarch the word "king" designates. As far as Josiah's account is concerned, the distribution of this feature is most noteworthy. It appears at the beginning of the narrative in 22:3 and is consistently held until 23:15. Then it disappears in 23:16–20, that is, in verses that may be judged secondary also for other reasons (e.g., vv. 16–18 are not part of the report on the cultic reform but a fulfillment notice linked to the oracle in 1 Kgs 13).[65] Subsequently the title "king" appears again in the celebration of the Passover in verses 21–23, before disappearing in verse 24, which seems to be an additional catalogue of Josiah's reform measures.[66] This observation does not mean that the text of 22:3–23:15 + 23:21–23 must be homogenous exactly as it currently stands, but basically it seems to constitute a literary unit.

Therefore, while certain parts of the account of Josiah's reign are probably secondary, the basic portrayal of the events leading to the cult reform, including Huldah's oracle, seems to be literarily more or less homogenous, and it thus most likely cannot stem from the seventh century.

10.5. Conclusion

The accounts of the reigns of Manasseh, Amon, and Josiah evince characteristics that point to their post-586 BCE composition. It seems likely that Manasseh and Josiah's accounts went through a secondary redaction, but there are no sufficient literary indices allowing for a reconstruction

---

64. Thomas Römer, "Transformations in Deuteronomistic and Biblical Historiography: On 'Book-Finding' and Other Literary Strategies," *ZAW* 109 (1997): 9. Cf. also Blanco Wissmann, *Er tat das Rechte*, 152–53.

65. O'Brien, *Deuteronomistic History Hypothesis*, 263–64; Römer, *So-Called Deuteronomistic History*, 161.

66. The secondary nature of v. 24 is recognized, by, e.g., O'Brien, *Deuteronomistic History Hypothesis*, 266–67; Eynikel, *Reform of King Josiah and the Composition of the Deuteronomistic History*, 350.

of a basic primitive text from which all the elements reflecting an exilic or Persian period origin would be absent. The attempts at such reconstructions arouse suspicion of being motivated by the pressure of broader redactional models.[67]

---

67. A note briefly touching on the account of Hezekiah's reign (that I otherwise avoided for reasons of space) might be added at this point. One of the general arguments for dating the first edition of Kings to the preexilic period is the idea that the historian writing in that time would have had better access to sources than a scribe working after the destruction of Jerusalem. Nevertheless, it seems quite clear that the scribes writing in the sixth century or later did have access to sources from the time of the monarchy. This is corroborated, e.g., by the narrative that immediately precedes Manasseh's account, i.e., the report of the visit of Merodach-Baladan's envoys to Hezekiah (1 Kgs 20:12–19). On the one hand, this text probably reflects a historical event, i.e., a diplomatic visit of the envoys of the Babylonian king Marduk-Apla-Iddina II (721–710 and 703) to Jerusalem under Hezekiah's reign. On the other hand, the whole text is clearly constructed so as to segue into a prediction of exile. It is impossible to reconstruct an older version of the text that would be part of the Josianic edition, and it is even hard to imagine why the Josianic historian would want to include this event in his work. Therefore, the information about the diplomatic visit of the Babylonian king's envoys most likely survived in a source, perhaps the annotated list of Judahite kings, until the exilic or Persian period, when it could be developed into a narrative leading to an anticipation of the exile.

Two Faces of Manasseh:
The Reception of Manasseh in the Early Jewish Literature

David Cielontko

King Manasseh is one of the most infamous kings of Judah. As the longest reigning ruler of the divided monarchy, the Deuteronomistic History portrays him as the king whose sins exceeded even those of Ahab, Ahaz, or Jeroboam and as the one responsible for the downfall of Judah and the exile. There has been much discussion as to whether ideologically tendentious biblical narratives represent something factual about the real Manasseh of history. His existence is supported by two Assyrian texts; the Esarhaddon annals, which claim that Manasseh was a vassal king of the city(-state) of Judah and, together with twenty-one other kings, had supported the building project of Esarhaddon's new palace; and the Assurbanipal annals, which describe Assurbanipal's first campaign against Egypt on which Manasseh participated with other vassal kings.[1] Therefore, his subjection to the Assyrian Empire to whom Judah was submitted as a vassal state is well grounded in the sources. Some scholars argue that his cultic and cultural openness that opposed Hezekiah's strict reforms was a clever political manoeuver toward Assyria and thus a pragmatic move to protect his people.[2] On the other hand, his motivation could have been far

---

This study was supported by the Charles University Grant Agency and Protestant Theological Faculty of the Charles University, project GA UK no. 728516. I am grateful to Kyle Parsons for proofreading the paper.

1. For Esarhaddon, see "The Syro-Palestinian Campaign; Prism B," *ANET*, 291. For Assurbanipal, see "Campaigns against Egypt, Syria, and Palestine; Cylinder C," *ANET*, 294.

2. See the discussion in Francesca Stavrakopoulou, *King Manasseh and Child Sacrifice: Biblical Distortions of Historical Realities*, BZAW 338 (Berlin: de Gruyter, 2004), 99–119; Lester L. Grabbe, *Ancient Israel: What Do We Know and How Do We Know*

less noble, as Gösta Ahlström suggested, he might simply have understood that any rebellion would be meaningless.[3]

As important as this reconstruction of the historical Manasseh is, it is not the aim of this study. Our present concern is to analyze the literary texts about Manasseh in early Jewish literature. These literary sources provide us with special insights into various ways traditions and recollections developed about this Judean king throughout the centuries. We exclude from this systematic inquiry Josephus since it has been thoroughly discussed elsewhere, and several mentions in rabbinic literature.[4] However, they will be repeatedly mentioned when they offer important parallels to the discussed texts. This study presents first and foremost a survey of the texts about Manasseh without ambition to offer any coherent theory on the development of the tradition in the light of historical and social contexts in which the discussed texts originated. We are rather skeptical about the possibility of such a task since in the case of most texts, we are unable to determine the date or provenience with any precision.[5] It might be conve-

---

It?, rev. ed., LHBOTS 393 (London: T&T Clark, 2017), 244–47; Israel Finkelstein and Neil A. Silberman, *The Bible Unearthed: Archaeology's New Vision of Ancient Israel and the Origin of Its Sacred Texts* (London: Simon & Schuster, 2001), 264–74; Finkelstein, "The Archaeology of the Days of Manasseh," in *Scripture and Other Artifacts: Essays on the Bible and Archaeology in Honor of Philip J. King*, ed. Michael D. Coogan, J. Cheryl Exum, and Lawrence E. Stager (Louisville: Westminster John Knox, 1994), 169–87; Yifat Thareani-Sussely, "The 'Archaeology of the Days of Manasseh' Reconsidered in the Light of Evidence from the Beersheba Valley," *PEQ* 139 (2007): 69–77; but also a different evaluation in Oded Lipschits, Omer Sergi, and Ido Koch, "Judahite Stamped and Incised Jar Handles: A Tool for Studying the History of Late Monarchic Judah," *TA* 38 (2011): 5–41; esp. 26–29.

3. Gösta W. Ahlström, *The History of Ancient Palestine*, JSOTSup 146 (Sheffield: Sheffield Academic, 1993), 730.

4. For Josephus, see Louis H. Feldmann, *Studies in Josephus' Rewritten Bible*, JSJSup 58 (Leiden: Brill, 1998), 416–26; Christopher Begg, *Josephus' Story of the Later Monarchy*, BETL 145 (Leuven: Peeters, 2000), 441–52. The material in rabbinic literature has been gathered in Louis Ginzberg, *The Legends of the Jews* (Philadelphia: Jewish Publication Society, 1909–1938), 6:370–76. See also David S. Sperling, "Manasseh," *EncJud* 13:452–53; and Pierre Bogaert, *L'Apocalypse Syriaque de Baruch: Introduction, traduction du syriaque et commentaire* (Paris: Cerf, 1969), 1:296–319.

5. See, e.g., Lowell K. Handy, "Rehabilitating Manasseh: Remembering King Manasseh in the Persian and Hellenistic Periods," in *Remembering Biblical Figures in the Late Persian and Early Hellenistic Periods: Social Memory and Imagination*, ed. Ehud Ben Zvi and Diana V. Edelman (Oxford: Oxford University Press, 2013), 221–35.

nient to notice that biblical narratives are already part of *Wirkungsgeschichte* of Manasseh, and, naturally, the portrayal of 2 Chronicles is dependent on 2 Kings. Nevertheless, both biblical narratives serve, for the most part, as a model for the later traditions that we are interested in. Therefore, we start our analysis with a brief discussion of them.

11.1. Manasseh in the Biblical Narratives

11.1.1. Presentation of Manasseh in the Biblical Narratives

The account of the Deuteronomist in 2 Kgs 21:1–18 paints a dark picture of this king of Judah. He is portrayed as an idolater who instituted the worship of the foreign gods, Baal and Asherah, in Jerusalem and rebuilt the high places that his father, Hezekiah, had previously destroyed. He has also made his son "pass through fire," practiced soothsaying, sorcery and divination (v. 6), and shed very much innocent blood until he filled Jerusalem with it (v. 16; 24:4).[6] As an avowed sinner and the most wicked king of Judah, Manasseh's deeds are likened to the bad kings Ahab (vv. 3, 13), Ahaz (v. 6), and Jeroboam in causing the downfall of the kingdom (cf. 13–14). He also stands in contrast to the good kings Hezekiah (vv. 2–3), David, and Solomon (v. 7).[7]

From a theological standpoint, the Deuteronomist explains the exile as a result of the accumulation of (predominantly) cultic sins of the Israelites and their kings against God. Manasseh serves as the climactic figure whose sins exceed everyone before him (2 Kgs 21:16) and whose

---

6. The Dtr terminology distinguishes between the practice of the nations who "burn in fire" (שרפו באש) their children in service of their gods (Deut 12:31; 2 Kgs 17:31) and the practice of apostate Israelites who "make pass through fire" (באש העביר) their children (2 Kgs 16:3; 21:6). Cf. Mordechai Cogan and Hayim Tadmor, *II Kings: A New Translation with Introduction and Commentary*, AB 11 (New York: Doubleday, 1988), 266. On the shedding of innocent blood, see Edgar Kellenberger, "Wessen unschuldiges Blut vergossen Manasse und Jojaqim?," in *A King Like All the Nations? Kingdoms of Israel and Judah in the Bible and History*, ed. Manfred Oeming and Petr Sláma, BVB 28 (Münster: LIT, 2015), 215–27.

7. Cf. Percy S. F. van Keulen, *Manasseh through the Eyes of the Deuteronomists: The Manasseh Account (2 Kings 21:1–18) and the Final Chapters of the Deuteronomistic History*, OTS 38 (Leiden: Brill, 1996), 144–58; Klaas Smelik, "The Portrayal of King Manasseh: A Literary Analysis of II Kings xxi and II Chronicles xxiii," in *Converting the Past: Studies in Ancient Israelite and Moabite Historiography*, ed. Klaas Smelik, OTS 28 (Leiden: Brill, 1992), 148–49.

wickedness reaches the level that God was not willing to pardon (2 Kgs 23:26; 24:3–4; cf. Jer 15:4). Not even the best king in the Deuteronomistic estimation, Josiah (2 Kgs 23:25), could change anything about God's impending judgment.

The Chronicles' narrative (2 Chr 33:1–20) offers a considerably different account of the Manasseh's reign. After the description of his sins, which, in the most cases, parallels the account of 2 Kings, the Chronicler narrates a different course of events.[8] As a consequence of ignoring the divine warning about his wrong deeds, Manasseh is immediately punished for wrongdoing by being arrested and deported to Babylon by the king of Assyria. In his own "exile,"[9] he prayed and cried out to God in distress having acknowledged that "the Lord was indeed God" (v. 13) and, in response, God brought him back to Jerusalem. Manasseh's conversion is afterward demonstrated by his deeds of restoration, which can be seen in his rebuilding the fortifications in Jerusalem, installing military commanders in all the fortified cities of Judah, purifying the cult in Jerusalem, and commanding Judah to worship Yahweh as the God of Israel (vv. 14–16). There is agreement that these unique verses to the Chronicles' narrative are interwoven with the theological vocabulary of the book.[10] Most of the scholars find here an expression of the so-called doctrine of immediate retribution, which, in this case, offers an explanation of the king's long reign.[11] Nevertheless, while Manasseh's repentance effectively counters his image as the worst king of the Judahite monarchy, some of his

---

8. However, Smelik notices that portrayal of Manasseh in the Chronicles is also less extremely negative with regard to the period before conversion. Smelik, "Portrayal of King Manasseh," 184.

9. The Chronicler here uses identical phraseology to that of Nebuchadnezzar's exile of Jehoiakim in 2 Chr 36:6 (ויאסרהו בנחשתים).

10. Ralph W. Klein, 2 Chronicles: A Commentary, Hermeneia (Minneapolis: Fortress, 2012), 473.

11. For the doctrine of immediate retribution, see also Sara Japhet, The Ideology of the Book of Chronicles and Its Place in Biblical Thought, 2nd ed. (Frankfurt: Lang, 1997), 165–76; Raymond B. Dillard, 2 Chronicles, WBC 15 (Waco, TX: Word, 1987), 76–81. This theological doctrine of the books of Chronicles has fundamental expression in 2 Chr 7:14 and 15:2 and is the most apparently present in the cases of late Solomon, Rehoboam, Abijah, Asa, Jehoshaphat, and Manasseh. However, there are also cases in which it does not apply. Cf. Klein, 2 Chronicles, 11–12. For his repentance as an explanation for his long reign, see Sara Japhet, 2 Chronik, HThKAT (Freiburg im Breisgau: Herder, 2003), 442–53.

earlier sins remain unrevoked and, therefore, he leaves a partially negative cultic legacy for his successors. After all, we read that despite all his restoration acts "the people continued sacrificing on the high places, though only to Yahweh, their God" (v. 17).[12]

11.1.2. Evaluation of Manasseh in the Biblical Narratives

Both accounts present highly stylized depictions of Manasseh. To make it even more apparent, it is instructive to compare the structures of both presentations. In the Deuteronomistic account, 2 Kgs 21:9, with its focus on Manasseh causing the whole nation to stray, is the center. On the other hand, Chronicles sets Manasseh's repentance as the climax.[13]

For both accounts, Manasseh is an important figure, theologically symbolizing something more significant than a king of the past. Deuteronomistic Manasseh represents Judah's most dangerous threat. He is presented as the arch-villain responsible for the fall of Judah, and his description serves as an everlasting warning reminding that there is a level of disobedience and provocation that God is not willing to pardon. For Chronicles, Manasseh is a paradigm for the experience that Judah itself would undergo in the following story. He is a symbol of the punished, the repentant, the restored, and the newly blessed Israel. Manasseh is seen as a penitent king whose prayer in distress was heard by God and whose reign became blessed because he changed his previous ways.[14]

For our inquiry, it is instructive to enlist the unique elements that are characteristic of only one of the traditions as the following texts are

---

12. See the nuanced discussion on Manasseh in Chronicles by Gary N. Knoppers, "Saint of Sinner? Manasseh in Chronicles," in *Rewriting Biblical History: Essays on Chronicles and Ben Sira in Honor of Pancratius C. Beentjes*, ed. Jeremy Corley and Harm van Grol, DCLS 9 (Berlin: de Gruyter, 2011), 211–29. Biblical quotations are from the NRSV, sometimes modified.

13. Philippe Abadie, "From the Impious Manasseh (2 Kings 21) to the Convert Manasseh (2 Chronicles 33): Theological Rewriting by the Chronicler," in *The Chronicler as Theologian: Essays in Honor of Ralph W. Klein*, ed. M. Patrick Graham, Steven L. McKenzie, and Gary N. Knoppers, JSOTSup 371 (Edinburgh: T&T Clark, 2003), 91–96; Smelik, "Portrayal of King Manasseh," 133, 170.

14. Dillard, *2 Chronicles*, 271; Mark J. Boda, "Identity and Empire, Reality and Hope in the Chronicler's Perspective," in *Community Identity in Judean Historiography: Biblical and Comparative Perspectives*, ed. Gary N. Knoppers and Kenneth A. Ristau (Winona Lake, IN: Eisenbrauns, 2009), 267–68.

usually dependent on the literary presentations of the Hebrew Bible. We have already mentioned the important elaboration of the story in Chronicles focusing on the king's repentance and reforms. In addition, there are two noteworthy elements of 2 Kings that have no counterparts in 2 Chronicles: (1) a prophetic oracle against Manasseh who is blamed for the coming destruction of Jerusalem and Judah and deportation of the people to exile (2 Kgs 21:10–15), (2) a remark on Manasseh shedding much innocent blood in Jerusalem (v. 16). All of these observations will be instructive in the following analysis.

11.2. The Reception of Manasseh in Early Jewish Literature

Now we can proceed to the reception of Manasseh in the texts of early Judaism. By early Jewish literature, we mean noncanonical Jewish writings from approximately the third century BCE to second century CE. Seven different texts from the selected period will be discussed. Unfortunately, we cannot arrange these texts chronologically since the dates are, in some cases, disputed. Therefore, on the grounds of preliminary observation of the content of these texts, we have decided to sort them according to their presentation of Manasseh, whether they present the Judean king as a positive or negative figure. These two distinct lines of depiction naturally result from the distinct content of the biblical accounts. It is interesting that these texts tend to exclusively portray Manasseh with no attention given to the specifics of other biblical tradition. Eventually, this one-sidedness allows us to outline the material in a suggested way. It is fair to acknowledge that the depiction by Josephus, which is not part of this discussion, does not fit well into this outline. However, this outline serves only as a manner of presentation. In the discussions, we will start with those texts that depict Manasseh as a negative figure.

11.2.1. Negative Depictions of Manasseh

This section will discuss three apocalypses and one legend. In the case of the Animal Apocalypse and the Apocalypse of Abraham, we deal with a methodologically questionable situation as Manasseh is not explicitly named, and therefore, we must acknowledge the fact that we are arguing in a sort of hermeneutical circle. However, the identification of the implicit referent as Manasseh is plausibly made on the basis of the interpretation of their presentation of the history of Israel.

11.2.1.1. The Animal Apocalypse

The very first text of our concern is an Enochic composition called the Animal Apocalypse. It is a historical apocalypse extant as a part of dream visions of the first book of Enoch.[15] The final form of the text comes from the time of the campaigns of Judas Maccabeus around 165–160 BCE.[16] The history presented in this vision is divided into three major eras: (1) from the creation to the flood, (2) from the renewal of the creation after the flood to the great judgment, (3) the second renewal after the judgment into an open future.[17] The vision is narrated allegorically by using animals instead of the biblical characters.[18] For example, Adam is represented by a white bull, Cain and Abel are black and red bullocks, the giants begotten by daughters of men are elephants, camels, and asses, the fallen angels are stars, Israel are sheep, the oppressing gentile nations are wild beasts, and so on.

As a part of a broader allegorical description of the period of the divided kingdom (1 En. 89.51–58), which could be summarized as an era of increasing degeneration, apostasy, and rejection of the prophetic call, verses 54–58 describe the last period of the history of Judah before the exile. This tendency to interpret the history as increasing in decadence is also evident in the complete neglect of the good kings: Hezekiah and Josiah. Although some suggested that this last section describes the Syro-Ephraimite war, it is more convincing to read it as a summary of the period during the reign of Manasseh according to 2 Kings.[19] There are several arguments supporting this reading: (1) it is described as a period of the

---

15. For the introduction to 1 Enoch, see George W. E. Nickelsburg, *Jewish Literature between the Bible and the Mishnah*, 2nd ed. (Minneapolis: Fortress, 2005), 43–53, 83–86, 110–14, 248–50.

16. For the discussion about the date of origin, see Patrick A. Tiller, *A Commentary on the Animal Apocalypse*, EJL 4 (Atlanta: Scholars Press, 1993), 61–79; See also George W. E. Nickelsburg, *1 Enoch 1: A Commentary on the Book of 1 Enoch*, Hermeneia (Minneapolis: Fortress, 2001), 360–63.

17. See Nickelsburg, *1 Enoch 1*, 354–55.

18. Tiller, *Commentary*, 21–60; on the identification, see Nickelsburg, *1 Enoch 1*, 358.

19. The author of Animal Apocalypse follows the biblical history according to the Deuteronomistic account. See Nickelsburg, *1 Enoch 1*, 358; Daniel Assefa, *L'Apocalypse des animaux (1Hen 85–90): Une propagande militaire?*, JSJSup 120 (Leiden: Brill, 2007), 158–59, 265–66. For reading this text as referring to the Syro-Ephraimite war,

worst apostasy (see below), (2) it is followed by the destruction of Judah and exile, and (3) verse 56 is apparently a paraphrase of 2 Kgs 21:14, however, in its own allegorical way:

> And I saw that he [God] abandoned that house of theirs and their tower, and he threw them all into the hands of the lions so that they might tear them in pieces and devour them—into the hands of all the beasts. (1 En. 89.56, trans. Nickelsburg)

> I [God] will abandon the remnant of my heritage, and give them into the hand of their enemies; they shall become a prey and a spoil to all their enemies. (2 Kgs 21:14)

In the Enochic text, the house and tower refer to Jerusalem and its temple, and the lions symbolize Babylonians. This section, which formally begins in verse 54 with an introductory "and after that," describes the climactic period of the apostasy of Israel, which is summarized as "they went astray in everything and their eyes were blinded." In the Animal Apocalypse, the images of blindness and straying from the path of God represent the sins of apostasy from the divinely revealed and sanctioned cult. The seriousness of the wrongdoing is expressed by a combination of both of the terms, which appear only in this case and in the story of the golden calf (89.32–35). Nevertheless, only in this place we find an intensification of the apostasy with the statement, "they went astray in *everything*."[20] Therefore, in the author's perspective, this last episode of the history of Judah is characterized as the worst. As a reaction to these sins, God leaves Jerusalem and the temple and abandons his "sheep" to the hands of the dire animals representing Egyptians (wolves), Ammonites (foxes), Arameans (leopards), Moabites (hyenas), and, foremost, Babylonians (lions) who start to tear Israel (sheep) into pieces. Hence, there is a clear connection between the sins of this last generation and the upcoming destruction of Judea and the exile. The section ends with Enoch's petition on behalf of Israel, but God's decree is irrevocable (cf. 2 Kgs 23:26; 24:3–4). For the author of this text, the situation during Manasseh's reign had a crucial impact on his lifetime as, according to his view, the cult has never been

---

see Tiller, *Commentary*, 317; Daniel C. Olson, *A New Reading of the Animal Apocalypse of 1 Enoch*, SVTP 24 (Leiden: Brill, 2013), 185.

20. Nickelsburg, *1 Enoch 1*, 384–86, emphasis added.

properly restored and therefore, the temple has been polluted since the time of Manasseh (89.73).[21]

In the Animal Apocalypse, the description of Manasseh's reign follows the Deuteronomistic account. This period is characterized as a time of the greatest apostasy in Israelite history and forms the climax of the increasing decadence of the kingdom of Judah. The anticlimactic good kings Hezekiah and Josiah are completely omitted, and Manasseh is blamed for the irreversible destruction of Judah and the exile.[22] The author relies solely on 2 Kings and there are no traces of Manasseh's conversion in the story. Deuteronomistic Manasseh fits well into this apocalyptic presentation of history. It is interesting that the author of this text brought one novelty to the tradition that is not found in either 2 Kings or 2 Chronicles but only in Ezek 9–10, concretely, that God in response to the wickedness abandons Jerusalem and its temple. The same idea will reappear in 2 Baruch.

11.2.1.2. The Apocalypse of Abraham

The Apocalypse of Abraham is another historical apocalypse narrating an account of Abraham's conversion from idolatry (chs. 1–8) and the revelations he received after ascending to heaven (chs. 9–32). The exact date of the composition is unknown, but it probably originated not long after the destruction of Jerusalem that is mentioned in chapter 27.[23]

The reference to Manasseh is again only indirect, as in the previous text. It appears in the second vision of Abraham, which presents history as a series of vignettes. After dealing with the fall of humanity (chs. 23–24), which opened questions about the nature of sin, Abraham sees the murder of Abel and human actions that represent impurity, theft, passion, and desire, as well as their punishment (ch. 24). The era of Manasseh belongs to the last segment of Abraham's vision focusing on the temple and its cult (ch. 25).

Abraham first sees a defiled earthly temple with an idol worshiped by a man and with boys being slaughtered on an altar in front of the face

---

21. See a similar tradition in rabbinic texts b. Yoma 9b; 21b; Pesiq. Rab. 35; Gen. Rab. 36:8.

22. The only possible reference to Josiah is made indirectly through a mention of "the wolves" as one of the beasts that tear sheep to pieces in v. 45. The wolves are the Egyptians (1 En. 89.13–27) and therefore the event referred to is most likely the campaign of Pharaoh Necho that resulted in the death of Josiah (2 Kgs 23:28–35).

23. Cf. Ryszard Rubinkiewicz, "Apocalypse of Abraham," OTP 1:683.

of that idol. After that, he sees a beautiful heavenly temple beneath God's throne with art and beauty. In the following explanation, God explains to him that the beautiful temple is God's own idea of the ideal priesthood where every man, king, or prophet could enter and dwell. However, the idol and the man who slaughters the boys make God angry. Subsequently, for these cultic abominations, the gentiles destroy Jerusalem and burn the temple (ch. 27).

The description of the man who worshiped the idol and slaughtered boys in chapter 25 accords with the image of Manasseh from 2 Kings.[24] Manasseh is here presented as a man of God's anger who caused the destruction of Jerusalem and the temple. The motif of slaughtered boys in front of an idol probably derives from Manasseh's sacrificing his own son (2 Kgs 21:6) or sons in the plural (2 Chr 33:6). The idol with a face reflects the development of the tradition from 2 Kgs 21:7 // 2 Chr 33:7. As we will see below, 2 Baruch contains a more expanded description of the idol. While identification of Manasseh as the cause of the destruction of Jerusalem comes undoubtedly from the Deuteronomistic version, the plural of boys might be influenced by the plural of 2 Chronicles. In this portrayal, similarly to the Animal Apocalypse, the apocalyptic historical overview skips the good kings, Hezekiah and Josiah, in order to culminate the wickedness during Manasseh's reign.

11.2.1.3. The Syriac Apocalypse of Baruch or 2 Baruch

Second Baruch is a pseudepigraphical text supposedly written by Baruch, the scribe of Jeremiah, which is set on the eve of the destruction of Jerusalem in 587 BCE. However, this text was composed sometime between the two Jewish wars in 70 and 132 CE.[25]

This extensive apocalypse is divided into seven units consisting of various genres such as narratives, conversations, laments, visions, and

---

24. See Nickelsburg, *Jewish Literature*, 287; Ryszard Rubinkiewicz, *L'Apocalypse D'Abraham: Introduction, texte critique, traduction et commentaire* (Lublin: Société des Lettres et des Sciences de l'Université Catholique de Lublin, 1987), 183.

25. See the discussion in Bogaert, *Apocalypse Syriaque*, 1:270–95. Bogaert tends to date it to the last decade of the first century. Gurtner suggests that the 'twenty-fifth year of Jeconiah' in 2 Bar. 1.1 refers to the year 95 CE as the date of origin, see Daniel M. Gurtner, "The 'Twenty-Fifth Year of Joconiah' and the Date of *2 Baruch*," *JSP* 18 (2008): 23–32.

prayers.[26] The longest unit spans through chapters 53–76 and describes a vision of the history of Israel presented as a cloud pouring twelve sets of alternating dark and bright waters on the earth. After these twelve showers, one additional dark shower appears describing the turbulent final period (chs. 69–71), which is immediately followed by the period of the messiah (chs. 72–74), who will inaugurate an era of peace and prosperity.

In the interpretation of this remarkable vision that angel Ramiel provides, the ninth black waters represent the days of Manasseh (chs. 64–65). It begins by listing his evil deeds: he acted very wickedly, killed the righteous, perverted judgment, shed innocent blood, violently polluted married women, overturned altars, abolished offerings, drove away the priests who ministered in the sanctuary, and he made a statue with five faces, four of them looked in four directions and the fifth looked up to challenge the zeal of the Mighty One. His impiety increased to such a degree that God's glory removed itself from the sanctuary. He was also blamed for the incoming judgment when Zion would be uprooted, and the remaining tribes of Israel would be carried away into captivity. His final habitation is said to be on fire.

Some of these charges just repeat those from the biblical tradition. The remarks on shedding innocent blood and blame for the destruction and exile point to 2 Kings as the source. Nevertheless, it also adds some new elements such as killing the righteous, perverting the judgment, violently polluting women, driving out priests, and making an idol with five faces, all of which are also known from other traditions. Manasseh is traditionally connected with the death of the righteous prophet Isaiah (cf. Heb 11:37; Liv. Pro. 1; b. Sanh. 103b; b. Yebam. 49b; Mart. Ascen. Isa. 5.1–2 [see below]).[27] In the case of b. Yebam. 49b and Martyrdom of Isaiah, he also acts in the role of judge who sentences the prophet. In the similar list of his evil deeds in the Martyrdom of Isaiah, we also find that he committed fornication (Mart. Ascen. Isa. 2:5) and tractate b. Sanh. 103b records that he "violated his sister." Although none of these match perfectly with the "violently polluting married women" of 2 Baruch, the tradition indeed

---

26. For the literary structure of the 2 Baruch see Tom W. Willett, *Eschatology in the Theodicies of 2 Baruch and 4 Ezra*, JSPSup 4 (Sheffield: JSOT Press, 1989), 80–95.

27. However, b. Sanh 103b refers to a different interpretation of the killing of righteous in the west (Palestine) where: "[It means] that he made an image as heavy as a thousand men, and every day it slew all of them" (trans. H. Freedman).

elaborates on his aggressive attitude toward women.[28] With regard to the peculiar idol that he made, Apocalypse of Abraham (see above) records that he set in the temple an idol with one face (Apoc. Ab. 25.2) and b. Sanh. 103b expounds this by noting that he made, at first, the idol with one face, but subsequently he remade it with four faces imitating the four figures on the divine throne of Ezek 1. The four-faced idol is also mentioned in the Peshitta of 2 Chr 33:7 and Deut. Rab. 2:20. The description of the idol in 2 Bar. 64.3 looks, therefore, to be a conflation of these traditions having the five faces with four facing the four cardinal points and one on top.

The most exciting part of the depiction of Manasseh in 2 Baruch begins at 64.7 where we read about his prayer in distress. In contrast to his righteous father, Hezekiah, who also prayed to God and was saved (2 Bar. 63), Manasseh is said to be an unworthy sinner to whom God's intervention had become only a sign of God's final punishment upon him, for he should have understood that "who is able to benefit is also able to punish" (64.10, trans. Klijn, OTP). Even though God saved Manasseh from his captivity, Manasseh did not change his ways and wrongly thought that God in his time would not hold him responsible for his sins (ch. 65). Manasseh's rescue from the Babylonian captivity is referred to here curiously as being saved from "the brazen horse that was about to be melted" (64.8).[29] This odd reference is clarified when read in the light of y. Sanh. 10.2 and the targum of Chronicles:

> They caught Manasse in ḥōḥîm (2 Chr 33:11). What are ḥōḥîm? Handcuffs. Rebbi Levi said, they made a bronze mule for him, put him inside, and started heating it from below. (trans. Guggenheimer)

> Then the Chaldeans made a bronze mule and bored many small holes in it. They shut him (Manasseh) up inside it and lit a fire all around it. When he was in distress, he sought help from all his idols which he had made, but there was no help forthcoming, for there is no profit in them.

---

28. Bogaert, Apocalypse Syriaque, 2:119.

29. On the possible origin of the motif as an adaptation of a well-known torturing instrument of Sycilian tyrant Phalaris in the shape of a brazen bull, see Gideon Bohak, "Classica et Rabbinica I: The Bull of Phalaris and the Tophet," JSJ 31 (2000): 203–16. The Arabic version of 2 Baruch reads "bronze bull" instead of "bronze mule." Cf. Frederik Leemhuis, Albertus F. J. Klijn, and Geert J. H. van Gelder, The Arabic Text of the Apocalypse of Baruch (Leiden: Brill, 1986), 98–99. The bull shape is also to be found in Midrash Haggadol of Gen 4:13.

Then he changed his mind and prayed before the Lord his God, and humbled himself greatly from before the Lord, the God of his fathers.... And he (God) made an opening and a gap in the heavens beneath the throne of his Memra, the mule was shattered, and he (Manasseh) came out from there. Then there went forth a wind from between the wings of cherubim, it blew him by the decree of the Memra of the Lord, and he returned to Jerusalem to his Kingdom.[30]

The portrayal of Manasseh in 2 Baruch gives an exciting insight into the development of the traditions about Manasseh at the end of the first century CE. The author of this apocalypse interacts with various traditions that have probably been in circulation. The quantity of traditions brought together in 2 Baruch can be compared only to the presentation of Manasseh in Josephus's *Jewish Antiquities* (10.37–48) who gathered a wide array of sources for his historical presentation. Second Baruch is also the only text of those surveyed here as presenting an evil Manasseh that deals with the king's repentance recorded in Chronicles. It refers to Manasseh's prayer but without the deeds of restoration and, thus, draws a picture of a disingenuous calculative penitent who, in his distress, calls upon God but eventually remains wicked.[31]

11.2.1.4. The Martyrdom of Isaiah

The Martyrdom of Isaiah is presumably a Jewish source of a significant part of the larger Christian composition known as the Ascension of Isaiah that was written in the beginning of the second century CE. In recent scholarship, it has repeatedly been denied that any form of an original Jewish source could be retrieved from the final composition. It is argued that if some Jewish source ever existed, it is now thoroughly interwoven into the Christian composition and, therefore, is impossible to extract.[32]

---

30. Derek R. G. Beattie and J. Stanley McIvor, eds., *The Targums of Chronicles and Ruth*, ArBib 19 (Edinburgh: T&T Clark, 1994), 230–31.

31. This depiction finds some similarities with the opinions of some masters in b. Sanh. 102b, 103a.

32. Cf. Mauro Pesce, "Presupposti per I'utilizzazione storica dell Ascensione di Isaia," in *Isaia, il Diletto e la Chiesa: Visione e esegesi profitica cristiano-primitive nell' Ascensione di Isaia*, ed. Mauro Pesce, Testi e ricerche di scienze religiose 20 (Brescia: Paidea, 1983), 13–48, esp. 35–45; Enrico Norelli, *Ascensio Isaiae: Commentarius*, 2 vols., CCSA 7–8 (Turnhout: Brepols, 1995), 1:46–52; Jonathan M. Knight, *The Ascen-*

This is significant and, as it goes, it looks convincing. At the same time, it is understandable why earlier scholarship found it compelling to distinguish a different source from the Christian text. The legend about Isaiah's conflict with Manasseh (chs. 1–3, 5) is only marginally connected to the later apocalyptic visions in chapters 6–11; further, chapter 4, which is thematically and stylistically close to the latter part, here clearly interrupts the compactness of the narrative. It is also noteworthy that most of the recent studies that discuss selected issues of this Christian apocalypse deal almost exclusively with chapters 4 and 6–11.[33] Therefore, we accept that there is no particular methodology that distinguishes any form of the original source with finite certainty; however, there are good reasons to believe that the legend of the first part of the Christian composition is a meaningful and compact narrative and, as such, could have existed in some form as a separate Jewish text (as in the case of some testaments of the Testaments of Twelve Patriarchs). Therefore, with these cautions, we include this legend in our inquiry.

The story begins in a testimonial setting when the old king Hezekiah summons his son Manasseh to hand him certain commands in the presence of the prophet Isaiah. Isaiah predicts that Manasseh will not obey these commands and, instead, he will become an instrument of Beliar and eventually put the prophet to death. Right after Manasseh succeeds his father on the throne, the prophecy begins to be fulfilled. Manasseh disobeys Hezekiah's commands, forsakes the worship of the God of his father and serves Satan and his angels. He also leads his house astray and turns Jerusalem into a center of apostasy, lawlessness, occult arts, fornication, and persecution of the righteous. Isaiah then withdraws from Jerusalem into the Judean wilderness, where he is accompanied by a group of faithful prophets who live only by wild herbs. Then the false

---

sion of Isaiah (Sheffield: Sheffield Academic, 1995), 21–23; Richard Bauckham, "The Ascension of Isaiah: Genre, Unity and Date," in The Fate of the Dead: Studies on the Jewish and Christian Apocalypses, ed. Richard Bauckham, NovTSup 93 (Leiden: Brill, 1998), 363–90; Robert G. Hall, "The Ascension of Isaiah: Community Situation, Date and Place in Early Christianity," JBL 109 (1990): 289–306. For an older perspective see Michael A. Knibb, "Martyrdom and Ascension of Isaiah," OTP 2:143–76; George W. E. Nickelsburg, "The Martyrdom of Isaiah," in Jewish Writings of the Second Temple Period, ed. Michael E. Stone, CRINT 2 (Philadelphia: Fortress, 1984), 52–56; André Caquot, "Bref Commentaire du 'Martyr d'Isaïe,'" Sem 23 (1973): 65–93.

33. E.g., the recent collection of studies in Jan N. Bremmer, Thomas R. Karmann, and Tobias Nicklas, eds., The Ascension of Isaiah, SECA 11 (Leuven: Peeters, 2016).

prophet Bechira (sometimes named Belkira or Melkira) appears on the scene; he is a descendant of the false prophet Zedekiah ben Chenanah, the opponent of the true prophet Michaiah ben Imlah from 1 Kgs 22:1–36. He discovers the hiding place of Isaiah and brings charges against him before Manasseh. Manasseh, driven by Beliar, who dwells in his heart, sentences Isaiah to death by being sawn asunder. As Isaiah is being tortured, Bechira, acting on behalf of Satan, attempts to get the prophet to recant but Isaiah refuses and in turn curses Bechira and all demonic powers and dies.

The story is a legendary expansion of 2 Kgs 21:16, which is understood as the biblical justification for Isaiah's martyrdom in the time of Manasseh. The list of Manasseh's sins in 2.4–6 is undoubtedly based on 2 Kgs 21:2–6, similar to the stereotypical contrast between the good and pious father, Hezekiah, and the wicked and impious son, Manasseh. This story does not contain any trace of Manasseh's penitence or other elements of Chronicles' version. Manasseh is pictured as a wicked man who consults with false prophets as did king Ahab (1 Kgs 22:1–36) and he becomes a tool of Satan who resides in his heart. By putting the righteous prophet Isaiah to death, who even during torture refuses to recant, Manasseh takes the position of God's adversary in the dualistic conflict of the story.

11.2.2. Positive Depictions of Manasseh

After reviewing the negative representations of Manasseh, we now proceed to texts that present Manasseh in more positive colors.

11.2.2.1. The (Greek) Prayer of Manasseh

The Prayer of Manasseh is a short pseudepigraphical Jewish work attributed to Manasseh in the form of a penitential psalm.[34] The prayer is an elaboration of a brief reference to Manasseh's remorseful prayer in 2 Chr 33:13, 18. It is akin to other early Jewish prayers with confessional ele-

---

34. See James H. Charlesworth, "The Prayer of Manasseh," *OTP* 2:625–33. A Hebrew version of this prayer has been found in the Cairo Genizah that likely dates to the tenth century CE. However, it is probably a retranslation from Syriac or Greek, not the Hebrew *Vorlage*. See Peter Schäfer and Shaul Shaked, eds., *Magische Texte aus der Kairoer Geniza*, vol. 2, TSAJ 64 (Tübingen: Mohr Siebeck, 1997), 51–53.

ments.[35] However, the closest parallel is Ps 51.[36] The oldest extant text of this prayer is in two early church teaching documents: the Didascalia Apostolorum, and the Apostolic Constitutions.[37] In addition, this prayer is a part of collections of odes appended to the book of Psalms in some Greek biblical manuscripts.[38] This text was originally composed in either Greek or a Semitic language. The brevity of this prayer makes any decision on this issue inconclusive, although most recent interpreters lean toward a Greek origin.[39] The original *Sitz im Leben* of the prayer is also dubious. In the Didascalia and the Apostolic Constitutions, the story of Manasseh and the prayer are parts of a longer instruction to bishops and provides the basis for accepting penitent sinners back into the church. On the other hand, the inclusion of the prayer into the odes suggests a liturgical context for the text. Both the instructional and liturgical context could be imagined as the original Jewish setting.[40]

Manasseh is only explicitly referred to in the superscription to the prayer, but the content has some very close ties to 2 Chr 33.[41] On the other hand, no specific elements of 2 Kings are present. At the beginning of

---

35. Ezra 9; Neh 9; Dan 9; Bar 1:15–3:8; LXX Dan 3; 4Q504; Ps. Sol. 9; 1QS I, 24–II, 1; CD XX, 28–30; 3 Macc 2:1–20. Cf. Pieter W. van den Horst and Judith H. Newman, *Early Jewish Prayers in Greek*, CEJL (Berlin: de Gruyter, 2008), 147.

36. Judith H. Newman, "The Form and Settings of the Prayer of Manasseh," in *The Development of Penitential Prayer in Second Temple Judaism*, vol. 2 of *Seeking the Favor of God*, ed. Mark J. Boda, Daniel K. Falk, and Rodney A. Warline, EJL 22 (Atlanta: Society of Biblical Literature, 2007), 105–25; Charlesworth, "Prayer of Manasseh," 630.

37. See van den Horst and Newman, *Early Jewish Prayers*, 153–55.

38. The oldest and most prominent one is the fifth-century Codex Alexandrinus; cf. van den Horst and Newman, *Early Jewish Prayers*, 156–58.

39. Cf. Charlesworth, "Prayer of Manasseh," 625–27; James R. Davila, "Is the Prayer of Manasseh a Jewish Work?," in *Heavenly Tablets: Interpretation, Identity and Tradition in Ancient Israel*, ed. Lynn LiDonnoci and Andrea Lieber, JSJSup 119 (Leiden: Brill, 2007), 75–85, esp. 75–76.

40. George W. E. Nickelsburg, "The Prayer of Manasseh," in *The Oxford Bible Commentary*, ed. John Barton and John Muddiman (Oxford: Oxford University Press, 2001), 771; See also Judith Newman, "Three Contexts for Reading Manasseh's Prayer in the Didascalia," *JCSSS* 7 (2007): 3–15.

41. The superscription in Codex A reads: "Προσευχή Μανασσή"; Codex T adds further clarification: "υἱός Ἐζεκίου." See the parallels: provoking: 2 Chr 33:6 // Pr Man 10; placing idols: 2 Chr 33:7 // Pr Man 10; being ensnared in chains: 2 Chr 33:11 // Pr Man 9b–10; humbling of Manasseh: 2 Chr 33:12 // Pr Man 11; terming God as God of ancestors: 2 Chr 33:12 // Pr Man 1.

the prayer, Manasseh acknowledges the Lord Almighty as the God of the patriarchs, the Creator of heaven and earth, and the God of mercy who instituted repentance (vv. 1–7). In the following confession, Manasseh affirms the divine constitution of repentance as not only for the righteous but also for sinners, such as himself (v. 8). He expresses his unworthiness and sinfulness about setting up desecrations and multiplying abominations that provoked God's wrath (cf. Apoc. Ab. 25.5–6; 2 Bar. 64.3–4). The petition starts with a description of external conditions that symbolizes the internal state. Manasseh "bent down the knee of his heart" begging for the kindness of God. The explicit confession is expressed as: "I have sinned, O Lord, I have sinned, and I acknowledge my transgressions" (v. 12, trans. van den Horst and Newman), which is followed by a petition for forgiveness: "Forgive me, Lord, forgive me!" (v. 13). The prayer then concludes with the expression of trust in the divine salvation as a result of God's mercy (v. 13d–14) and with Manasseh's vow to praise God for all the days of his life (v. 15a) that is appended with a doxology (v. 15b).

Manasseh of the Prayer of Manasseh is then an example of a petitioner. By imitating the structure of Ps 51, the exemplary penitential prayer of the Hebrew Bible, the author probably meant to produce another remarkable prayer of a well-known figure with an ambivalent story. The sins of Manasseh are expressed only generally, and therefore, they could be appropriated by any repenting sinner. Especially powerful are repeated sections in his confession and petition (vv. 9, 12, 13). Manasseh, as the petitioner speaking in the first person, is thus portrayed as a positive example for repentant people of Israel similar to David in Ps 51.

11.2.2.2. The Prayer of Manasseh in 4Q381

There is another pseudepigraphical penitential prayer called the Prayer of Manasseh in Qumran scroll 4Q381. This scroll is written in Hebrew and is paleographically dated to approximately 75 BCE.[42] Its superscription reads "Prayer of Manasseh, king of Judah when the king of Assyria put him in prison" (תפלה למנשה מלך יהודה בכלו אתו מלך אשור) and therefore betrays knowledge of the story from 2 Chr 33. However, except for this superscription, this prayer shares nothing with the Greek prayer. It is not

---

42. Esther Eshel et al., *Qumran Cave 4 VI: Poetical and Liturgical Texts, Part 1*, DJD XI (Oxford: Clarendon, 1998), 88–89.

completely certain which fragments of 4Q381 belong to this prayer. While it undoubtedly begins at 4Q381 33, 8, it is very likely that frag. 45a+b belongs to the same prayer and perhaps frag. 47 as well. Both of them share much of the same terminology with 2 Chr 33, albeit without direct reference to Manasseh.[43] Moreover, the content of the prayer is sometimes hard to follow because of many lacunae. Nevertheless, it can be recovered that it is a penitential prayer of the individual, the king Manasseh, situated in the story of 2 Chr 33 when the king has been imprisoned by the king of Assyria. The psalm begins with the acknowledgement of God as the God of mercy, who brings salvation to the sinner. This leads Manasseh to submit himself to God for his sins. The confession follows as Manasseh expresses that he multiplied guilt and his soul will not have a part in the eternal joy (33, 9–10). The exile is mentioned, although the meaning of the fragmentary line is not clear. However, it seems to refer to the exile of Judah caused by Manasseh, similarly as in the Deuteronomistic account.[44] Further, he admits his sins in the holy place and that he did not serve the Lord (33, 11). In the fragments 45a+b and 47, Manasseh purifies himself from abominations that he was acquainted with and he humbles his soul before God. The plot of those who conspire against him is referred to but Manasseh confesses that he trusts in God and his judgment. The prayer concludes with an emphasis on God's mercifulness and graciousness and with Manasseh's vow to walk in God's truth.

This Qumran prayer is thus another penitential prayer ascribed to Manasseh that provides wording for the prayer alluded to in 2 Chr 33:13, 18. Like the Greek pseudepigraphical prayer, it portrays Manasseh as a positive example of a petitioner confessing his sins. However, Mika Pajunen sees one crucial difference between the Qumran prayer and the Greek prayer in the broader engagement of the Qumran prayer with different facets of

---

43. See Mika S. Pajunen, "The Prayer of Manasseh in 4Q381 and the Account of Manasseh in 2 Chronicles 33," in *The Scrolls and Biblical Traditions: Proceedings of the Seventh Meeting of the IOQS in Helsinki*, ed. George J. Brooke et al., STDJ 103 (Leiden: Brill, 2012), 149–57; these fragments are also grouped together in the reconstruction by Hartmut Stegemann in Eillen M. Schuller, *Non-Canonical Psalms from Qumran: A Pseudepigraphic Collection*, HSS 28 (Atlanta: Scholars Press, 1986), 267–83; See also Eshel, *Qumran Cave 4 VI*, 122–23; 132–33.

44. 4Q381 33, 10: "... [ ]ואו גלו י[כי ..." While it is possible to reconstruct "for my *sins* they went into exile" as the extant suffix allows, this reconstruction is only a conjecture.

Manasseh's reign.[45] The Qumran prayer not only refers to Manasseh's sins, punishment, and repentance, but it also recounts the conspiracy against the king and his plans after he returns from captivity. In particular, in the section 45, 2–3, we read about the plot against Manasseh[46] and two other sections display Manasseh as teaching something about his sinfulness and about God's willingness to accept true repentance (45, 1 and 47, 3). These instruction sections bring this prayer closer to a didactic setting. It is striking that both of these, otherwise unknown elements of the tradition, have parallels in Josephus's account. According to *A.J.* 10.40, Manasseh was captured by the king of Assyria by treachery (δόλῳ ληφθέντα) and, in *A.J.* 10.43, it is said that Manasseh taught the people (τὸ πλῆθος ἐδίδασκε) to show gratitude to God and to keep God's favor throughout their whole lives.[47] These two common notions could suggest that Josephus could have been aware of some traditions common to this prayer or even of the prayer itself.[48] Nevertheless, this prayer presents Manasseh as an example of a penitent whose experience legitimized him to instruct the others about God's mercifulness. Besides, it is another witness to the development of the traditions of Manasseh.

11.2.2.3. Apostolic Constitutions 7.37

The last text to be discussed describing Manasseh is found in the aforementioned early Christian teaching document, the Apostolic Constitutions. For more than a century it has been recognized that some of the prayers

---

45. Pajunen, "Prayer of Manasseh in 4Q381," 158–60.

46. "And they conspire to lock me up" (ועלי יזמו להסגירני).

47. Another possible allusion to the capture by trap is in the short recension of Tob 14:10 (e.g., MSS Vaticanus, Alexandrinus, Venetus) that reads: "Μανασσης ... ἐσώθη ἐκ παγίδος θανάτου." However, the presence of Manasseh (the king of Judah) in that context is odd. Cf. Carey A. Moore, *Tobit: A New Translation with Introduction and Commentary*, AB 40A (New York: Doubleday, 1996), 292–93. For Manasseh as a teacher, see Begg, *Josephus' Story*, 447–50; Feldmann, *Studies in Josephus' Rewritten Bible*, 417–18. In b. Sanh. 102b and 103b, Manasseh is depicted as a great scholar learned in interpretation of Leviticus and halakic matters.

48. Pajunen, "Prayer of Manasseh in 4Q381," 161. Josephus similarly concludes that Manasseh as a repentant is worthy of imitation: "In fact he underwent such a change of heart in these respects and lived the rest of his life in such a way as to be accounted a blessed and enviable man after the time when he began to show piety toward God" (*A.J.* 10.45 [Marcus, LCL]).

from book 7 of the Apostolic Constitutions could be remnants of Jewish synagogue prayers.[49] The prayers in Apos. Con. 7.33–37 are parallel to the first six of the Seven Benedictions for Sabbaths and Festivals of the Jewish prayer book. However, they contain various Christian interpolations in their present form.[50]

The reference to Manasseh is in Apos. Con. 7.37 where he is enlisted in the catalogue of the righteous Israelites of the past. It is not entirely decidable whether this list originally belonged to the Jewish prayer or is redactional. The redactor of these prayers had a penchant for listing heroes of Hebrew Bible (e.g., 7.33.4–6; 7.38.2), but similar lists are common to the Jewish tradition.[51]

The prayer opens with an appeal to God to accept Israel's prayers just as he accepted the sacrifices and prayers of the righteous heroes of the past. The list of examples runs from Abel to Mattathias, the leader of Maccabees, and his sons. It contains prominent figures of Jewish history such as Abraham, Isaac, Jacob, Moses, Joshua, Samuel, David, Elijah, Hezekiah, Josiah, and Ezra (7.33.2–4). Manasseh unexpectedly appears in the list of the righteous, although he is usually accompanied by more negative heroes such as Ahab or Jeroboam.[52] In this reference, it is said that God accepted the prayer "of Manasseh in the land of the Chaldeans after his transgression" (7.33.3), which clearly points to the Chronicles version of the story. Therefore, what was only implicitly assumed in the two previous prayers is here stated explicitly: Manasseh, as an example of the righteous repentant, should be remembered as an important figure of Israel's past alongside heroes such as Abraham, Moses, David, or, ironically, Manasseh's father, Hezekiah.

---

49. On the history of research of these prayers cf. van den Horst and Newman, *Early Jewish Prayers*, 9–22. For a very thorough analysis of the evidence, see Esther G. Chazon, "A 'Prayer Alleged to Be Jewish' in the *Apostolic Constitutions*," in *Things Revealed: Studies in Early Jewish and Christian Literature in Honor of Michael E. Stone*, ed. Esther G. Chazon, David Satran, and Ruth Clements, JSJSup 89 (Leiden: Brill, 2004), 261–77.

50. See the suggested criteria of authenticity in David Fiensy, *Prayers Alleged to Be Jewish: An Examination of the Constitutiones Apostolorum*, BJS 65 (Chico, CA: Scholars Press, 1985), 165–67.

51. Van den Horst and Newman, *Early Jewish Prayers*, 86–87.

52. E.g., b. Sanh. 103b, y. Sanh. 10.2, where all these kings are said to have no portion in the world to come. See also the other black waters in 2 Baruch.

11.3. Conclusions

Two different biblical representations of Manasseh in the biblical narratives give rise to two very distinct ways this king has been remembered. Most of the depictions elaborate only on one of the biblical stories. Apparently, the bad ones follow 2 Kings and the good ones 2 Chronicles. The only exceptions are 2 Baruch, which acknowledges Manasseh's prayer, and probably 4Q381 with its reference to the exile. Furthermore, all the texts presenting negative portrayals of Manasseh were apocalypses or texts, at least, situated in the apocalyptic worldview. Historical apocalypses offer a theological explanation for the present crisis in broader historical context. This crisis is usually the result of an increasing decline in the faithfulness of Israel and an increase in apostasy from proper worship and keeping the law. Manasseh, as the evil corruptor of temple worship and the law, with the reputation for causing the downfall of Judah, was an ideal candidate to be put at the climax of these historical narratives; especially in those apocalypses that address the ensuing crisis after the fall of Jerusalem and its temple in 70 CE. Noticeably, the texts presenting positive depiction were all prayers. If God was willing to forgive the sins of someone as corrupt as Manasseh, it is convenient to pray in the same words as he did, or at least to remind God of his great mercy that was shown to Manasseh and expect the same kind of mercy.

The surveyed texts are also important witnesses to the development of the traditions of Manasseh within early Judaism. In most of the texts, Manasseh was not a crucial figure of the narratives; or, to put it differently, the narratives were not primarily about Manasseh. This means that most of the inventions could reflect more about the development of the tradition than on deliberate authorial creations. Therefore, the depictions serve predominantly as windows into the ongoing process of the growing tradition about Manasseh. This is also apparent from the fact that most of the novelties were attested in more than one text. However, in the case of the Martyrdom of Isaiah and, probably, both of the prayers, we should give more credit to the creativity of the authors. Nevertheless, it is impressive that during several centuries Manasseh became known for killing the righteous prophet Isaiah, abusing women (or even his sister), being a satanic tool, or making an obscure (one to) five-faced idol. And yet, at the same time, he is renowned as one of the most notable examples of a righteous repentant, great teacher and scholar, and thus a man worthy of imitation. The stark difference between these distinct presentations could be partially explained by the different contexts and genres of the texts. However, the nature of our evidence does not allow us to describe the development in a more concrete way, for example, a linear way from bad to good.

Finally, most of the biblical characters in early Jewish literature became a sort of cypher for a particular field of knowledge or behavior. Thus, for example, Moses became known as the scribe of torah, Enoch as the revealer of heavenly mysteries, Levi as the priest, Solomon as the sage who handed down wisdom, David as the author of Psalms and as a messianic figure, and so on. Yet, there is something unique about Manasseh as there is no other figure remembered in such distinctive ways: on the one hand, as the most wicked sinner, murderer, and the one responsible for one of the biggest catastrophes of the Jewish history; on the other hand, as a righteous example and a teacher for the subsequent generations.

Bibliography

Abadie, Philippe. "From the Impious Manasseh (2 Kings 21) to the Convert Manasseh (2 Chronicles 33): Theological Rewriting by the Chronicler." Pages 89–104 in *The Chronicler as Theologian: Essays in Honor of Ralph W. Klein*. Edited by M. Patrick Graham, Steven L. McKenzie, and Gary N. Knoppers. JSOTSup 371. Edinburgh: T&T Clark, 2003.

Achtemeier, Elizabeth. *Minor Prophets I*. Grand Rapids: Baker, 2012.

ʿAdawi, Zubair. "Jerusalem, Ras el-ʿAmud (A)." *HA* 125 (2013): https://tinyurl.com/SBL2643a.

Aharoni, Miriam. "An Iron Age Cylinder Seal." *IEJ* 46 (1996): 52–54.

Aharoni, Miriam, and Yohanan Aharoni. "The Stratification of Judahite Sites in the Eighth and Seventh Centuries BCE." *BASOR* 224 (1976): 73–90.

Aharoni, Yohanan. "Arad." Pages 74–89 in *Encyclopedia of Archaeological Excavations in the Holy Land*. Edited by Michael Avi-Yonah. Englewood Cliffs: Prentice-Hall, 1978.

———. "Arad: Its Inscriptions and Temple." *BA* 31 (1968): 1–32.

———. "Excavations at Tel Beer-sheba." *BA* 35 (1972): 111–27.

———. *Excavations at Ramat Raḥel I: Seasons 1959 and 1960*. Centro di Studi Semitici, Serie Archaeologica 2. Rome: Università degli studi, Centro di studi semitici, 1962.

———. *Excavations at Ramat Raḥel II: Seasons 1961 and 1962*. Centro di Studi Semitici, Serie Archaeologica 6. Rome: Università degli studi, Centro di studi semitici, 1964.

———. "The Horned Altar of Beer-sheba." *BA* 37 (1974): 2–6.

———. *The Land of the Bible*. Philadelphia: Westminster, 1979.

———. "The Sanctuary and High Place." Pages 26–32 in *Investigation at Lachish? The Sanctuary and the Residency (Lachish V)*. Publications of the Institute of Archaeology 4. Tel Aviv: Gateway, 1975.

———. "Stratification of the Site." Pages 4–8 in *Beer-Sheba I: Excavations at Tel Beer-Sheba, 1969–1971 Seasons*. Edited by Yohanan Aharoni. Publications of the Institute of Archaelogy 2. Tel Aviv: Tel Aviv University, Institute of Archaeology, 1973.

Aḥituv, Shmuel, Esther Eshel, and Zeʾev Meshel. "The Inscriptions." Pages 73–142 in *Kuntillet ʿAjrud (Ḥorvat Teman): An Iron Age II Religious Site on the Judah-Sinai Border*. Edited by Ze'ev Meshel and Liora Freud. Jerusalem: Israel Exploration Society, 2012.

Ahlström, Gösta W. *The History of Ancient Palestine*. JSOTSup 146. Sheffield: Sheffield Academic, 1993.

Albright, William F. "Astarte Plaques and Figurines from Tel Beit Mirsim." Pages 107–20 in *Mélanges syriens offerts à monsieur René Dussaud*. Edited by Académie des inscriptions & belles-lettres. Paris: Geuthner, 1939.

———. *Excavations and Results at Tell el-Fûl (Gibeah of Saul)*. AASOR 4. New Haven: Yale University Press, 1924.

Albright, William F., James L. Kelso, and J. Palin Thorley. *The Iron Age*. Vol. 3 of *The Excavation of Tel Beit Mirsim*. AASOR 21–22. New Haven: American Schools of Oriental Research, 1943.

Amiran, Ruth. *Ancient Pottery of the Holy Land: From Its Beginning in the Neolithic Period to the End of the Iron Age*. Ramat Gan: Massada, 1969.

Amiran, Ruth, and I. Dunayevsky. "The Assyrian Open-Court Building and Its Palestinian Derivatives." *BASOR* 149 (1958): 25–32.

Amit, David, and Irit Yezerski. "An Iron Age II Cemetery and Wine Presses at an-Nabi Danyal." *IEJ* 51 (2001): 171–93.

Andersen, Francis I., and David Noel Freedman. *Micah: A New Translation with Introduction and Commentary*. AB 24E. New York: Doubleday, 2000.

Ashcroft, Bill, Gareth Griffiths, and Helen Tiffin. *The Empire Writes Back: Theory and Practice in Post-colonial Literatures*. 2nd ed. London: Routledge, 2004.

———. *Post-colonial Studies: The Key Concepts*. London: Routledge, 2013.

Assefa, Daniel. *L'Apocalypse des animaux (1 Hen 85–90): Une propagande militaire? Approches narrative, historico-critique, perspectives theologiques*. JSJSup 120. Leiden: Brill, 2007.

Aurelius, Erik. *Zukunft jenseits des Gerichts: Eine redaktionsgeschichtliche Studie zum Enneateuch*. BZAW 319. Berlin: de Gruyter, 2003.

Avigad, Nachman. *Corpus of West Semitic Stamp Seals*. Rev. and completed by Benjamin Sass. Jerusalem: Israel Exploration Society, 1997.

Bagg, Ariel M. "Assyria and the West: Syria and the Levant." Pages 268–74 in *A Companion to Assyria*. Edited by Eckart Frahm. BCAW. Hoboken, NJ: Wiley & Sons, 2017.

———. *Die Assyrer und das Westland: Studien zur historischen Geographie und Herrschaftspraxis in der Levante im 1. Jt. v.u.Z.* OLA 216. Leuven: Peeters, 2011.

———. "Palestine under Assyrian Rule: A New Look at the Assyrian Imperial Policy in the West." *JAOS* 133 (2013): 119–44.

Barkay, Gabriel. "Burial Caves and Burial Practices in Judah in the Iron Age." Pages 96–164 in *Graves and Burial Practices in Israel in the Ancient Period*. Edited by Itamar Singer. Jerusalem: Yad Ben Zvi, 2004.

———. "The Iron Age III: The Babylonian Period." In *Is It Possible to Define the Pottery of the Sixth Century B.C.E. in Judeah?* [Hebrew] Edited by Oded Lipschits. Booklet of lecture summaries from the conference held in Tel Aviv University, 21.10.1998. Tel Aviv, 1998.

Barkay, Gabriel, Alexander Fantalkin, and Oren Tal. "A Late Iron Age Fortress North of Jerusalem." *BASOR* 328 (2002): 49–71.

Barr, James. "Historical Reading and the Theological Interpretation of Scripture." Pages 30–51 in *The Scope and Authority of the Bible*. London: SCM, 1980.

Bartlett, John R. *Edom and the Edomites*. JSOTSup 77. Sheffield: JSOT Press, 1989.

Baruch, Yuval, and Joe Uziel. "Tell el-Ful and Its Environs during the Second Temple and Late Roman Period." Pages 163–83 in *New Studies on Jerusalem 21*. Edited by Eyal Baruch and Avraham Faust. Ramat Gan: Bar-Ilan University, 2015.

Bauckham, Richard. "The Ascension of Isaiah: Genre, Unity and Date." Pages 363–90 in *The Fate of the Dead: Studies on the Jewish and Christian Apocalypses*. Edited by Richard Bauckham. NovTSup 93. Leiden: Brill, 1998.

Beʾeri, Ron. "Jerusalem, Shuʿfat Ridge." *HA* 124 (2012): https://tinyurl.com/SBL2643b.

Beattie, Derek R., and J. Stanley McIvor, eds. *The Targums of Chronicles and Ruth*. ArBib 19. Edinburgh: T&T Clark, 1994.

Beck, Pirhiya. "A Neo-Assyrian Bulla." Pages 194–96 in *Ḥorvat ʿUza and Ḥorvat Radum: Two Fortresses in the Biblical Negev*. Edited by Itzhaq Beit-Arieh. Sonia and Marco Nadler Institute of Archaeology Monograph Series 25. Tel Aviv: Emery and Claire Yass Publications in Archaeology, 2007.

Becking, Bob. "The Betrayal of Edom: Remarks on a Claimed Tradition." *HTS* 72 (2016): 1–4.

Begg, Christopher. *Josephus' Story of the Later Monarchy*. BETL 145. Leuven: Peeters, 2000.

Beit-Arieh, Itzhak. "Tel-'Ira and Horvat 'Uza: Negev Sites in the Late Israelite Period" [Hebrew]. *Cathedra* 42 (1987): 34–38.

———. *Tel 'Ira: A Stronghold in the Biblical Negev*. Monograph Series of the Institute of Archaeology 15. Tel Aviv: Institute of Archaeology of Tel Aviv University, 1999.

Ben-Ami, Doron. *Jerusalem Excavations in the Tyropoeon Valley (Givʿati Parking Lot)*. IAAR 52. Jerusalem: Israel Antiquities Authority, 2013.

Ben-Shlomo, David. "Jerusalem's Trade Networks in the Iron Age II as Seen through the Archaeometric Analysis of Pottery" [Hebrew]. Pages 177–87 in vol. 11 of *New Studies in the Archaeology of Jerusalem and Its Region: Collected Papers*. Edited by Yuval Gadot, Yehiel Zelinger, Katia Cytryn-Silverman, and Joseph Uziel. Jerusalem, 2017.

Ben Zvi, Ehud. *A Historical-Critical Study of the Book of Zephaniah*. BZAW 198. Berlin: de Gruyter, 1991.

———. *Micah*. FOTL 21B. Grand Rapids: Eerdmans, 2000.

Berlejung, Angelika. "The Assyrians in the West: Assyrianization, Colonialism, Indifference, or Development Policy?" Pages 21–60 in *Congress Volume Helsinki 2010*. Edited by Martti Nissinen. VTSup 148. Leiden: Brill, 2012.

Billig, Yaʿakov. "Jerusalem, Bet Ha-Kerem, Preliminary Report." *HA* 123 (2011): https://tinyurl.com/SBL2643c.

Bin-Nun, Shoshana R. "Formulas from Royal Records of Israel and of Judah." *VT* 18 (1968): 414–32.

Biran, Avraham. "Tel-'Ira and 'Aroʿer towards the End of the Judean Monarchy" [Hebrew]. *Cathedra* 42 (1987): 26–33.

Blanco Wissmann, Felipe. *"Er tat das Rechte...": Beurteilungskriterien und Deuteronomismus in 1Kön 12–2Kön 25*. ATANT 93. Zurich: TVZ, 2008.

Blenkinsopp, Joseph. "Remembering Josiah." Pages 236–56 in *Remembering Biblical Figures in the Late Persian and Early Hellenistic Period: Social Memory and Imagination*. Edited by Diana V. Edelman and Ehud Ben Zvi. Oxford: Oxford University Press, 2013.

Bocher, Efrat, and Liora Freud. "Persian Period Settlement in the Rural Jerusalem Hinterland" [Hebrew]. Pages 147–58 in *New Studies on*

Jerusalem 22. Edited by Eyal Baruch and Avraham Faust. Ramat Gan: Rennert Center for Jerusalem Studies, 2017.

Bocher, Efrat, and Oded Lipschits. "The Corpus of *yršlm* Stamp Impressions—The Final Link." *TA* 40 (2013): 99–116.

Boda, Mark J. "Identity and Empire, Reality and Hope in the Chronicler's Perspective." Pages 249–72 in *Community Identity in Judean Historiography: Biblical and Comparative Perspectives*. Edited by Gary N. Knoppers and Kenneth A. Ristau. Winona Lake, IN: Eisenbrauns, 2009.

Bogaert, Pierre. *L'Apocalypse Syriaque de Baruch: Introduction, traduction du syriaque et commentaire*. 2 vols. SC 144, 145. Paris: Cerf, 1969.

Bohak, Gideon. "Classica et Rabbinica I: The Bull of Phalaris and the Tophet." *JSJ* 31 (2000): 203–16.

Boness, Doron, and Yuval Goren. "Petrographic Study of the Iron Age and Persian Period Pottery at Ramat Raḥel." In *Ramat Raḥel V*. Edited by Oded Lipschits and Yuval Gadot. Forthcoming.

Borowski, Oded. "Hezekiah's Reforms and the Revolt against Assyria." *BA* 58 (1995): 148–55.

Brandl, Baruch. "Bullae with Figurative Decoration." Pages 58–74 in *Inscriptions*. Vol. 6 of *Excavations at the City of David 1978–1985 Directed by Yigael Shiloh*. Edited by Donald T. Ariel. Qedem 41. Jerusalem: Institute of Archaeology, Hebrew University of Jerusalem, 2000.

Bremmer, Jan N., Thomas R. Karmann, and Tobias Nicklas, eds. *The Ascension of Isaiah*. SECA 11. Leuven: Peeters, 2016.

Brettler, Mark Zvi. "Redaction, History, and Redaction-History of Amos in Recent Scholarship." Pages 103–12 in *Israel's Prophets and Israel's Past: Essays on the Relationship of Prophetic Texts and Israelite History in Honor of John H. Hayes*. Edited by Brad E. Kelle and Megan B. Moore. LHBOTS 446. London: T&T Clark, 2006.

Briffa, Josef M. "The Figural World of the Southern Levant during the Late Iron Age." PhD diss., UCL Institute of Archaeology, 2017.

Bunimovitz, Shlomo, and Zvi Lederman, eds. *Tel Beth-Shemesh: A Border Community in Judah; Renewed Excavations 1990–2000; The Iron Age*. Vol 2. Sonia and Marco Nadler Institute of Archaeology Monograph Series 34. Winona Lake, IN: Eisenbrauns, 2016.

Cahill, Jane M. "Rosette-Stamped Handles." Pages 85–108 in *Inscriptions*. Vol. 6 of *Excavations at the City of David 1978–1985 Directed by Yigal Shiloh*. Edited by Donald T. Ariel. Qedem 41. Jerusalem: Institute of Archaeology, Hebrew University of Jerusalem, 2000.

———. "Rosette Stamp Seal Impressions." Pages 85–98 in *The Finds from Areas A, W and X-2*. Vol. 2 of *Jewish Quarter Excavations in the Old City of Jerusalem*. Edited by Hillel Geva. Jerusalem: Israel Exploration Society, 2003.

———. "Rosette Stamp Seal Impression from Ancient Judah." *IEJ* 45 (1995): 230–52.

———. "Royal Rosettes Fit for a King." *BAR* 23.5 (1997): 48–57, 68–69.

Campbell, Edward F. *Text*. Vol. 1 of *Shechem III: The Stratigraphy and Architecture of Shechem/Tell Balatah*. ASORAR 6. Boston: American Schools of Oriental Research, 2002.

Čapek, Filip. "David's Ambiguous Testament: The Role of Joab in 1 Kings 2:1–12." *Communio Viatorum* 52 (2010): 4–26.

———. "The Shephelah in the Iron Age I and IIA: A New Survey of the Emergence of the Early Kingdom of Judah." *Oriental Archive* 80 (2012): 475–504.

Caquot, André. "Bref Commentaire du 'Martyr d'Isaïe.'" *Sem* 23 (1973): 65–93.

Carroll, Robert P. "Jewgreek and Greekjew: The Hebrew Bible Is All Greek to Me; Reflections on the Problematics of Dating the Origins of the Bible in Relation to Contemporary Discussions of Biblical Historiography." Pages 91–107 in *Did Moses Speak Attic? Jewish Historiography and Scripture in the Hellenistic Period*. Edited by Lester L. Grabbe. JSOTSup 317. Sheffield: Sheffield Academic, 2001.

Chadwick, Jeff R. "Discovering Hebron: The City of the Patriarchs Slowly Yields Its Secrets." *BAR* 31.5 (2005): 24–33, 70–71.

Chandler, Daniel. *Semiotics: The Basics*. 2nd ed. London: Routledge, 2007.

Charlesworth, James H. "The Prayer of Manasseh." *OTP* 2:625–33.

Chazon, Esther G. "A 'Prayer Alleged to Be Jewish' in the *Apostolic Constitutions*." Pages 261–77 in *Things Revealed: Studies in Early Jewish and Christian Literature in Honor of Michael E. Stone*. Edited by Esther G. Chazon, David Satran, and Ruth Clements. JSJSup 89. Leiden: Brill, 2004.

Cogan, Mordechai, and Hayim Tadmor. *II Kings: A New Translation with Introduction and Commentary*. AB 11. New York: Doubleday, 1988.

Coggins, Richard J. *Joel and Amos*. NCB. Sheffield: Sheffield Academic, 2000.

Cooley, Jeffrey L. "Astral Religion in Ugarit and Ancient Israel." *JNES* 70 (2011): 281–87.

Cross, Frank Moore. *Canaanite Myth and Hebrew Epic: Essays in the History of the Religion of Israel.* Cambridge: Harvard University Press, 1973.

Crowfoot, John Winter, Grace M. Crowfoot, and Kathleen M. Kenyon. *The Objects from Samaria.* Samaria-Sebaste 3. London: Palestine Exploration Fund, 1957.

Darby, Erin. *Interpreting Judean Pillar Figurines: Gender and Empire in Judean Apotropaic Ritual.* FAT 2/69. Tübingen: Mohr Seibeck, 2014.

Davidovich, Uri, et al. "Salvage Excavation at Ramot Forest and Ramat Bet-Hakerem: New Data Regarding Jerusalem's Periphery during the First and Second Temple Periods" [Hebrew]. Pages 35–111 in *New Studies on Jerusalem 11.* Edited by Eyal Baruch and Avraham Faust. Ramat Gan: Bar-Ilan University, 2006.

Davila, James R. "Is the Prayer of Manasseh a Jewish Work?" Pages 75–85 in *Heavenly Tablets: Interpretation, Identity and Tradition in Ancient Israel.* Edited by Lynn LiDonnoci and Andrea Lieber. JSJSup 119. Leiden: Brill, 2007.

Day, John. *Yahweh and the Gods and Goddesses of Canaan.* JSOTSup 265. Sheffield: Sheffield Academic, 2000.

De Groot, Alon. "Discussion and Conclusions." Pages 141–84 in *Area E; Stratigraphy and Architecture.* Vol. 7A of *Excavation at the City of David 1978–1985 Directed by Yigal Shiloh.* Edited by Alon De Groot and Hannah Bernick-Greenberg. Qedem 53. Jerusalem: Institute of Archaeology, Hebrew University of Jerusalem, 2012.

De Groot, Alon, and Donald T. Ariel. "Ceramic Report." Pages 91–154 in *Extramural Areas.* Vol. 5 of *Excavations at the City of David 1978–1985 Directed by Yigal Shiloh.* Qedem 40. Edited by Donald T. Ariel. Jerusalem: Institute of Archaeology, Hebrew University of Jerusalem, 2000.

De Groot, Alon, and Hannah Bernick-Greenberg, eds. *Area E; Stratigraphy and Architecture.* Vol. 7A of *Excavations at the City of David 1978–1985 Directed by Yigal Shiloh.* Qedem 53. Jerusalem: Institute of Archaeology, Hebrew University of Jerusalem, 2012.

———. "The Pottery of Strata 12–10 (Iron Age IIB)." Pages 57–198 in *Area E; The Finds.* Vol. 7B of *Excavations at the City of David 1978–1985 Directed by Yigal Shiloh.* Edited by Alon De Groot and Hannah Bernick-Greenberg. Qedem 54. Jerusalem: Institute of Archaeology, Hebrew University of Jerusalem, 2012.

De Groot, Alon, and Michal Weinberger-Stern. "Wine, Oil and Gibeonites: Iron II–III at Kh. el-Burj, Northern Jerusalem" [Hebrew]. Pages

95–102 in *New Studies on Jerusalem 19*. Edited by Eyal Baruch and Avraham Faust. Ramat Gan: Bar-Ilan University, 2013.

De Groot, Alon, and Zvi Greenhut. "Moza—A Judahite Administrative Center near Jerusalem" [Hebrew]. Pages 7–14 in *New Studies on Jerusalem 8*. Edited by Eyal Baruch and Avraham Faust. Ramat Gan: Bar-Ilan University, 2002.

De Groot, Alon, Hillel Geva, and Irit Yezerski. "Iron Age Pottery." Pages 1–49 in *The Finds from Areas A, W and X-2*. Vol. 2 of *Jewish Quarter Excavations in the Old City of Jerusalem*. Edited by Hillel Geva. Jerusalem: Israel Exploration Society, 2003.

Delamarter, Steve. "The Death of Josiah in Scripture and Tradition: Wrestling with the Problem of Evil?" *VT* 54 (2004): 29–60.

Dever, William G. *Did God Have a Wife? Archaeology and Folk Religion in Ancient Israel*. Grand Rapids: Eerdmans, 2005.

Dever, William G., H. Darrell Lance, and G. Ernest Wright. *Gezer I: Preliminary Report of the 1964–66 Seasons*. Jerusalem: Glueck School of Biblical Archaeology, 1970.

Dietrich, Walter. *Prophetie und Geschichte: Eine Redaktionsgeschichtliche Untersuchung zum deuteronomistischen Geschichtswerk*. FRLANT 108. Göttingen: Vandenhoeck & Ruprecht, 1972.

Dillard, Raymond B. *2 Chronicles*. WBC 15. Waco, TX: Word, 1987.

Dothan, Trude, and Seymour Gitin. "Tel Miqne/Ekron: The Rise and Fall of a Philistine City." *Qadmoniot* 105–106 (1996): 2–28.

Dreytza, Manfred. *Buch Micha*. Witten: Brockhaus, 2009.

Eco, Umberto. *A Theory of Semiotics*. Bloomington: Indiana University Press, 1976.

Edelman, Diana. "Hezekiah's Alleged Cultic Centralization." *JSOT* 32 (2008): 395–434.

Edelstein, Gershon. "A Terraced Farm at er-Ras." *Atiqot* 40 (2000): 39–63.

Edelstein, Gershon, and Mordechai Kislev. "Mevasseret Yerushalayim: The Ancient Settlement and Its Agricultural Terraces." *BA* 44 (1981): 53–56.

Edelstein, Gershon, Ianir Milevski, and Sara Aurnat. *Villages, Terraces and Stone Mounds: Excavations at Manahat, Jerusalem, 1987–1989*. IAAR 3. Jerusalem: Israel Antiquities Authority, 1998.

Eisenberg, Emanuel. "The Fortifications of Hebron in the Bronze Age" [Hebrew]. *ErIsr* 30 (2011): 14–32.

———. "Naḥal Rephaim: A Bronze Age Village in Southwestern Jerusalem" [Hebrew]. *Qadmoniot* 103–104 (1993): 82–95.

————. *The 1999 Excavations at Tel Hebron*. Forthcoming.

Eisenberg, Emanuel, and David Ben-Shlomo, eds. *Tel Hevron 2014 Excavations: Final Report*. Ariel: Ariel University Press, 2017.

Eisenberg, Emanuel, and Ella Nagorski. "Tel Hebron." *HA* 114 (2002): 91–92.

Elat, Moshe. "The Economic Relations of the Neo-Assyrian Empire with Egypt." *JAOS* 98 (1978): 20–34.

————. "International Commerce in Palestine under the Assyrian Rule." Pages 67–88 in *Commerce in Palestine throughout the Ages*. Edited by Benjamin Zeev Kedar, Trude Dothan, and Shmuel Safrai. Jerusalem: Yad Ben Zvi, 1990.

Elgart-Sharon, Yelena. "Settlement Patterns and Land Use in the Upper Soreq Area: Longue Durée Approach" [Hebrew]. MA thesis, Tel Aviv University, 2017.

Eliyahu-Behar, Adi, Naama Yahalom-Mack, and David Ben-Shlomo. "Excavation and Analysis of an Early Iron Age Lime Kiln." *IEJ* 67 (2017): 14–31.

Eshel, Esther, et al. *Qumran Cave 4 VI: Poetical and Liturgical Texts, Part 1*. DJD XI. Oxford: Clarendon, 1998.

Eshel, Itzhak, and Kay Prag, eds. *The Iron Age Cave Deposits on the South-East Hill and Isolated Burials and Cemeteries Elsewhere*. Vol. 4 of *Excavations by K. M. Kenyon in Jerusalem 1961–1967*. Oxford: Oxford University Press, 1995.

Eynikel, Erik. *The Reform of King Josiah and the Composition of the Deuteronomistic History*. OTS 33. Leiden: Brill, 1996.

Fantalkin, Alexander. "Coarse Kitchen and Household Pottery as an Indicator for Egyptian Presence in the Southern Levant: A Diachronic Perspective." Pages 233–41 in *Ceramics, Cuisine and Culture: The Archaeology and Science of Kitchen Pottery in the Ancient Mediterranean World*. Edited by Michela Spataro and Alexandra Villing. Oxford: Oxbow, 2015.

————. "Contacts between the Greek World and the Southern Levant during the Seventh–Sixth Centuries BCE." PhD diss., Tel Aviv University, 2008.

————. "Why Did Nebuchadnezzar II Destroy Ashkelon in Kislev 604 B.C.E.?" Pages 87–111 in *The Fire Signals of Lachish: Studies in the Archaeology and History of Israel in the Late Bronze Age, Iron Age, and Persian Period in Honor of David Ussishkin*. Edited by Israel Finkelstein and Nadav Na'aman. Winona Lake, IN: Eisenbrauns, 2011.

Faust, Avraham. "Differences in Family Structure between Cities and Villages in Iron Age II." *TA* 26 (1999): 233–52.

———. "Jerusalem's Countryside during the Iron Age II–Persian Period Transition" [Hebrew]. Pages 83–89 in *New Studies on Jerusalem 7*. Edited by Avraham Faust and Eyal Baruch. Ramat Gan: Bar-Ilan University

———. "Jerusalem's Hinterland and the City's Status in the Bronze and Iron Ages" [Hebrew]. *ErIsr* 28 (2007): 165–72.

———. "Judah in the Sixth Century BCE: Continuity or Break?" *ErIsr* 29 (2009): 339–47.

———. "Settlement and Demography in Seventh-Century Judah and the Extent and Intensity of Sennacherib's Campaign." *PEQ* 140 (2008): 168–94.

———. "Settlement, Economy, and Demography under Assyrian Rule in the West: The Territories of the Former Kingdom of Israel as a Test Case." *JAOS* 135 (2015): 765–89.

Faust, Avraham, and Ehud Weiss. "Judah, Philistia and the Mediterranean World: Reconstructing the Economic System of the Seventh Century BCE." *BASOR* 338 (2005): 71–92.

Faust, Avraham, and Esther Eshel. "An Inscribed Bulla with Grazing Doe from Tel 'Eton." Pages 63–70 in *Puzzling the Past: Studies in Northwest Semitic Languages and Literature in Honor of Bruce Zuckerman*. Edited by Marilyn J. Lunberg, Steven Fine, and Wayne T. Pitard. CHANE 55. Leiden: Brill, 2012.

Faust, Avraham, and Shlomo Bunimovitz. "The Four Room House: Embodying Iron Age Israelite Society." *NEA* 66 (2003): 22–31.

Faust, Avraham, Haya Katz, Yair Sapir, Assaf Avraham, Ofer Marder, Guy Bar-Oz, Ehud Weiss, Chen Auman-Chazan, Anat Hartmann-Shenkman, Tehila Sadiel, Oren Vilany, Michael Tserasky, Pariente Sarah, Oren Ackerman, Natasha Timmer, Ofir Katz, Dafna Langgut, and Mordechay Benzaquen. "The Birth, Life and Death of an Iron Age House at Tel 'Eton, Israel: A Preliminary Analysis." *Levant* 49 (2017): 136–73.

Feig, Nurit. "The Agricultural Settlement in the Jerusalem Area in Iron Age II" [Hebrew]. Pages 3–7 in *Recent Innovations in the Study of Jerusalem I*. Edited by Zeev Safrai, and Avraham Faust. Ramat Gan: Bar-Ilan University, 1995.

———. "The Environs of Jerusalem in the Iron Age II" [Hebrew]. Pages 387–409 in *The History of Jerusalem: The Biblical Period*. Edited by Shmuel Ahituv and Amihai Mazar. Jerusalem: Yad Ben Zvi, 2000.

———. "Khirbat er-Ras, Jerusalem: Iron Age and Ottoman-Period Remains." *HA* 128 (2016): https://tinyurl.com/SBL2643d.

Feldmann, Louis H. *Studies in Josephus' Rewritten Bible.* JSJSup 58. Leiden: Brill, 1998.

Fiaccavento, Chiara, Daria Montanari, and Gaia Ripepi. "The MB III Rampart and Cyclopean Wall of Tell es-Sultan/Jericho." *Scienze dell'Antichità* 19 (2013): 58–61.

Fiensy, David. *Prayers Alleged to Be Jewish: An Examination of the Constitutiones Apostolorum.* BJS 65. Chico, CA: Scholars Press, 1985.

Finkelstein, Israel. "The Archaeology of the Days of Manasseh." Pages 169–87 in *Scripture and Other Artifacts: Essays on the Bible and Archaeology in Honor of Philip J. King.* Edited by Michael D. Coogan, J. Cheryl Exum, and Lawrence E. Stager. Louisville: Westminster John Knox, 1994.

———. "Comments on the Date of Late-Monarchic Judahite Seal Impressions." *TA* 39 (2012): 203–11.

———. "Edom in the Iron I." *Levant* 24 (1992): 159–66.

———. *The Forgotten Kingdom: The Archaeology and History of Northern Israel.* ANEM 5. Atlanta: Society of Biblical Literature, 2013.

———. "Jerusalem and Judah 600–200 BCE: Implications for Understanding Pentateuchal Texts." Pages 3–18 in *The Fall of Jerusalem and the Rise of the Torah.* Edited by Peter Dubovský, Dominik Markl, and Jean-Pierre Sonnet. FAT 107. Tübingen: Mohr Siebeck, 2016.

Finkelstein, Israel, and Dafna Langgut. "Climate, Settlement History, and Olive Cultivation in the Iron Age Southern Levant." *BASOR* 379 (2018): 153–69.

Finkelstein, Israel, and Nadav Na'aman. "The Shephelah of Judah in the Late Eighth and Early Seventh Century BCE: An Alternative View." *TA* 31 (2004): 60–79.

Finkelstein, Israel, and Neil A. Silberman. *The Bible Unearthed: Archaeology's New Vision of Ancient Israel and the Origin of Its Sacred Texts.* London: Simon & Schuster, 2001.

———. *David and Solomon: In Search of the Bible's Sacred Kings and the Roots of Western Tradition.* New York: Free Press, 2006.

Finkelstein, Israel, and Yuval Gadot. "Mozah, Nephtoah and Royal Estates in the Jerusalem Highlands." *Semitica et Classica* 8 (2015): 227–34.

Finkelstein, Israel, Shlomo Bunimovitz, and Zvi Lederman. *Shiloh: The Archaeology of a Biblical Site.* Sonia and Marco Nadler Institute of

Archaeology Monograph Series 10. Tel Aviv: Institute of Archaeology Tel Aviv University, 1993.

Fischer, Georg. *Jeremia 1–25*. HThKAT. Vienna: Herder, 2005.

Fleischer, Gunther. *Von Menschenverkäufern, Baschankühen und Rechts-verkehren: Die Sozialkritik des Amosbuches in historisch-kritischer, sozialgeschichtlicher und archäologischer Perspektive*. BBB 74. Frank-furt: Athenäum, 1989.

Frahm, Eckart. "The Neo-Assyrian Period (ca. 1000–609)." Pages 161–208 in *A Companion to Assyria*. Edited by Eckart Frahm. BCAW. Hobo-ken, NJ: Wiley & Sons, 2017.

———. "Revolts in the Neo-Assyrian Empire: A Preliminary Discourse Analysis." Pages 76–89 in *Revolt and Resistance in the Ancient Classi-cal World and the Near East: In the Crucible of Empire*. Edited by John J. Collins and J. G. Manning. CHANE 85. Leiden: Brill, 2016.

Franken, Hendricus J. *A History of Pottery and Potters in Ancient Jerusa-lem: Excavations by K. M. Kenyon in Jerusalem 1961–1967*. London: Equinox, 2005.

Franken, Hendricus J., and Margreet L. Steiner, eds. *The Iron Age Extra-mural Quarter on the South-East Hill*. Vol. 2 of *Excavation in Jerusalem 1961–1967*.Oxford: Oxford University Press, 1990.

Freedman, David Noel, and Rebecca Frey. "False Prophecy Is True." Pages 82–87 in *Inspired Speech: Prophecy in the Ancient Near East; Essays in Honor of Herbert B. Huffmon*. Edited by John Kaltner and Louis Stul-man. JSOTSup 378. London: T&T Clark, 2004.

Freud, Liora. "The Longue Durée of the Seventh Century BCE: A Study of the Iron Age Pottery Vessels from Ramat Raḥel" [Hebrew]. MA thesis, Tel Aviv University, 2011.

———. "Judahite Pottery of the Transition Phase between the Iron Age and Persian Period" [Hebrew]. PhD diss., Tel Aviv University, 2018.

———. "Pottery of the Iron Age: Typology and Summary." Pages 254–65 in *Ramat Raḥel III: Final Publication of Yohanan Aharoni's Excavations (1954, 1959–1962)*. Edited by Oded Lipschits, Yuval Gadot, and Liora Freud. Sonia and Marco Nadler Institute of Archaeology Monograph Series 35. Winona Lake, IN: Eisenbrauns, 2016.

———. "Production and Widespread Use of Holemouth Vessels in Jeru-salem and Its Environs in the Iron Age II: Typology, Chronology, and Distribution" [Hebrew]. Pages 93–110 in vol. 11 of *New Studies in the Archaeology of Jerusalem and Its Region: Collected Papers*. Edited by

Yuval Gadot, Yehiel Zelinger, Katya Cytryn-Silberman, and Joe Uziel. Jerusalem, 2017.

Fulton, Deirdre N., Yuval Gadot, Assaf Kleiman, Liora Freud, Omri Lernau, and Oded Lipschits. "Feasting in Paradise: Feast Remains from the Iron Age Palace of Ramat Raḥel and Their Implications." *BASOR* 374 (2015): 29–48.

Gaarder, Jostein. *I et speil, i en gåte*. Oslo: Aschehoug, 1993.

Gadot, Yuval. "In the Valley of the King: Jerusalem's Rural Hinterland in the Eighth–Fourth Centuries BCE." *TA* 42 (2015): 3–26.

Gadot, Yuval, and Efrat Bocher. "The Introduction of the Open-Court-yard Building to the Jerusalem Landscape and Judean-Assyrian Inter-action." Pages 205–27 in *Archaeology and History of Eighth-Century Judah: Papers in Honor of Oded Borowski*. Edited by Zev I. Farber and Jacob L. Wright. ANEM 23. Atlanta: SBL Press, 2018.

Gadot, Yuval, and Joe Uziel. "The Monumentality of Iron Age Jerusalem Prior to the Eighth Century BCE." *TA* 44 (2017): 123–40.

Gadot, Yuval, Liora Freud, Oren Tal, and Itamar Taxel. "Sub-Sectors ACS1; ACS2." Pages 97–172 in *Ramat Raḥel III: Final Publication of Yohanan Aharoni's Excavations (1954, 1959–1962)*. Edited by Oded Lipschits, Yuval Gadot, and Liora Freud. Sonia and Marco Nadler Institute of Archaeology Monograph Series 35. Winona Lake, IN: Eisenbrauns, 2016.

Gadot, Yuval, Yelena Elgart-Sharon, Nitsan Ben-Melech, Uri Davidovich, Gideon Avni, Yoav Avni, and Naomi Porat. "OSL Dating of Pre Ter-raced and Terraced Landscape: Land Transformation in Jerusalem's Rural Hinterland." *Journal of Archaeological Science Report* 21 (2018): 575–83.

Garfinkel, Yosef, and Sa'ar Ganor. *Excavation Report 2007–2008*. Vol. 1 of *Khirbet Qeiyafa*. Jerusalem: Israel Exploration Society, 2009.

Geva, Hillel. "Jerusalem's Population in Antiquity: A Minimalist View." *TA* 41 (2014): 131–60.

———. "Western Jerusalem at the End of the First Temple Period in Light of the Excavations in the Jewish Quarter." Pages 183–208 in *Jerusalem in Bible and Archaeology: The First Temple Period*. Edited by Andy G. Vaughn and Ann E. Killebrew. SymS 18. Atlanta: Society of Biblical Literature, 2003.

Gilbert-Peretz, Diana. "Ceramic Figurines." Pages 29–41 in *Various Reports*. Vol. 4 of *Excavations at the City of David 1978–1985 Directed by Yigal Shiloh*. Edited by Donald T. Ariel and Alon De Groot. Qedem

35. Jerusalem: Institute of Archaeology, Hebrew University of Jerusalem, 1996.

Gilboa, Ayelet. "Assyrian Pottery in Dor and Notes on the Status of the City During the Period of Assyrian Rule" [Hebrew]. *ErIsr* 25 (1996): 122–35.

Ginzberg, Louis, *The Legends of the Jews*. 7 vols. Philadelphia: Jewish Publication Society, 1909–1938.

Gitin, Seymour. "Iron Age IIC: Judah." Pages 345–63 in *The Ancient Pottery of Israel and Its Neighbors from the Iron Age through the Hellenistic Periods*. Edited by Seymour Gitin. Vols. 1–2. Jerusalem: Israel Exploration Society, 2015.

———. "The Neo-Assyrian Empire and Its Western Periphery: The Levant, with a Focus on Philistine Ekron." Pages 77–103 in *Assyria 1995: Proceedings of the Tenth Anniversary Symposium of the Neo-Assyrian Text Corpus Project, Helsinki, September 7–11, 1995*. Edited by Simo Parpola and Robert M. Whiting. Helsinki: Neo-Assyrian Text Corpus Project, 1997.

———. "The Philistines in the Prophetic Texts: An Archaeological Perspective." Pages 273–90 in *Hesed ve-Emet: Studies in Honor of Ernest S. Frerichs*. Edited by Jodi Magness and Seymour Gitin. BJS 320. Atlanta: Scholars Press, 1998.

———. "Temple Complex 650 at Ekron: The Impact of Multi-Cultural Influences on Philistine Cult in the Late Iron Age." Pages 223–56 in *Temple Building and Temple Cult: Architecture and Cultic Paraphernalia of Temples in the Levant (2.–1. Mill. B.C.E.)*. Edited by Jens Kamlah. ADPV 41. Wiesbaden: Harrassowitz, 2012.

Goren, Yuval. "Excursus: Petrographic Analysis of the *lmlk* and Official Sealed Jar Handles from the Renewed Excavations." Pages 502–4 in vol. 2 of *Tel Beth-Shemesh A Border Community in Judah: Renewed Excavations 1990–2000; The Iron Age*. Edited by Shlomo Bunimovitz and Zvi Lederman. Sonia and Marco Nadler Institute of Archaeology Monograph Series 34. Winona Lake, IN: Eisenbrauns, 2016.

Gorzalczany, Amir. "Appendix: Petrographic Analysis of Persian-Period Vessels." Pages 51–56 in *Area E; The Finds*. Vol. 7B of *Excavations at the City of David 1978–1985 Directed by Yigal Shiloh*. Edited by Alon De Groot and Hannah Bernick-Greenberg. Qedem 54. Jerusalem: Institute of Archaeology, Hebrew University, 2012.

Grabbe, Lester L. *Ancient Israel: What Do We Know and How Do We Know It?* London: T&T Clark, 2007. Rev. ed. 2017.

———, ed. *Good Kings and Bad Kings: The Kingdom of Judah in the Seventh Century BCE*. LHBOTS 393. London: T&T Clark, 2005.

Graesser, Carl F. "Standing Stones in Ancient Palestine." *BA* 35.2 (1972): 33–63.

Greenberg, Raphael, and Gilad Cinamon. "Excavations at Rogem Gannim, Jerusalem: Installations of the Iron Age, Persian, Roman and Islamic Periods." *Atiqot* 66 (2011): 79–106.

———. "Rock-Cut Installations from the Iron Age, Persian and Roman Periods." *Atiqot* 66 (2011): 79–106.

———. "Stamped and Incised Jar Handles from Rogem Ganim, and Their Implications for the Political Economy of Jerusalem, Late Eighth–Early Fourth Centuries BCE." *TA* 33 (2006): 229–43.

Greenhut, Zvi. "Impressed and Incised Sherds." Pages 129–37 in *Salvage Excavations at Tel Moza: The Bronze and Iron Age Settlements and Later Occupations*. Edited by Zvi Greenhut and Alon De Groot. IAAR 39. Jerusalem: Israel Antiquities Authority, 2009.

Greenhut, Zvi, and Alon De Groot. *Salvage Excavations at Tel Moza: The Bronze and Iron Age Settlements and Later Occupations*. IAAR 39. Jerusalem: Israel Antiquities Authority, 2009.

Greimas, Algirdas J. "La structure élémentaire de la signification en linguistique." *L'Homme* 3.3 (1964): 5–17.

Groß, Melanie. "Ḥarrān als kulturelles Zentrum in der altorientalischen Geschichte und sein Weiterleben." Pages 139–54 in *Kulturelle Schnittstelle: Mesopotamien, Anatolien, Kurdistan; Geschichte; Sprachen; Gegenwart*. Edited by Lea Müller-Funk, Stephan Procházka, Gebhard J. Selz, and Anna Telič. Vienna: Instituts für Orientalistik der Universität Wien, 2014.

Guggenheimer, Heinrich W. *The Jerusalem Talmud, Fourth Order: Neziqin; Tractates Sanhedrin, Makkot, and Horaiot*. Berlin: de Gruyter, 2010.

Gurtner, Daniel M. "The 'Twenty-Fifth Year of Joconiah' and the Date of *2 Baruch*." *JSP* 18 (2008): 23–32.

Hall, Robert G. "The Ascension of Isaiah: Community Situation, Date and Place in Early Christianity." *JBL* 109 (1990): 289–306.

Halpern, Baruch, and André Lemaire. "The Composition of Kings." Pages 123–53 in *The Books of Kings: Sources, Composition, Historiography and Reception*. Edited by André Lemaire and Baruch Halpern. VTSup 129. Leiden: Brill, 2010.

Hammond, Philip C. "Hebron." *RB* 72 (1965): 267–70.

———. "Hebron." *RB* 73 (1966): 566–69.

Handy, Lowell K. "Rehabilitating Manasseh: Remembering King Manasseh in the Persian and Hellenistic Periods." Pages 221–35 in *Remembering Biblical Figures in the Late Persian and Early Hellenistic Periods: Social Memory and Imagination*. Edited by Diana V. Edelman and Ehud Ben Zvi. Oxford: Oxford University Press, 2013.

Herzog, Ze'ev. "The Fortress Mound at Arad: An Interim Report." *TA* 29 (2002): 3–109.

———. "Perspectives on Southern Israel's Cult Centralization: Arad and Beer-sheba." Pages 169–99 in One God–One Cult–One Nation: Archaeological and Biblical Perspectives. Edited by Reinhard G. Kratz and Hermann Spieckermann. BZAW 405. Berlin: de Gruyter, 2010.

Herzog, Ze'ev, and Lily Singer-Avitz, eds. *Beer-Sheba III: The Early Iron IIA Enclosed Settlement and the Late Iron IIA–Iron IIB Cities*. Sonia and Marco Nadler Institute of Archaeology Monograph Series 33. Winona Lake, IN: Eisenbrauns, 2016.

Herzog, Ze'ev, Miriam Aharoni, Anson F. Rainey, and Shmuel Moshkovitz. "The Israelite Fortress at Arad." *BASOR* 254 (1984): 1–34.

Hoffmann, Hans-Detlef. *Reform und Reformen: Untersuchungen zu einem Grundthema der deuteronomistischen Geschichtsschreibung*. ATANT 66. Zurich: TVZ, 1980.

Holland, Thomas A. "A Study of Palestinian Iron Age Baked Clay Figurines, with Special Reference to Jerusalem Cave 1." *Levant* 9 (1977): 121–55.

———. "A Typological and Archaeological Study of Human and Animal Representations in the Plastic Art of Palestine during the Iron Age." PhD diss., Oxford University, 1975.

Holloway, Steven Winford. "Harran: Cultic Geography in the Neo-Assyrian Empire and Its Implications for Sennacherib's Letter to Hezekiah in 2 Kings." Pages 276–314 in *The Pitcher Is Broken: Memorial Essays for Gösta Ahlström*. Edited by Steven Winford Holloway and Lowell K. Handy. JSOTSup 190. Sheffield: Sheffield Academic, 1995.

Horst, Pieter W. van den, and Judith H. Newman. *Early Jewish Prayers in Greek*. CEJL. Berlin: de Gruyter, 2008.

Houston, Walter J. *Contending for Justice: Ideologies and Theologies of Social Justice in the Old Testament*. New York: T&T Clark, 2006.

Ilan, Tal. "Huldah, the Deuteronomic Prophetess of the Book of Kings." *Lectio Difficilior* 11 (2010). https://tinyurl.com/SBL2643j.

Israel Antiquities Authority. "A Gate-Shrine Dating to the First Temple Period Was Exposed in Excavations of the Israel Antiquities Authority in the Tel Lachish National Park." https://tinyurl.com/SBL2643e.

Japhet, Sara. *2 Chronik*. HThKAT. Freiburg im Breisgau: Herder, 2003.

———. *The Ideology of the Book of Chronicles and Its Place in Biblical Thought*. 2nd ed. Frankfurt: Lang, 1997.

Katz, Haya. *"A Land of Grain and Wine … A Land of Olive Oil and Honey": The Economy of the Kingdom of Judah* [Hebrew]. Jerusalem: Yad Ben Zvi, 2008.

Katzenstein, H. Jacob. "Gaza in the Neo-Babylonian Period (626–539 B.C.E.)." *Transeu* 7 (1994): 35–49.

Keefe, Alice A. *Woman's Body and the Social Body in Hosea*. JSOTSup 338. Sheffield: Sheffield Academic, 2001.

Keel, Othmar. *Die Geschichte Jerusalems und die Entstehung des Monotheismus*. Göttingen: Vandenhoeck & Ruprecht, 2007.

———. *Goddesses and Trees, New Moon and Yahweh: Ancient Near Eastern Art and the Hebrew Bible*. JSOTSup 261. Sheffield: Sheffield Academic, 1998.

———. *Von Tel el-ʿIdham bis Tel Kitan*. Vol. 5 of *Corpus der Stempelsiegel-Amulette aus Palästina/Israel: Von den Anfängen bis zur Perserzeit*. OBO.SA 35. Fribourg: Academic Press; Göttingen: Vandenhoeck & Ruprecht, 2017.

———. *Von Tel Gamma bis Chirbet Husche*. Vol. 4 of *Corpus der Stempelsiegel-Amulette aus Palästina/Israel: Von den Anfängen bis zur Perserzeit*. OBO.SA 33. Fribourg: Academic Press; Göttingen: Vandenhoeck & Ruprecht, 2013.

———. *Von Tell Abu Farağ bis ʿAtlit*. Vol. 1 of *Corpus der Stempelsiegel-Amulette aus Palästina/Israel: Von den Anfängen bis zur Perserzeit*. OBO.SA 13. Fribourg: Academic Press; Göttingen: Vandenhoeck & Ruprecht, 1997.

———. *Von Tell el-Farʿa-Nord bis Tell el-Fir*. Vol. 3 of *Corpus der Stempelsiegel-Amulette aus Palästina/Israel: Von den Anfängen bis zur Perserzeit*. OBO.SA 31. Fribourg: Academic Press; Göttingen: Vandenhoeck & Ruprecht, 2010.

Keel, Othmar, and Christoph Uehlinger. *Gods, Goddesses, and Images of God in Ancient Israel*. Minneapolis: Fortress, 1998.

———. *Göttinnen, Götter und Gottessymbole: Neue Erkenntnisse zur Religionsgeschichte Kanaans und Israels aufgrund bislang unerschlossener ikonographischer Quellen*. 4th ed. QD 134. Freiburg: Herder, 1999.

Kelle, Brad E. *Hosea 2: Metaphor and Rhetoric in Historical Perspective.* AcBib 20. Atlanta: Society of Biblical Literature, 2005.

Kellenberger, Edgar. "Wessen unschuldiges Blut vergossen Manasse und Jojaqim?" Pages 215–27 in *A King like All the Nations? Kingdoms of Israel and Judah in the Bible and History.* Edited by Manfred Oeming and Petr Sláma. BVB 28. Münster: LIT, 2015.

Kenyon, Kathleen. "Excavation in Jerusalem 1967." *PEQ* 100 (1968): 97–111.

Kessler, Rainer. *Staat und Gesellschaft im vorexilischen Juda: Vom 8. Jahrhundert bis zum Exil.* VTSup 47. Leiden: Brill, 1992.

Keulen, Percy S. F. van. *Manasseh through the Eyes of the Deuteronomists: The Manasseh Account (2 Kings 21:1–18) and the Final Chapters of the Deuteronomistic History.* OTS 38. Leiden: Brill, 1996.

Kisilevitz, Shua. "Cultic Finds from the Iron Age in the Excavations at Moza." Pages 38–46 in vol. 7 of *New Studies in the Archaeology of Jerusalem and Its Region: Collected Papers.* Edited by Guy D. Stiebel, Orit Peleg-Barkat, Doron Ben-Ami, and Yuval Gadot. Jerusalem, 2014.

———. "The Iron IIA Judahite Temple at Tel Moza." *TA* 42 (2015): 147–64.

Klein, Ralph W. *2 Chronicles: A Commentary.* Hermeneia. Minneapolis: Fortress, 2012.

Kletter, Raz. *Economic Keystones: The Weight System of the Kingdom of Judah.* JSOTSup 276. Sheffield: Sheffield Academic, 1998.

———. *The Judean Pillar-Figurines and the Archaeology of Asherah.* BARIS 636. Oxford: Tempus Reparatum, 1996.

———. "Pots and Polities: Material Remains of Late Iron Age Judah in Relation to Its Political Borders." *BASOR* 314 (1999): 19–54.

———. "Selected Material Remains of Judah at the End of the Iron Age in Relation to Its Political Borders." PhD diss., Tel Aviv University, 1995.

Kletter, Raz, and Katri Saarelainen. "Horses and Riders and Riders and Horses." Pages 197–224 in *Family and Household Religion: Toward a Synthesis of Old Testament Studies, Archaeology, Epigraphy, and Cultural Studies.* Edited by Rainer Albertz, Beth Alpert Nakhai, Saul M. Olyan, and Rüdiger Schmitt. Winona Lake, IN: Eisenbrauns, 2014.

Kloner, Amos. *Survey of Jerusalem: The Northwestern Sector, Introduction and Indices.* Archaeological Survey of Israel. Jerusalem: Israel Antiquities Authority, 2003.

Knauf, Axel E. "The Glorious Days of Manasseh." Pages 164–88 in *Good Kings and Bad Kings: The Kingdom of Judah in the Seventh Century BCE.* Edited by Lester L. Grabbe. LHBOTS 393. London: T&T Clark,

Knibb, Michael A. "Martyrdom and Ascension of Isaiah." *OTP* 2:143–76.

Knight, Jonathan M. *The Ascension of Isaiah*. Sheffield: Sheffield Academic, 1995.

Knoppers, Gary N. "Saint of Sinner? Manasseh in Chronicles." Pages 211–29 in *Rewriting Biblical History: Essays on Chronicles and Ben Sira in Honor of Pancratius C. Beentjes*. Edited by Jeremy Corley and Harm van Grol. DCLS 9. Berlin: de Gruyter, 2011.

———. "Theories of the Redaction(s) of Kings." Pages 69–88 in *The Books of Kings: Sources, Composition, Historiography and Reception*. Edited by André Lemaire and Baruch Halpern. VTSup 129. Leiden: Brill, 2010.

Koch, Ido. "New Light on the Glyptic Finds from Late Iron Age Jerusalem and Judah" [Hebrew]. Pages 29–44 in vol. 12 of *New Studies in the Archaeology of Jerusalem and Its Region: Collected Papers*. Edited by Joe Uziel, Yuval Gadot, Yehiel Zelinger, Orit Peleg, and Oren Gutfeld. Jerusalem, 2018.

———. "Rosette Stamp Impressions." Pages 371–88 in *Ramat Raḥel III: Final Publication of Yohanan Aharoni's Excavations (1954, 1959–1962)*. Edited by Oded Lipschits, Yuval Gadot, and Liora Freud. Sonia and Marco Nadler Institute of Archaeology Monograph Series 35. Winona Lake, IN: Eisenbrauns, 2016.

Koch, Ido, and Lidar Sapir-Hen. "Beersheba–Arad Valley during the Assyrian Period." *Sem* 60 (2018): 427–52.

Koch, Ido, and Oded Lipschits. "The Rosette Stamped Jar Handle System and the Kingdom of Judah at the End of the First Temple Period." *ZDPV* 129 (2013): 55–78.

Köckert, Matthias. "Zum literargeschichtlichen Ort des Prophetengesetzes Dtn 18 zwischen dem Jeremiabuch und Dtn 13." Pages 80–100 in *Liebe und Gebot: Studien zum Deuteronomium; Festschrift zum 70. Geburtstag von Lothar Perlitt*. Edited by Reinhard Gregor Kratz and Hermann Spieckermann. FRLANT 190. Göttingen: Vandenhoeck & Ruprecht, 2000.

Koen, Karleen. *Through a Glass Darkly*. New York: Doubleday, 1986.

Koenen, Klaus. *Bethel: Geschichte, Kult und Theologie*. OBO 192. Fribourg: Presses Universitaires; Göttingen: Vandenhoeck & Ruprecht, 2003.

Kogan-Zehavi, Elena. "The Rural Settlement in the Judaean Foothills in the Persian and Early Hellenistic Periods, in Light of the Excavations in Ramat Beit Shemesh" [Hebrew]. Pages 120–33 in vol. 8 of

New Studies in the Archaeology of Jerusalem and Its Region: Collected Papers. Edited by Guy D. Stiebel, Orit Peleg-Barkat, Doron Ben-Ami, and Yuval Gadot. Jerusalem, 2014.

Laato, Antti. *Josiah and David Redivivus: The Historical Josiah and the Messianic Expectations of Exilic and Postexilic Times.* ConBOT 33. Stockholm: Almquist & Wiksell, 1992.

Lanfranchi, Giovanni B. "Greek Historians and the Memory of the Assyrian Court." Pages 39–65 in *Der Achämenidenhof/The Achaemenid Court: Akten des 2. Internationalen Kolloquiums zum Thema "Vorderasien im Spannungsfeld klassischer und altorientalischer Überlieferungen" Landgut Castelen bei Basel, 23.–25. Mai 2007.* Edited by Bruno Jacobs and Robert Rollinger. Classica et Orientalia 2. Wiesbaden: Harrassowitz, 2010.

Langgut, Dafna, and Oded Lipschits. "Dry Climate during the Early Persian Period and Its Impact on the Establishment of Idumea." *Transeu* 49 (2017): 135–62.

Langgut, Dafna, Israel Finkelstein, Thomas Litt, Frank Harald Neumann, and Mordechai Stein. "Vegetation and Climate Changes during the Bronze and Iron Ages (~3600–600 BCE) in the Southern Levant Based on Palynological Records." *Radiocarbon* 57 (2015): 217–35.

Leemhuis, Frederik, Albertus F. J. Klijn, and Geert J. H. Van Gelder. *The Arabic Text of the Apocalypse of Baruch.* Leiden: Brill, 1986.

Lehmann, Gunnar. "Area E." Pages 73–87 in *Tel Kabri: The 1986–1993 Excavation Seasons.* Edited by Aharon Kempinski. Sonia and Marco Nadler Institute of Archaeology Monograph Series 20. Tel Aviv: Emery and Claire Yass Publications in Archaeology, Institute of Archaeology, Tel Aviv University, 2002.

Lemaire, André. "Les inscriptions de Khirbet el-Qôm et l'Asherah de Yhwh." *RB* 84 (1977): 595–608.

———. "Vers l'Histoire de la Rédaction des Livres des Rois." *ZAW* 98 (1986): 221–36.

Lescow, Theodor. "Das vorexilische Amosbuch: Erwägungen zu seiner Kompositionsgeschichte." *BN* 93 (1998): 23–55.

Levinson, Bernard M., and Jeffrey Stackert. "Between the Covenant Code and Esarhaddon's Succession Treaty: Deuteronomy 13 and the Composition of Deuteronomy." *JAJ* 3 (2012): 123–40.

Lipschits, Oded. "Achaemenid Imperial Policy, Settlement Processes in Palestine, and the Status of Jerusalem in the Middle of the Fifth Century BCE." Pages 19–52 in *Judah and the Judeans in the Persian Period.*

Edited by Oded Lipschits and Manfred Oeming. Winona Lake, IN: Eisenbrauns, 2006.

———. *The Age of Empires: History and Administration in Judah in Light of the Stamped Jar Handles* [Hebrew]. Jerusalem: Yad Ben Zvi, 2018.

———. "The Changing Faces of Kingship in Judah under Assyrian Rule." Pages 116–38 in *Changing Faces of Kingship in Syria-Palestine 1500–500 BCE.* Edited by Agustinus Gianto and Peter Dubovský. AOAT 459. Münster: Ugarit-Verlag, 2018.

———. "Demographic Changes in Judah between the Seventh and the Fifth Centuries BCE." Pages 323–76 in *Judah and the Judeans in the Neo-Babylonian Period.* Edited by Oded Lipschits and Joseph Blenkinsopp. Winona Lake, IN: Eisenbrauns, 2003.

———. *The Fall and Rise of Jerusalem: The History of Judah under Babylonian Rule.* Winona Lake, IN: Eisenbrauns, 2005.

———. "On Cash-Boxes and Finding or Not Finding Books: Jehoash's and Josiah's Decisions to Repair the Temple." Pages 239–54 in *Essays on Ancient Israel in Its Near Eastern Context: A Tribute to Nadav Na'aman.* Edited by Yairah Amit, Ehud Ben Zvi, Israel Finkelstein, and Oded Lipschits. Winona Lake, IN: Eisenbrauns, 2006.

———. "Persian Period Judah: A New Perspective." Pages 187–212 in *Texts, Contexts and Readings in Postexilic Literature: Explorations into Historiography and Identity Negotiation in Hebrew Bible and Related Texts.* Edited by Louis Jonker. FAT 2/53. Tübingen: Mohr Siebeck, 2011.

———. "Shedding New Light on the Dark Years of the 'Exilic Period': New Studies, Further Elucidation, and Some Questions Regarding the Archaeology of Judah as an 'Empty Land.'" Pages 57–90 in *Interpreting Exile: Interdisciplinary Studies of Displacement and Deportation in Biblical and Modern Contexts.* Edited by Brad E. Kelle, Frank R. Ames, and Jacob L. Wright. AIL 10. Atlanta: Society of Biblical Literature, 2011.

———. "Was There a Royal Estate in Ein-Gedi by the End of the Iron Age and During the Persian Period?" [Hebrew]. Pages 31–42 in *Jerusalem and Eretz Israel (Arie Kindler Volume).* Edited by Joshua Schwartz, Zohar Amar, and Irit Ziffer. Tel Aviv: Eretz Israel Museum and The Ingeborg Center for Jerusalem Studies, 2000.

Lipschits, Oded, and David Amit. "Eighteen Stamped Jar Handles Not Published So Far" [Hebrew]. Pages 179–98 in *New Studies in Jerusalem 17.* Edited by Eyal Baruch and Avraham Faust. Ramat Gan: Rennert Center for Jerusalem Studies, 2011.

Lipschits, Oded, and David S. Vanderhooft. *Yehud Stamp Impressions: A Corpus of Inscribed Stamp Impressions from the Persian and Hellenistic Periods in Judah.* Winona Lake, IN: Eisenbrauns, 2011.

Lipschits, Oded, and Yuval Gadot. "Ramat Rahel and the Emeq Rephaim Sites: Links and Interpretations" [Hebrew]. Pages 88–96 in vol. 2 of *New Studies in the Archaeology of Jerusalem and Its Region: Collected Papers.* Edited by David Amit and Guy Stiebel. Jerusalem, 2008.

Lipschits, Oded, Nitsan Shalom, Noa Shatil, and Yuval Gadot. "Judah in 'the Long Third Century': An Archaeological Perspective" [Hebrew]. Pages 134–52 in vol. 8 of *New Studies in the Archaeology of Jerusalem and Its Region: Collected Papers.* Edited by Guy D. Stiebel, Orit Peleg-Barkat, Doron Ben-Ami, and Yuval Gadot. Jerusalem, 2014.

Lipschits, Oded, Omer Sergi, and Ido Koch. "Judahite Stamped and Incised Jar Handles: A Tool for the Study of the History of Late Monarchic Judah." *TA* 38 (2011): 5–41.

———. "Royal Judahite Jar Handles: Reconsidering the Chronology of the *lmlk* Stamp Impressions." *TA* 37 (2010): 3–32.

Lipschits, Oded, Yuval Gadot, and Liora Freud. *Ramat Rahel III: Final Publication of Yohanan Aharoni's Excavations (1954, 1959–1962).* Sonia and Marco Nadler Institute of Archaeology Monograph Series 35. Winona Lake, IN: Eisenbrauns, 2016.

Lipschits, Oded, Yuval Gadot, Benjamin Arubas, and Manfred Oeming. "Palace and Village, Paradise and Oblivion: Unraveling the Riddles of Ramat Rahel." *NEA* 74 (2011): 1–49.

———. *What Are the Stones Whispering? Ramat Rahel: 3000 Years of Forgotten History.* Winona Lake, IN: Eisenbrauns 2017.

Liverani, Mario. *Israel's History and the History of Israel.* London: Equinox, 2005.

Lowery, Richard H. *The Reforming Kings: Cults and Society in First Temple Judah.* JSOTSup 120. Sheffield: Sheffield Academic, 1991.

Mackerle, Adam. *Ámos: Když Bůh musí řvát jako lev.* Prague: Česká biblická společnost, 2017.

———. "Kniha Abdijáš: Co má Starý zákon proti Edómu? (Abd 1,1–21)." Pages 193–205 in *Obtížné oddíly Zadních proroků.* Edited by M. Prudký. Kostelní Vydří: Karmelitánské nakladatelství, 2016.

———. "Možnosti a úskalí práce s hebrejským textem." Pages 30–48 in *Jednota v mnohosti: Zborník z Teologickej konferencie mladých vedeckých pracovníkov.* Edited A. Biela, R. Schön, and J. Badura. Bratislava: Univerzita Komenského v Bratislave, 2012.

Maeir, Aren M., and Itzik Shai. "Reassessing the Character of the Judahite Kingdom: Archaeological Evidence for Non-Centralized, Kinship-Based Components." Pages 323–40 in *From Sha'ar Hagolan to Shaaraim: Essays in Honor of Prof. Yosef Garfinkel.* Edited by Sa'ar Ganor, Igor Kreimerman, Katharina Streit, and Madeleine Mumcuoglu. Jerusalem: Israel Exploration Society, 2016.

Magen, Yitzhak, and Israel Finkelstein, eds. *Archaeological Survey of the Hill Country of Benjamin* [Hebrew]. Jerusalem: Israel Antiquities Authority, 1993.

Markoe, Glenn. *Phoenician Bronze and Silver Bowls from Cyprus and the Mediterranean.* Berkeley: University of California Press, 1985.

Master, Daniel M. "From the Buqe'ah to Ashkelon." Pages 305–17 in *Exploring the Longue Durée: Essays in Honor of Lawrence E. Stager.* Edited by David Schloen. Winona Lake, IN: Eisenbrauns, 2009.

Mastin, Brian A. "Yahweh's Asherah, Inclusive Monotheism and the Question of Dating." Pages 326–51 in *In Search of Pre-Exilic Israel: Proceedings of the Oxford Old Testament Seminar.* Edited by John Day. JSOTSup 406. London: T&T Clark, 2004.

May, Natalya. "Giv'at Ḥoma." [Hebrew]. *HA* 107 (1997): 93–94.

Mayes, Andrew D. H. *The Story of Israel between Settlement and Exile: A Redactional Study of the Deuteronomistic History.* London: SCM, 1983.

Mazar, Amihai. *Archaeology of the Land of the Bible.* ABRL. New York: Doubleday, 1990.

———. "The Northern Shephelah in the Iron Age: Some Issues in Biblical History and Archaeology." Pages 247–67 in *Scriptures and Other Artifacts, Essays on the Bible and Archaeology in Honor of Philip J. King.* Edited by Michael D. Coogan, J. Cheryl Exum, and Lawrence E. Stager. Louisville: Westminster John Knox, 1994.

Mazar, Amihai, and Nava Panitz-Cohen. *Timnah (Tel Batash) II: The Finds from the First Millennium BCE (Text, Plates).* Qedem 42. Jerusalem: Institute of Archaeology, Hebrew University of Jerusalem, 2001.

Mazar, Eilat. *Area G.* Vol. 1 of *The Summit of the City of David Excavations 2005–2008: Final Reports.* Jerusalem: Shoham Academic Research and Publication, 2015.

Mazar, Eilat, and Benjamin Mazar. *Excavations in the South of the Temple Mount: The Ophel of Biblical Jerusalem.* Qedem 29. Jerusalem: Institute of Archaeology, Hebrew University of Jerusalem, 1989.

Mazor, Gaby. "A Farmhouse from the Late Iron Age and Second Temple Period in 'French Hill,' North Jerusalem" [Hebrew]. *Atiqot* 54 (2007): 1*–14*.

McCown, Chester Charlton. *Tell en-Nasbeh I: Excavated under the Direction of the Late William Frederic Bade.* New Haven: American Schools of Oriental Research, 1947.

McKenzie, Steven L. "The Trouble with Kingship." Pages 286–314 in *Israel Constructs Its History: Deuteronomistic Historiography in Recent Research.* Edited by Albert de Pury, Thomas Römer, and Jean-Daniel Macchi. JSOTSup 306. Sheffield: Sheffield Academic, 2000.

Meier, John P. *Mentor, Message, and Miracles.* Vol. 2 of *A Marginal Jew: Rethinking the Historical Jesus.* ABRL. New York: Doubleday, 1994.

Mendelsohn, Isaac. "Guilds in Ancient Palestine." *BASOR* 80 (1940): 17–21.

Mizrahi, Sivan, and Renee Forestani. "Jerusalem, Ramot Alon, Preliminary Report." *HA* 128 (2016): https://tinyurl.com/SBL2643f.

Mizrahi, Sivan, Natalya Katanelson, and Donald T. Ariel. "Jerusalem, Ramot Alon." *HA* 128 (2016): https://tinyurl.com/SBL2643g.

Moore, Carey A. *Tobit: A New Translation with Introduction and Commentary.* AB 40A. New York: Doubleday, 1996.

Moore, Megan Bishop. "Writing Israel's History Using the Prophetic Books." Pages 23–36 in *Israel's Prophets and Israel's Past: Essays on the Relationship of Prophetic Texts and Israelite History in Honor of John H. Hayes.* Edited by Brad E. Kelle and Megan B. Moore. LHBOTS 446. London: T&T Clark, 2006.

Moorey, Peter Roger Stuart. *Idols of the People: Miniature Images of Clay in the Ancient Near East.* Schweich Lectures. Oxford: Oxford University Press, 2003.

Moyal, Yigal, and Avraham Faust. "Jerusalem and Its Daughters: Moza, Ramat Rahel, and Jerusalem's Hinterland in the Seventh Century BCE" [Hebrew]. Pages 25–46 in *New Studies on Jerusalem 21.* Edited Eyal Baruch and Avraham Faust. Ramat Gan: Bar-Ilan University, 2015.

Na'aman, Nadav. "The Abandonment of Cult Places in the Kingdoms of Israel and Judah as Acts of Cult Reform." *UF* 34 (2002): 585–602.

———. "An Assyrian Residence at Ramat Rahel?" *TA* 28 (2001): 260–80.

———. "The Brook of Egypt and Assyrian Policy on the Border of Egypt." *TA* 6 (1979): 68–90.

———. "Esarhaddon's Treaty with Baal and Assyrian Provinces along the Phoenician Coast." *RSF* 22 (1994): 3–8.

———. "Hezekiah and the Kings of Assyria." *TA* 21 (1994): 235–54.

———. "The Kingdom of Judah under Josiah." *TA* 18 (1991): 3–71.

———. "The *lmlk* Seal Impressions Reconsidered." *TA* 43 (2016): 111–25.

———. "The Negev in the Last Century of the Kingdom of Judah" [Hebrew]. *Cathedra* 42 (1987): 3–15.

———. "Population Changes in Palestine Following the Assyrian Deportations." *TA* 20 (1993): 104–24.

———. "Province System and Settlement Pattern in Southern Syria and Palestine in the Neo-Assyrian Period." Pages 103–15 in *Neo-Assyrian Geography*. Edited by Mario Liverani. Quaderni di geografia storica 5. Rome: Università di Roma, Istituto di studi del Vicino Oriente, 1995.

———. "Royal Inscriptions and the Histories of Joash and Ahaz, Kings of Judah." *VT* 48 (1998): 333–49.

———. "The Sources Available for the Author of the Book of Kings." Pages 105–20 in *Recenti Tendenze nella Riccostruzione della Storia Antica d'Israele: Convegno internazionale (Roma, 6–7 marzo 2003)*. Edited Mario Liverani. Contributi del Centro Linceo Interdisciplinare "Beniamino Segre" 110. Roma: Accademia Nazionale dei Lincei, 2005.

———. "The Temple Library of Jerusalem and the Composition of the Book of Kings." Pages 129–52 in *Congress Volume Leiden 2004*. Edited by André Lemaire. VTSup 109. Leiden: Brill, 2006.

———. "Two Notes on the History of Ashkelon and Ekron in the Late Eighth–Seventh Century B.C.E." *TA* 25 (1998): 219–27.

———. "When and How Did Jerusalem Become a Great City? The Rise of Jerusalem as Judah's Premier City in the Eighth–Seventh Centuries B.C.E." *BASOR* 347 (2007): 21–56.

Nadelman, Yonatan. "Iron Age II Clay Figurine Fragments from the Excavations." Pages 123–27 in *Excavations in the South of the Temple Mount: The Ophel of Biblical Jerusalem*. Edited by Eilat Mazar and Benjamin Mazar. Qedem 29. Jerusalem: Institute of Archaeology, Hebrew University of Jerusalem, 1989.

Nagorski, Alla, and Zvi Greenhut. "Iron Age and Second Temple-Period Remains at Ras el-ʿAmud, Jerusalem" [Hebrew]. *Atiqot* 80 (2015): 1*–21*.

Nelson, Richard D. *The Double Redaction of the Deuteronomistic History*. JSOTSup 18. Sheffield: JSOT Press, 1981.

Newman, Judith. "The Form and Settings of the Prayer of Manasseh." Pages 105–25 in *The Development of Penitential Prayer in Second Temple Judaism*. Vol. 2 of *Seeking the Favor of God*. Edited by Mark J. Boda, Daniel K. Falk, and Rodney A. Warline. EJL 22. Atlanta: Society of Biblical Literature, 2007.

———. "Three Contexts for Reading Manasseh's Prayer in the Didascalia." *JCSSS* 7 (2007): 3–15.

Nickelsburg, George W. E. *1 Enoch 1: A Commentary on the Book of 1 Enoch*. Hermeneia. Minneapolis: Fortress, 2001.

———. *Jewish Literature between the Bible and the Mishnah: A Historical and Literary Introduction*. 2nd ed. Minneapolis: Fortress, 2005.

———. "The Martyrdom of Isaiah." Pages 52–56 in *Jewish Writings of the Second Temple Period: Apocrypha, Pseudepigrapha, Qumran Sectarian Writings, Philo, Josephus*. Edited by Michael E. Stone. CRINT 2. Philadelphia: Fortress, 1984.

———. "The Prayer of Manasseh." Pages 770–73 in *The Oxford Bible Commentary*. Edited by John Barton and John Muddiman. Oxford: Oxford University Press, 2001.

Norelli, Enrico. *Ascensio Isaiae: Commentarius*. 2 vols. CCSA 7–8. Turnhout: Brepols, 1995.

Noth, Martin. *The Deuteronomistic History*. 2nd ed. JSOTSup 15. Sheffield: Sheffield Academic, 1991.

O'Brien, Mark A. *The Deuteronomistic History Hypothesis: A Reassessment*. OBO 92. Fribourg: Presses Universitaires; Göttingen: Vandenhoeck & Ruprecht, 1989.

Oded, Bustenay. *Mass Deportations and Deportees in the Neo-Assyrian Empire*. Wiesbaden: Reichert, 1979.

Ofer, Avi. "Hebron." *NEAEHL* 2:606–9.

———. "The Highland of Judah during the Biblical Period." 2 vols. PhD diss., Tel Aviv University, 1993.

———. "Tel Hebron" [Hebrew]. *HA* 90 (1988): 47–48.

Olson, Daniel C. *A New Reading of the Animal Apocalypse of 1 Enoch*. SVTP 24. Leiden: Brill, 2013.

Onn, Alexander, and Yehuda Rapuano. "Jerusalem—Kh. er-Ras." *ESI* 13 (1993): 71.

Ornan, Tallay. "The Beloved, Neʿehevet, and Other Does: Reflections on the Motif of the Grazing or Browsing Wild Horned Animal." Pages 279–302 in *Alphabets, Texts and Artifacts in the Ancient Near East:*

Studies Presented to Benjamin Sass. Edited by Israel Finkelstein, Christian Robin, and Thomas Römer. Paris: Van Dieren, 2016.

———. "The Complex System of Religious Symbols: The Case of the Winged Disc in Ancient Near Eastern Imagery of the First Millennium BCE." Pages 207–41 in *Crafts and Images in Contact: Studies on Eastern Mediterranean Art of the First Millennium BCE.* Edited by Claudia E. Suter and Christoph Uehlinger. OBO 210. Fribourg: Academic Press; Göttingen: Vandenhoeck & Ruprecht, 2005.

———. "Ištar as Depicted on Finds from Israel." Pages 235–56 in *Studies in the Archaeology of the Iron Age in Israel and Jordan.* Edited by Amihai Mazar. JSOTSup 331. Sheffield: Sheffield Academic, 2001.

———. "The Mesopotamian Influence on West Semitic Inscribed Seals: A Preference for the Depiction of Mortals." Pages 52–73 in *Studies in the Iconography of Northwest Semitic Inscribed Seals.* Edited by Benjamin Sass and Christoph Uehlinger. OBO 125. Fribourg: Academic Press; Göttingen: Vandenhoeck & Ruprecht, 1993.

———. "Mesopotamian Influence on the Glyptic of Israel and Jordan in the First Millennium B.C." PhD diss., Tel Aviv University, 1997.

———. "On the Dating of Some Middle Assyrian Cylinder Seals." *NABU* 3 (2003): 71–73.

Pajunen, Mika S. "The Prayer of Manasseh in 4Q381 and the Account of Manasseh in 2 Chronicles 33." Pages 143–61 in *The Scrolls and Biblical Traditions: Proceedings of the Seventh Meeting of the IOQS in Helsinki.* Edited by George J. Brooke, Daniel K. Falk, Eibert J. C. Tigchelaaar, and Molly M. Zahn. STDJ 103. Leiden: Brill, 2012.

Pakkala, Juha. "Why the Cult Reforms in Judah Probably Did Not Happen." Pages 201–35 in *One God–One Cult–One Nation: Archaeological and Biblical Perspectives.* Edited by Reinhard G. Kratz and Hermann Spieckermann. BZAW 405. Berlin: de Gruyter, 2010.

Panitz-Cohen, Nava, and Amihai Mazar. *Timnah (Tel Batash) III: The Finds from the First Millennium BCE.* Qedem 45. Jerusalem: Institute of Archaeology, Hebrew University of Jerusalem, 2006.

Park, Aaron W. *The Book of Amos as Composed and Read in Antiquity.* StBibLit 37. New York: Lang, 2004.

Parker, Bradley J. *The Mechanics of Empire: The Northern Frontier of Assyria as a Case Study in Imperial Dynamics.* Helsinki: Neo-Assyrian Text Corpus Project, 2001.

Parpola, Simo. "Assyria's Expansion in the Eighth and Seventh Centuries and Its Long-Term Repercussions in the West." Pages 99–111 in *Sym-*

biosis, Symbolism, and the Power of the Past: Canaan, Ancient Israel, and Their Neighbors from the Late Bronze Age through Roman Palaestina. Edited by William Dever and Seymour Gitin. Winona Lake, IN: Eisenbrauns, 2003.

Paul, Shalom. *Amos: A Commentary on the Book of Amos.* Hermeneia. Minneapolis: Fortress, 1991.

Peirce, Charles S. *Principles of Philosophy.* Vol. 1 of *Collected Papers of Charles Sanders Peirce.* Edited by C. Hartshorne and P. Weiss. Cambridge: Harvard University Press, 1931.

Pesce, Mauro. "Presupposti per l'utilizzazione storica dell Ascensione di Isaia." Pages 13–76 in *Isaia, il Diletto e la Chiesa: Visione ed esegesi profetica cristiano-primitive nell' Ascensione di Isaia.* Edited by Mauro Pesce. Testi e ricerche di scienze religiose 20. Brescia: Paidea, 1983.

Pietsch, Michael. "Prophetess of Doom: Hermeneutical Reflections on the Huldah Oracle (2 Kings 22)." Pages 71–80 in *Soundings in Kings: Perspectives and Methods in Contemporary Scholarship.* Edited by Mark Leuchter and Klaus-Peter Adam. Minneapolis: Fortress, 2010.

Pratt, Mary Louise. *Imperial Eyes: Travel Writing and Transculturation.* 2nd ed. London: Routledge, 2008.

Premnath, Devadasan N. *Eighth Century Prophets: A Social Analysis.* St. Louis: Chalice, 2003.

Priest, John. "Huldah's Oracle." *VT* 30 (1980): 366–68.

Pritchard, James B. *Palestinian Figurines in Relation to Certain Goddesses Known through Literature.* AOS 24. New Haven: American Oriental Society, 1943.

Provan, Ian W. *Hezekiah and the Books of Kings: A Contribution to the Debate about the Composition of the Deuteronomistic History.* BZAW 172. Berlin: de Gruyter, 1988.

Radner, Karen. "Economy, Society, and Daily Life in the Neo-Assyrian Period." Pages 209–28 in *A Companion to Assyria.* Edited by Eckart Frahm. BCAW. Hoboken, NJ: Wiley & Sons, 2017.

———. "Provinz. C. Assyrien." *RLA* 11:42–68.

———. "Revolts in the Assyrian Empire: Succession Wars, Rebellions Against a False King and Independence Movements." Pages 41–54 in *Revolt and Resistance in the Ancient Classical World and the Near East: In the Crucible of Empire.* Edited by John J. Collins and J. G. Manning. CHANE 85. Leiden: Brill, 2016.

Rapuano, Yehuda, and Alexander Onn. "An Iron Age Structure from Shu'afat Ridge, Northern Jerusalem." *Atiqot* 47 (2004): 119–29.

Redford, Donald B. *Egypt, Canaan, and Israel in Ancient Times.* Princeton: Princeton University Press, 1992.

Regev, Johanna, Joe Uziel, Nahshon Szanton, and Elizabetta Boaretto. "Absolute Dating of the Gihon Spring Fortifications, Jerusalem." *Radiocarbon* 59 (2017): 1171–93.

Reich, Ronny. *Excavating the City of David: Where Jerusalem's History Began* [Hebrew]. Jerusalem: Israel Exploration Society, 2011.

Reich, Ronny, and Eli Shukron. "Jerusalem, City of David." *HA* 114 (2003): 92–94.

———. "A New Segment of the Middle Bronze Fortification in the City of David." *TA* 37 (2010): 141–53.

Robinson, Gnana. "The Origin and Development of the Old Testament Sabbath: A Comprehensive Exegetical Approach." PhD diss., Hamburg, 1975.

Rollston, Christopher A. "The Rise of Monotheism in Ancient Israel: Biblical and Epigraphic Evidence." *SCJ* 6 (2003): 95–115.

Römer, Thomas. "The Rise and Fall of Josiah." Pages 329–40 in *Rethinking Israel: Studies in the History and Archaeology of Ancient Israel in Honor of Israel Finkelstein.* Edited by Oded Lipschits, Yuval Gadot, and Matthew J. Adams. Winona Lake, IN: Eisenbrauns, 2017.

———. *The So-Called Deuteronomistic History: A Sociological, Historical and Literary Introduction.* London: T&T Clark, 2005.

———. "Transformations in Deuteronomistic and Biblical Historiography: On 'Book-Finding' and Other Literary Strategies." *ZAW* 109 (1997): 1–11.

Ron, Zvi. "Agricultural Terraces in the Judean Mountains." *IEJ* 16 (1966): 111–22.

Rottzoll, Dirk U. *Studien zur Redaktion und Komposition des Amosbuchs.* BZAW 243. Berlin: de Gruyter, 1996.

Rubinkiewicz, Ryszard. "Apocalypse of Abraham." *OTP* 2:689–705.

———. *L'Apocalypse D'Abraham: Introduction, texte critique, traduction et commentaire.* Lublin: Société des Lettres et des Sciences de l'Université Catholique de Lublin, 1987.

Rückl, Jan. "Aspects of Prologue Formulae in Kings." Pages 159–74 in *A King Like All the Nations: Kingdoms of Israel and Judah in the Bible and History.* Edited by Manfred Oeming and Petr Sláma. BVB 28. Münster: LIT, 2015.

———. *A Sure House: Studies on the Dynastic Promise to David in the Books of Samuel and Kings.* OBO 281. Fribourg: Academic Press; Göttingen: Vandenhoeck & Ruprecht, 2016.

Rudolph, Wilhelm. *Micha–Nahum–Habakuk–Zephanja.* KAT 13.3. Berlin: Evangelische Verlagsanstalt, 1977.

Sack, Ronald H. "Nebuchadnezzar II and the Old Testament: History versus Ideology." Pages 221–33 in *Judah and the Judeans in the Neo-Babylonian Period.* Edited by Oded Lipschits and Joseph Blenkinsopp. Winona Lake, IN: Eisenbrauns, 2003.

Saussure, Ferdinand de. *Course in General Linguistics.* Edited by C. Bally and A. Sechehaye. Translated by R. Harris. London: Duckworth, 1983.

Schäfer, Peter, and Shaul Shaked, eds. *Magische Texte aus der Kairoer Geniza.* Vol. 2. TSAJ 64. Tübingen: Mohr Siebeck, 1997.

Schart, Aaron. *Die Entstehung des Zwölfprophetenbuchs: Neubearbeitungen von Amos im Rahmen schriftenübergreifender Redaktionsprozesse.* BZAW 260. Berlin: de Gruyter, 1998.

Schipper, Bernd. "Egypt and the Kingdom of Judah under Josiah and Jehoiakim." *TA* 37 (2010): 200–226.

———. "Egyptian Imperialism after the New Kingdom: The Twenty-Sixth Dynasty and the Southern Levant." Pages 268–90 in *Egypt, Canaan and Israel: History, Imperialism, Ideology and Literature; Proceedings of a Conference at the University of Haifa, 3–7 May 2009.* Edited by Shay Bar, Dan'el Kahan, and Judith J. Shirley. CHANE 52. Leiden: Brill, 2011.

Schuller, Eillen M. *Non-Canonical Psalms from Qumran: A Pseudepigraphic Collection.* HSS 28. Atlanta: Scholars Press, 1986.

Seger, Joe D. "The MB II Fortifications at Shechem and Gezer: A Hyksos Retrospective." *ErIsr* 12 (1975): 34*–45*.

Seligman, Jon. "A Late Iron Age Farmhouse at Ras Abu Maʿaruf, Pisgat Zeʾev A." *Atiqot* 25 (1994): 63–75.

Sellers, Ovid R. *The Citadel of Beth-Zur.* Philadelphia: Westminster, 1933.

Sergi, Omer. "*lmlk* Stamp Impressions." Pages 287–341 in *Ramat Raḥel III: Final Publication of Yohanan Aharoni's Excavations (1954, 1959–1962).* Edited by Oded Lipschits, Yuval Gadot, and Liora Freud. Sonia and Marco Nadler Institute of Archaeology Monograph Series 35. Winona Lake, IN: Eisenbrauns, 2016.

Sergi, Omer, Abraham Karasik, Yuval Gadot, and Oded Lipschits. "The Royal Judahite Storage Jar: A Computer Generated Typology and Its Archaeological and Historical Implications." *TA* 39 (2012): 64–92

Shiloh, Yigal. *Excavations at the City of David I 1978–1982: Interim Report of the First Five Seasons.* Qedem 19. Jerusalem: Hebrew University, 1984.

———. "A Group of Hebrew Bullae from the City of David." *IEJ* 36 (1986): 16–38.

Simian-Yofre, Horacio. *Amos: Nuova versione, introduzione e commento.* Libri Biblici Primo Testamento 15. Milan: Paoline, 2002.

Singer-Avitz, Lily. "The Pottery of Megiddo Strata III–II and a Proposed Subdivision of the Iron IIC Period in Northern Israel." *BASOR* 372 (2014): 123–45.

Ska, Jean Louis. *Introduzione alla lettura del Pentateuco: Chiavi per l'interpretazione dei primi cinque libri della Bibbia.* Bologna: Dehoniane, 1998.

Smelik, Klaas. "The Portrayal of King Manasseh: A Literary Analysis of II Kings xxi and II Chronicles xxiii." Pages 129–89 in *Converting the Past: Studies in Ancient Israelite and Moabite Historiography.* Edited by Klaas Smelik. OTS 28. Leiden: Brill, 1992.

Smend, Rudolph. *Die Entstehung des Alten Testaments.* ThW 1. Stuttgart: Kohlhammer, 1978.

Sperling, David S. "Manasseh." *EncJud* 13:452–53.

Stade, Bernhard. "Miscellen." *ZAW* 6 (1886): 156–89.

Stager, Lawrence E. "The Archaeology of the Family in Ancient Israel." *BASOR* 260 (1985): 1–35.

———. "Ashkelon and the Archaeology of Destruction: Kislev 604 BCE." *ErIsr* 25 (1996): 61*–74*.

Stavrakopoulou, Francesca. *King Manasseh and Child Sacrifice: Biblical Distortions of Historical Realities.* BZAW 338. Berlin: de Gruyter, 2004.

Steiner, Margreet L. *The Settlement in the Bronze and Iron Ages.* Vol. 3 of *Excavations by Kathleen M. Kenyon in Jerusalem 1961–1967.* Copenhagen International Series 9. London: Sheffield Academic, 2001.

———. "Two Popular Cult Sites of Ancient Palestine: Cave 1 in Jerusalem and E 207 in Samaria." *SJOT* 11 (1997): 16–28.

Stern, Ephraim. *The Assyrian, Babylonian, and Persian Periods (732–332 B.C.E.).* Vol. 2 of *Archaeology of the Land of the Bible.* ABRL. New York: Doubleday, 2001.

———. "Assyrian and Babylonian Elements in the Material Culture of Palestine in the Persian Period." *Transeu* 7 (1994): 51–62.

———. "The Dor Province in the Persian Period in the Light of the Recent Excavations at Dor." *Transeu* 2 (1990): 147–55.

———. *En-Gedi Excavations I–Conducted by B. Mazar and I Dunayevsky: Final Report (1961–1965)*. Jerusalem: Israel Exploration Society, 2007.

———. "From Many Gods to the One God: The Archaeological Evidence." Pages 395–403 in One God–One Cult–One Nation: Archaeological and Biblical Perspectives. BZAW 405. Edited by Reinhard G. Kratz and Hermann Spieckermann. Berlin: de Gruyter, 2010.

———. "Hazor, Dor and Megiddo in the Time of Ahab and under Assyrian Rule." *IEJ* 40 (1990): 12–30.

———. "The Jericho Region and the Eastern Border of the Judean Kingdom in Its Last Days" [Hebrew]. *ErIsr* 24 (1993): 192–97.

———. "Persian Period." Pages 565–617 in vol. 2 of *The Ancient Pottery of Israel and Its Neighbors from the Iron Age through the Hellenistic Period*. Edited by Seymour Gitin. Jerusalem: Israel Exploration Society, 2015.

Steymans, Hans U. "Deuteronomy 28 and Tell Tayinat." *VeEc* 34 (2013): 1–13.

Storchan, Benyamin. "Jerusalem, Ramat Shelomo." *HA* 129 (2017): https://tinyurl.com/SBL2643h.

Stuart, Douglas. *Hosea–Jonah*. WBC 31. Waco, TX: Word, 1987.

Tadmor, Hayim. "The Assyrian Campaigns to Philistia" [Hebrew]. Pages 261–85 in *The Military History of the Land of Israel in Biblical Times*. Edited by Joseph Liver. Tel Aviv: Bialik, 1964.

———. "On the History of Samaria in the Biblical Period" [Hebrew]. Pages 67–74 in *Eretz Shomron: The Thirtieth Archaeological Convention, September 1972*. Edited by Joseph Aviram. Jerusalem: Israel Exploration Society, 1973.

Talshir, Zipora. "The Three Deaths of Josiah and the Strata of Biblical Historiography (2 Kings XXIII 29–30; 2 Chronicles XXXV 20–5; 1 Esdras I 23–31." *VT* 46 (1996): 213–36.

Tatum, Lynn. "Jerusalem in Conflict: The Evidence for the Seventh-Century B.C.E. Religious Struggle over Jerusalem." Pages 291–306 in *Jerusalem in Bible and Archaeology: The First Temple Period*. Edited by Andrew G. Vaughn and Ann E. Killebrew. SymS 18. Atlanta: Society of Biblical Literature, 2003.

Tebes, Juan Manuel. "The Edomite Involvement in the Destruction of the First Temple: A Case of Stab-in-the-Back Tradition?" *JSOT* 36 (2011): 219–55.

Thareani-Sussely, Yifat. "The 'Archaeology of the Days of Manasseh' Reconsidered in the Light of Evidence from the Beersheba Valley." *PEQ* 139 (2007): 69–77.

Thareani-Sussely, Yifat, and Nadav Na'aman. "Dating the Appearance of Imitations of Assyrian Ware in Southern Palestine." *TA* 33 (2006): 61–82.

Thomas, Benjamin D. *Hezekiah and the Compositional History of the Book of Kings.* FAT 2/63. Tübingen: Mohr Siebeck, 2014.

Tiller, Patrick A. *A Commentary on the Animal Apocalypse.* EJL 4. Atlanta: Scholars Press, 1993.

Ulrich, Eugene. *The Biblical Qumran Scrolls: Transcriptions and Textual Variants.* VTSup 134. Leiden: Brill, 2010.

Ussishkin, David. *The Renewed Archaeological Excavations at Lachish (1973–1994).* 4 vols. Sonia and Marco Nadler Institute of Archaeology Monograph Series 22. Tel Aviv: Emery and Claire Yass Publications in Archaeology, 2004.

———. "Synopsis of Stratigraphical, Chronological, and Historical Issues." Pages 50–119 in vol. 1 of *The Renewed Archaeological Excavations at Lachish (1973–1994).* Edited by David Ussishkin. Sonia and Marco Nadler Institute of Archaeology Monograph Series 22. Tel Aviv: Emery and Claire Yass Publications in Archaeology, 2004.

———. "Was Jerusalem a Fortified Stronghold in the Middle Bronze Age? An Alternative View." *Levant* 48 (2016): 135–51.

Uziel, Joe, and Nahshon Szanton. "New Evidence of Jerusalem's Urban Development in the Ninth Century BCE." Pages 429–39 in *Rethinking Israel: Studies in the History and Archaeology of Ancient Israel in Honor of Israel Finkelstein.* Edited by Oded Lipschits, Yuval Gadot, and Matthew J. Adams. Winona Lake, IN: Eisenbrauns, 2017.

———. "Recent Excavations near the Gihon Spring and Their Reflection on the Character of Iron II Jerusalem." *TA* 42 (2015): 233–50.

Vainstub, Daniel, and David Ben-Shlomo. "A Hebrew Seal and an Ostracon from Tel Hebron." *IEJ* 66 (2016): 151–60.

Van Seters, John. *The Biblical Saga of King David.* Winona Lake, IN: Eisenbrauns, 2009.

———. *In Search of History: Historiography in the Ancient World and the Origins of Biblical History.* New Haven: Yale University Press, 1983.

Vanderhooft, David S. *The Neo-Babylonian Empire and Babylon in the Latter Prophets.* HSM 59. Atlanta: Scholars Press, 1999.

Varšo, Miroslav. *Abdiáš, Jonáš, Micheáš.* Komentáre k Starému zákonu 2. Trnava: Dobrá kniha, 2010.

Veijola, Timo. *Die Ewige Dynastie: David und die Entstehung seiner Dynastie nach der deuteronomistischen Darstellung.* Helsinki: Suomalainen Tiedakatemia, 1975.

Vitto, Fanny. "A First Century CE Mint South of Jerusalem? Archaeological Context." Pages 7*–15* in vol. 5 of *New Studies in the Archaeology of Jerusalem and Its Region: Collected Papers.* Edited by D. Amit, G. D. Stiebel, and O. Peleg-Barkat. Jerusalem, 2011.

Waltke, Bruce K. *A Commentary on Micah.* Grand Rapids: Eerdmans, 2007.

Weiser, Artur. *Die Propheten Hosea, Joel, Amos, Obadja, Jona, Micha.* Vol. 1 of *Das Buch der zwölf kleinen Propheten.* ATD 24. Göttingen: Vanderhoeck & Ruprecht, 1974.

Weksler-Bdolah, Shlomit. "'Alona." *HA* 19 (1997): 68*–70*.

Wilkinson, T. J., Jason Ur, Eleanor Barbanes Wilkinson, and Mark Altaweel. "Landscape and Settlement on the Neo-Assyrian Empire." *BASOR* 340 (2005): 23–56.

Willett, Tom W. *Eschatology in the Theodicies of 2 Baruch and 4 Ezra.* JSPSup 4. Sheffield: JSOT Press, 1989.

Willis, John T. "Structure of Micah 3–5 and the Function of Micah 5:9–14 in the Book." *ZAW* 81 (1969): 191–214.

Winderbaum, Ariel. "The Iconic Seals and Bullae of the Iron Age." Pages 363–419 in vol. 1 of *The Summit of the City of David Excavations 2005–2008: Final Reports.* Edited by Eilat Mazar. Jerusalem: Shoham Academic Research and Publications, 2015.

Wolff, Hans Walter, *Dodekapropheton 2: Joel und Amos.* 3rd ed. BKAT 2. Neukirchen-Vluyn: Neukircher Verlag, 1985.

———. *Dodekapropheton 4: Micha.* BKAT 4. Neukirchen-Vluyn: Neukircher Verlag, 1982.

Wolff, Sam, and Alon Shavit. "Tel Ḥamid." *HA* 109 (1999): 68*–70*.

Yadin, Yigal. "The Nature of the Settlements during the Middle Bronze IIA Period in Israel and the Problem of the Aphek Fortifications." *ZDPV* 94 (1978): 1–23.

Yellin, Joseph, and Jane M. Cahill. "Rosette-Stamped Handles: Instrumental Neutron Activation Analysis." *IEJ* 54 (2004): 191–213.

Yezerski, Irit. "Iron Age II Pottery." Pages 84–93 in *Area E and Other Studies.* Vol. 3 of *Jewish Quarter Excavations in the Old City of Jerusalem.* Edited by Hillel Geva. Jerusalem: Israel Exploration Society, 2006.

―――. "Pottery of Stratum V." Pages 86–129 in *En-Gedi Excavations I: Final Report (1961–1965)*. Edited by Ephraim Stern. Jerusalem: Israel Exploration Society, 2007.

Yezerski, Irit, and Eilat Mazar. "Iron Age III Pottery." Pages 243–98 in *Area G*. Vol. 1 of *The Summit of the City of David Excavations 2005–2008: Final Reports*. Edited by Eilat Mazar. Jerusalem: Shoham Academic Research and Publication, 2015.

Yezerski, Irit, and Hillel Geva. "Iron Age II Clay Figurines." Pages 63–84 in *The Finds from Areas A, W and X-2*. Vol. 2 of *Jewish Quarter Excavations in the Old City of Jerusalem*. Edited by Hillel Geva. Jerusalem: Israel Exploration Society, 2003.

Young, Robb Andrew. *Hezekiah in History and Tradition*. VTSup 155. Leiden: Brill, 2012.

Zapassky, Elena. "Volume Estimation of Four Iron Age Holemouth Jars." Pages 111–14 in *Salvage Excavations at Tel Moza: The Bronze and Iron Age Settlements and Later Occupations*. Edited by Zvi Greenhut and Alon De Groot. IAAR 39. Jerusalem: Israel Antiquities Authority, 2009.

Ziffer, Irit. "Iron Age Stamp Seals, A Cylinder Seal, and Impressions." Pages 514–23 in *Tel Malḥata: A Central City in the Biblical Negev*. Edited by Itzhaq Beit-Arieh and Liora Freud. Sonia and Marco Nadler Institute of Archaeology Monograph Series 32. Winona Lake, IN: Eisenbrauns, 2015.

Zilberbod, Irina. "Jerusalem, Givʿat Shaʾul, Final Report." *HA* 127 (2015): https://tinyurl.com/SBL2643i.

Zimhoni, Orna. "The Pottery of Levels III and II." Pages 1643–1788 in vol. 4 of *The Renewed Archaeological Excavations at Lachish (1973–1994)*. Edited by David Ussishkin. Sonia and Marco Nadler Institute of Archaeology Monograph Series 22. Tel Aviv: Emery and Claire Yass Publications in Archaeology, 2004.

―――. *Studies in the Iron Age Pottery of Israel: Typological, Archaeological, and Chronological Aspects*. Institute of Archaeology of Tel Aviv University Occasional Publications 2. Tel Aviv: Tel Aviv University, Institute of Archaeology, 1997.

―――. "Two Ceramic Assemblages from Lachish Levels III and II." *TA* 17 (1990): 3–52.

Zorn, Jeffery R. "Mizpah: Newly Discovered Stratum Reveals Judah's Other Capital." *BAR* 23.5 (1997): 28–38, 66.

Contributors

Josef Mario Briffa, SJ (briffa@biblico.it) is Lecturer in Archaeology, Ancient History and Sacred Scripture at the Pontifical Biblical Institute in Rome and Jerusalem and Director of Academic Programmes in Jerusalem. He holds a Licentiate in Sacred Scripture (2012) from the same institute and a PhD from the Institute of Archaeology, University College London. His dissertation, "The Figural World of the Southern Levant during the Late Iron Age" (2017), is currently being prepared for publication. Briffa has coauthored a "Catalogue of Artefacts from Malta in the British Museum" (2017). He has excavated in Malta and Israel and is currently a staff member of the Lautenschläger Azekah Expedition. He is also a Roman Catholic priest.

David Cielontko (david.cielontko@gmail.com) is a PhD candidate at the Charles University, Prague, and a researcher in the Centre for Classical Studies at the Institute of Philosophy of the Czech Academy of Sciences. He is currently completing a dissertation entitled "Social Reality of the Parables of Enoch." His research interests lie in the various aspects of Second Temple Judaism, early Christianity, and theoretical issues of interpretation of ancient texts.

Filip Čapek (capek@etf.cuni.cz) is Associate Professor at the Department of Old Testament Studies of Protestant Theological Faculty, Charles University, Prague, and Researcher of the Centre of Biblical Studies of Czech Academy of Sciences. His current research in archaeology is focused on transformations of cult in Judah in the Iron Age and in biblical studies on sapiential texts of late third and early second centuries BCE. He is the author of the *Hermeneutics of the Hebrew Bible: Canon as Interpretative Possibility Elucidated with Help of Works of B. S. Childs and J. A. Sanders* [Czech] (2005), *Qoheleth: Unsettled Book for Unsettled Times* [Czech] (2016), and *Archeology, History and Formation of Identity of Ancient*

Israel [Czech] (2018). He took part in archaeological campaigns in Ramat Raḥel, Khirbet Qeiyafa, the City of David, and Naḥal Rephaim. He coordinates as an institutional partner Czech participation in the Tel Moza Excavation Project (since 2019) and in the Lautenschläger Azekah Expedition (since 2013).

Liora Freud (freudliora@gmail.com) is a project coordinator at the Sonia and Marco Nadler Institute of Archaeology of Tel Aviv University. She is the registrar and pottery expert of the Lautenschläger Azekah Expedition, directed by Oded Lipschits, Manfred Oeming and Yuval Gadot, and is currently coordinating the publication of the finds from the renewed excavations at Ramat Raḥel (2005–2010). Her PhD dissertation, titled "Judahite Pottery in the Transitional Phase between the Iron Age and the Persian Period: Jerusalem and Environs," focused on Babylonian period pottery. She started her speciality in ancient pottery, mainly of the Iron Age, while working for many years with the late Itzhak Beit-Arieh, and she participated in the publications of many sites in the Beersheba Valley.

Yuval Gadot (ygadot@gmail.com) is the head of the Jacob M. Alkow Department of Archaeology and Ancient Near Eastern Cultures at Tel-Aviv University. Since 2013 he has directed Tel-Aviv University excavations at the City of David and co-directed the Lautenschläger Azekah Expedition. His research in Jerusalem includes excavations of the city's ancient core together with interdisciplinary study of the rural landscape surrounding it. Gadot obtained his PhD in 2004 from Tel-Aviv University with a dissertation titled "Continuity and Change: The Transition between the Late Bronze Age and the Iron Age in Israel Central Coastal Plain." The work included the first full publication of the excavations at Tel Aphek and a regional study of trends in the material culture as they understood in relation to historical events. Gadot's edited *The Bronze Age Cemetery at ʿAra* (2014) and coedited *Ramat Raḥel III: Final Publication of Yohanan Aharoni's Excavations (1954, 1959–1962)* (2016) and *Rethinking Israel*, a volume published in honor of Israel Finkelstein.

David Gellman (davidgel@israntique.org.il) is an archaeologist working for the Jerusalem branch of the Israel Antiquities Authority, currently excavating in the Old City of Jerusalem. He is also a master's degree student in the Institute of Archaeology and Ancient Near East in the Hebrew University in Jerusalem, researching the Late Bronze Age in the Judean Shephelah.

Ido Koch (idokoch@tauex.tau.ac.il) is a Senior Lecturer at the Department of Archaeology and Ancient Near Eastern Cultures at Tel Aviv University and codirector of the Tel Hadid Expedition. He is the author of *The Shadow of Egypt* [Hebrew] (2018), a comprehensive study of local reactions to Egyptian colonialism during the Late Bronze Age. His current research interests include the impact of Assyrian colonialism on the southern Levant, seals and sealings across the ages, and archaeology of religion.

Oded Lipschits (lipschit@tauex.tau.ac.il) is a professor of Jewish History in the Department of Archaeology and Ancient Near Eastern Cultures at Tel-Aviv University, where he also serves as the Director of the Sonia and Marco Nadler Institute of Archaeology, the Incumbent of the Austria Chair of the Archeology of the Land of Israel in the Biblical Period, and the head of the international MA and PhD program in Ancient Israel Studies. He directed the excavations at Ramat Raḥel (2005–2010), and since 2012 he has been codirector of the Lautenschläger Azekah Expedition. He created an online MOOC course ("The Fall and Rise of Jerusalem: The History of Judah under Babylonian Rule") based on his 2005 book with the same name. Among his numerous books and more than 150 scientific papers, one can mention his coauthored *Yehud Stamp Impressions: A Corpus of Inscribed Stamp Impressions from the Persian and Hellenistic Periods in Judah* (2011) and *What Are the Stones Whispering? Ramat Raḥel: 3000 Years of Forgotten History* (2017), as well as his forthcoming *The Age of Empires: History and Administration in Judah in Light of the Stamped Jar Handles (between the Eighth and the Second Centuries BCE)*.

Adam Mackerle (mackerle@tf.jcu.cz) is Assistant Professor of the Old Testament at the Faculty of Theology of the University of Southern Bohemia, in the Czech Republic. His interests focus mainly on the corpus of the Minor Prophets viewed from different perspectives. He recently published a commentary titled *Amos: When God Has to Roar Like a Lion* [Czech] (2017) and a monograph titled *Ethical Apects of Preexilic Minor Prophets* [Czech] (2019) in which he analyzes how the books of Hosea, Amos, Micah, and Zephaniah can be used in contemporary ethical discourse.

Sivan Mizrahi (sivanmi@israntique.org.il) is a field excavator and researcher for the Israel Antiquity Authority. She is also a PhD student in archaeology at Ben-Gurion University of the Negev, researching the Early Bronze Age II–III rural settlements in the Lachish region.

David Rafael Moulis (david.moulis@gmail.com) is a Researcher at the Department of Old Testament Studies, Protestant Theological Faculty of Charles University, Prague. In recent years he has participated in the archaeological projects in Jerusalem, Tel Azekah, Tel Moza, Ein el-Jarba, and Naḥal Rephaim. He is particularly focused on the study of transitions and developments of the cult in Iron Age Judah. He is author of "Hezekiah's Religious Reform—In the Bible and Archaeology" (2017) and "Tel Jerusalem: The Place Where It All Began (Archaeological Remains from the Epipaleolithic Period to the Iron Age II Period)" (2014).

Jan Rückl (janrucklsafarik@gmail.com) is a researcher and lecturer at the Protestant Theological Faculty at Charles University in Prague. He is the author of *A Sure House: Studies on the Dynastic Promise to David in the Books of Samuel and Kings* (2016), a commentary on the book of Haggai [Czech] (2018), and several studies on the textual and redactional history of various texts in the Former and Latter Prophets.

David Ben-Shlomo (davben187@yahoo.com) in Associate Professor of archaeology at Ariel University and the head of the Land of Israel Studies and Archaeology Department and the Institute of Archaeology at Ariel University. His current research focuses on the material culture in Judah during the Iron Age, in particular in the Jordan Valley region. Another focus of his research is compositional and provenance analysis of pottery and ceramic objects in antiquity. He recently published a volume titled *The Iron Age Pottery of Jerusalem: An Archaeological and Technological Study* (2019). Prior to this his research focused on the Philistine material culture as well as iconography and cult in the Iron Age Levant. He directed excavations at Tel Hebron, Khirbet Mastarah, and Aujah el-Foqa. His scientific publications include nine books and numerous articles.

Ancient Sources Index

Personal and Place Names Index

Modern Authors Index

CPSIA information can be obtained
at www.ICGtesting.com
Printed in the USA
LVHW071044260623
750795LV00004B/36